Contents

Your handbook cover

About the cover

Ed Kluz is an English artist whose work focuses on perceptions of the past through the reimagining of historic landscapes, buildings and objects. He has a curiosity for the obscure and overlooked, and draws inspiration from old forms of architectural representation, early photography, film and theatre.

This year's handbook cover has been created by artist Ed Kluz, inspired by the many sites and objects in our care.

Can you find the below sites, people and objects on the handbook cover? We have included a royal crown to celebrate the coronation of King Charles III in 2023.

Caryatids at **Audley End House** (p.138)

Quarry Gardens, **Belsay Hall** (p.272)

Bolsover Castle and Venus fountain (p.166)

The Royal Oak, **Boscobel House** (p.186)

Carisbrooke Castle gateway (p.80)

Coventina relief panel, **Carrawburgh Roman Fort** (p.262)

Charles Darwin (p.54)

Clifford's Tower (p.210)

Facepot, **Corbridge** (p.260)

Dover Castle (p.50)

Dido Belle (p.26)

Mah-Jongg the lemur from **Eltham Palace and Gardens** (p.22)

Abbot's crozier from **Furness Abbey** (p.244)

Hadrian's Wall (p.250)

Samson and Lion roof boss, **Hailes Abbey** (p.106)

Iron Bridge (p.189)

Kenwood (p.26)

Queen Victoria (p.76)

Reculver Towers (p.61)

Royal crown

Chinese lacquer screen, **Marble Hill** (p.30)

Stonehenge (p.122)

Tintagel Castle's bridge (p.94)

Duke of Wellington's boots from **Walmer Castle** (p.64)

Archer Pavilion, **Wrest Park** (p.132)

Visit english-heritage.org.uk/2023-handbook to discover more.

Welcome

This handbook is your indispensable guide to the hundreds of sites in our care – all of which you, as Members, can visit for free, and as many times as you like.

Inside, you'll not only find practical information about the sites, but also intriguing introductions to their histories, and a useful overview of what you'll discover on your days out. There are plenty of exciting new ways to step into England's story up and down the country this year and for you to get maximum value from your membership.

In Kent, we're unearthing the unique story of **Richborough Roman Fort and Amphitheatre**. From this spring, you'll be able to explore its fascinating story as never before, thanks to a new museum housing fascinating archaeological finds, a recreated wooden gatehouse, and new information panels.

In Northumberland, a major project is set to transform **Belsay Hall, Castle and Gardens** when it's completed in the summer. We have replaced the roof of the neo-Grecian hall, replanted the formal gardens and installed new displays and trails to help visitors of all ages explore the castle and grounds. There will also be a new café and playground, and thanks to new paths, ramps and facilities, the whole site will be much more accessible to many more people.

You'll also find revamped exhibitions and new experiences at **Wroxeter Roman City** in Shropshire, **Witley Court** in Worcestershire, **Grime's Graves** in Norfolk and **Lindisfarne Priory** and **Warkworth Castle** in Northumberland.

A new chapter in England's story will be written this year when the country celebrates the coronation of King Charles III. We're planning our own special commemoration – you can keep up to date with all our latest plans and announcements by signing up to the Members' e-newsletter.

As ever, our *Members' Magazine* is a wonderful source of year-round inspiration and in-depth insight into all things English Heritage.

English Heritage is a charity, and, as a Member, you play a vital part in our important work. Thanks to you, we're able to protect our nation's precious past and encourage more people to visit, value and enjoy it for themselves.

Kate Mavor
Chief Executive

Membership

Your membership is helping to care for over 400 historic sites across the country. Every day, you're playing a vital role in keeping the story of England alive for future generations. Thank you for your support.

Read all about it

The *Members' Magazine** comes out several times a year and is packed with inspiration and ideas for making the most of your membership. Be the first to hear about new Members' Rewards, special events and the latest news by signing up to the Members' e-newsletter at **english-heritage.org.uk/newsletter**

For families

Every Member can bring up to six children to visit our sites for free. Children must be under 18 and within your family group. Younger Members will also love the Kids' Area, which features lots of fun activities and crafts to do at home. Simply visit **english-heritage.org.uk/ members** to register and log in.

Free parking

Members can get free parking at the majority of our sites by displaying a current car sticker (free parking does not apply at sites or car parks that are not managed by English Heritage).

Events

Members enjoy free or discounted entry to a whole host of fantastic days out – see p.10 for details, or visit **english-heritage.org.uk/events**

Members' Area

Check out your dedicated Members' Area on our website to find specially curated articles, videos and quizzes – along with back issues of the magazine.

Loyalty rewarded

If you've been an English Heritage Member beyond your first renewal, you can now get 10% off in most of our shops and cafés (local exclusions and restrictions may apply), as well as our online shop.

Exclusive Members' events

As a Member, you can delve far deeper into our sites. Our experts will invite you behind the scenes, let you handle artefacts, lead you in workshops and take you on walking tours. We have events across the country every year. Look out for these in your magazine and Members' Area.

Members' Rewards

Our Members' Rewards programme gives you access to a wide range of exclusive competitions, deals and special offers, which are updated throughout the year at **english-heritage.org.uk/ rewards**

More days out

Your membership card opens doors to many other associated attractions and properties – either at no extra charge or for a discounted rate. See p.282 or check the online Members' Area.

Share your experience

Follow us on Facebook, Twitter and Instagram – we love to hear about your days out, as well as your recommendations and general tips for making the most of your membership.

*The *Members' Magazine* is mailed directly to UK Members, and to Life Members overseas.

Eltham Palace and Gardens, London

Wrest Park, Bedfordshire

Planning your visit

This section contains important information about planning your visit and helpful contact details.

Access

Our handbook listings indicate accessible areas of our properties with the use of the ♿ symbol. If you have a disability, your carer or companion is always admitted free. Many of our sites have accessible parking.

For more detail on access for families and visitors with disabilities at our sites, please call us on 0370 333 1181.

Email us at customers@english-heritage.org.uk, or visit english-heritage.org.uk

Book your visit online

You don't need to book your ticket in advance, but you'll always get the best price and guaranteed entry by booking online ahead of your visit. You can, however, still turn up without a booking, unless otherwise stipulated.

We can't take bookings over the phone, but please get in touch if you have difficulties booking online.

If you have booked a time slot for a free visit you can no longer make, please cancel it online. This will free up the space for someone else to visit. If you have booked for an event with an additional charge or paid for a non-member friend, please note that we are unable to cancel and refund your payment.

Remember to bring your membership card with you, along with a copy of your ticket confirmation email – either as a printout or on your phone.

Catering and picnics 🍴🍽🧺

Many of our properties offer delicious home-made food and drink.

Don't forget, if you've been an English Heritage Member beyond your first renewal, you can now get 10% off in our shops and cafés (local exclusions and restrictions may apply), as well as our online shop.

You're welcome to picnic in the grounds of most of our properties.

Audley End House and Gardens, Essex

Tintagel Castle, Cornwall

Dogs

We welcome dogs on leads wherever possible, but please see individual property listings and look out for the dog symbol. Assistance dogs are welcome at all sites.

Families and children

With towering castles and underground passages, tales of royal revels and wartime heroes, our sites provide endless adventures for children. From gardens to coastlines, we offer spectacular outdoor locations for fun, exploration and picnics. Alongside our events, exhibitions and interactive displays you'll also find fantastic family-friendly resources at many of our properties. To ensure everyone is safe while having fun, children visiting sites must be accompanied by an adult. For larger groups, please ensure there is a sensible ratio of adults to children.

If you are visiting as part of a large family group and not all visitors are Members, you may qualify for a 15% group booking discount (10% for Stonehenge). Visit **english-heritage.org.uk/visit/group-visits**

We also offer free self-led educational visits to all of our sites, and Discovery Visit workshops at others. Whether you're homeschooling or your children attend as part of a class trip, these experiences support the National Curriculum across a range of subjects and all key stages. We also have a variety of free downloadable teaching resources. Find out more at **english-heritage.org.uk/education**

Guides and tours

You'll find guidebooks, audio tours and multimedia guides at many of our sites. We also provide audio guides and trails for children (some available in different languages). All of our paying sites, and a few of our free-to-enter sites, have guidebooks – almost 100 of these are 'Red Guides', with their distinctive red spines. Written by experts, all of our guidebooks feature a tour of the site together with an in-depth history of the people who lived and worked there. Packed with plans, reconstruction drawings, eyewitness accounts and beautiful photography, they make essential reading as well as brilliant souvenirs of your visit. Many of our sites provide guided tours, please speak to a member of staff to see what is available on the day. Short histories and descriptions of our free-to-enter sites are also available on our website. Dive deeper into the hidden histories of our sites with the *Speaking with Shadows* and weekly English Heritage podcasts, both available for free on major podcast platforms.

Photography

In some properties we don't allow photography, due to the sensitive nature of some materials. Non-commercial photography is welcome in the gardens and grounds of all our sites.

Safety and smoking ⚠

Due to their historic nature, some of our sites have potentially hazardous features – please pay attention to all safety notices on site. If you have any doubts, our staff can always advise on safety issues. Please wear suitable footwear to avoid accidents, and do not climb on walls or monuments. In areas of woodland deer pasture there may be a slight risk of ticks, so keep vulnerable parts of your body covered and/or use insect repellent. Smoking or vaping is not permitted inside any of our properties.

Travel and transport

Where possible in the property listings, we have provided local train information. For bus travel, please visit **traveline.info**, where you can search for our sites and get the most up-to-date times and routes. Alternatively you can call Traveline on 0871 200 22 33 (calls cost 12p plus your phone company's access charge). For cycle routes, call 0300 303 2604 or visit **sustrans.org.uk**. OS Landranger/Explorer map references have also been supplied for each property.

Admission prices

As a Member, entry to our sites will be free for yourself and everyone covered by your membership. In addition to site access, we offer a variety of events on certain days that are either free or reduced cost to our Members. Please see the website for the latest details. All site admission prices can be found online and will apply to anyone that is not a Member.

Admission categories: Adult; Concession (over 65s, Jobseekers and students with relevant ID); Child (age 5-17, under 5s go free); Family tickets admit one or two adults and up to three children (ticket categories may vary at properties not managed by us).

Overseas Visitors Pass

Visitors from overseas planning to visit a number of properties may save money with an Overseas Visitors Pass (OVP). These provide admission to all English Heritage properties marked with the OVP symbol over a 9- or 16-day period. Call 0370 333 1181 or visit **english-heritage.org.uk/ovp**

Gift Aid

UK taxpayers choosing a 'with donation' ticket and Gift Aiding their admission allow us to claim an additional 25p for every £1. This helps us to look after the historic places in our care, and keep the story of England alive for future generations. Admission tickets 'without donation' are also available; the same right of admission applies. Please also remember to Gift Aid your membership; it really does make a big difference to our work. Call 0370 333 1181 or visit **english-heritage.org.uk/giftaid**

Keeping you safe

All of our sites have uneven surfaces due to their historic and/or outdoor nature, so please wear appropriate footwear. Please observe site signage, barriers and staff instructions. Please supervise children closely. Metal detecting, smoking, fires, BBQs and unauthorised commercial photography and drones are prohibited at all our properties. We continue to aim to keep all visitors safe from Covid and follow the latest guidance at all times.

Free parking

Members enjoy free parking at the majority of our sites by displaying a current car sticker. Free parking does not apply at sites that are not managed by English Heritage. Full details of parking can be found in the individual listings in this handbook.

Sign up for events updates

Get regular events updates sent straight to your inbox. Just visit **english-heritage.org.uk/newsletter** to register. You can also keep up to date with our events programme at **english-heritage.org.uk/events** or check the latest copy of your *Members' Magazine*.

Events

Welcome to another exciting year of events to inspire the whole family. From exciting jousts and battle re-enactments to Members' exclusive events offering intimate behind-the-scenes access to our sites, we'll have something for Members of all ages to enjoy.

Historical re-enactments

Once again, you'll be able to enjoy the sight of knights clashing at a joust or tournament. Romans will patrol **Hadrian's Wall** (p.250) and Second World War guns will fire at **Dover Castle** (p.50). Be swept away this summer by stories of pirates and the high seas at some of our coastal sites, and of course don't miss our epic re-enactment of the **Battle of Hastings** (p.70) in October.

Events for all the family

Learn what it takes to be a pirate, try your hand at archery, enjoy Victorian pastimes and join historical characters in a medieval court. For a quieter time, take tours of our gardens and sites led by our experts and volunteers.

Easter adventure quests

Join us on an egg-citing quest during the Easter holiday. Intrepid adventurers who complete their mission will get a certificate to prove it, and there may even be a prize too!

Fighting knights

Our brave knights will take on the ultimate challenge at our fiery series of Knights' Tournaments and Legendary Jousts this summer.

Halloween events

Get into the spirit of Halloween and hunt for ghosts as darkness descends on a ruined castle. Discover spine-tingling tales of ghostly apparitions, dastardly deeds and ghoulish goings-on, or kick up crackling leaves with the kids and get creative with fancy dress and spooky trails.

Exclusive events for Members

Every year we put on unique events exclusively for Members. Meet the experts, find out what it takes to care for our sites and discover the histories of some of England's most fascinating places. Visit the Members' Area of the website or check your *Members' Magazine* for full details. In April 2023 we will be holding our **Members' Week**, with a special programme of events around the country just for you.

Shop with us

From traditional treats like ginger wine and lemon curd to artisan gifts inspired by our sites, our shops offer an inspiring, imaginative and unusual alternative to the high street, with ideas that cover all ages and all interests.

Each of our shops has a unique range of products inspired by the stories of our sites – expect art deco cups at **Eltham Palace** (p.22), Victorian kitchenware at **Audley End** (p.138) and gardening tools at **Belsay Hall** (p.272). Whichever site you visit, you can expect a warm welcome from our staff and a wide selection of items, with everything from jewellery to homeware, history books to memorabilia, and food and drink to toys, games and fancy dress.

Our shops are the perfect places to pick up one of our famous Red Guides. These beautifully illustrated guidebooks feature maps, reconstructions and historical images, taking you on an expert tour of each site and telling fascinating stories along the way.

You'll also find our range of award-winning food and drink. Our alcoholic drinks are a particular highlight, with traditional fruit wines and a wide selection of meads. Mead is the world's oldest

alcoholic drink, and we sell more of this delectable nectar than anyone else. Many of our sites offer free tastings of all our wines and meads – the perfect way to get a flavour of the past.

There's plenty for our younger visitors and Members to enjoy, including board games, jigsaw puzzles, wooden armour, swords, books and cuddly toys.

Don't forget, Members in their second year onwards can get 10% off in shops as part of our loyalty discount.

Find out more

Our online gift shop features an extensive range of products and online exclusives at english-heritageshop.org.uk

Kenwood, London

Boscobel House and The Royal Oak, Shropshire

Eat with us

Whether you are looking for a cup of tea, slice of cake or a more substantial lunch, we have over 30 cafés and tearooms across the country to choose from.

Our cafés, tearooms and kiosks can be found at sites across the country. At each, you'll find plenty of tasty treats and refreshing drinks to help fuel your adventure. Whether you're taking in the view at **Tintagel's** Beach Café (p.94), relaxing in the Walled Garden at **Wrest Park** (p.132) or enjoying a Roman burger at **Birdoswald Roman Fort** (p.254) on **Hadrian's Wall** (p.250), you can relax in the knowledge that all the money we raise from our food and drink helps care for England's story. We seek out high-quality ingredients from local producers, and hold all our suppliers across the country to strict welfare and environmental standards. Wherever we can, we use ingredients grown on site – visit **Audley End House** (p.138) or **Walmer Castle** (p.64), for instance, and you could find yourself tucking into that day's harvest from the kitchen garden. **Check the website before you visit to find out the latest information.**

A few of our favourites

- Tuck into traditional cornish pasties and light bites at **Tintagel Castle's** Beach Café, with views out to sea and of the bridge

- Treat yourself to a locally produced ice cream at **Osborne's** beach pavilion on the Isle of Wight
- Admire the grand Riding House from **Bolsover Castle's** tearoom with a cake and a cuppa
- Enjoy eating at **Eltham Palace**
- Savour a proper Sunday lunch in the Brew House Café at **Kenwood**
- Enjoy your lunch while savouring wide-ranging views of **Rievaulx Abbey**
- Keep watch over **Hadrian's Wall** during your lunch break at **Birdoswald Roman Fort**
- Try out delicious dishes in the baronial setting of **Framlingham Castle's** atmospheric café

Members in their second year onwards can enjoy 10% off in cafés as part of our loyalty discount (local restrictions may apply).

Handy tip

When using your handbook look out for these icons in the site information panels:

🍴 Café   Tearoom

Audley End House and Gardens, Essex

Walmer Castle and Gardens, Kent

Stay with us

Stay in the places where history happened with our holiday cottages at sites across the country.

Why stay with us?

One of the great benefits of a stay in our cottages is that you have access to the grounds once the public have gone home. Relax in the peace of **Rievaulx Abbey** (p.222), take an evening stroll along the beach at **Osborne** (p.76) or watch the sun rise over the parade ground at **Pendennis Castle** (p.92). You can also enjoy watching the sunset from **St Mawes** (p.96) as you look out to sea, or take a quiet walk through the serene gardens at **Walmer Castle** (p.64), **Audley End** (p.138) and **Mount Grace Priory** (p.218). Get away from the everyday by crossing the dramatic causeway to stay in the Coastguard's Cottage at **Lindisfarne Priory** (p.276), or command fine views of the English Channel at **Dover Castle** (p.50) as you wake up within the walls of the 'Key to England'.

A number of our cottages have been recently refurbished, see properties marked with a *.

Find out more

Browse and book our available cottages at english-heritage.org.uk/holidaycottages or call 0370 333 1181

South East
Battle Abbey* South Lodge

Carisbrooke Castle*
The Bowling Green Apartment

Dover Castle* The Sergeant
Major's House & Peverell's Tower

Osborne* Pavilion Cottage &
No. 1 & No. 2 Sovereign's Gate

Walmer Castle* The Garden
Cottage & The Greenhouse
Apartment

South West
Pendennis Castle The Custodian's
House & Callie's Cottage

St Mawes Fort House

East of England
Audley End House* Cambridge
Lodge & Head Gardener's House

Wrest Park* Gardener's House

East Midlands
Hardwick Old Hall East Lodge

Kirby Hall* Peacock Cottage

West Midlands
Witley Court* Pool House

Yorkshire
Mount Grace Priory* Prior's Lodge

Rievaulx Abbey* Refectory Cottage

North East
Lindisfarne Priory Coastguard's
Cottage

Wellington Arch, London

Hiring a property

For a historic celebration

From iconic London landmarks to medieval castles, an 18th-century villa to Queen Victoria's seaside retreat, host your event in the places where history happened.

Our rich historical settings are perfect for everything from corporate away-days and business meetings to lavish dinners and spectacular showcases. Whether you are looking to host a small private event or a large-scale extravaganza, we have a range of venues guaranteed to make your event unique and memorable.

For a memorable wedding day

Your wedding day is everlasting. It's the start of the next chapter of your story. It's a moment captured in time – through pictures that stand for a lifetime and memories re-lived for years to come.

English Heritage's historic wedding venues share this unique sense of the everlasting. With castles rising above the sea, royal retreats and sweeping views of age-old gardens, our venues give you a connection to the past and an inspiring setting for your future.

Properties for hire

With a collection of properties across England alongside a suite of award-winning accredited suppliers, our expert team is on hand to help ensure that your event is perfect.

Find out more

T. 0300 020 0017
W. english-heritage.org.uk/venuehire
E. hospitality@english-heritage.org.uk

Eltham Palace and Gardens, Greenwich

WELCOME TO
LONDON

LONDON

With countless grand buildings and nearly 1,000 blue plaques, England's capital city is a real treasure-trove for history lovers.

In the heart of the city, climb the iconic **Wellington Arch** (p.32), step inside one of the few surviving parts of the medieval Westminster Palace (**Jewel Tower**, p.29) or discover the dazzling London home of the Duke of Wellington (**Apsley House**, p.20).

Further afield, explore the riverside retreat of one of Georgian high society's most remarkable women (**Marble Hill**, p.30) or an art deco mansion that rose beside the remains of a medieval royal palace (**Eltham Palace and Gardens**, p.22). Famous Old Masters line the walls of **Kenwood** (p.26), a country house in the London suburbs, while rare renaissance artworks glitter behind the handsome brick facade of **Ranger's House** (p.31).

Explore London's streets and squares to discover blue plaques commemorating connections with a huge variety of people from the past (p.34). Members can enjoy exclusive blue plaque walks with a historian – visit **english-heritage.org.uk/members-events** to find out more.

Apsley House

Eltham Palace and Gardens

Ranger's House – the Wernher Collection

APSLEY HOUSE

HYDE PARK – W1J 7NT

Revel in the dazzling interiors, glittering treasures and fabulous art collections of the Duke of Wellington's Apsley House. Enjoy the multimedia guide, and find out how the 'Iron Duke' entertained in the grandest style.

Home of the first Duke of Wellington and his descendants, and popularly known as 'Number 1 London', Apsley House stands right in the heart of the capital at Hyde Park Corner. It is London's only surviving aristocratic townhouse open to visitors today. Originally designed by Robert Adam for Baron Apsley – from whom it takes its name – it was lavishly and fashionably extended and remodelled for Wellington by Benjamin Wyatt between 1819 and 1829.

Wellington is most famous for defeating Napoleon at the Battle of Waterloo in 1815, the culmination of a brilliant military career. But he was also a major politician, becoming Prime Minister in 1828. Reflecting the duke's rising status, Apsley House's magnificent interiors provided the perfect backdrop for entertaining, particularly at the annual Waterloo Banquets, which commemorated the great victory, held here every year from 1820 until the Duke's death in 1852.

Highlights include the grandiose Dining Room, with its breath-taking crystal chandelier and the fabulous thousand-piece gilt Portuguese tableware service, one of many treasures presented to Wellington by grateful people, rulers and nations. These include the amazing silver-gilt Waterloo Shield, depicting ten of Wellington's victories, given in 1822 by the merchants and bankers of London.

The mansion's interior displays nearly 3,000 fine paintings, sculptures and works of art in silver and porcelain, including Wellington's outstanding picture collection. Many of its paintings came from the Spanish Royal Collection, rescued from the fleeing Joseph Bonaparte after the Battle of Vitoria and later given to Wellington by the King of Spain. Paintings by many famous artists – including Velázquez, Rubens, Goya, Titian and Breughel – hang throughout the first-floor rooms, and you can also admire the famous portraits of Wellington by Goya and Sir Thomas Lawrence. Wellington added purchases and commissions of his own, including portraits of his comrades-in-arms. A colossal nude statue by Canova of Wellington's rival Napoleon dominates the stairwell at the centre of the house – which had to be reinforced to support its great weight.

When the seventh Duke of Wellington gave the house to the nation in 1947, the family retained the private rooms, which they still use today. This makes Apsley House the only property cared for by English Heritage in which the owner's family still lives.

Apsley House offers multimedia guides for adults and children.

Complete your experience by crossing the road to Wellington Arch, one of London's most iconic landmarks, which also honours the famous duke. You'll also discover more about Wellington at his country house, Walmer Castle in Kent.

Please note: Photography in the house is not permitted.

OPENING TIMES

Open varying days 1 Apr-28 Mar

Site closed 24 Dec-1 Jan

See website for latest opening times

Last entry 30 mins before closing

VISIT US

Address: Apsley House, 149 Piccadilly, Hyde Park Corner, London W1J 7NT

Direction: Adjacent to Hyde Park Corner tube station, next to the entrance to Hyde Park

Train: Victoria ½ mile

Bus: Visit traveline.info or tfl.gov.uk/plan-a-journey

Tube: Hyde Park Corner

Tel: 020 7499 5676

By being a Member, you save up to £60 (price of a family ticket) when you visit **Apsley House** and **Wellington Arch.**

NON-MEMBERS

See website for entry prices

Pre-booked guided tours are available for groups. Visit english-heritage.org.uk/traveltrade/apsleyhouse or call the site on 020 7499 5676

ACQ 1947 | OVP

Disabled access very limited. Please phone property for information.

MAP PAGE 304 (3E)

OS MAP 176, 161/173: TQ284799

ELTHAM PALACE AND GARDENS

GREENWICH – SE9 5QE

At Eltham Palace you'll discover what 1930s millionaires could achieve when they built and furnished a mansion regardless of expense. It's a triumph of style, taste and ahead-of-the-time home comforts, with wonderful gardens and a children's play area. Come and experience a unique art deco extravaganza.

Stephen and Virginia Courtauld created a uniquely memorable masterpiece when they built their mansion adjoining the Great Hall of medieval Eltham Palace. Completed in 1936, the exterior of the new house was built in sympathy with the old hall. But its interior is an outstanding showcase of 1930s high fashion.

An introductory film uncovers the history of the palace, how it was created, and how the Courtaulds lived in it. Multimedia handsets draw you into 1930s society, and help you experience what it was like to be a guest here. Visual guides to each room help you admire the mansion's striking art deco design details.

What impresses most is the house itself. The dining room is an art deco tour de force, with bird's-eye maple veneered walls, a shimmering aluminium-leaf ceiling and black-and-silver doors portraying animals and birds. Still more exotic is Virginia Courtauld's bathroom, with onyx bath and sink and gold-plated bath taps.

You can also take a look into her walk-in wardrobe, next to her bedroom. It displays glamorous period dresses based on those she wore, and you can try on replica 1930s clothes and accessories. Explore her nephews' bedrooms and bathroom, complete with an innovative shower. It's one of a pioneering range of ultra-modern conveniences you'll find in this lavishly 'high-tech' home, including underfloor heating, a centralised vacuum cleaner and a built-in audio system.

Admire the 1930s Map Room, reflecting the Courtaulds' exotic holidays, often involving pioneering travel by air. Also on view are a luxury wartime air-raid shelter and a billiard room, with a mural featuring the family's pet lemur, Mah-Jongg.

For a complete contrast with the 1930s rooms, step into the Great Hall – the only substantially remaining part of the medieval royal palace of Eltham. It has a magnificent hammer beam roof, built for Edward IV in the 1470s. Henry VIII spent much of his childhood at Eltham.

Be sure to leave time to wander the palace's beautiful gardens, including the fragrant sunken Rose Garden and the Rock Garden with its cascade. They've been replanted and re-presented in the style commissioned by the Courtaulds.

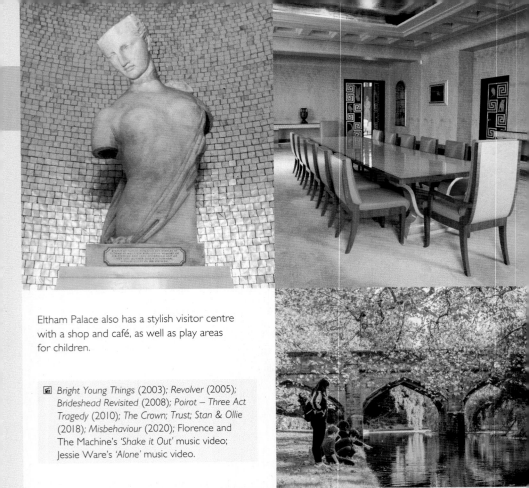

Eltham Palace also has a stylish visitor centre with a shop and café, as well as play areas for children.

 Bright Young Things (2003); *Revolver* (2005); *Brideshead Revisited* (2008); *Poirot – Three Act Tragedy* (2010); *The Crown; Trust; Stan & Ollie* (2018); *Misbehaviour* (2020); Florence and The Machine's *'Shake it Out'* music video; Jessie Ware's *'Alone'* music video.

OPENING TIMES

Open varying days 1 Apr-28 Mar

Site closed 24-25 Dec

See website for latest opening times

Last entry 30 mins before closing

VISIT US

Address: Court Yard, Eltham, London SE9 5QE

Direction: Off Court Rd SE9, Jct 3 on the M25, then A20 to Eltham. Please use satnav postcode SE9 5NP to help direct you straight to the car park

Train: Mottingham ½ mile walk (best for visitor centre entrance). Eltham Station is also ½ mile walk

Bus: Visit traveline.info or tfl.gov.uk/plan-a-journey

Tel: 0370 333 1181

SAVE TODAY By being a Member, you save up to £60 (price of a family ticket) when you visit **Eltham Palace and Gardens**.

NON-MEMBERS

See website for entry prices

Please note: Members may be charged for special events

ACQ.1995

Pushchairs and large rucksacks need to be left at the entrance of the house.

Parking: charges apply to non-members, free for Members with valid English Heritage car sticker.

Some restrictions on photography in the house.

MAP PAGE 305 (4F)
OS MAP 177, 162: TQ424740

english-heritage.org.uk

CHISWICK HOUSE & GARDENS

CHISWICK – W4 2RP

Chiswick House is a neo-Palladian villa designed and built by Richard Boyle, 3rd Earl of Burlington, in the 18th century. After travelling to Italy in his youth, Burlington was inspired to bring the grandeur of ancient Rome home to London. His close friend, the architect and gardener William Kent, not only played a huge role in decorating the interior of the house but also designed the grounds.

Today Chiswick House & Gardens covers 65 acres in west London, from the manicured Italian Garden to the untamed Wilderness. Explore the restored gallery rooms, and learn about the people who shaped Chiswick House over the last 300 years. Look out for seasonal exhibitions delving deeper into their stories. Following your visit to the house, head over to the award-winning Kitchen Garden, both a place of sanctuary and a hive of activity for local community groups. Constantly changing with the seasons, admire the range of fruit, vegetables and cut flowers, lovingly tended by a fantastic team of gardeners. Our organic garden produce is dependent on seasonal availability, please see website for latest timings.

Visit in February to March to see the renowned spring blooms.

The RIBA award-winning café serves coffee and homemade cakes and a range of delicious lunch items. The café is next to the children's play area – perfect for using up a little energy before heading home. Check the Chiswick House & Gardens website to find out what's on.

Managed by Chiswick House & Gardens Trust in partnership with English Heritage.
chiswickhouseandgardens.org.uk

Available for corporate and private hire – visit chiswickhouseandgardens.org.uk for details.
Licensed for civil wedding ceremonies.

OPENING TIMES

Kitchen Garden and Conservatory

1 Apr–29 Oct, Thu–Sun	11am–4pm
30 Oct–28 Mar	Closed

House

1 Apr–24 May	Closed
25 May–1 Oct, Thu–Sun	11am–4pm
2 Oct–28 Mar	Closed
Last entry 30 mins before closing	
Gardens are open all year round	7am–dusk

Occasionally the house, conservatory or gardens are closed for private events – please check chiswickhouseandgardens.org.uk prior to visiting

Group bookings: house and gardens available for private tours and group bookings all year round, seven days a week. Email groups@chgt.org.uk to find out more

VISIT US

Direction: Burlington Lane, Chiswick, London W4 2RP

Train: Chiswick ¼ mile walk (10 mins)

Bus: Visit traveline.info or tfl.gov.uk/plan-a-journey

Tube: Turnham Green 1 mile then bus E3

Tel: 020 3141 3352

NON-MEMBERS

See website for entry prices

Free guided tours – see website for details

Entry to the gardens (excluding Kitchen Garden) is free; donations welcome

National Art Pass holders free entrance to the house

Members may be charged for special events

ACQ 1956

Disabled access to ground floor only.

Dogs are welcome in the gardens.
Assistance dogs allowed inside the house.

Parking (charges apply: pay with PayByPhone app – disabled bays available) – off Westbound A4. Satnav: W4 2RP.

Photography is permitted in the gardens and some parts of the house.

Caution: deep water, steep stairs.

MAP PAGE 304 (3E)   OS MAP 176, 161: TQ210775

KENWOOD

HAMPSTEAD – NW3 7JR

Kenwood is among the finest of all the great houses in our care. Its breathtaking interiors and fabulous world-class art collection are free for everyone to enjoy. The neo-Classical villa and its tranquil parkland are favourites with visitors seeking relief from the bustle of central London, and there's plenty here for families to discover together.

Crowning Hampstead Heath, Kenwood was remodelled by Robert Adam between 1764 and 1779 for William Murray, first Earl of Mansfield, creating the imposing mansion that greets visitors today.

Most striking of all Kenwood's glories is its suite of magnificent Robert Adam rooms: the Entrance Hall, Great Staircase, Anteroom, and his masterpiece, the Great Library, lavishly restored as they originally appeared over two centuries ago.

Kenwood also famously displays the Iveagh Bequest, an internationally renowned art collection assembled by brewing magnate Edward Cecil Guinness, 1st Earl of Iveagh, and bequeathed to the nation, along with the Kenwood estate, in 1927. It features paintings by Rembrandt, Van Dyck, Vermeer, Gainsborough, Reynolds, Turner and Constable. A lift to the first floor provides access to the Suffolk Collection of Stuart portraits, with full-length paintings of extravagantly dressed Jacobean courtiers. Ask our volunteer explainers about the house and its paintings.

Interpretation helps you discover the story of Kenwood and its people, from Lord Mansfield and his mixed-race great-niece, Dido Belle, to Lord Iveagh, Kenwood's great benefactor. There are also family activities in the housekeeper's room.

Kenwood's 112-acre parkland, landscaped by Humphry Repton, is renowned for its fine views over London. There's plenty to explore and admire: sculptures by Henry Moore and Barbara Hepworth, lakeside walks and paths meandering through ancient woodland, a Site of Special Scientific Interest. Don't miss the conserved ornamental 18th-century dairy, which once supplied the mansion with fresh produce and included a space for the ladies of the house to take tea and indulge in the fashionable pastime of butter making (please check with the site for opening details).

You can also download our free app before visiting: **english-heritage.org.uk/kenwood**

Please note: Photography in the house is limited.

🎬 *Notting Hill* (1999); *Mansfield Park* (1999); *Scenes of a Sexual Nature* (2006); *Venus* (2006).

© By kind permission of the Earl of Mansfield, Scone Palace, Perth, Scotland

OPENING TIMES

House

Open daily 1 Apr-28 Mar

House closed 24-26, 31 Dec & 1 Jan

Brew House Café and Steward's Room Café

Open daily 1 Apr-28 Mar

Café closed 24-25 & 31 Dec

Garden Shop and Orangery Shop

Open daily 1 Apr-28 Mar

Shops closed 24-25 & 31 Dec

See website for latest opening times

Estate open from 8am to dusk (closed 25 Dec) – see park entrance for closing time

Last entry 30 mins before closing

From Nov until Mar, the house, shops and cafés will close 15 mins prior to the estate closing time

Talks and tours throughout the week, please see website for further details

VISIT US

Address: Kenwood, Hampstead NW3 7JR

Direction: Hampstead Lane

Train: Gospel Oak or Hampstead Heath (both London Overground)

Bus: Visit traveline.info

Tube: Golders Green or Archway then bus 210

Tel: 0370 333 1181

NON-MEMBERS

Entry to the house and grounds is free; donations welcome

Pre-booked guided tours may be available for groups, please email bookings@english-heritage.org.uk or call 0370 333 1181 for latest information

Disabled access (lift to all floors for visitors with a disability or mobility requirements; toilets).

Dogs: in certain areas within the grounds dogs can be let off leads. Only assistance dogs are allowed inside the house.

Parking: charges apply to non-members, free for Members with valid English Heritage car sticker. Disabled bays available. Call 020 3282 8361 or look at our website for accessibility information.

MAP PAGE 304 (3E)
OS MAP 176, 173: TQ271874

CHAPTER HOUSE AND PYX CHAMBER

WESTMINSTER ABBEY – SW1P 3PA

Built in 1250, the Chapter House was used for monks' daily meetings, and sometimes by medieval parliaments. A beautiful vaulted building, it displays a medieval tiled floor and spectacular wall paintings.

Under the care and management of the Dean and Chapter of Westminster.

OPENING TIMES

Open varying days 1 Apr-28 Mar

Site closed 2 Apr, 24-25 Dec & 1 Jan

See website for latest opening times

May be closed at short notice on state and religious occasions

VISIT US

Direction: Within Westminster Abbey. Members who do not wish to visit the rest of the abbey: enter Dean's Yard from Broad Sanctuary and turn left across the square to find the cloisters. All other visitors should use the normal visitor entry point for the abbey

Train: Victoria and Charing Cross

Bus: Visit traveline.info

Tube: Westminster and St James's Park

Tel: 020 7222 5152

NON-MEMBERS

Buy ticket from Westminster Abbey or online

ACQ.1872 Chapter House

ACQ.1901 Pyx Chamber

MAP PAGE 304 (3E)
OS MAP 176/177, 161/173: TQ299795

COOMBE CONDUIT

KINGSTON UPON THAMES – KT2 7HE

Two brick-walled chambers, connected by an underground passage. Part of a system collecting spring water and channelling it to Hampton Court Palace.

Managed by the Kingston upon Thames Society.

COOMBE CONDUIT

OPENING TIMES

See website for latest opening times

VISIT US

Direction: Coombe Lane West close to corner with Lord Chancellor Walk

Train: Norbiton ¾ mile or Raynes Park 1 mile then bus 57

Bus: Visit traveline.info

Tube: Wimbledon then bus 57

Tel: 020 8549 4586

ACQ.1978 Caution: deep water.
Disabled access (exterior only).

MAP PAGE 304 (4E)
OS MAP 176, 161: TQ204698

HARMONDSWORTH GREAT BARN

HILLINGDON – UB7 0AQ

Medieval timber-framed barn, built 1426-27. One of the largest barns ever built in England, and among the least altered medieval buildings in Britain. Managed by the Friends of the Great Barn at Harmondsworth.

OPENING TIMES

See website for latest opening times

VISIT US

Direction: Located in High Street, Harmondsworth Village

Train: West Drayton 2 miles

Bus: Visit traveline.info

Tube: Heathrow Terminals 1, 2, 3 – 2 miles

Tel: 0370 333 1181

ACQ.2012

MAP PAGE 304 (3E)
OS MAP 176, 160: TQ056778

LONDON WALL

TOWER HILL – EC3N 4DJ

The best-preserved remnant of the Roman wall which formed part of the eastern defences of Roman Londinium. Built c. AD 200.

OPENING TIMES

Any reasonable daylight hours

VISIT US

Direction: Located outside Tower Hill Underground station, EC3

Train: Fenchurch Street ¼ mile or London Bridge 1 mile

Bus: Visit traveline.info

Tube: Tower Hill

DLR: Tower Gateway

Tel: 0370 333 1181

ACQ.1953

Caution: falling masonry.

MAP PAGE 305 (3F)
OS MAP 176/177, 173: TQ336807

WINCHESTER PALACE

SOUTHWARK – SE1 9DG

Part of the 12th-century great hall of Winchester Palace, London mansion of the Bishops of Winchester, including a striking rose window.

Managed by Bankside Open Spaces Trust.

OPENING TIMES

Any reasonable daylight hours

VISIT US

Direction: On Clink Street close to corner with Stoney Street (between *Golden Hinde* replica ship and the Clink Prison Museum)

Train/Tube: London Bridge ¼ mile

Bus: Visit traveline.info

Tel: 0370 333 1181

ACQ.1967

Featured in new *Palaces of the Bishops of Winchester* guidebook.

MAP PAGE 305 (3F)
OS MAP 176/177, 173: TQ325803

JEWEL TOWER

—— WESTMINSTER – SW1P 3JX ——

Tucked away between the Houses of Parliament and Westminster Abbey, the Jewel Tower is an easily overlooked but precious fragment of English history. It also offers you magnificent views of the Houses of Parliament.

The Tower was built in c. 1365 as the 'Jewel House' to safeguard Edward III's silver plate and royal treasures. It's the sole surviving remnant of the 'Privy Palace', the private royal apartments within the great medieval Palace of Westminster. It's also the only part of the palace complex which survived the disastrous fire of 1834 and is regularly open to the public.

Displaying a finely carved medieval vault, its 14th-century architecture remains largely unaltered, with an anti-clockwise spiral staircase. You can still see the excavated remains of its original moat. The tower later became a royal Tudor lumber room, whose contents included dolls discarded by Henry VIII's daughters. Subsequently it housed the House of Lords records and then the National Weights and Measures Office, determining the value of weights and measures for Britain and its empire.

You can explore the Tower's history and changing roles over the centuries across three floors of displays. Outstanding among its collection are the Westminster Capitals, eight rare and beautifully carved early Norman sculptures made in the 1090s, which once adorned William Rufus's Westminster Hall. Admire the Palace of Westminster Sword, part of a richly decorated Anglo-Saxon weapon. A screen offers you digital reconstructions of Westminster Hall, St Stephen's church and the Palace of Westminster before the 1834 fire.

Light refreshments are available.

OPENING TIMES
Open varying days 1 Apr-28 Mar

Site closed 24-26 Dec & 1 Jan

See website for latest opening times

Last entry 30 mins before closing

VISIT US
Direction: Located on Abingdon Street, opposite the southern end of the Houses of Parliament (Victoria Tower)

Train: Victoria and Charing Cross ¾ mile, Waterloo 1 mile

Bus: Visit traveline.info

Tube: St James's Park and Westminster ¼ mile

Tel: 020 7222 2219

NON-MEMBERS
See website for prices

By being a Member, you save up to **£24.50** (price of a family ticket) when you visit Jewel Tower

New café with indoor and outdoor seating.

Disabled access (limited).

MAP PAGE 304 (3E)
OS MAP 176/177,
161/173: TQ301793

MARBLE HILL

—————— TWICKENHAM – TW1 2NL ——————

A beautiful Palladian mansion set in riverside parkland, Marble Hill is the last complete survivor of the elegant 18th-century villas which bordered the Thames between Richmond and Hampton Court.

It was begun in 1724 for Henrietta Howard, Countess of Suffolk, a remarkable woman of letters and friend of some of England's greatest writers. The house and gardens were planned by fashionable connoisseurs, including the poet Alexander Pope.

Marble Hill was intended as an Arcadian retreat from crowded 18th-century London. There can be few places in England which better evoke the atmosphere of Georgian fashionable life.

🎬 *Nanny McPhee Returns* (2010); *Vanity Fair* (2018); *Harlots* (2019).

MARBLE HILL REVIVED

The £8 million Marble Hill Revived project is complete, so the house, gardens and park are open to explore, free, five days a week for seven months of the year. Thanks to generous grants from the National Lottery Heritage Fund and Community Fund, and the help of nearly 250 volunteers, we've restored the house and its interiors, telling the story of Henrietta and how she triumphed over deafness and an abusive husband. We've also recreated the core of the gardens as she would have known them, planted over 350 trees, opened up woodland areas and wildflower meadows and enhanced nature conservation and biodiversity. There's a family trail, sport and play facilities, a café and much more to enjoy.

OPENING TIMES

House
Open varying days 1 Apr-5 Nov

Site closed 6 Nov-28 Mar

See website for latest opening times

Park open 7am-dusk
Please be aware some areas of the park may be temporarily closed for restoration work

Coach House Café
Open varying days 1 Apr-28 Mar

Café closed 25 Dec

See website for latest opening times

Entry to the House and grounds is free; donations welcome. Pre-booked group tours may be available

Last entry 30 mins before closing

VISIT US

Direction: Richmond Road, Twickenham, London

Train: St Margaret's, Twickenham or Richmond

Bus: Visit traveline.info for the latest bus timetables and routes

Tube: Richmond 1 mile

Tel: 020 8892 1900

Café: please check website for details.

Disabled access (exterior, ground floor and first floor only; toilets). There are hard paths throughout the park, but some areas have uneven ground.

Dogs: in certain areas within the grounds dogs can be let off leads. Only assistance dogs are allowed inside the house.

Parking: charges apply to non-members, free for Members with valid English Heritage car sticker.

MAP PAGE 304 (4E)
OS MAP 176, 161: TQ173736

english-heritage.org.uk

Wernher Collection

RANGER'S HOUSE THE WERNHER COLLECTION

———— GREENWICH PARK – SE10 8QX ————

The Wernher Collection is one of the greatest private art collections ever assembled in Europe. Enhanced interpretation guides you through its diverse wonders, displayed within a mansion which doubled as the exterior of the *Bridgerton* home in the Netflix series.

Gathered by fabulously wealthy diamond magnate Sir Julius Wernher (1850-1912), the collection is showcased in an elegant Georgian villa, once the official residence of the 'Ranger of Greenwich Park'. It includes nearly 700 varied works of art, including early religious paintings and Dutch Old Masters, fine Renaissance bronzes and silver treasures, and the life-sized erotic statue, *The Love of Angels*. You'll also see Botticelli's *Madonna of the Pomegranate*, recently discovered to be from the painter's own workshop.

The 120 pieces of medieval and Renaissance jewellery – the largest collection in England – feature pendants set with a galaxy of precious stones. There are tapestries with scenes of Chinese life, a mechanical travelling cabinet whose drawers pop out, and rarely seen paintings by famous artists.

Sir Julius developed his keen eye for fine craftsmanship while assessing diamonds. He could afford to buy the very best, and his passion was for what he called the 'splendidly ugly' – tiny, unusual artworks expertly crafted in rich materials. You'll discover an enamelled gold skull pendant, a minute boxwood coffin with intricate contents, and a 2nd-century BC Greek gold earring of the goddess Victory. Everyone will have their favourite. What will yours be?

Explore a preview of highlights from the collection on our website english-heritage.org.uk/rangers-house-history

Please note: Photography in the house is not permitted.

🎬 *Belle* (2013); *Bridgerton* (2020-).

OPENING TIMES

Open varying days 1 Apr-5 Nov

Site closed 6 Nov-28 Mar

See website for latest opening times

Last entry 30 mins before closing

VISIT US

Address: Chesterfield Walk, Blackheath, London

Direction: Ranger's House is on Chesterfield Walk and overlooks the junction of General Wolfe Road and Shooters Hill Road

DLR: Deptford Bridge then bus 53, or 20 min walk from Cutty Sark

Train: Blackheath ¾ mile

Bus: Visit traveline.info for the latest bus timetables and routes

River: Greenwich Pier

Tel: For enquiries, please call Eltham Palace on 020 8294 2548

NON-MEMBERS

See website for entry prices

By being a Member you save up to **£41.50** (price of a family ticket) when you visit **Ranger's House**

ACQ 1986 ♿ 🏛 🚶 🚻 ✉ ♿ OVP

MAP PAGE 305 (4F)
OS MAP 177, 161/162: TQ388769

WELLINGTON ARCH

HYDE PARK – W1J 7JZ

Walk into this famous landmark to gain wonderful views over Royal London from the balconies, and see the Household Cavalry riding past. Enjoy four floors of fascinating exhibitions within and discover the vital part played by the Royal Artillery in the First World War.

Set in the heart of the capital at Hyde Park Corner, opposite Apsley House, Wellington Arch is one of London's most iconic monuments. It's crowned by the largest bronze sculpture in Europe, depicting the Angel of Peace descending on the 'Quadriga' – or four-horsed chariot – of War.

The balconies just below the sculpture offer you glorious panoramas over the Royal Parks and central London. It's a unique spot from which to view the Household Cavalry passing beneath, to and from the Changing of the Guard at Horse Guards Parade.

On the first floor within the arch, you'll discover a display revealing its fascinating and sometimes surprising story. Originally intended as a grand outer entrance to Buckingham Palace, it later took on the role of a victory arch proclaiming Wellington's triumph over Napoleon, and once housed London's smallest police station. By 1883, however, the arch was causing traffic bottlenecks. So it was moved, stone by stone, some 100 metres (328 feet) to its current position. The great bronze Quadriga sculpture, by Adrian Jones, was added

in 1912. Jones had been a cavalry veterinary officer, and the sculpture's horses reflect his deep knowledge of equine anatomy.

On the second floor, you'll find a display about the Royal Regiment of Artillery, 1914-1918. Mounted in partnership with the Royal Artillery, it commemorates the wartime sacrifice of over 49,000 artillerymen, and considers how they were remembered by the nearby Royal Artillery Memorial, controversial because it was the first war memorial in Britain to depict a fallen soldier. The exhibition also focuses on the human aspect, highlighting the story of Gunner Stone, VC, and includes rarely seen artefacts from the Ypres battlefields.

Combine your trip to Wellington Arch with a visit to the Duke of Wellington's London residence, Apsley House, just opposite.

DON'T MISS

The exhibition on the first floor, which gives you some fascinating insights into the history of Wellington Arch. Find out how and why the arch was moved from one side of Hyde Park to the other. Did you know that it once had a huge statue of the Duke of Wellington on top, provoking violent controversy? Wellington Arch may be small, but it has a big history.

OPENING TIMES

Open varying days 1 Apr-28 Mar

Site closed 24-26, 31 Dec & 1 Jan

See website for latest opening times

Last entry 30 mins before closing

May close due to corporate or private hire events

VISIT US

Address: Wellington Arch, Apsley Way, Hyde Park Corner, London W1J 7JZ

Direction: Hyde Park Corner, W1J

Train: Victoria ½ mile

Bus: Visit traveline.info or tfl.gov.uk/plan-a-journey

Tube: Hyde Park Corner, adjacent

Tel: 020 7930 2726

SAVE TODAY

By being a Member, you save up to £60 (price of a family ticket) when you visit **Apsley House** and **Wellington Arch.**

NON-MEMBERS

See website for entry prices

Pre-booked guided tours are available for groups. For group visits, go to english-heritage.org.uk/visit/places/wellington-arch/plan-your-visit/group-visits/ or call Apsley House on 020 7499 5676

[ACQ.1999] [♿] [E] [🖼] [⊗] [📷] [⚠] [OVP]

MAP PAGE 304 (3E)

OS MAP 176, 161/173: TQ284798

BLUE PLAQUES

Blue plaques commemorate famous people and fascinating buildings – and, most often, mark the link between the two. They are an attractive reminder of the inspiring and interesting stories that lie behind the brick, stone and stucco of our streetscapes.

London's blue plaques scheme, founded in 1866, is believed to be the oldest of its kind in the world – and has inspired many similar programmes across the UK and abroad. English Heritage has run the scheme since 1986, and there are now over 980 official plaques in Greater London.

The London plaques celebrate all areas of human endeavour and reflect London's past and present as an international city of enormous diversity and talent. Plaques put up in recent years have commemorated an amazing range of figures – from sporting greats such as footballer Bobby Moore, to modern musical legends like John Lennon, Bob Marley and Freddie Mercury, as well as the suffragettes Emmeline and Christabel Pankhurst, and stars of the stage and screen, including Ava Gardner, Margaret Lockwood and Sir John Gielgud.

Sometimes historical events or groups of people are commemorated, rather than individuals. Examples are the plaque that marks the house in which the artists of the Pre-Raphaelite Brotherhood gathered in Gower Street, Bloomsbury, and the blue roundel at Alexandra Palace – from where the world's first regular high-definition television broadcasts were transmitted.

Several plaques of this variety went up in 2022, including that which memorialises the Match Girls' Strike of 1888 – when young women workers at the Bryant and May factory in Bow took action to win improved pay and conditions – and the roundel that marks the former Ayahs' Home in

Hackney, where displaced nannies and nursemaids from Asia found refuge. The former headquarters of the National Union of Women's Suffrage Societies in Westminster has likewise been commemorated.

Among the individuals honoured with plaques in the last year were Dadabhai Naoroji, the first Asian MP to be popularly elected to the House of Commons, at his old house in Penge; the philosopher Sir Isaiah Berlin, in Holland Park, and the pattern designer Enid Marx, in Islington.

FIND OUT MORE

Our guidebook, *The English Heritage Guide to London's Blue Plaques*, is available at the English Heritage online shop and in all good bookshops. A map-linked blue plaques app may be downloaded at the app store for both Apple and Android phones and tablets, and each official London plaque has its own page on the English Heritage website.

GET INVOLVED

The scheme relies entirely on private donations and almost all plaques originate from a proposal from a member of the public. To be considered for a blue plaque, a person must have been dead for 20 years, and an authentic building holding strong associations with them must survive in London. If you would like to nominate someone for a blue plaque in London, go to **english-heritage.org.uk/propose-a-plaque**

Help us continue this work by making a donation today: **english-heritage.org.uk/support-the-scheme**

THE
AYAHS'
HOME
for nannies
and nursemaids
from Asia
was based here
1900-1921

ENGLISH HERITAGE
DADABHAI
NAOROJI
1825 ~ 1917
Indian Nationalist
and MP
lived here

ENGLISH HERITAGE
The
MATCH
GIRLS' STRIKE
took place here at the
Bryant and May works
in 1888

ENGLISH HERITAGE
ENID
MARX
1902 - 1998
Pattern designer,
illustrator and
artist
lived and worked here
from 1965

LONDON STATUES AND MONUMENTS

Explore central London to discover 47 statues and monuments which honour famous historical figures from all over the world, from monarchs and generals to explorers and nurses. They also include some outstanding 20th-century war memorials, including the iconic Cenotaph.

The statues and monuments in English Heritage's care include masterpieces of sculpture and architecture. Many depict monarchs and aristocrats, generals and statesmen, nurses and explorers. These reflect the values of the times in which they were made and unveiled. These values may not align with those some people hold today, particularly when commemorating Britain's history as an imperial power. Only four women are commemorated – two queens and the nurses Florence Nightingale and Edith Cavell. The monuments include the famous Cenotaph and the Royal Artillery Memorial, still the settings for ceremonies of remembrance each year.

Find out more at **english-heritage.org.uk/ london-statues-and-monuments**

THE CAPITAL'S STATUES AND MONUMENTS

Belgian Gratitude Memorial
Victoria Embankment, WC2N

Captain Scott
Waterloo Place, SW1

Carabiniers' Memorial
Chelsea Embankment, SW3

Cenotaph
Whitehall, SW1

Chindit Memorial
Victoria Embankment, SW1

Christopher Columbus
Belgrave Square, SW1

Duke of Cambridge
Whitehall, SW1

Duke of Devonshire
Whitehall, SW1

Duke of Kent
Crescent Gardens (locked),
Portland Place, W1

Duke of Wellington
Apsley Way, W1

Earl Haig
Whitehall, SW1

Edith Cavell
St Martin's Place, WC2

Field Marshal Bernard Montgomery
Whitehall, SW1

Florence Nightingale
Waterloo Place, SW1

General de Gaulle
Carlton Gardens, SW1

General de San Martin
Belgrave Square, SW1

General Gordon
Victoria Embankment, SW1

George Washington
Trafalgar Square, WC2

Guards Crimean War Memorial
Waterloo Place, SW1

King Charles I
Whitehall, SW1

King Edward VII
Waterloo Place, SW1

King George II
Golden Square, W1

King George III
Cockspur St, SW1

King James II
National Gallery,
Trafalgar Square, WC2

Cenotaph

Marble Arch

Royal Artillery Memorial

Statues in Waterloo Place

King William III
St James's Square, SW1

Lord Curzon
Carlton House Terrace, SW1

Lord Herbert
Waterloo Place, SW1

Lord Napier of Magdala
Queen's Gate, SW7

Lord Portal
Victoria Embankment, SW1

Lord Trenchard
Victoria Embankment, SW1

Machine Gun Corps Memorial
Apsley Way, W1

Marble Arch **W1**

Queen Anne
Queen Anne's Gate, SW1

Queen Anne (formerly identified
as Queen Charlotte)
Queen Square, WC1

Robert Clive
King Charles St, SW1

Royal Artillery Memorial
Apsley Way, W1

Samuel Plimsoll
Victoria Embankment, SW1

Simón Bolívar
Belgrave Square, SW1

Sir Arthur Harris
St Clement Danes, WC2

Sir Colin Campbell
Waterloo Place, SW1

Sir John Franklin
Waterloo Place, SW1

Sir John Lawrence
Waterloo Place, SW1

Sir Walter Ralegh
**Old Royal Naval College,
Greenwich, SE10**

Sir Thomas Cubitt
St George's Drive, Pimlico, SW1

Viscount Alanbrooke
Whitehall, SW1

Viscount Slim
Whitehall, SW1

Wellington Arch and Quadriga
Apsley Way, W1

english-heritage.org.uk

WELCOME TO THE
SOUTH EAST

Osborne, Isle of Wight

South East

The South East of England has experienced events that have defined the country's history.

The fort at **Richborough** (p.59) marks the landing place of Roman invaders in AD 43, while in 1066 William the Conqueror disembarked his troops at **Pevensey Castle** (p.73) before his epic battle for the crown at **Hastings** (p.70). And after centuries of guarding the English Channel from atop the White Cliffs, **Dover Castle** (p.50) played a crucial part in the Second World War.

Henry VIII guarded his realm with coastal forts, including **Deal Castle** (p.48) and **Walmer Castle and Gardens** (p.64), now transformed into a comfortable country house with spectacular gardens.

History was also made at **Down House** (p.54), the family home of Charles Darwin. Other sites shine light on very different family lives, from **Lullingstone Roman Villa** (p.58) to **Osborne** (p.76), the seaside home of Victoria and Albert.

Dover Castle, Kent

Osborne, Isle of Wight

Walmer Castle and Gardens, Kent

DONNINGTON CASTLE

BERKSHIRE – RG14 2LE

The striking, twin-towered, 14th-century gatehouse of this castle, later the focus of a Civil War siege and battle, survives amid impressive earthworks.

OPENING TIMES

Any reasonable daylight hours, exterior viewing only

Car park open daily   7am-7pm

VISIT US

Direction: 1 mile N of Newbury, off B4494

Train: Newbury 1¼ miles

Bus: Visit traveline.info for the latest bus timetables and routes

[ACQ.1952] [&] [♠] [P] [⚠]

Disabled access (Caution: steep slopes within grounds).

Parking: charges apply to non-members, free for Members with valid English Heritage car sticker.

MAP PAGE 304 (4C)
OS MAP 174, 158: SU461692

HAMPSHIRE

BISHOP'S WALTHAM PALACE

HAMPSHIRE – SO32 1DH

The ruins of a medieval palace of the bishops of Winchester, the subject of a recent major restoration project. Much of what survives is the work of William Wykeham, bishop from 1367. The ground floor of the farmhouse, adapted from the palace's lodging range, houses the Bishop's Waltham Town Museum.

BISHOP'S WALTHAM PALACE

Download a free audio tour from our website.

OPENING TIMES

Grounds
Open daily 1 Apr-28 Mar

Site closed 25 Dec

Farmhouse Museum
Open varying days 1 May-30 Sep

See website for latest opening times

VISIT US

Direction: In Bishop's Waltham

Train: Botley 3½ miles

Bus: Visit traveline.info for the latest bus timetables and routes

Tel: 0370 333 1181

[ACQ.1952] [🏰] [&] [♠] [📷] [P] [🚻] [⚠]

Disabled access (grounds only).

Dogs on leads (restricted areas only).

Museum (limited opening hours).

Featured in new *Palaces of the Bishops of Winchester* guidebook.

Caution: deep water, unguarded drops.

MAP PAGE 304 (5C)
OS MAP 185, 119: SU552174

CALSHOT CASTLE

HAMPSHIRE – SO45 1BR

This Tudor artillery fort, built to defend the approaches to Southampton, later saw service in both World Wars.

Managed by Hampshire County Council.

OPENING TIMES

See website for latest opening times

VISIT US

Direction: On spit, 2 miles SE of Fawley, off B3053

CALSHOT CASTLE

Train: Beaulieu Road 10 miles, Southampton 15 miles

Bus: Visit traveline.info for the latest bus timetables and routes

Tel: 023 8089 2023; when castle is closed, please call 023 8089 2077

NON-MEMBERS

See website for entry prices

[ACQ.1964] [&] [E] [📷] [♠] [♦] [😊] [P]
[📷] [&] [⚠]

Disabled access (part of the Courtyard, toilets and some exhibtion space).

Parking charges apply.

Caution: deep water, steep stairs.

MAP PAGE 304 (6C)
OS MAP 196, OL22/OL29/119: SU489025

FLOWERDOWN BARROWS

HAMPSHIRE – SO22 6PS

Three Bronze Age burial mounds, including two bowl barrows and the largest and finest disc barrow in Hampshire.

OPENING TIMES

Any reasonable daylight hours

VISIT US

Direction: Off B3049, out of Winchester to Littleton; at crossroads in centre of village

Train: Winchester 2 miles

Bus: Visit traveline.info for the latest bus timetables and routes

Tel: 0370 333 1181

[ACQ.1972] [🐕]

MAP PAGE 304 (5C)
OS MAP 185, 132: SU459320

FORT BROCKHURST
HAMPSHIRE – PO12 4DS

One of the best surviving of the artillery forts built to protect Portsmouth's vital harbour during the 1850s-60s, when invasion by Napoleon III's France was expected. It's largely unaltered, and you can still see the moated keep, parade ground and emplacements for formidable heavy guns.

OPENING TIMES

Exterior:
Any reasonable daylight hours

Interior: Apr-Oct, 2nd and 4th Sat of the month   11am-3pm

Due to occasional operational changes, we advise visitors to check website in advance

Additional opening times during Gosport Heritage Open Days – please check website

VISIT US

Direction: Off A32, in Gunner's Way, Elson; on N side of Gosport

Train: Fareham 3 miles

Bus: Visit traveline.info for the latest bus timetables and routes

Tel: 0370 333 1181

ACQ.1963 🔲 ♿ 👁 🅿 🎦 ⚠️

Disabled access (grounds and parts of ground floor only).

Dogs on leads (grounds only).

Parking: charges apply to non-members, free for Members with valid English Heritage car sticker.

Caution: deep water, unguarded drops, steep stairs.

> MAP PAGE 304 (6C)
> OS MAP 196, OL29/119:
> SU596021

THE GRANGE AT NORTHINGTON
HAMPSHIRE – SO24 9TG

Set like a lakeside temple in a landscaped park, the Grange at Northington is among the foremost examples of the Greek Revival style in England, remodelled after 1808.

🎦 *Onegin*, with Ralph Fiennes.

OPENING TIMES

Exterior only:
Open daily 1 Apr-28 Mar*

Site closed 24-26 Dec & 1 Jan

See website for latest opening times

*Closes early for Opera evenings in June and July

VISIT US

Direction: Located 4 miles N of New Alresford, off B3046 along a farm track – 450 metres (493 yards). Follow brown signs not sat nav

Train: Winchester 8 miles

Bus: Visit traveline.info for the latest bus timetables and routes

Tel: 0370 333 1181

ACQ.1975 ♿ 🎦 👁 🅿 🎦 ⚠️

Disabled access (with assistance, steep steps to terrace).

Caution: unguarded drops, steep stairs.

> MAP PAGE 304 (5C)
> OS MAP 185, 132: SU562362

HURST CASTLE
HAMPSHIRE – SO41 0TP

HURST CASTLE

Among the most advanced of Henry VIII's artillery fortresses, later strengthened by immense 19th-century gun emplacements, Hurst Castle helped defend the Solent up until the Second World War. You can now visit the Tudor keep, where Charles I was imprisoned in 1648, and the 19th-century east wing has been conserved.

Managed by Hurst Castle Ferries.

OPENING TIMES

See website for latest opening times

Opening times are weather dependent throughout the year. Call 01590 642500 to check before you visit

VISIT US

Direction: 2-mile walk on shingle spit from Milford on Sea. Best approached by ferry from Keyhaven. Ferry departs 10am then approx. every 20 minutes, charges apply – see hurstcastle.co.uk

Train: Lymington Town 6½ miles

Bus: Visit traveline.info for the latest bus timetables and routes

Tel: 01590 642500

NON-MEMBERS

See website for entry prices

ACQ.1933 🔲 🎦 🇪 🎦 🚶 🚶 🗺 🎦 📷 💮 ⚠️

Dogs on leads.

Castle Café open 1 Apr-5 Nov (not managed by English Heritage).

Parking (charge payable) Keyhaven SO41 0TP.

Caution: deep water, unguarded drops, steep stairs.

> MAP PAGE 304 (6B)
> OS MAP 196, OL22/OL29:
> SZ318897

DON'T FORGET

Remember to take your membership card.

KING JAMES'S AND LANDPORT GATES, PORTSMOUTH

HAMPSHIRE – PO1 2EJ

Two ornamental gateways, formerly part of Portsmouth's defences. King James's Gate (1687) has been moved, but Georgian Landport Gate (1760), once the principal entrance to Portsmouth, remains in its original position.

OPENING TIMES

Exterior from roadside only: Any reasonable daylight hours

VISIT US

Direction: King James's Gate forms the officers' entrance to United Services Recreation Ground, Burnaby Rd; Landport Gate as above, men's entrance on St George's Road

Train: Portsmouth Harbour ¼ mile

Bus: Visit traveline.info for the latest bus timetables and routes

Tel: 0370 333 1181

ACQ.1930

Caution: beware of traffic.

> MAP PAGE 304 (6C)
> OS MAP 196, OL29/119
> KING JAMES'S GATE: SZ636999
> LANDPORT GATE: SZ634998

MEDIEVAL MERCHANT'S HOUSE, SOUTHAMPTON

HAMPSHIRE – SO14 2AT

Among the oldest surviving merchant's houses in England, this partly timber-framed combination of home, shop and warehouse was originally built in about 1290. Now vividly recreated as it looked in the mid-14th century, with replica furnishings.

OPENING TIMES

Open varying days 1 Apr-1 Oct

Site closed 2 Oct-28 Mar

See website for latest opening times

VISIT US

Direction: 58 French St, ¼ mile S of city centre, just off Castle Way (between High St and Bugle St)

Train: Southampton ¾ mile

Bus: Visit traveline.info for the latest bus timetables and routes

Tel: 023 8022 1503

Local Tourist Information: Southampton: 023 8083 3333

NON-MEMBERS

See website for entry prices

ACQ.1973 OVP

Disabled access (two steps). Ground floor only.

> MAP PAGE 304 (6B)
> OS MAP 196, OL22: SU419112

NETLEY ABBEY

HAMPSHIRE – SO31 5FB

The most complete surviving Cistercian monastery in southern England, with much of its big 13th-century church, cloister and monastic buildings still standing. Later converted into a Tudor mansion, now largely vanished. The abbey's Romantic Gothic ruins inspired many artists and writers, including Constable, Turner and Jane Austen. Download a free audio tour from our website.

OPENING TIMES

Open daily 1 Apr-28 Mar

Site closed 25 Dec

See website for latest opening times

VISIT US

Direction: In Netley; 4 miles SE of Southampton, facing Southampton Water

Train: Netley 1 mile

Bus: Visit traveline.info for the latest bus timetables and routes

Tel: 0370 333 1181

ACQ.1922 P

Gravel car park, limited spaces. Caution: falling masonry.

> MAP PAGE 304 (6C)
> OS MAP 196, OL22: SU453090

ROYAL GARRISON CHURCH, PORTSMOUTH

HAMPSHIRE – PO1 2NJ

The roofed and furnished chancel of a church constructed c. 1212 and damaged by 1941 bombing. Recent conservation work has seen it enhanced with a new chancel screen, refreshed decoration and step-free access.

OPENING TIMES

See website for latest opening times

VISIT US

Direction: In Portsmouth; on Grand Parade S of High St

Train: Portsmouth Harbour ¾ mile

Bus: Visit traveline.info

Tel: 0370 333 1181

ACQ.1970   🚻   ⛔   **P**

Parking charges apply on the Parade Ground opposite the church.

> MAP PAGE 304 (6C)
> OS MAP 196, OL29/119: SZ633992

SILCHESTER ROMAN TOWN WALLS AND AMPHITHEATRE

HAMPSHIRE – RG7 2HP

An Iron Age tribal centre, Silchester became the important Roman town of Calleva Atrebatum. The complete circuit of its walls, 1½ miles long, can be traced, although

SILCHESTER ROMAN TOWN WALLS AND AMPHITHEATRE

no buildings within survive. Outside are remains of a Roman amphitheatre. Download a free audio tour from our website.

OPENING TIMES

Any reasonable daylight hours

Car park	
1 Apr-30 Sep, daily	8am-7pm
1 Oct-28 Mar, daily	8.30am-4pm

VISIT US

Direction: On a minor road, 1 mile E of Silchester

Train: Bramley or Mortimer, both 2¾ miles

Bus: Visit traveline.info for the latest bus timetables and routes

Tel: 0370 333 1181

ACQ.1965   🚻   🏪   **P**   ⚠

There is no parking at the amphitheatre, visitors should park at the main car park for the Roman Town. Prior notice of tall vehicles (i.e. coaches and minibuses) wishing to park in the car park is needed. Car park operated by Hampshire County Council – please contact 0118 970 0132 to open height barrier.

Caution: unguarded drops, steep stairs.

> MAP PAGE 304 (4C)
> OS MAP 175, 159: SU639624

SOUTHWICK PRIORY

HAMPSHIRE – PO17 6EB

Remains of a wealthy Augustinian priory, originally founded at Portchester: once a famous place of pilgrimage. Only part of the refectory wall survives.

OPENING TIMES

Any reasonable daylight hours

VISIT US

Direction: Access via footpath from Priory Road, opposite village car park

Bus: Visit traveline.info for the latest bus timetables and routes

Tel: 0370 333 1181

ACQ.1970   🚻   **P**   ⚠

Parking in village car park.

Caution: falling masonry.

> MAP PAGE 304 (6C)
> OS MAP 196, 119: SU629084

TITCHFIELD ABBEY

HAMPSHIRE – PO15 5RA

The ruins of a 13th-century abbey of Premonstratensian canons, later converted into a Tudor mansion. The church was rebuilt as a grand turreted gatehouse. Download a free audio tour from our website.

OPENING TIMES

Open daily 1 Apr-28 Mar

Site closed 25-26 Dec

See website for latest opening times

VISIT US

Direction: Located ½ mile N of Titchfield, off A27, along Mill Lane, opposite Fisherman's Rest pub

Train: Fareham 2 miles

Bus: Visit traveline.info for the latest bus timetables and routes

Tel: 0370 333 1181

ACQ.1923   &   🚻   **P**   ⚠

Disabled access (with assistance, steep steps to terrace).

Car park accessed via narrow entrance through high wall.

Parking: charges apply to non-members, free for Members with valid English Heritage car sticker.

Caution: steep stairs.

> MAP PAGE 304 (6C)
> OS MAP 196, 119: SU542067

PORTCHESTER CASTLE

———— HAMPSHIRE – PO16 9QW ————

Set within the most magnificently complete Roman fort walls in northern Europe, this medieval castle became a crowded prisoner of war camp. Our dramatic displays immerse you in the story of the African-Caribbean soldiers held here during the Napoleonic wars.

Much the best-preserved of the Roman 'Saxon Shore' forts, Portchester retains most of its Roman defences, including 16 towers. During the 12th century a Norman castle with a powerful keep was built in one corner, developing into a 14th-century royal palace.

Later, the castle was transformed into a vast prisoner of war camp. During the Napoleonic Wars up to 8,000 captives were held here. Our displays examine how they fought poverty and boredom and retained their national identity.

On the keep's ground floor, you'll find a representation of the theatre where French prisoners performed plays. On the upper floors, surround sound effects evoke the prisoners' sea journey to Britain.

Another arresting installation highlights Portchester's most surprising prisoners, around 2,000 African-Caribbean soldiers captured while fighting for the French on St Lucia in the Caribbean. You'll discover how they encountered kindness as well as cruelty and prejudice. Find more about them at english-heritage.org.uk/black-prisoners

Climb to the roof of the 30-metre (100 feet) high keep for breathtaking views of the Roman fort, with the great sweep of Portsmouth harbour beyond.

OPENING TIMES

Open daily 1 Apr-5 Nov

Open varying days 6 Nov-28 Mar

Site closed 24-25 Dec

See website for latest opening times

VISIT US

Direction: On the S side of Portchester off A27; Junction 11 on M27

Train: Portchester 1 mile

Bus: Visit traveline.info for the latest bus timetables and routes

Tel: 023 9237 8291

NON-MEMBERS

See website for entry prices

By being a Member, you save up to **£32.50** (price of a family ticket) when you visit **Portchester Castle**

ACQ.1926 🎧 ♿ 🐕 ▮ E 🚼 🖥 🚹 🚻 P 🎪 📷 OVP

Caution: relatively steep stairs to the exhibitions on upper floors of the keep.

Disabled access (grounds and lower levels only).

Dogs on leads (outer grounds only).

Toilets (facilities are in the car park, owned and managed by Fareham Borough Council).

MAP PAGE 304 (6C)
OS MAP 196, OL29/119: SU625046

WOLVESEY CASTLE (OLD BISHOP'S PALACE)
HAMPSHIRE – SO23 9NB

An important residence of the wealthy bishops of Winchester since Anglo-Saxon times, standing near to Winchester Cathedral. The extensive surviving ruins date largely from the 12th century. Download a free audio tour from our website.

OPENING TIMES

Open daily 1 Apr-28 Mar

Site closed 25-26 Dec

See website for latest opening times

VISIT US

Direction: 600 metres SE of Winchester Cathedral, next to the Bishop's Palace; access from College St

Train: Winchester ¾ mile

Bus: Visit traveline.info for the latest bus timetables and routes

Tel: 0370 333 1181

ACQ.1962 🎧 ♿ 🐕 🎁 🖼 ⚠

Please do not climb on the walls.

No access to the adjacent garden (private property).

Featured in new *Palaces of the Bishops of Winchester* guidebook.

Caution: deep water, falling masonry.

MAP PAGE 304 (5C)
OS MAP 185, 132: SU484291

BAYHAM OLD ABBEY KENT – TN3 8LP

One of southern England's finest monastic ruins, Bayham Abbey was founded in the early 13th century by Robert de Thurnham for the Premonstratensian 'white canons'. Renowned for the quality and richness of their architecture, these impressive ruins include much of the church, chapter house and picturesque 14th-century gatehouse. The secluded nature of the site is enhanced by views of the picturesque landscape designed by Humphry Repton, creating a beautiful and tranquil experience.

OPENING TIMES

Open daily 1 Apr-31 Oct

Open varying days 1 Nov-28 Mar

Second hand bookshop
Sat-Sun   11am-3pm

Short talks, Sat   1pm-3pm

See website for latest opening times

VISIT US

Direction: 1¾ miles W of Lamberhurst, off B2169

Train: Frant 4 miles then bus 256

Bus: Visit traveline.info

Tel: 0370 333 1181

ACQ.1961 ♿ 🎁 P 🖼 ⚠

Parking: charges apply to non-members, free for Members with valid English Heritage car sticker.

Caution: deep water, unguarded drops.

MAP PAGE 305 (5G)
OS MAP 188, 136: TQ650365

DEAL CASTLE

KENT – CT14 7BA

Lively storytelling, displays and activities help you explore every corner of Deal Castle, the biggest and most elaborate of all Henry VIII's coastal artillery forts.

As you enter this formidable fortress, you'll be faced by a replica Tudor cannon. It's a reminder that Deal was one of the revolutionary new-style artillery castles built from 1539 by Henry VIII to counter a threatened invasion by European Catholic powers. Flanked by neighbouring Walmer Castle and now-vanished Sandown Castle, all linked by defensive earthworks, it was the crucial centrepiece of three forts whose heavy guns commanded the vital sheltered anchorage between the hazardous Goodwin Sands and the shore. Its distinctive multi-lobed design provided all-round firepower from a total of over 140 guns, arranged in five tiers.

On its squat rounded bastions – intended to minimise the effect of incoming cannonballs – you'll find 'Guarding the Downs', one of the displays which vividly illustrate how the castle worked.

Within the keep, the core of the fortress, you'll find 'Henry VIII's Castle of War', throwing light on the world of 1539 and how Deal fitted into it. A huge illustrated jigsaw-style map of Europe lays out the international situation when the castle was built. Sit on the thrones of Henry, his nervous fourth wife, Anne of Cleves, or his opponents the Pope, the Emperor and the King of France; pick up the earphones and you'll hear each one's thoughts. Nearby, there's a 3D jigsaw model of the castle to assemble. In neighbouring rooms you'll discover site-finds of Tudor weaponry from Camber Castle, another of Henry's forts, including pike heads, armour-piercing arrows, and equipment for cannons and muskets.

If you want to try defending the castle yourself, go down to the castle basement to 'Explore and Defend the Rounds'. This dark, narrow and winding passage encircles the whole castle, and is equipped with 53 ports for handguns to mow down any attackers who reached the dry moat. If you dare to venture into the Rounds, you can borrow wellies (the passage floor can be wet after rain) and a replica musket from racks near the entrances. Look out for the wind-up listening devices, which let you eavesdrop on two soldiers during the Civil War siege of 1648, when the castle saw hard fighting. Don't get lost!

To find out more about the fort's later history, climb the spiral stairs to the Georgian panelled rooms of the keep's upper floor. Here the 'Captains of Deal' display tells you about the commanders and garrison soldiers of the castle from Tudor times until the 20th century. You can read 'conversations' between contrasting captains, and hear the thoughts of others. Don't miss the room highlighting the graffiti written or scratched on the castle roof over the centuries, where you can leave your own mark on paper to add to Deal Castle's fascinating history.

The castle stands right next to Deal's attractive beach, and there are fine sea views from the ramparts. A cycle path links Deal and Walmer Castles (p.64) along the beachfront.

english-heritage.org.uk

OPENING TIMES

Open daily 1 Apr-5 Nov

Open varying days 6 Nov-28 Mar

Site closed 24-25 Dec

See website for latest opening times

Last entry 30 mins before closing

VISIT US

Address: Marine Road, Deal,
Kent CT14 7BA

Direction: SW of Deal town centre

Train: Deal ½ mile

Bus: Visit traveline.info for the latest
bus timetables and routes

Tel: 01304 372762

By being a Member, you save up to £32.50 (price of a family ticket) when you visit **Deal Castle**.

NON-MEMBERS

See website for entry prices

ACQ.1904 🎧 ♿ 🔦 E 📖 🚶 🚻 🐕 P 📷 ⚠ OVP

Disabled access (courtyards and ground
floor only, parking available).

Parking: charges apply to non-members,
free for Members with valid English Heritage
car sticker and free ticket from the machine
(3 hours maximum stay). See signs on
arrival for details.

MAP PAGE 305 (4J)
OS MAP 179, 150: TR378522

DOVER CASTLE

KENT – CT16 1HU

Crowning the White Cliffs high above the Channel, Dover's majestic fortress offers visitors an unparalleled journey into the past, from Roman times via medieval sieges to the Second World War and beyond.

Renowned as 'the Key to England', Dover Castle boasts a long and immensely eventful 2,000-year history. Its spectacular site still displays a Roman lighthouse and an Anglo-Saxon church. Begun soon after 1066, it became a medieval royal castle-palace of immense strength. In the labyrinthine tunnels beneath it, Vice Admiral Ramsay planned the miraculous rescue of the British Army from Dunkirk in 1940. It later concealed a secret Cold War bunker.

MEDIEVAL ROYAL PALACE

Dover Castle is first and foremost the strongest medieval fortress in England, created by King Henry II and his Plantagenet successors in the 12th and 13th centuries. Mutually supporting circuits of towered walls made it the very first 'concentric' castle in Europe. At its heart stands the mighty keep – the Great Tower. Built between 1180 and 1185, this symbol of kingly power was also a palace designed for royal ceremony.

The interior of the Great Tower palace has been recreated as it might have appeared when newly completed. Entering the Great Tower, you'll find projected figures, which bring to life your journey round the vibrantly recreated and colourfully furnished rooms of the palace, from kitchens and royal bedchambers to the impressive King's Hall.

You can follow the dramatic story of Henry II and his turbulent brood in an introductory exhibition, 'A Family at War', and a virtual tour reveals the Great Tower to those unable to explore it.

EPIC SIEGES

Climb to the Great Tower's roof for panoramic views over the castle's immense complex of medieval fortifications. These saw desperate fighting during the epic sieges of 1216-17, when the castle resisted ten months of attack by a French army. Intrepid visitors can descend into the Medieval Tunnels, burrowed beneath the castle during and after the siege.

THE FIRST WORLD WAR

During the First World War, Dover was officially designated as a Fortress, with the castle as its military headquarters. The Fire Command Post recreates this dramatic chapter in its history. Explore what it was like to work here, try communicating in Morse code, learn semaphore and discover how to spot enemy or friendly ships.

To counter the new threat of aerial attack, the fortress mounted pioneering anti-aircraft guns. Now it's home to the only working British 3-inch anti-aircraft gun in the world, which performs regular firing demonstrations on selected weekends in summer.

Exploring the maze of intriguing and sometimes eerie tunnels beneath Dover Castle, burrowed at times of crisis both for the fortress and the nation it defended. The atmospheric Medieval Tunnels were cut during and after the epic sieges of 1216-17. When French invasion threatened during the Napoleonic Wars, they were enlarged into 'bomb proof' underground barracks for up to 2,000 defending troops.

When even greater danger to castle and nation loomed in 1940, the extended Secret Wartime Tunnels became the nerve-centre of Operation Dynamo – the rescue of the British army from Dunkirk. Witness the drama of the evacuation in the very place where it was planned, and relive the tension in the Underground Hospital. Later still, and right up until 1984, the tunnels housed a secret Cold War government bunker. See if you and your team can solve the clues and crack the codes to reach the bunker in our immersive escape room experience.

Peverell's Tower was at one time a prison. Today it makes a perfect romantic castle tower for two.

The *Sergeant Major's House* is surrounded by hundreds of years of history. This spacious four-storey Georgian residence sleeps six. Great for families, it even has its own secret games room.

See p.13 for details on staying at Dover and our other holiday cottages.

STAY WITH US

THE SECOND WORLD WAR: RESCUE FROM DUNKIRK

Dover Castle's defences were even more sorely tested in the darkest days of the Second World War, when tunnels deep beneath the castle became Vice Admiral Bertram Ramsay's bomb-proof naval headquarters.

On 26 May 1940, Ramsay began the rescue of the British Army and its allies, trapped at Dunkirk and fighting for their lives. The task of rescuing them – 'Operation Dynamo' – demanded sending a huge improvised fleet of ships across the Channel, under attack from air, sea and land. The British Army in France depended upon it.

Make the adventurous journey into the Wartime Tunnels and immerse yourself in the drama of the daring evacuation that followed. Film presentations vividly recreate the run-up to Dunkirk. Then, in the very place where Operation Dynamo was planned, witness the astounding rescue from the eastern breakwater and beaches happening all around you.

You can also take a fascinating guided tour of the Underground Hospital within the tunnels, reliving the tension as a surgeon battles to save an injured pilot. Find out more about the 'Miracle of Dunkirk' in the 'Wartime Tunnels Uncovered' exhibition, featuring the recorded voices of many who actually took part.

After Dunkirk, the tunnels played a leading role in the elaborate deception which fooled the enemy about the true target of the D-Day invasions.

Later still, during the 1960s Cold War, they hosted a top-secret government bunker.

Both the Great Tower Café and the NAAFI Restaurant have been reinvigorated. Menus in the Great Tower Café include more family-friendly options, and the NAAFI has enhanced takeaway and sit-down meal options.

See our website for dates when you can meet costumed live interpreters in the Great Tower, bringing to life the reign of Henry II.

All this, and very much more, makes it well worth enjoying a whole day of discovery at Dover Castle. There are lots of refreshment stops, and an ice cream van in summer. Our new nine-seater electric bus is available to help those who need assistance to get around this vast and intriguing fortress.

🎬 *The Other Boleyn Girl* (2008); *Into the Woods* (2014); *Avengers: Age of Ultron* (2015); *Wolf Hall* (2015); *The Crown* (2016); *King Lear* (2018)

OPENING TIMES

Open daily 1 Apr-5 Nov

Open varying days 6 Nov-28 Mar

Site closed 24-25 Dec

See website for latest opening times

Last entry 1 hour before closing

VISIT US

Address: Dover Castle, Castle Hill, Dover, Kent CT16 1HU

Direction: E of Dover town centre

Train: Dover Priory 1½ miles

Bus: Visit traveline.info for the latest bus timetables and routes

Tel: 0370 333 1181

Local Tourist Information: Dover: 01304 205108

NON-MEMBERS

See website for entry prices

Additional charges for Members and non-members apply for the Bunker (discount for Members) and may apply on event days.

Please see the Dover Castle website for information on accessibility. Mobility scooters are available and should be booked in advance.

Dogs are welcome on a lead at all times, although not permitted in the Great Tower and Secret Wartime Tunnels (apart from assistance dogs).

We advise you to wear comfortable shoes.

MAP PAGE 305 (5J)
OS MAP 179, 138: TR325419

SAVE TODAY By being a Member, you save up to £86 (price of a family ticket) when you visit **Dover Castle**.

The Great Tower is self-guided. Stewards in the tower are always on hand to answer any questions. Access to the Operation Dynamo experience in the Secret Wartime Tunnels is by guided tour only. Due to the immersive nature of these visits, no independent guiding is allowed in these areas. However, tour leaders of groups of younger visitors must stay with their parties at all times. Access to the Underground Hospital (separate access from Operation Dynamo) is by guided tour only (limited to 30 people and lasting approximately 20 minutes). At peak times, there may be queues at the popular tunnel experiences. Groups of 11+ can call and book ahead for a group discount on admission. Car parks open at site opening time. Last tunnel tours depart one hour before closing.

HOME OF CHARLES DARWIN, DOWN HOUSE

KENT – BR6 7JT

Experience the Victorian country house where the world was changed. Explore the home of Charles Darwin and his family at your own pace.

A delightful place in itself to visit, Down House is a site of outstanding international significance. Here the famous naturalist Charles Darwin lived with his family for 40 years, worked on his revolutionary theories, and wrote *On the Origin of Species by Means of Natural Selection* – the book which shook the Victorian world and has influenced thinking ever since.

You'll find Darwin's work and personality vividly reflected throughout the house and grounds. The handheld tour, narrated by Sir David Attenborough and Andrew Marr, guides you round the family rooms as well as the garden. It includes commentaries by experts, animations, film footage and games for all the family.

The ground floor rooms have been recreated as they appeared when he lived here with his indefatigably supportive wife, Emma, and their many children. They include the 'Old Study' where Darwin wrote his most famous books, still displaying his chair, writing board and many personal items. You can also visit the family's drawing room – with Emma's grand piano – billiard room and dining room. Upstairs, his bedroom has been recreated as when he rested there. It gives a detailed insight into Darwin's personal side – from the non-scientific books he enjoyed reading

to his taste for Old Master prints. A refuge when he was suffering from poor health, it also enabled him to keep an eye on his garden experiments from the room's large bay windows. A soundscape lets you listen in on Emma reading to her husband.

'UNCOVERING ORIGIN' EXHIBITION

The award-winning exhibition on the house's first floor covers Darwin's life, his scientific work, and the controversy that it provoked. Beginning with an introduction to Darwin and the impact of his theories, the displays continue with his famous five-year voyage aboard the *Beagle* in 1831-36, including a full-scale recreation of his on-board cabin. You'll discover how Darwin's observations of wildlife during the voyage influenced his thinking, and how an insect bite may have triggered the ill-health which plagued him all his life. Further displays highlight *On the Origin of Species*, which immediately sold out its first edition and consolidated Darwin's international recognition and notoriety.

The Darwin children's schoolroom celebrates family life at Down House. There's also an education room available for family learning, and a resources room for those interested in delving deeper includes digitised versions of Darwin's journals and notebooks.

EXPERIMENTS IN THE GARDENS

By no means the stereotypically stern Victorian father, Darwin involved his children in his practical experiments in the extensive gardens of Down House. This was his 'outdoor laboratory' and the place where he made many of his discoveries. You can now follow these via the multimedia guide, beginning with Darwin's 'weed garden' illustrating the struggle for existence in nature.

The sundial amid pretty flowerbeds highlights Emma Darwin's role as a gardener, a surviving mulberry tree recalls family traditions, and a 'lawn experiment' investigates proliferation of plant species. Visit the nearby glasshouse to see some of Darwin's most fascinating experiments, and the working observation beehive in the laboratory. Explore our new interactive panels in the gardens and the laboratory, which help to bring Darwin's experiments to life.

After a tour of the extensive kitchen gardens, you reach what is for many a place of pilgrimage: the wooded Sandwalk. This was Darwin's famous 'thinking path', which he paced for five laps a day while working out his theories.

Stop off at the tearoom, in Darwin's kitchen area, for a refreshing break before exploring the grounds.

Please note: No photography is allowed inside the house.

HELPING BUTTERFLIES

Many butterfly species are in serious trouble. To help them, partners including the London Wildlife Trust have begun to create a Butterfly Bank at Down House. Wildflowers seeded on this chalk bank will support existing local butterfly populations and attract new species. But it will take some time to establish, so watch that space...

OPENING TIMES

Open daily 1 Apr-5 Nov

Open varying days 6 Nov-28 Mar

Site closed 24-25 Dec

See website for latest opening times

VISIT US

Address: Down House, Luxted Road, Downe, Kent BR6 7JT

Direction: Luxted Road, Downe; off A21 or A233. Some satellite navigation systems will not accurately navigate you to site. Please plan your route in advance

Train: Orpington 3¾ miles, Bromley South 5½ miles

Bus: R8 and 146 service Down House, for more information visit **traveline.info**

Tel: 01689 859119

NON-MEMBERS

See website for entry prices

SAVE TODAY

By being a Member, you save up to £60 (price of a family ticket) when you visit Home of Charles Darwin, Down House.

ACQ.1996 🎧 📷 ♿ 🏛 E ❄ 💻 🚼
🚹 🚻 🚫 P 🅿 📷 💳 👍 OVP

Disabled access: level access throughout the house and gardens (excluding sandwalk). Two designated blue badge spaces in car park. Wheelchair hire available.

Audio tour is the multimedia tour.

Dogs (except assistance dogs) are not allowed on site at any time and must not be left unattended in the car park.

Parking available but can be limited at busy times. Coach parking available for one coach, must be booked in advance.

No smoking or vaping anywhere on site, including gardens.

MAP PAGE 305 (4F)
OS MAP 177/187,147: TQ431611

DYMCHURCH MARTELLO TOWER
KENT – TN29 0NU

One of 103 ingeniously designed artillery towers built between 1805 and 1812 at vulnerable points around the south and east coasts, to resist threatened Napoleonic invasion. It's been re-equipped with its single roof-mounted cannon, which could be rotated to fire in any direction. The small garrison occupied 'bomb-proofed' rooms within.

Open in partnership with the Friends of Martello 24.

OPENING TIMES
Exterior only:
Any reasonable daylight hours

Interior:
Open varying days 1 Apr-31 Oct

See website for latest opening times

Bespoke visits for groups of 10 or more by appointment, please email theromneymarsh.net/ visitmartello24#bespoke

VISIT US
Direction: Access from Dymchurch High Street

Train: Sandling 7 miles; Dymchurch (Romney, Hythe and Dymchurch Railway) ¾ mile

Bus: Visit traveline.info for the latest bus timetables and routes

Tel: 01787 366604

ACQ.1959 **E** ⊗ ⚠

Caution: steep stairs.

MAP PAGE 305 (5H)
OS MAP 189, 138: TR102292

EYNSFORD CASTLE
KENT – DA4 0AA

The substantial walls of a very early Norman 'enclosure castle', begun c. 1085-87 and unusually little altered. In an attractive village setting.

OPENING TIMES
Open daily 1 Apr-28 Mar

Site closed 25 & 26 Dec

See website for latest opening times

VISIT US
Direction: In Eynsford, off A225

Train: Eynsford 1 mile

Bus: Visit traveline.info

Tel: 0370 333 1181

ACQ.1948 ♿ ⊗ **P** ⚠

Caution: deep water, steep stairs.

MAP PAGE 305 (4F)
OS MAP 177, 162: TQ542658

FAVERSHAM STONE CHAPEL (OUR LADY OF ELVERTON)
KENT – ME13 0TB

Ruins of a small Anglo-Saxon and medieval chapel, incorporating the remains of a pagan Romano-British mausoleum. Near the probable site of the Roman town of Durolevum.

OPENING TIMES
Any reasonable daylight hours

FAVERSHAM STONE CHAPEL

VISIT US
Direction: In field immediately N of A2 just W of Ospringe and opposite Faversham Road

Train: Faversham 1½ miles

Bus: Visit traveline.info for the latest bus timetables and routes

Tel: 0370 333 1181

ACQ.1972 ♘ ⚠

Access is across a field.

Caution: beware of traffic.

MAP PAGE 305 (4H)
OS MAP 178, 149: TQ992613

HORNE'S PLACE CHAPEL
KENT – TN26 2AL

Rare survival of a domestic chapel, built for William Horne in 1366 and attached to his manor house, which was attacked during the Peasants' Revolt of 1381. (House and chapel are privately owned.)

OPENING TIMES
By appointment only. Please phone Customer Services on 0370 333 1181

Open Sep Heritage Open Days only. See website for latest opening times

VISIT US
Direction: 1½ miles N of Appledore

Train: Appledore 2½ miles

Bus: Visit traveline.info for the latest bus timetables and routes

Tel: 0370 333 1181

ACQ.1950 ⊗ ⚠ OVP

Caution: steep stairs.

MAP PAGE 305 (5H)
OS MAP 189, 125: TQ958309

LULLINGSTONE ROMAN VILLA

—— KENT – DA4 0JA ——

Among the most exciting Roman villa survivals in Britain, Lullingstone Roman Villa's vivid displays and interpretation give you a unique insight into Roman domestic life over three centuries.

The villa was begun in about AD 100, and developed to suit successive wealthy owners. These may have included the family of Pertinax, Roman Emperor for just 87 days in AD 193. Additions included a heated bath suite and a remarkable underground pagan 'cult room', including a wall painting of water deities, by far the oldest painting in English Heritage's care.

The villa reached its luxurious zenith in the mid-4th century, when a big new dining room was added. This displays spectacular mosaics, including Europa and Jupiter, and Bellerophon killing the Chimera. By now Christians, the owners also created a 'house-church' above the pagan cult room: wall paintings discovered here are among the earliest evidence of Christianity in Britain, but pagan worship may also have continued, suggesting a relaxed relationship between the old and new faiths.

All this is clearly interpreted in the galleries overlooking the excavated remains, where you'll see finds including adult and infant skeletons. Modern children and adults can play Roman board games, handle original building materials and try on Roman costumes. See the villa come to life in a film and light show that illuminates excavated areas and reveals how they were once used.

OPENING TIMES

Open daily 1 Apr-5 Nov

Open varying days 6 Nov-28 Mar

Site closed 24-26 Dec & 1 Jan

See website for latest opening times

VISIT US

Direction: ½ mile SW of Eynsford, off J3 of M25, A20 towards West Kingsdown, A225 to Eynsford

Train: Eynsford 2 miles

Bus: Visit traveline.info for the latest bus timetables and routes

Tel: 01322 863467

NON-MEMBERS

See website for entry prices

By being a Member, you save up to £36.50 (price of a family ticket) when you visit **Lullingstone Roman Villa**

ACQ 1958 🔊 ♿ 🎁 🍴 E 📷 ♿ OVP

Dogs on leads (restricted areas only).

Parking: charges apply to non-members, free for Members with valid English Heritage car sticker.

MAP PAGE 305 (4F)
OS MAP 177/188, 147/162: TQ530651

RICHBOROUGH ROMAN FORT AND AMPHITHEATRE

KENT – CT13 9JW

Evocatively sited amid the East Kent marshes, Richborough Roman Fort is the most symbolically important of all Roman sites in Britain, witnessing both the beginning and the end of Roman rule here.

Here the invading Roman forces first came ashore in AD 43. Later an important port of entry to Roman Britain, it became the site of one of the most powerful 'Saxon Shore' forts, long sections of whose stone walls still stand high. It was also one of the last Roman forts to be regularly occupied: there was still a large Roman population here in the early 5th century.

NEW FOR 2023

In spring 2023 a major new project will be completed, transforming the experience of visiting Richborough by highlighting its leading role in the history of Roman Britain. We're creating a replica of a Roman gateway and a section of the rampart which protected the Roman invasion beachhead in AD 43. The museum is being transformed while new information panels, family trail and audio guides, as well as accessible paths will make Roman Richborough easier to explore and understand for more people. There'll also be a new pathway enabling visitors to stand on the site of the Roman amphitheatre nearby, and a programme of activities for local schools and the wider community.

OPENING TIMES

Fort: See website for latest opening times

Amphitheatre: Any reasonable time in daylight hours, access across grazed land from footpath; please call 01304 612013 for details

VISIT US

Direction: At the A256/A257 roundabout, head for Sandwich then turn left onto Richborough Road and proceed for approx. 1 mile

Train: Sandwich 2 miles

Bus and riverbus: Visit traveline.info (bus) and visitkent.co.uk and cptcolinsriverbus.co.uk (both riverbus) for details

Tel: 01304 612013

NON-MEMBERS

See website for entry prices

By being a Member, you save up to £32.50 (price of a family ticket) when you visit **Richborough Roman Fort and Amphitheatre**

ACQ.1912

Dogs on leads (restricted areas only).

New guidebook.

MAP PAGE 305 (4J) OS MAP 179, 150
FORT: TR324602
AMPHITHEATRE: TR321598

KIT'S COTY HOUSE AND LITTLE KIT'S COTY HOUSE
KENT – ME20 7EZ

The remains of two megalithic burial chambers. Impressive Kit's Coty has three uprights and a massive capstone. Little Kit's Coty House, alias the Countless Stones, is now a jumble of sarsens.

OPENING TIMES
Any reasonable daylight hours

VISIT US
Direction: W of A229, 2 miles N of Maidstone

Train: Aylesford 2½ miles

Bus: Visit traveline.info for the latest bus timetables and routes

Tel: 0370 333 1181

ACQ.1883 🐕 ⚠ Caution: beware of traffic.

MAP PAGE 305 (4G)
OS MAP 178/188, 148
KIT'S COTY HOUSE: TQ745608
LITTLE KIT'S COTY HOUSE: TQ744604

KNIGHTS TEMPLAR CHURCH, DOVER
KENT – CT17 9DP

Foundations of a small medieval chapel with a distinctive round nave, a feature associated with the military order of Knights Templar.

OPENING TIMES
Any reasonable daylight hours

VISIT US
Direction: On the Western Heights above Dover

Train: Dover Priory ¾ mile

KNIGHTS TEMPLAR CHURCH

Bus: Visit traveline.info for the latest bus timetables and routes

Tel: 0370 333 1181

ACQ.1968 🐕 P ⚠
Parking (on the road).
Caution: unguarded drops.

MAP PAGE 305 (5J)
OS MAP 179, 138: TR313407

MAISON DIEU
KENT – ME13 8TS

This attractive flint and timber-framed medieval building was part of a much larger complex, including a Canterbury pilgrims' hostel, a royal lodging and a school. It houses a museum including archaeological finds made here and at a nearby Roman cemetery. Managed by the Maison Dieu Museum Trust.

OPENING TIMES
See website for latest opening times

VISIT US
Direction: On main A2 on W corner of Water Lane in village of Ospringe. Public car park 300yds W

Train: Faversham ¾ mile

Bus: Visit traveline.info for the latest bus timetables and routes

Tel: 01795 601714

NON-MEMBERS
See website for entry prices

ACQ.1947 📷 🚶 🚶 📷 ❌ 📷 ⚠
Caution: steep stairs.

MAP PAGE 305 (4H)
OS MAP 178, 149: TR003609

MILTON CHANTRY
KENT – DA12 2BH

Retaining its 14th-century timber roof, this was in turn a hospital, chantry chapel, pub, barracks and Second World War gas decontamination chamber.

Managed by Gravesham Borough Council.

OPENING TIMES
See website for latest opening times

VISIT US
Direction: In New Tavern Fort Gardens; E of central Gravesend, off A226

Train: Gravesend ¾ mile

Bus: Visit traveline.info for the latest bus timetables and routes

Tel: 01474 337600

ACQ.1972 🎧 📷 🐾 ⚠
Caution: steep stairs.

MAP PAGE 305 (4G)
OS MAP 177/178, 162/163: TQ653743

OLD SOAR MANOR
KENT – TN15 0QX

A small but complete portion of a stone manor house built c. 1290.

Managed by the National Trust on behalf of English Heritage.

OPENING TIMES
Open daily 1 Apr-30 Sep (closed Tue)

Site closed 1 Oct-28 Mar

See website for latest opening times

VISIT US
Direction: 1 mile E of Plaxtol

Train: Borough Green and Wrotham 2½ miles

Bus: Visit traveline.info for the latest bus timetables and routes

Tel: 01732 810378

ACQ.1948 🐾 P ⚠ Parking (limited).
Dogs on leads (grounds only).
Caution: steep stairs.

MAP PAGE 305 (4G)
OS MAP 188, 147/148: TQ619541

RECULVER TOWERS AND ROMAN FORT

KENT – CT6 6SS

Twin 12th-century towers of an atmospheric ruined seaside church, enclosing traces of a Saxon monastery. Within the partly visible walls of one of the first Roman 'Saxon Shore' forts. Download a free audio tour from our website.

OPENING TIMES

Exterior only: Any reasonable daylight hours

VISIT US

Direction: At Reculver, 3 miles E of Herne Bay; signed off Thanet Way A299

Train: Herne Bay 4 miles

Bus: Visit traveline.info for the latest bus timetables and routes

Tel: 0370 333 1181

ACQ.1925 ♿ 🐕 📷 ⚠

Disabled access (grounds only – long slope up from car park).

Parking (pay and display), toilets and a café are available at nearby Reculver Visitor Centre (not managed by English Heritage).

Caution: steep slopes.

MAP PAGE 305 (4J)
OS MAP 179, 150: TR228693

ST AUGUSTINE'S ABBEY CONDUIT HOUSE

KENT – CT1 1QH

The Conduit House is part of the monastic waterworks that supplied nearby St Augustine's Abbey.

OPENING TIMES

Exterior only: Any reasonable daylight hours

VISIT US

Direction: In King's Park. Approx. 5-10 min walk from St Augustine's Abbey. Please call or ask at the Abbey for directions

Train: Canterbury East and West, both ¾ mile

Bus: Visit traveline.info for the latest bus timetables and routes

Tel: 0370 333 1181

ACQ.1977 🐕 P ⚠

Parking (on street only).

Caution: deep water.

MAP PAGE 305 (4H)
OS MAP 179, 150: TR159580

ST AUGUSTINE'S CROSS

KENT – CT12 5JB

This Anglo-Saxon style Victorian cross marks what is traditionally believed to be the site of St Augustine's landing in England in AD 597. Nearby was the stream where he allegedly baptised his first English convert.

ST AUGUSTINE'S CROSS

OPENING TIMES

Any reasonable daylight hours

VISIT US

Direction: Cliffs End, Thanet, 2 miles E of Minster off B29048

Train: Minster 2 miles

Bus: Visit traveline.info

Tel: 0370 333 1181

ACQ.1912 ♿ 🐕

MAP PAGE 305 (4J)
OS MAP 179, 150: TR340642

ST JOHN'S COMMANDERY

KENT – CT15 7HG

The 13th-century chapel and hall of a 'Commandery' of Knights Hospitallers, later converted into a farmhouse. Features a medieval crown-post roof and 16th-century ceilings.

OPENING TIMES

By appointment only. To arrange your visit phone 07712 899290

Open weekends of Sep (Heritage Open Days) 10am-4pm

See website for latest opening times

VISIT US

Direction: 2 miles NE of Densole, off A260

Train: Kearsney 4 miles; Folkestone Central 6 miles

Bus: Visit traveline.info for the latest bus timetables and routes

ACQ.1978 🐕 P ⚠

Dogs on leads (grounds only).

Caution: steep stairs.

MAP PAGE 305 (5J)
OS MAP 179/189, 138: TR232440

ROCHESTER CASTLE

KENT – ME1 1SW

Discover the tallest Norman keep in England, the target of famous medieval sieges.

Dominating the bridge where the road from London to Dover crossed the river Medway, Rochester Castle was among the most strategically important fortresses in medieval England. In 1136 William of Corbeil, Archbishop of Canterbury, completed the great stone keep at the command of Henry I. At 37.7 metres (125 feet) high, it was probably the tallest castle keep ever built.

In 1215, garrisoned by rebel barons, the castle endured an epic siege by King John. He used 'the fat of 40 pigs' to fire a mine burrowed beneath the keep, bringing its south-east corner crashing down. Even then the defenders held out behind a stout wall within the building, living on water and horsemeat until finally starved out.

You can still see how the demolished corner tower was rebuilt – it's rounded, not square like the rest – before the keep endured a second siege in 1264, when it beat off an assault by Simon de Montfort's rebel army.

Exploring Rochester's keep shows you why it was so hard to take. After entering the forebuilding at first floor level, you can climb some 200 spiralling steps, winding from the basement cesspit up to the battlements. On the way you'll pass the chapel, displaying a model of the whole castle and a cutaway of the keep. Next comes the vast galleried great hall with its round-headed Norman arches, one of the most impressive spaces in any English castle. Then you climb past the third floor to the keep roof. Enjoy breathtaking views over the nearby cathedral, the historic core of Rochester and the broad sweep of the Medway whose crossing this noble fortress once guarded.

Managed by Medway Council.

OPENING TIMES

See website for latest opening times

Last entry 45 mins before closing

Due to events that take place in July adjacent to the castle, it may be necessary to close early on some days. Please check the website for details

VISIT US

Direction: By Rochester Bridge (A2): Junction 1 of M2 and Junction 2 of M25. Signposted from A228 Rochester by-pass

Train: Combined train/bus station, 5 minute walk from castle

Bus: Visit traveline.info for the latest bus timetables and routes

Tel: 01634 332901

NON-MEMBERS

See website for entry prices

Audio tours (small charge).

Dogs on leads (grounds only).

Events (not English Heritage).

Toilets (in castle grounds).

No disabled access to keep.

Caution: steep stairs, falling masonry.

MAP PAGE 305 (4G)
OS MAP 178, 148/163: TQ741686

english-heritage.org.uk

ST AUGUSTINE'S ABBEY

—— KENT – CT1 1PF ——

Explore this ancient monastery, an outstandingly important landmark in English history.

Founded in AD 598 by St Augustine himself, this once-great abbey proclaims the rebirth of Christianity in southern England. The pagan King Aethelberht of Kent, then the most powerful of the Anglo-Saxon monarchs, married a Christian princess from France. Soon afterwards he accepted baptism by Augustine, a missionary from Rome. He thus became the first Christian Anglo-Saxon ruler.

To mark his conversion, Aethelberht gave Augustine land to build this very first monastery in Anglo-Saxon England. Displaying a wonderful variety of site finds – including personal possessions and intriguing artefacts from graves – the big site museum traces how the Saxon monastery was magnificently rebuilt by the Normans before becoming a Tudor royal palace and Stuart garden.

Using award-winning state-of-the-art technology, adults and children aged ten and over can also take a personal virtual reality tour of the abbey as it looked in about 1500; a fascinating and absorbing experience.

Be sure to explore the extensive and atmospheric abbey ruins in person, too. They're set against a backdrop of Canterbury's medieval buildings, with the cathedral towers soaring in the distance. Guided by the audio tour, you'll discover excavated remains of the oldest Anglo-Saxon churches in England. These were overlaid after 1072 by the huge Norman monastery with its cathedral-sized church, whose crypt and other features you can still clearly see.

The cradle of revived English Christianity, this tranquil but immensely significant place shouldn't be missed by visitors to the Canterbury World Heritage Site.

OPENING TIMES
Open daily 1 Apr–5 Nov

Open varying days 6 Nov–28 Mar

Site closed 24-26 Dec & 1 Jan

See website for latest opening times

VISIT US
Direction: In Canterbury, ¼ mile east of city centre

Train: Canterbury East and West, both ¾ mile

Bus: Visit traveline.info for the latest bus timetables and routes

Tel: 01227 767345

Local Tourist Information:
Canterbury: 01227 862162

NON-MEMBERS
See website for entry prices

By being a Member, you save up to **£32.50** (price of a family ticket) when you visit **St Augustine's Abbey**

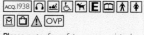

Please note: for safety reasons, virtual reality viewers cannot be used by children under ten.

Disabled access (all site can be viewed, but some steps).

Pay and display parking nearby. Long-stay Park and Ride at New Dover Road and Wincheap.

MAP PAGE 305 (4H)
OS MAP 179, 150: TR155578

WALMER CASTLE AND GARDENS

KENT – CT14 7LJ

There's plenty to see and do at Walmer Castle, a Tudor artillery fort turned elegant stately home set amid delightful and immensely varied gardens. We've revealed areas of the pleasure grounds inaccessible for over a century, including the long-lost chalk quarry Glen Garden, added imaginative play spaces for children in the Woodland Walk and created the attractive Glasshouse Café by the Kitchen Garden.

'The most charming marine chateau that ever was' – as a friend of the Duke of Wellington described it – Walmer Castle began in 1539-40 as one of Henry VIII's Tudor artillery forts defending the Downs, a crucial sheltered anchorage. But within the distinctive 'clover leaf' shell characteristic of Tudor forts, you'll discover the comfortable and fashionable rooms of a country house. For almost three centuries, it's been the official residence of the Lord Warden of the Cinque Ports, an office granted to some of Britain's most celebrated people, including Sir Winston Churchill and Queen Elizabeth the Queen Mother.

Displays highlight the Duke of Wellington, Lord Warden for 23 years until his death here, aged 83, in 1852. You'll see his spartan bedroom, complete with the original armchair in which he died, and a pair of his 'Wellington boots'. Tracing other famous Lords Warden, more rooms are set as in Georgian times, and as during the First World War, when the castle was a hub for high-level conferences. Look out for the second-hand bookshop in the basement.

Recent garden developments recreate the vision of Lord Warden William Pitt the Younger, a former Prime Minister, and his niece and hostess Lady Hester Stanhope. In 1805, they transformed a former chalk quarry on the boundary of the 8-acre gardens into a romantic Glen, now rejuvenated for you to enjoy. The steps descending into it are steep, but there's a viewing platform and accessible vistas from the top. You'll reach the Glen by the winding Woodland Walk, set with surprises and creative play spaces for children – including a wobbly bridge, climbing frames and a quirky oversized swing.

Nearer the house, you'll find the formal Broadwalk, flanked by vividly planted herbaceous borders and the famous Cloud Hedges; the tranquil Queen Mother's Garden, created to honour her 95th birthday (look out for the bronze corgi on a bench); and the fully working Kitchen Garden, whose flowers, vegetables and fruit you can admire from our light and airy Glasshouse Café. It also supplies produce for the produce stall and the Lord Warden's Tearoom.

STAY WITH US

Walmer Castle's holiday cottages, the *Greenhouse Apartment* and the *Garden Cottage*, both offer great views over the Kitchen Garden and are only a few minutes' walk from the beach.

See p.13 for details on staying at Walmer and our other holiday cottages.

OPENING TIMES

Open daily 1 Apr-5 Nov*

Open varying days 6 Nov-28 Mar

Site closed 24-25 Dec

See website for latest opening times

Last entry 1 hour before closing

*Closed from 7-9 July when Lord Warden is in residence

VISIT US

Address: Walmer Castle, Kingsdown Road, Deal, Kent CT14 7LJ

Direction: On coast S of Walmer, on A258; Junction 13 of M20 or from M2 to Deal

Train: Walmer 1 mile

Bus: Visit traveline.info for the latest bus timetables and routes

Tel: 01304 364288

Local Tourist Information:
Deal: 01304 369576 and
Dover: 01304 205108

NON-MEMBERS

See website for entry prices

SAVE TODAY By being a Member, you save up to £52.50 (price of a family ticket) when you visit **Walmer Castle and Gardens.**

ACQ.1904

Caution: steep steps to and within Glen. Stout footwear recommended.

Disabled access (three ground-floor display rooms, tearooms, shop courtyard and garden only; parking available across the road from castle). Mobility scooters and wheelchairs available on loan. No access to Glen or moat garden. Steep steps to second-hand bookshop in basements.

Please note: dogs (except registered assistance dogs) not allowed in grounds at any time. No smoking or vaping anywhere on site, including gardens.

Parking located at the beach opposite (free for Members with valid car sticker). Limited disabled parking on site.

No coach parking at the site.

MAP PAGE 305 (4J)
OS MAP 179, 138: TR378501

ST LEONARD'S TOWER

KENT – ME19 6PD

An early and well-preserved example of a small freestanding Norman tower keep, surviving almost to its original height.

OPENING TIMES

Exterior only: Any reasonable daylight hours

VISIT US

Direction: Nr West Malling, on unclassified road W of A228

Train: West Malling 1 mile

Bus: Visit traveline.info for the latest bus timetables and routes

Tel: 0370 333 1181

ACQ.1937 🐕 P ⚠ Parking (limited).

Caution: falling masonry.

> **MAP PAGE 305 (4G)**
> OS MAP 178/188, 148: TQ676571

SUTTON VALENCE CASTLE

KENT – ME17 3LW

The ruins of a small 12th-century Norman keep, with panoramic views over the Weald.

OPENING TIMES

Any reasonable daylight hours

VISIT US

Direction: 5 miles SE of Maidstone, in Sutton Valence village, on A274

Train: Headcorn 4 miles, Hollingbourne 5 miles

Bus: Visit traveline.info for the latest bus timetables and routes

Tel: 0370 333 1181

ACQ.1976 🐕 ⚠

Caution: steep slopes, steep stairs.

No nearby parking, pedestrian access only. Parking in the village is recommended.

> **MAP PAGE 305 (4G)**
> OS MAP 188, 137: TQ815491

TEMPLE MANOR

KENT – ME2 2AH

Part of a Knights Templar manor house, built c. 1240, with a first floor hall displaying traces of wall paintings.

TEMPLE MANOR

Managed by Medway Council.

OPENING TIMES

See website for latest opening times

For group visits call 01634 332901

VISIT US

Direction: Located in Strood (Rochester), off A228

Train: Strood ¾ mile

Bus: Visit traveline.info for the latest bus timetables and routes

ACQ.1950 🏠 🐕 P 👤 ⚠

Disabled access (grounds only).

Dogs on leads (grounds only). Assistance dogs welcome across the site.

Caution: steep stairs.

> **MAP PAGE 305 (4G)**
> OS MAP 178, 148/163: TQ733685

UPNOR CASTLE

KENT – ME2 4XG

Set in a riverside village, this Elizabethan artillery fort was built to protect warships in Chatham dockyard. Its furious cannonade failed to stop the Dutch severely damaging the anchored English fleet in 1667. An exhibition highlights the raid.

Managed by Medway Council.

OPENING TIMES

See website for latest opening times

Last entry 45 mins before closing

VISIT US

Direction: At Upnor, on unclassified road off A228

Train: Strood 2 miles

UPNOR CASTLE

Bus: Visit traveline.info

Tel: 01634 332902 or when castle is closed 01634 332901

NON-MEMBERS

See website for entry prices

ACQ.1961 🎧 ♿ E 🖥 🧍 👤 😊 P
📷 ⚠ OVP

Audio guide (small charge).

Disabled access (grounds only).

Parking at a slight distance from castle -- park before village (not English Heritage).

Caution: steep stairs.

> **MAP PAGE 305 (4G)**
> OS MAP 178, 163: TQ759706

WESTERN HEIGHTS, DOVER

KENT – CT17 9DZ

A huge fortification constructed during the Napoleonic Wars and completed in the 1860s, designed to protect Dover from French invasion.

Managed by Western Heights Preservation Society.

OPENING TIMES

Exterior only: Any reasonable daylight hours

Tours of the Drop Redoubt: Guided tours are held on the 3rd Sunday of the month from Apr-Sep, 11am and 2pm. Places must be pre-booked. Visit doverwesternheights.org for details and additional opening times

VISIT US

Direction: Above Dover town on W side of harbour

Train: Dover Priory ¾ mile

Bus: Visit traveline.info for the latest bus timetables and routes

Tel: 01304 211067

 ACQ.1968 🅿 ⚠

Unsuitable for visitors who use wheelchairs or have limited mobility.

Caution: unguarded drops, steep stairs.

MAP PAGE 305 (5J)
OS MAP 179, 138: TR312408

OXFORDSHIRE

ABINGDON COUNTY HALL MUSEUM
OXFORDSHIRE – OX14 3HG

Designed by colleagues of Sir Christopher Wren, this delightful 17th-century 'English Baroque' building houses the Abingdon Museum, and has fine rooftop views.

Managed by Abingdon Town Council.

OPENING TIMES

See website for latest opening times

VISIT US

Direction: In Abingdon, 7 miles south of Oxford; in Market Place

Train: Radley 2½ miles

Bus: Visit traveline.info for the latest bus timetables and routes

Tel: 01235 523703

ABINGDON COUNTY HALL MUSEUM

ENTRY

Free entry to museum. Roof access Apr-Sep weather permitting

Adult	£2
English Heritage Members and Children (over 6 years old only)	£1

ACQ.1952 🚶 🚼 📧 🐕 💻

Limited access to museum floors (no lift).

Caution: steep stairs.

MAP PAGE 304 (3C)
OS MAP 164, 170: SU498971

DEDDINGTON CASTLE
OXFORDSHIRE – OX15 0TE

Extensive earthwork remains of an 11th-century castle, associated with Odo, Bishop of Bayeux, half-brother of William the Conqueror.

Managed by Deddington Parish Council.

OPENING TIMES

Any reasonable daylight hours

VISIT US

Direction: S of B4031 on E side of Deddington; 17 miles N of Oxford

Train: King's Sutton 5 miles

Bus: Visit traveline.info for the latest bus timetables and routes

ACQ.1951 ⚑ ⚠

Caution: steep slopes.

MAP PAGE 304 (2C)
OS MAP 151, 191: SP472316

MINSTER LOVELL HALL AND DOVECOTE
OXFORDSHIRE – OX29 0RR

MINSTER LOVELL HALL AND DOVECOTE

The extensive and picturesque ruins of a 15th-century riverside manor house, including a fine hall, south-west tower and complete nearby dovecote. The home of Richard III's henchman Lord Lovell.

OPENING TIMES

Any reasonable daylight hours

Dovecote – exterior viewing only

VISIT US

Direction: Adjacent to Minster Lovell Church; 3 miles W of Witney, off A40

Train: Charlbury 7 miles

Bus: Visit traveline.info for the latest bus timetables and routes

ACQ.1937 Minster Lovell Hall

ACQ.1957 Dovecote ⚑ 🏛 ⚠

Guidebook (from St Kenelm's Church).

Caution: deep water.

Please do not climb on the walls.

MAP PAGE 304 (2B)
OS MAP 164, 180: SP325113

NORTH HINKSEY CONDUIT HOUSE
OXFORDSHIRE – OX2 9AS

Roofed conduit for Oxford's first water mains, constructed during the early 17th century.

Managed by Oxford Preservation Trust.

OPENING TIMES

Exterior viewing only:
See website for latest opening times

VISIT US

Direction: In North Hinksey off A34; 1½ miles W of Oxford. Located off track leading from Harcourt Hill

Train: Oxford (1½ miles)

Bus: Visit traveline.info for the latest bus timetables and routes

ACQ.1973 ⚑ ⚠ Caution: deep water.

No nearby parking, pedestrian access only.

MAP PAGE 304 (3C)
OS MAP 164, 180: SP495050

NORTH LEIGH ROMAN VILLA

OXFORDSHIRE – OX29 6QE

The remains of a large, well-built Roman courtyard villa, with a nearly complete mosaic tile floor, patterned in reds and browns.

OPENING TIMES

Grounds open any reasonable daylight hours. See website for details of mosaic house open days

VISIT US

Direction: 2 miles N of North Leigh; 10 miles W of Oxford, off A4095

Train: Hanborough 3½ miles

Bus: Visit traveline.info for the latest bus timetables and routes

ACQ.1952 🏕 P ⚠

Pedestrian access only from main road – 550 metres (600 yards). Track is steep and rough.

Steps to reach mosaic building.

Parking (lay-by, not in access lane).

Caution: unguarded drops.

MAP PAGE 304 (2B)
OS MAP 164, 180: SP397154

ROLLRIGHT STONES

OXFORDSHIRE – OX7 5QB

Traditionally a petrified monarch and his courtiers, the Rollright Stones include the King's Men stone circle, the Whispering Knights burial chamber and the King Stone. They span nearly 2,000 years of Neolithic and Bronze Age development.

Managed and owned by the Rollright Trust.

ROLLRIGHT STONES

OPENING TIMES

Entry at any reasonable time all year by permission of The Rollright Trust and English Heritage

VISIT US

Direction: Off unclassified road between A44 and A3400, 3 miles NW of Chipping Norton, near villages of Little Rollright and Long Compton

Train: Moreton-in-Marsh 6½ miles

Bus: Visit traveline.info for the latest bus timetables and routes

Contact: sitemanager@rollright stones.co.uk

ENTRY

Admission charges apply to English Heritage Members and non-members

Adults/Concessions	£1
Children	50p

ACQ.1883 🏕 P ⚠

Parking (in lay-by).

Dogs welcome on leads except inside the stone circle.

Caution: beware of traffic.

MAP PAGE 304 (2B)
OS MAP 151, OL45/191:
SP297309

UFFINGTON CASTLE, WHITE HORSE AND DRAGON HILL

OXFORDSHIRE – SN7 7QJ

Atmospheric sites along the Ridgeway. Uffington 'Castle' is a large Iron Age hillfort, Dragon Hill a natural mound. The famous White Horse is the oldest chalk-cut hill figure in Britain, perhaps over 3,000 years old.

UFFINGTON CASTLE

Managed by the National Trust on behalf of English Heritage.

OPENING TIMES

Any reasonable daylight hours

VISIT US

Direction: S of B4507, 7 miles W of Wantage. Ridgeway National Trail runs directly past the site

Bus: Visit traveline.info for the latest bus timetables and routes

Tel: 01793 762209

ACQ.1936 🏕 🐎 P ⚠

Parking in NT White Horse car park. Pay and display or free to English Heritage Members displaying valid car sticker or with current membership card.

Caution: steep slopes.

MAP PAGE 304 (3B)
OS MAP 174, 170: SU301866

WAYLAND'S SMITHY

OXFORDSHIRE – SN7 7QJ

An atmospheric Neolithic long barrow on the Ridgeway, named after the Saxon smith-god Wayland.

Managed by the National Trust on behalf of English Heritage.

OPENING TIMES

Any reasonable daylight hours

VISIT US

Direction: On the Ridgeway (closed to vehicles); ¾ mile NE of B4000, Ashbury – Lambourn Road

Bus: Visit traveline.info for the latest bus timetables and routes

ACQ.1922 🏕 P ⚠

Parking in NT White Horse car park (then 1 mile walk along Ridgeway). Pay and display but free to English Heritage Members displaying valid car sticker.

Caution: unguarded drops.

MAP PAGE 304 (3B)
OS MAP 174, 170: SU281854

FARNHAM CASTLE KEEP
SURREY – GU9 0AG

The impressive motte and shell keep of a castle founded in 1138 by Henry of Blois, Bishop of Winchester. A viewing platform reveals the buried remains of an earlier tower.

Managed by Farnham Castle Ltd.

OPENING TIMES

See website for latest opening times

Last entry 30 mins before closing

Guided tours of the Bishop's Palace are available on select Wednesday afternoons only, starting at 2pm (last tour starts at 3.30pm) for an additional fee. For details and to book a tour, visit farnham-castle.com (spaces are limited)

VISIT US

Direction: ½ mile north of Farnham off A287

Train: Farnham ¾ mile

Bus: Visit traveline.info for the latest bus timetables and routes

Tel: 01252 721194

ACQ.1933 | E | 🏠 | 🚶 | ⚠️ | 🐕 | P | ♿ | ⚠️

Parking for blue badge holders only.

Featured in new *Palaces of the Bishops of Winchester* guidebook.

Caution: steep stairs.

MAP PAGE 304 (4D)
OS MAP 186, 145: SU837473

WAVERLEY ABBEY
SURREY – GU9 8EP

Remains of the monastic buildings and church of the very first abbey of Cistercian monks to be built in Britain, founded in 1128 and largely rebuilt in the 13th century. Set by a peaceful loop of the River Wey.

Download a free audio tour from our website.

📷 *Elizabeth; Snow White and the Huntsman* (2014); *The Mummy* (2017); *Cursed* (2020); *Midsomer Murders;* BBC Series, *Howards End*.

OPENING TIMES

Any reasonable daylight hours

VISIT US

Direction: 2 miles SE of Farnham, off B3001; off Junction 10 of M25

Train: Farnham 2 miles

Bus: Visit traveline.info for the latest bus timetables and routes

Tel: 0370 333 1181

ACQ.1961 | 🐕 | 🚻 | 🚗 | P | ⚠️

Parking (limited).

Access is through two kissing gates and across uneven ground. Cattle may be grazing around footpaths to abbey.

Caution: deep water, falling masonry.

MAP PAGE 304 (5D)
OS MAP 186, 145: SU868453

CAMBER CASTLE
EAST SUSSEX – TN31 7TD

Ruins of an unusually unaltered artillery fort, built by Henry VIII to guard Rye. Limited opening times, but regular guided walks around Rye Harbour Nature Reserve include the castle.

Managed by Rye Harbour Nature Reserve.

OPENING TIMES

Aug-Oct open on the first Sat of the month for guided tour starting at 2pm prompt. Meet at the castle, but please be aware there is no vehicular access to the site and the nearest parking is a 1 mile walk away. In addition there are regular guided walks around the Rye Harbour Nature Reserve that include the castle. Please check website or visit sussexwildlifetrust. org.uk/visit/ryeharbour

VISIT US

Direction: 1 mile walk across fields, off the A259; 1 mile S of Rye, off Harbour Road. No vehicle access. Follow the public footpath from Brede Lock

Train: Rye 1¼ miles

Bus: Visit traveline.info for the latest bus timetables and routes

Tel: Nature reserve office number 01797 227784 (Mon-Fri, 9am-5pm only)

NON-MEMBERS

See website for entry prices

ACQ.1967 | 🐕 | 🐕 | ⚠️

Caution: Unguarded drops, falling masonry.

Cattle and sheep may be grazing around footpaths to castle.

MAP PAGE 305 (5H)
OS MAP 189, 125: TQ922185

1066 BATTLE OF HASTINGS, ABBEY AND BATTLEFIELD

EAST SUSSEX – TN33 0AE

There are so many ways to enjoy the scene of England's most renowned and crucial battle. Alongside the battlefield you can also explore abbey ruins and the intriguing traces of a country house, as well as interactive displays in the beautiful abbey gatehouse. An all-round great experience, this vast and varied site provides a unique day out for the whole family.

Its history began on the fateful 14th of October 1066, when after many hours of hard fighting William the Conqueror's Norman invaders finally defeated King Harold Godwinson's English army in this very place. You can discover the dramatic story of the epic conflict in the visitor centre, where a host of interactives, displays of Norman and Anglo-Saxon weaponry, and a compelling film recount the background to the battle, the fighting, and how the Norman victory transformed the nation's history.

Accompanied by an audio tour, which recreates the sounds of combat, you can stand on the abbey terrace to view the slope where the Normans advanced against the hilltop English shield wall. Or you can choose to walk more of the battlefield, using the 'Battlefield 1066' family trails to hunt out dramatic wooden figures including a Norman mounted knight and archer as well as a Saxon axeman and standard bearer.

The turning point of the battle came when Harold Godwinson was killed, perhaps struck in the eye by an arrow. You can stand by the spot where he fell, later marked by the high altar of Battle Abbey, the great monastery William founded as a penance for the terrible bloodshed of the battle and a memorial to the dead. All around, the abbey's ruins stand ready to explore, notably the great dormitory range with its atmospheric pillared and vaulted undercrofts, built just below the place where the English army awaited attack.

As the symbol of Norman triumph, Battle Abbey enjoyed enormous wealth and influence, symbolised by the Great Gatehouse. Built in about 1338, it's among the finest medieval monastic portals in Britain. You can climb to its rooftop for astonishing views over the pretty town of Battle, the abbey ruins, and the landscape of the fighting. Don't miss our displays in the splendidly recreated gatehouse chambers. They vividly illustrate how the abbey operated and ruled its wide estates, and how its monks lived from day to day.

STAY WITH US

South Lodge is a former gatehouse, which sleeps four and comes with its own fully enclosed garden. There is so much to see and experience here, but nothing beats soaking up the atmosphere as the evening sun lights up the mellow stone of the beautiful abbey ruins.

See p.13 for details on staying at **Battle** and our other holiday cottages.

Site-finds, handling replicas and imaginative interactives share stories of monastic health, worship, finance, manuscript production, writing and much more. You can listen to part of a monastic service, hear a specially recorded carol found in an early 16th-century Battle manuscript, design your own coat of arms to add to the abbey's roll of knights, look down a monks' garderobe loo, try your hand at reassembling a stained glass window and open drawers and boxes to make discoveries of your own.

The displays also trace how, after its suppression by Henry VIII, the abbey became a grand country house. You'll find intriguing survivors of this later life as you wander the extensive grounds, including a thatched ornamental Regency dairy, an underground icehouse, and the Duchess of Cleveland's tranquil, hidden Walled Garden, now replanted with local species of fruit trees and equipped with beehives.

With so much to see, do and experience throughout the site, you'll need a break in our big café, with indoor and outdoor seating among the trees near the gatehouse. There's an imaginative children's playground nearby, with timber play stations inspired by the site's history to climb and swing on – just one of the many activities that children can enjoy as part of their day out.

Set amid pretty countryside, the renowned battlefield, the medieval abbey, clues to vanished country house life and much more await your exploration here. So be sure to leave plenty of time for your visit.

OPENING TIMES

Open daily 1 Apr–5 Nov

Open varying days 6 Nov–28 Mar

Site closed 24-25 Dec

See website for latest opening times

VISIT US

Address: Battle Abbey, High Street, Battle, East Sussex TN33 0AE

Direction: In Battle, at south end of High St. Take the A2100 off the A21

Train: Battle ½ mile

Bus: Visit traveline.info for the latest bus timetables and routes

Tel: 0370 333 1181

Local Tourist Information:
Hastings: 0303 003 8265
Rye: 01797 223902

NON-MEMBERS

See website for entry prices

SAVE TODAY

By being a Member, you save up to £52.50 (price of a family ticket) when you visit **Battle of Hastings, Abbey and Battlefield.**

ACQ.1976 🎧 ♿ ⛰ ♿ 🍽 🎒 ▣ E
♿ ▢ ⌂ 🥾 🚶 🚻 ⚓ P 🏛 📷
🍴 ♿ ⚠ OVP

Audio tours (suitable for families and for those in wheelchairs or with learning difficulties. Also available in Dutch, French, German, Japanese and Spanish). Audio tours are complimentary but will not be issued on special events days.

Disabled access (grounds and visitor centre).

Parking: charges apply to non-members. Free for Members, but limited to 6 hours with a timed ticket from the machine and displayed alongside a valid car sticker.

MAP PAGE 305 (6G)
OS MAP 199, 124: TQ749157

PEVENSEY CASTLE

—— EAST SUSSEX – BN24 5LE ——

Massive Roman fortress, strong medieval castle and emergency Second World War stronghold, Pevensey Castle has witnessed over 1,700 years of history. Engaging displays tell its long story.

Begun in about AD 290, Pevensey was the largest of the Roman 'Saxon Shore' fortresses; its hugely impressive walls, over 500 metres (1,640 feet) long, still stand almost to their full height. Here, in 1066, William the Conqueror landed to begin his invasion of England, building a fortress within the Roman defences. By the 13th century this had developed into an important medieval castle guarding the coast, whose powerful gatehouse and towered walls endured several long sieges. After centuries of abandonment, the ancient stronghold was pressed back into service in 1940, with machine gun posts cleverly camouflaged into its walls.

In our exhibitions, you'll discover stories of massacre, sieges and royal prisoners. Find out how British, Canadian and US Second World War soldiers interacted with local people, and see a recreated 1940 commander's office. Children can crack the Pevensey Castle Code, and look into a dungeon and recently opened medieval basement room.

Thanks to your support, we've recently completed the removal of vegetation from the castle walls, and the expert conservation of the Pevensey cannon.

OPENING TIMES

Open daily 1 Apr-5 Nov

Open Sat-Sun 6 Nov-28 Mar

Site closed 24-26 Dec & 1 Jan

See website for latest opening times

VISIT US

Direction: Off A259 between villages of Pevensey and Westham

Train: Pevensey & Westham ½ mile

Bus: Visit traveline.info for the latest bus timetables and routes

Tel: 01323 762604

NON-MEMBERS

See website for entry prices

By being a Member, you save up to **£28.50** (price of a family ticket) when you visit **Pevensey Castle**

ACQ.1925 🏠 🅷 E 🚻 🎞 💷 📷 ⚠ OVP

Free on-street parking in Pevensey and Westham villages. Car park (charged) is not managed by English Heritage and not free for Members.

Toilets in Pevensey village.

MAP PAGE 305 (6G)
OS MAP 199, 123/124: TQ645048

BOXGROVE PRIORY WEST SUSSEX – PO18 0EE

BRAMBER CASTLE
WEST SUSSEX – BN44 3WE

The remains of a Norman motte-and-bailey castle on the banks of the River Adur, founded by William de Braose c. 1073. The earthworks are dominated by a towering wall of the keep-gatehouse.

OPENING TIMES
Any reasonable daylight hours

VISIT US
Direction: On W side of Bramber village, off A283

Train: Shoreham-by-Sea 4½ miles

Bus: Visit **traveline.info** for the latest bus timetables and routes

Tel: 0370 333 1181

ACQ.1975 🐕 **P** ⚠

Parking (limited). Parking: charges apply to non-members, free for Members with valid English Heritage car sticker.

Caution: steep slopes, unguarded drops, falling masonry.

MAP PAGE 304 (6E)
OS MAP 198, 122: TQ185107

CHECK ONLINE
Pre-booking for visits to our staffed sites may be required, check our website for the latest guidance.

In a beautiful setting at the foot of the South Downs, the small Benedictine priory of Boxgrove was founded in about 1117.

Its principal remains are the lodging house for guests and travellers, roofless but standing to full height at the gable ends, and the priory church. This lovely building (not in the guardianship of English Heritage) became Boxgrove's parish church at the Dissolution of the Monasteries.

Today you can explore the church's splendid 12th-century chancel, central tower and unusual transepts, which survive complete, along with an early Tudor chantry chapel with fine Renaissance carvings. There's a model of the monastic buildings in the church.

Nearby, in Boxgrove gravel pit, archaeological excavation (funded by English Heritage) produced much the oldest human bones yet discovered in England: dating from around 500,000 years ago, they belonged to a 1.8-metre (6-foot) tall man.

OPENING TIMES
Any reasonable daylight hours

VISIT US
Direction: N of Boxgrove; 4 miles E of Chichester, on minor road off A27

Train: Chichester 4 miles

Bus: Visit **traveline.info** for the latest bus timetables and routes

Tel: 0370 333 1181

ACQ.1977 🐕 **P** ⚠

Caution: falling masonry.

MAP PAGE 304 (6D)
OS MAP 197, 121: SU908076

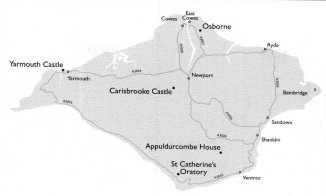

ST CATHERINE'S ORATORY
ISLE OF WIGHT – PO38 2JB

This medieval octagonal lighthouse tower was built in 1328 as penance for plundering church property – casks of wine – from a ship wrecked nearby.

Managed by the National Trust on behalf of English Heritage.

OPENING TIMES
Any reasonable daylight hours

VISIT US
Direction: E of Blackgang roundabout, off A3055. Approx. ¼ mile ascent across fields

Train: Shanklin 9 miles

Bus: Visit traveline.info for the latest bus timetables and routes

Ferry: West Cowes 14 miles, East Cowes 14 miles (both Red Funnel – Tel: 0844 844 9988); Yarmouth 15 miles (Wightlink – Tel: 0333 999 7333)

Tel: 0370 333 1181

ACQ.1952 🦌🏠🐑 P ⚠

Caution: steep slopes.
Cattle and sheep graze on the hillside and footpaths leading to the Oratory.

MAP PAGE 304 (7C)
OS MAP 196, OL29: SZ494773

APPULDURCOMBE HOUSE
ISLE OF WIGHT – PO38 3EW

The imposing, partly restored shell of Appuldurcombe, once the grandest mansion on the Isle of Wight. Still an outstanding example of English baroque architecture, it stands amid 11 acres of Capability Brown-designed ornamental grounds. The 1701 east wing has been re-roofed. Sir Richard Worsley, whose marital antics deliciously outraged Georgian England, extended the house in the 1770s.

OPENING TIMES
Open varying days 1 Apr-31 Oct

Site closed 1 Nov-28 Mar

See website for latest opening times

VISIT US
Direction: Wroxall ½ mile, off B3327

Train: Shanklin 3½ miles then bus 3

Bus: Visit traveline.info

Ferry: Ryde 11 miles (Wightlink 0333 999 7333; Hovercraft 0345 222 0461); West Cowes 12 miles, East Cowes 12 miles (Red Funnel 0844 844 9988)

Tel: 0370 333 1181

ACQ.1952 ♿🦌🏠🐑 P ⚠

Caution: cattle and sheep may be grazing around footpaths to Freemantle Gate.
Uneven surfaces and steep steps.
Car park closes at 5pm.

MAP PAGE 304 (7C)
OS MAP 196, OL29: SZ543800

OSBORNE

ISLE OF WIGHT – PO32 6JX

Osborne opens a unique window on the private family life of Queen Victoria and Prince Albert, revealing how the royal couple worked and relaxed, and how their children entertained themselves. Victoria's palatial holiday home also offers a beach, acres of grounds and gardens, and a new tree trail for families. There's lots of entertainment for visitors of all ages.

Shared with the couple's nine children, Osborne originated with the queen's desire for a 'place of one's own – quiet and retired'. Knowing and liking the Isle of Wight from childhood visits, she and Albert were determined to own a property there. In 1845 they bought Osborne, and plans for a new mansion began at once. Eventually a pair of Italianate towers dominated the landscape, looking out on the Solent. Albert lavished tremendous care on designing the surrounding gardens.

The lower terrace has intimate links with the young royal couple, still in their early thirties when they created it. Victoria bought the bronze statue of Andromeda at the Great Exhibition of 1851. She loved to relax in the Shell Alcove, now returned to its original colour scheme. We've also restored the terrace's 'Osborne yellow' walls while carefully preserving the magnolia and myrtle, which are offspring of original plantings by the royal pair.

Inside, Osborne's staterooms abound in opulent design and decoration. Marble sculptures line the Grand Corridor, and portraits and frescos are reminders of the family's links to the crowned heads of Europe, and of the worldwide extent of the British Empire. Many artefacts at Osborne are on loan from the Royal Collection.

Most lavish of all, the Durbar Room reflects Victoria's pride in her title Empress of India, granted in 1877. In 1890 she ordered a new banqueting chamber to be built in the 16th-century North Indian style, and symbols of India appear everywhere, with a splendid peacock standing proudly over the chimneypiece. You can also admire an outstanding collection of Indian treasures. Displays help you understand Victoria's relationship with the Empire, and give children the chance to encounter history.

Elsewhere in the house, you can go behind the scenes to visit more intimate royal family apartments. Visit the queen's sitting room, see Victoria's personal bathtub in the dressing room and, next door, the bedroom where she died on 22 January 1901. The queen kept Prince Albert's private suite just as it was in his lifetime, and many of the things he used at Osborne still lie where he left them.

Take a further step into the Victorian royal family's private life by exploring Osborne's vast and beautiful grounds, where there's a new tree trail. Family visitors shouldn't miss the Swiss Cottage, domain of the royal children. A purpose-built playhouse where they learnt 'normal' life skills,

english-heritage.org.uk

Our new tree trail, highlighting 25 special Osborne trees, including rare or exotic specimens and trees planted by the royal family to mark momentous occasions. Twelve of the trees also feature in our new family trail; each tree offers its own activity for families to enjoy – from creating an artwork using found objects to taking a selfie to celebrate Queen Victoria's Jubilees.

STAY WITH US

No 1 & No 2 Sovereign's Gate both sleep four. The stunning building was built for Queen Victoria and Prince Albert as the ceremonial entrance to Osborne for visiting heads of state. **Pavilion Cottage** sleeps four. Built in the early 1900s, this former Cricket Pavilion brims with period character. After the public leave, explore the tranquil grounds and enjoy the spectacular views across the Solent.

See p.13 for details on staying at Osborne and our other holiday cottages.

the Swiss Cottage includes a room dressed as on 11 July 1861, when the children prepared afternoon tea for their parents, not long before Prince Albert's tragically premature death.

Explore the once-private royal museum, full of strange objects from all over the world. It was originally created for the collections of the royal children, highlighting the fact that children's love of collecting oddities is nothing new. The Swiss Cottage play area is inspired by the royal children's toy fort.

From the Swiss Cottage Quarter you can make your way to the queen's once strictly private beach, where her children learnt to swim. Its attractions include the restored royal bathing machine, and you can recreate a Victorian beach holiday by relaxing in deckchairs and enjoying traditional seaside refreshments from the beach

café. The beach is a ¾ mile walk from the house; a mobility service runs at peak times.

There are plenty of other opportunities to enjoy delicious food and drink across the estate. The café in the Petty Officers' Quarters offers light lunches and snacks with handmade cakes and pastries, while the Terrace Restaurant, set on the lower terraces, offers light lunches and all-day cream teas in a relaxed environment. And the Gazelle House – behind the Swiss Cottage and next door to the children's play and picnic area – is the perfect spot to stop off for a takeaway service of cold snacks and refreshments, with Osborne-made cakes, sandwiches and children's lunch boxes. You're also welcome to enjoy a picnic throughout the grounds.

🎬 *Mrs Brown* (1997); *Victoria and Abdul* (2017); ITV Series *Victoria*.

OPENING TIMES

House and Grounds
Open daily 1 Apr-5 Nov

Site closed 6-10 Nov

Last entry to house and grounds is
1 hour before site closes

Ground Floor House and Grounds
(excluding Swiss Cottage & Museum)
Open varying days 11 Nov-28 Mar

Site closed 24-25 Dec

Last entry to house and grounds is
1 hour before site closes

See website for latest opening times

VISIT US

Address: York Avenue, East Cowes,
Isle of Wight PO32 6JX

Direction: 1 mile SE of East Cowes.
For satnav use postcode PO32 6JT

Train: Ryde Esplanade 7 miles

Bus: Visit traveline.info for the latest
bus timetables

Ferry: East Cowes 1½ miles
(Red Funnel – Tel: 0844 844 9988);
Fishbourne 4 miles; Ryde 7 miles
(Wightlink – Tel: 0333 999 7333)

Hovertravel: 0345 222 0461

Tel: 0370 333 1181

Local Tourist Information:
Visit Isle of Wight: 01983 813813
visitisleofwight.co.uk

SAVE TODAY

By being a Member, you save up to £76 (price of a family ticket) when you visit **Osborne**.

NON-MEMBERS

See website for entry prices

Pushchairs are not permitted within the
house, but are welcome in the gardens.

Disabled access – manual wheelchair access
to the first floor is via a lift although large
motorised wheelchairs are unable to access
the first floor (too narrow in places). Manual
wheelchairs are available to borrow on a
first come, first served basis. Small mobility
scooters are permitted only on the ground
floor of the house, and can be used in
the gardens.

MAP PAGE 304 (6C)
OS MAP 196, OL29: SZ516948

CARISBROOKE CASTLE

ISLE OF WIGHT – PO30 1XY

Guardian of the Isle of Wight for over a thousand years, Carisbrooke Castle is a fascinatingly varied place to visit. Begun soon after the Norman Conquest, it's been in turn a medieval stronghold, an Elizabethan artillery fortress, a king's prison and an Edwardian royal residence. There's a keep to climb for panoramic views and a colourful history to explore. It's also the home of the famous Carisbrooke donkeys.

This great hilltop-crowning fortress originated in Anglo-Saxon times as an earthwork defence against Viking raids. Soon after 1066, the Normans built a castle within it to secure their hold on the Isle of Wight, granted in 1100 to the Norman family of de Redvers. They raised the great Norman shell keep on its towering mound, and after 1262 the formidable Countess Isabella de Fortibus rebuilt the principal accommodation and service buildings.

In 1377, following the addition of its double-towered 14th-century gatehouse, Carisbrooke Castle experienced its only siege, beating off a French raiding force. After the Spanish Armada passed alarmingly close in 1588, the castle was updated as an artillery fortification by surrounding it with 'bastioned' earthworks nearly a mile long, still impressively visible.

Most famous among the castle's varied cast of past residents was Charles I, who was imprisoned here in 1647-48 after his defeat in the Civil War. At first comfortably accommodated in the Constable's Lodging – and provided with his own bowling green, which you can still try out today – he later became a closely guarded captive. He made two unsuccessful attempts to escape, one being foiled only when he became wedged in the window bars. All this time he was plotting to renew the war. Growing impatient with his intrigues, Parliament eventually ordered him taken to London, where he was tried and executed.

Much later, Princess Beatrice, Queen Victoria's youngest and favourite daughter and Governor of the Isle of Wight between 1896-1944, made Carisbrooke Castle her summer home. She also commissioned the altar painting in the castle chapel, in memory of a son killed in action in 1914. The chapel is now the Isle of Wight's county war memorial, honouring over 2,000 local people killed in both World Wars.

The award-winning Edwardian-style Princess Beatrice Garden, designed by Chris Beardshaw, was inspired by the princess, and includes a fountain and plantings in the rich colours of the royal arms. We are grateful to the late Mrs Dorothy Frazer, whose generous bequest and devotion to the island made the creation of this garden possible.

english-heritage.org.uk

STAY WITH US

The **Bowling Green Apartment** sleeps a family of four in contemporary comfort on the second floor of the 19th-century former service block. Enjoy the excitement of staying in a castle after dark.

See p.13 for details on staying at Carisbrooke and our other holiday cottages.

The castle's most beloved modern residents are undoubtedly the renowned Carisbrooke donkeys. These happy animals still demonstrate the tread wheel, which originally raised water 49 metres (160 feet) from the castle well. Today's donkeys have to work much less hard, and you can hear their story in a film hosted by Jupiter the cartoon donkey, voiced by locally raised comedian Phill Jupitus.

Don't miss the Charles I memorabilia and changing exhibitions in the Carisbrooke Castle Museum.

OPENING TIMES

Open daily 1 Apr-5 Nov

Open varying days 6 Nov-28 Mar

Site closed 24-25 Dec

See website for latest opening times

Last entry 1 hour before closing

VISIT US

Address: Carisbrooke Castle, Castle Hill, Newport, Isle of Wight PO30 1XY

Direction: 1¼ miles SW of Newport. Follow signs to Carisbrooke village, then castle

Train: Ryde Esplanade 9 miles

Bus: Visit traveline.info for the latest bus timetables and routes

Ferry: West Cowes 5 miles, East Cowes 6 miles (both Red Funnel – 0844 844 9988); Fishbourne 6 miles, Ryde 8 miles, Yarmouth 9 miles (Wightlink – Tel: 0333 999 7333)

Tel: 01983 522107

Local Tourist Information: 01983 813813

SAVE TODAY By being a Member, you save up to £47 (price of a family ticket) when you visit **Carisbrooke Castle.**

NON-MEMBERS

See website for entry prices

ACQ.1856

Disabled access (grounds and lower levels only).

Tearooms open daily Apr-Oct and weekends during winter (close 1 hour before site closes). 26 Dec-1 Jan, 11am-3pm.

Parking: charges apply to non-members, free for Members with valid English Heritage car sticker.

MAP PAGE 304 (6C)
OS MAP 196, OL29: SZ486878

YARMOUTH CASTLE

ISLE OF WIGHT – PO41 0PB

Built following a French raid on the Isle of Wight, Yarmouth Castle was designed to protect strategic Yarmouth harbour and (in conjunction with Hurst Castle – see p.43 – on the mainland) to defend the western end of the Solent against invasion fleets.

The last and most advanced addition to Henry VIII's chain of coastal artillery forts, it was completed after his death in 1547. Unlike Henry's earlier circular forts – such as Deal and Pendennis castles – Yarmouth Castle is a square blockhouse. It has a heavy gun battery to the front and the first new-style 'arrowhead' bastion built in England protecting its most exposed angle against land attack. In the 1560s its central courtyard was filled in to provide a solid gun platform. Again altered during the 17th century, it was garrisoned until 1885 and re-used during both World Wars.

Inside, you can discover atmospheric recreations of how rooms were used in the 16th century, and an exhibition about the many wrecks in 'Yarmouth Roads', the treacherous stretch of sea which the castle overlooks. There is also a magnificent picnic site, with views over the Solent.

OPENING TIMES

Open daily 1 Apr-5 Nov

Site closed 6 Nov-28 Mar

See website for latest opening times

VISIT US

Direction: In Yarmouth town centre, adjacent to car ferry terminal. Located just off Quay Street, up the short walkway and through the main gates into the castle

Train: Lymington Pier adjoins the ferry berth for the Wightlink service to Yarmouth

Bus: Visit traveline.info for the latest bus timetables and routes

Ferry: Yarmouth, adjacent (Wightlink – Tel: 0333 999 7333)

Tel: 01983 760444

NON-MEMBERS

See website for entry prices

By being a Member, you save up to £24.50 (price of a family ticket) when you visit **Yarmouth Castle**

ACQ.1913

Disabled access (part of ground floor only).

New guidebook.

No parking at site: parking 5 minutes walk away (not managed by English Heritage).

MAP PAGE 304 (6B)   OS MAP 196, OL29: SZ354898

WELCOME TO THE

SOUTH WEST

Pendennis Castle, Cornwall

South West

89-96: see Isles of Scilly pages 126-127

72, 73, 82, 83, 84, 85, 86, 87, 88
see Stonehenge and Avebury
pages 117-125

SOUTH WEST

History and legend come together at historic places across the South West.

Arthurian tales swirl around the clifftop castle of **Tintagel** (p.94), while the region is home to three major stone circles, including **Avebury** (p.118) and the world-famous **Stonehenge** (p.122). With its immersive exhibition and recreated Neolithic round houses, Stonehenge makes for an unmissable family day out.

Wander the rugged remains of an Iron Age village at **Chysauster** (p.89) or walk the walls of medieval castles at **Restormel** (p.91) and **Launceston** (p.90). Explore the defences of Tudor fortresses at **Dartmouth** (p.98) and **St Mawes** (p.96) and see how **Pendennis Castle** (p.92) developed to face the threat of invasion over the centuries.

If you're in search of quiet reflection, soak up the peaceful atmospheres of the abbeys of **Hailes** (p.106), **Muchelney** (p.112) and **Cleeve** (p.109).

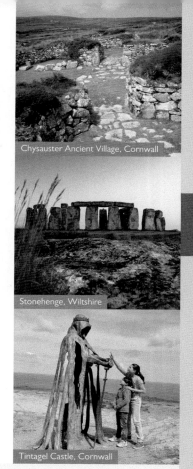

Chysauster Ancient Village, Cornwall

Stonehenge, Wiltshire

Tintagel Castle, Cornwall

SIR BEVIL GRENVILLE'S MONUMENT

BATH & NE SOMERSET – BA1 9DD

Erected to commemorate the heroism of a Royalist commander and his Cornish pikemen at the Battle of Lansdown, 1643.

OPENING TIMES

Any reasonable daylight hours

VISIT US

Direction: Located 4 miles NW of Bath on the N edge of Lansdown Hill, near the road to Wick

Train: Bath Spa 4½ miles

Bus: Visit **traveline.info** for the latest bus timetables and routes

ACQ.1953 🎯 P

Parking (in lay-by).

> MAP PAGE 303 (3H)
> OS MAP 172, 155: ST722703

STANTON DREW CIRCLES AND COVE

BATH & NE SOMERSET – BS39 4EW

The third largest collection of prehistoric standing stones in England. It includes the Great Circle – among the biggest in the country – two smaller circles and a three-stone 'cove'. Recent surveys prove they were part of a much more elaborate ritual site.

STANTON DREW CIRCLES AND COVE

OPENING TIMES

Cove: Any reasonable daylight hours

Two main stone circles: admission fee of £1 charged by landowner

Site closed 25 Dec

VISIT US

Direction: Cove: in the garden of the Druid's Arms public house. Circles: E of Stanton Drew village

Train: Bristol Temple Meads 7 miles

Bus: Visit **traveline.info** for the latest bus timetables and routes

Cove: parking at Druid's Arms. Stones: limited parking at entrance to Stones field.

> MAP PAGE 303 (3H)
> OS MAP 172/182, 154/155
> COVE: ST597631
> CIRCLES: ST601633

STONEY LITTLETON LONG BARROW

BATH & NE SOMERSET – BA2 8NR

One of the finest accessible examples of a Neolithic chambered tomb, with its multiple burial chambers open to view.

OPENING TIMES

Any reasonable daylight hours

VISIT US

Direction: 1 mile S of Wellow off A367. Narrow lane west of village leads to small parking area (1 mile)

Train: Bath Spa 6 miles

Bus: Visit **traveline.info** for the latest bus timetables and routes

ACQ.1884 🎯 🎯 P ⚠

Parking (limited). ¼ mile walk uphill from parking area.

Caution: steep slopes.

Note: visitors are advised to bring a torch.

> MAP PAGE 303 (3H)
> OS MAP 172, 142: ST735572

TEMPLE CHURCH

BRISTOL – BS1 6HS

The 'leaning tower' and walls of a large late-medieval church – originally founded by the Knights Templar – which survived Second World War bombing. Following recent conservation, plans to transform it into a community space are under way.

OPENING TIMES

Exterior only: Any reasonable daylight hours

VISIT US

Direction: Located in Temple St, off Victoria St

Train: Bristol Temple Meads ¼ mile

Bus: Visit **traveline.info** for the latest bus timetables and routes

ACQ.1958 ♿ 🎯 ⚠

Some steps and uneven flagstones around church.

Caution: unguarded drops.

> MAP PAGE 303 (3H)
> OS MAP 172, 154/155: ST593727

CORNWALL

BALLOWALL BARROW

CORNWALL – TR19 7NP

In a spectacular position, this large Bronze Age burial mound was reconstructed by Victorian Cornish antiquarian William Borlase. Managed by the National Trust on behalf of English Heritage.

OPENING TIMES

Any reasonable daylight hours

VISIT US

Direction: 1 mile W of St Just

Train: Penzance 8 miles

Bus: Visit **traveline.info** for the latest bus timetables and routes

ACQ.1954 🎯 P ⚠

Parking limited.

Caution: unguarded drops, falling rocks.

> MAP PAGE 302 (7A)
> OS MAP 203, 102: SW355312

CARN EUNY ANCIENT VILLAGE
CORNWALL – TR20 8RB

Among the best-preserved ancient villages in the South West, occupied from Iron Age until late Roman times.

Managed by the Cornwall Heritage Trust.

OPENING TIMES
Any reasonable daylight hours

VISIT US
Direction: 1½ miles W of Sancreed along narrow but signed lanes

Train: Penzance 6 miles

Bus: Visit traveline.info for the latest bus timetables and routes

ACQ.1957 🍴 📷 🚻 P ⚠

Parking (limited) in Brane, 600 metres (660 yards) walk to site.

Joint guidebook for sale at Chysauster.

Caution: unguarded drops.

MAP PAGE 302 (7A)
OS MAP 203, 102: SW402288

DUPATH WELL
CORNWALL – PL17 8AD

A charming well-house of c. 1500, standing over an ancient spring believed to cure whooping cough.

Managed by the Cornwall Heritage Trust.

OPENING TIMES
Any reasonable daylight hours

VISIT US
Direction: 1 mile E of Callington off A388

Train: Gunnislake 4½ miles

Bus: Visit traveline.info for the latest bus timetables and routes

ACQ.1937 🍴 P

Parking at farmyard entrance.

MAP PAGE 302 (6D)
OS MAP 201, 108: SX375692

CHYSAUSTER ANCIENT VILLAGE
CORNWALL – TR20 8XA

An elevated viewing platform offers you a bird's-eye view of Chysauster, one of the finest examples of a Romano-British village in Britain. Set in beautiful countryside rich in wildlife, the village probably originated as an Iron Age settlement in about 400 BC. Some 50 to 70 people may have lived here in Roman times, before Chysauster was abandoned for unknown reasons during the 3rd century AD. A site model gives you more insights into this ancient settlement and its unique prehistoric landscape.

The village includes substantial remains of nine stone-walled 'courtyard houses', a type found only on the Land's End peninsula and the Isles of Scilly. Lining a 'village street', each had an open central courtyard surrounded by thatched rooms. There's also the entrance to a 'fogou', an underground passage distinctive to west Cornwall sites. Their purpose remains a mystery.

OPENING TIMES
Open daily 1 Apr-5 Nov

Site closed 6 Nov-28 Mar

See website for latest opening times

Last entry 30 mins before closing

VISIT US
Direction: Located 2½ miles NW of Gulval, off B3311

Train: Penzance 3½ miles

Bus: Visit traveline.info for the latest bus timetables and routes

Tel: 07470 115475

Local Tourist Information:
Penzance: 01736 335530

NON-MEMBERS
See website for entry prices

By being a Member, you save up to £24.50 (price of a family ticket) when you visit **Chysauster Ancient Village**

ACQ.1931 ♿ 🍴 🔇 📷 🚶 ↟ P 🖼
📷 ⚠ OVP

Warning: uphill walk from car park, via gravel track including steps.

MAP PAGE 302 (7B)
OS MAP 203, 102: SW472350

HALLIGGYE FOGOU

CORNWALL – TR12 6AF

The largest of the mysterious underground passages or 'fogous' associated with Cornish Iron Age settlements. Whether they were refuges, storage chambers or shrines is uncertain.

Managed by the Trelowarren Estate.

OPENING TIMES

Any reasonable daylight hours May-Sep. No access inside fogou Oct-Apr inclusive

VISIT US

Direction: Approximately 1 mile south-east of Garras off B3293, enter the Trelowarren estate by the gatehouses. After 0.8 miles, turn right at crossroads and find parking area on the right, where a panel shows the route to the fogou. See website for further details

Train: Penryn 14 miles

Bus: Visit **traveline.info** for the latest bus timetables and routes

ACQ.1979 🕇 P ⚠

Limited parking.
Caution: steep stairs.
Visitors are strongly advised to bring a torch.

> MAP PAGE 302 (7B)
> OS MAP 203, 103: SW713239

THE HURLERS STONE CIRCLES

CORNWALL – PL14 5LE

Three late Neolithic or early Bronze Age stone circles arranged in a line, a grouping very rare in England.

Once believed to be men turned to stone for playing the Cornish game of hurling on a Sunday.

Managed by the Cornwall Heritage Trust.

OPENING TIMES

Any reasonable daylight hours

VISIT US

Direction: Located ½ mile NW of Minions, off B3254

THE HURLERS STONE CIRCLES

Train: Liskeard 7 miles

Bus: Visit **traveline.info** for the latest bus timetables and routes

ACQ.1935 🕇 🐾 P ⚠

Parking ¼ mile walk.

> MAP PAGE 302 (6D)
> OS MAP 201, 109: SX258714

KING DONIERT'S STONE

CORNWALL – PL14 6RU

Two richly carved pieces of a 9th-century cross, commemorating Dumgarth, British King of Dumnonia, died c. AD 875.

Managed by the Cornwall Heritage Trust.

OPENING TIMES

Any reasonable daylight hours

VISIT US

Direction: 1 mile NW of St Cleer, off B3254

Train: Liskeard 7 miles

Bus: Visit **traveline.info** for the latest bus timetables and routes

ACQ.1933 🕇 P

Parking (in lay-by).

> MAP PAGE 302 (6D)
> OS MAP 201, 109: SX236688

LAUNCESTON CASTLE

CORNWALL – PL15 7DR

Set on a tall mound dominating the town, with an unusual keep consisting of a 13th-century round tower inside an earlier shell keep. A gatehouse became a notorious prison. New interpretation traces the castle's varied history, featuring site finds, fresh reconstruction drawings, graphic displays and stories,

---

LAUNCESTON CASTLE

with poetry by the much-loved Launceston poet Charles Causley. His favourite cat, Rupert leads a new family trail.

With thanks to the Charles Causley Trust and Launceston Town Council.

🎬 *The Trouble With Maggie Cole* (2020).

OPENING TIMES

Open daily 1 Apr-5 Nov

Site closed 6 Nov-28 Mar

See website for latest opening times

Last entry 30 mins before closing

VISIT US

Direction: In Launceston town centre

Bus: Visit **traveline.info** for the latest bus timetables and routes

Tel: 01566 772365

Local Tourist Information:
Launceston: 01566 772321

NON-MEMBERS

See website for entry prices

ACQ.1952 ♿ 🕇 E 🖼 ◻ 🔼 🚻
⚠ OVP

No disabled access to keep. Low light levels on stairs leading to the view.

Refreshments available.

> MAP PAGE 302 (5D)
> OS MAP 201, 112: SX331846

PENHALLAM MANOR

CORNWALL – EX22 6XW

The low, grass-covered, complete ground-plan of a moated 13th-century manor house, in a delightful woodland setting.

OPENING TIMES

Any reasonable daylights hours

Car park	
Apr-Oct	10am-6pm
Nov-Mar	10am-4pm

VISIT US

Direction: Signposted from Week St Mary, off a minor road. From A39 heading north turn right at Treskinnick Cross

PENHALLAM MANOR

Bus: Visit **traveline.info** for the latest bus timetables and routes

ACQ.1981 🍴 **P** ⚠

Limited parking (15-minute walk from the car park along a forest track).

Caution: deep water.

> MAP PAGE 302 (5D)
> OS MAP 190, 111: SX224974

RESTORMEL CASTLE

CORNWALL – PL22 0EE

Restormel's great 13th-century circular keep stands on an earlier Norman mound, on top of a high spur beside the River Fowey. Twice visited by the Black Prince, it finally saw action during the Civil War. Commanding fantastic views, it makes an excellent picnic spot. A trail leads to the Duchy of Cornwall Nursery across the valley.

OPENING TIMES

Open daily 1 Apr-5 Nov

Site closed 6 Nov-28 Mar

See website for latest opening times

Last entry 30 mins before closing

VISIT US

Direction: Located 1½ miles N of Lostwithiel, off A390

Train: Lostwithiel 1½ miles

Bus: Visit **traveline.info** for the latest bus timetables and routes

Tel: 01208 872687

Local Tourist Information
Lostwithiel: 01208 872207

NON-MEMBERS

See website for entry prices

ACQ.1925 ♿ 🍴 📷 🚽 🚹 🛗 **P** ⛩
📷 ⚠ OVP

Access via a stock grazing area. Sensible footwear is strongly advised, due to grassy areas around the site.

No powered mobility scooters.

Refreshments available.

> MAP PAGE 302 (6C)
> OS MAP 200, 107: SX104614

ST BREOCK DOWNS MONOLITH

CORNWALL – PL30 5PN

Cornwall's largest prehistoric standing stone, originally weighing nearly 17 tonnes, on the summit of St Breock Downs.

Managed by the Cornwall Heritage Trust.

OPENING TIMES

Any reasonable daylight hours

VISIT US

Direction: 3½ miles SW of Wadebridge. 2 miles SW of Burlawn, on road to Rosenannon. Follow finger post, then turn right for approx. 500 metres

Train: Roche 5½ miles

Bus: Visit **traveline.info** for the latest bus timetables and routes

ACQ.1965 🍴 **P**

Parking in lay-by.

> MAP PAGE 302 (6C)
> OS MAP 200, 106: SW968683

ST CATHERINE'S CASTLE

CORNWALL – PL23 1JH

One of two small artillery forts built by Henry VIII to defend Fowey Harbour, consisting of two storeys with gunports at ground level.

OPENING TIMES

Any reasonable daylight hours

VISIT US

Direction: 1½ miles SW of Fowey along a woodland path off Readymoney Road

Train: Par 4 miles

Bus: Visit **traveline.info** for the latest bus timetables and routes

ACQ.1909 🍴 **P** ⚠

Parking (Readymoney Cove Car Park, Fowey, ¾ mile walk). Charged.

Caution: steep slopes, unguarded drops, steep stairs.

Please do not climb on the walls.

> MAP PAGE 302 (6C)
> OS MAP 200/204, 107: SX119509

TREGIFFIAN BURIAL CHAMBER

CORNWALL – TR19 6ER

Remains of a Neolithic chambered tomb, with a stone-lined entrance passage leading into the central chamber.

Managed by the Cornwall Heritage Trust.

OPENING TIMES

Any reasonable daylight hours

VISIT US

Direction: Located 2 miles SE of St Buryan, on B3315

Train: Penzance 5½ miles

Bus: Visit **traveline.info** for the latest bus timetables and routes

ACQ.1971 🐕 **P** ⚠

Parking (in lay-by).

Caution: unguarded drops.

> MAP PAGE 302 (7A)
> OS MAP 203, 102: SW431244

TRETHEVY QUOIT

CORNWALL – PL14 5JY

An impressive Neolithic burial chamber, 2.7 metres (8ft 11in) high. Five standing stones are surmounted by a huge capstone.

Managed by the Cornwall Heritage Trust.

OPENING TIMES

Any reasonable daylight hours

VISIT US

Direction: 1 mile NE of St Cleer, near Darite; off B3254

Train: Liskeard 3½ miles

Bus: Visit **traveline.info** for the latest bus timetables and routes

ACQ.1931 🍴 🚽 **P** ⚠

Limited parking.

Please do not climb on the stones.

> MAP PAGE 302 (6D)
> OS MAP 201, 109: SX259688

PENDENNIS CASTLE

CORNWALL – TR11 4NQ

In a strikingly beautiful setting, Pendennis Castle offers you exciting first-hand experiences of history. You can discover how historic guns worked, look out for enemies on the horizon and meet characters from its dramatic past. There's also a castle-themed soft play area.

Set on a picturesque rocky headland, Pendennis Castle has plenty of space for families to explore together, and commands breathtaking views over Falmouth, the Fal estuary and the sea. It was begun by Henry VIII in the 1540s, when Cornwall was in the front line of the Tudor conflict between England, France and Spain. Along with its sister castle, St Mawes, on the far side of the estuary, it guarded the vital anchorage of Carrick Roads. You'll witness how it was updated again and again to face new threats over the centuries, right up to the Second World War and after.

In the Tudor keep or 'gun tower', the core and oldest part of the fortress, immerse yourself in the drama as a possible enemy ship is sighted and the gunners rush to their stations. Climb to the top of the round keep for panoramic views.

Threatened again by Spanish landings in Elizabethan times, Henry VIII's fort was expanded to defend the whole headland, producing the extensive fortress you see today.

During the First World War Pendennis became the headquarters of 'Fortress Falmouth'. Hands-on displays recreate parts of the fortress as they were in 1914-18. Exhibits include the letters of Battery Quartermaster Sergeant 'Tommy' Thomas, who died of wounds in France, aged 27. They're now back in the very room where some were written.

Highlighting the castle's original Tudor, Napoleonic, Victorian and 20th-century guns, an intriguing display traces how its artillery developed to meet the changing threat of ever more deadly enemy weapons. Join one of our fascinating volunteer-led talks to discover how our historic guns work (check with staff on arrival for timings).

A Castle Explorers family trail guides you around the fortress. Follow the tunnel down to the Half Moon Battery and you'll be transported back to the Second World War. In the underground magazine, you might even get recruited into a gun-firing team. In the meticulously recreated Battery Observation Post bunker, you can scan the horizon for enemy ships and eavesdrop on telephone conversations between the commander and the gun crews.

Take a break from watching out for enemies on the horizon in the café, offering delicious meals and snacks inspired by the castle's heritage.

Picturesque Pendennis can also serve as a spectacular venue – from a dramatic coastal wedding to a memorable corporate event. The pre-bookable education suite fits up to 35 children.

Combine your trip to Pendennis with a visit to her sister fortress at St Mawes (p.96).

STAY WITH US

Enjoy the grounds and be in the heart of the action on event days when you stay in the *Custodian's House* or *Callie's Cottage* on the castle lawns. Both offer ideal bases from which to explore this picturesque part of southern Cornwall.

See p.13 for details on staying at **Pendennis** and our other holiday cottages.

OPENING TIMES

Open daily 1 Apr–5 Nov

Open varying days 6 Nov–28 Mar

Site closed 24–25 Dec

See website for latest opening times

Last entry 30 mins before closing

The castle may close from 4pm on Saturdays if a wedding is booked. Please check with the site in advance

The castle keep may close for 1 hour if an event is booked

Free guided tours of the Half Moon Battery and Tudor gun tower. Check availability on arrival

VISIT US

Address: Pendennis Castle, Falmouth, Cornwall TR11 4NQ

Direction: Follow the A39 through Falmouth and then follow the signs for 'scenic route'. For satnav to main car park use TR11 4NQ or for drop-off zone/limited disabled parking use TR11 4LP

Train: Falmouth Docks ½ mile

SAVE TODAY By being a Member, you save up to £47 (price of a family ticket) when you visit **Pendennis Castle**.

Bus: Visit traveline.info for the latest bus timetables and routes

Tel: 01326 316594

Local Tourist Information: Falmouth: 01326 741194

NON-MEMBERS

See website for entry prices

Wheelchair access to the grounds, but steep slopes or drops in places. There is also full wheelchair access to the shop, tearoom, weapons of war display and barracks.

Tearoom closes ½ hour before the castle.

MAP PAGE 302 (7C)
OS MAP 204, 103/105: SW824318

TINTAGEL CASTLE

CORNWALL – PL34 0HE

Linked by long tradition with the legend of King Arthur, romantically sited Tintagel was a focus of princely power during a shadowy era of Cornish history. A spectacular footbridge now connects its rocky headland and island, letting you explore this fabled place as our ancestors once did.

Tintagel means 'the fortress with the narrow entrance' – a slender neck of land which, according to legend, could be defended by just three men. During the 5th to 7th centuries, the island fortress was the stronghold of post-Roman Cornish rulers. Ongoing archaeological excavations prove it was the home of a high-status community with strong links to the Mediterranean.

Memories of Tintagel's past glories inspired many legends, most famously linking it with King Arthur. In the 12th century, Geoffrey of Monmouth wrote that Duke Gorlois of Cornwall shut his wife Ygraine away here to protect her from the lusts of Uther Pendragon, King of Britain. But Merlin magically transformed Uther into the likeness of Ygraine's husband: he slept with her here, and fathered Arthur.

Staking his claim to a part in Arthurian legend, Richard, Earl of Cornwall – Henry III's immensely wealthy younger brother – built a castle here in the 1230s. Its atmospheric ruins stand partly on the mainland and partly on the island: in medieval times the two halves were connected by a bridge.

For the first time in over 500 years, a daringly designed footbridge re-establishes this long-lost connection. Some 68 metres (223 feet) long, it's crafted of oak and steel, and floored with 40,000 local Delabole slate tiles. At its exact centre is a gasp-inducing 4cm gap, symbolising the transition from present to past and history to legend. The Tintagel bridge was made possible by the support of Julia and Hans Rausing.

Over on the rocky island, you'll discover the ruins of the castle hall and evocative traces of 5th- to 7th-century houses. A medieval garden with 'story stones' remembers Tintagel's links to the tale of the doomed lovers Tristan and Iseult. All around are spectacular coastal views.

Complete your exploration in the exhibition, where you'll see fascinating artefacts discovered here and a 3D model revealing how Tintagel developed through time. Imaginative book sculptures trace how this romantic site inspired writers from medieval Malory to Victorian Tennyson.

Children will love the beach below the castle (only accessible at low tide after a climb over rocks) with Merlin's Cave to explore. Everyone will enjoy our Beach Café, with its varied menu focused on locally sourced Cornish treats.

Please note: Entrance to the castle is managed through timed tickets, and due to limited availability, booking in advance online is strongly recommended. Go to **english-heritage.org.uk/tintagel** for the latest information and to book.

OPENING TIMES

Open daily 1 Apr–5 Nov

Open varying days 6 Nov–28 Mar

Site closed 24–25 Dec

See website for latest opening times

Last entry 1 hour before closing

VISIT US

Address: Tintagel Castle, Castle Road, Tintagel, Cornwall PL34 0HE

Direction: On Tintagel Head, 600 metres (660 yards) along steep, uneven track from Tintagel; no vehicles except Land Rover service (not managed by English Heritage and extra charge payable)

Bus: Visit traveline.info

Tel: 01840 770328

NON-MEMBERS

See website for entry prices

Limited availability – pre-booking strongly recommended. See website for latest information

SAVE TODAY

By being a Member, you save up to £60 (price of a family ticket) when you visit **Tintagel Castle**.

ACQ. 1931

We have introduced step-free access to the island via our new footbridge. However, there are no step-free routes around the island itself, so disabled access is limited from this point. Access is possible to the exhibition, Beach Café and shop. Please see website for full details.

Parking (600 metres (660 yards) in the village) – not managed by English Heritage

MAP PAGE 302 (5C)
OS MAP 200, 111: SX049891

🎬 The Kid Who Would Be King (2019).

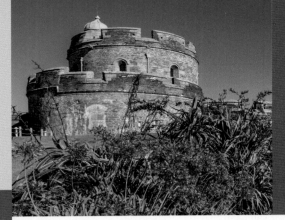

ST MAWES CASTLE

——— CORNWALL – TR2 5DE ———

Beautifully positioned overlooking the Fal estuary, St Mawes Castle is the best-preserved and most elaborately decorated of Henry VIII's Tudor artillery forts. Enhanced presentation highlights its stories for family explorers.

Along with Pendennis Castle on the other side of the estuary, St Mawes guarded the important anchorage of Carrick Roads. Mounting heavy ship-sinking guns, it was one of the chain of forts built to counter an invasion threat from Catholic Europe. Displays reveal how the ambitious Cornish merchant Thomas Treffry of Fowey masterminded its building, bedecking it with carvings praising the Tudor dynasty and becoming its first captain.

A model introduces the castle's charming clover-leaf design, hands-on games help families discover its ornate sculptures, and audio tracks bring Tudor characters to life.

The castle's re-presented collection of historic guns tells the story of how St Mawes guarded the Cornish coast for over 450 years, right up to 1956.

There are wonderful views of the sea and passing ships from the battlements. Add to your adventures by travelling to the castle by ferry.

OPENING TIMES

Open daily 1 Apr-5 Nov

Open varying days 6 Nov-28 Mar

Site closed 24-26 Dec

See website for latest opening times

Last entry 30 mins before closing

The castle may be closed on a Saturday if an event is booked. Please check with the property in advance

VISIT US

Direction: In St Mawes on A3078

Train: Penmere (Falmouth), 4 miles via Prince of Wales Pier and ferry

Bus: Visit traveline.info for the latest bus timetables and routes

Ferry: St Mawes passenger ferry from Falmouth or King Harry Car Ferry from Feock

Tel: 01326 270526

Local Tourist Information:
St Mawes: 01326 270440

NON-MEMBERS

See website for entry prices

By being a Member, you save up to **£28.50** (price of a family ticket) when you visit **St Mawes Castle**

ACQ.1961 ⛴ 🍴 🖥 🏠 👤 👥 P 🪑 🚻 ♿ ⚠ OVP

Parking: charges apply to non-members, free for Members with valid English Heritage car sticker.

MAP PAGE 302 (7C)
OS MAP 204, 105: SW841328

BERRY POMEROY CASTLE

DEVON – TQ9 6LJ

The perfect romantic ruin, tucked away in woodland. Within the 15th-century walls of the Pomeroy family castle looms the dramatic ruined shell of the great Elizabethan and Jacobean mansion of the Seymours, never completed.

OPENING TIMES

Open daily 1 Apr-5 Nov

Open varying days 6 Nov-28 Mar

Site closed 24-26 Dec & 1 Jan

See website for latest opening times

Last entry 30 mins before closing

VISIT US

Direction: 2½ miles E of Totnes off A385

Train: Totnes 3½ miles

Bus: Visit traveline.info for the latest bus timetables and routes

Tel: 01803 866618

NON-MEMBERS

See website for entry prices

ACQ.1977

Wheelchair and rugged mobility scooter access (grounds and ground floor only). **Please note:** a couple of helpers (or a scooter with enough power) and a chair with enough ground clearance advised, as it is quite difficult to get up the stepped ramp at the main gate.

Limited parking (no coach access). The car park is located at the end of a single track drive with passing places.

Tearooms (not managed by English Heritage) Tel: 01803 849473 for opening times.

MAP PAGE 303 (6F)
OS MAP 202, OL20/110: SX839623

BLACKBURY CAMP

DEVON – EX24 6JE

An Iron Age hillfort with impressive ramparts and defended single entrance. Now a picturesque spot for a picnic, surrounded by woodland.

OPENING TIMES

Any reasonable daylight hours

VISIT US

Direction: Off B3174/A3052

Train: Honiton 6½ miles

Bus: Visit traveline.info for the latest bus timetables and routes

ACQ.1930

Caution: steep slopes.

MAP PAGE 303 (5G)
OS MAP 192/193, 115: SY187924

DARTMOUTH, BAYARD'S COVE FORT

DEVON – TQ6 9AX

Small Tudor artillery fort guarding Dartmouth's inner harbour, picturesquely sited on the quayside.

See also Dartmouth Castle, p.98.

OPENING TIMES

Any reasonable daylight hours

VISIT US

Direction: Located in Dartmouth, on the riverside

Train: Kingswear Station on the Torbay & Paignton Railway and then catch the Dartmouth Lower Ferry or Passenger Ferry

Bus: Visit traveline.info for the latest bus timetables and routes

ACQ.1954

Caution: steep stairs, sheer drop into water.

Please do not climb on the walls.

MAP PAGE 303 (6F)
OS MAP 202, OL20: SX879509

KIRKHAM HOUSE, PAIGNTON

DEVON – TQ3 3AX

Late medieval house, restored in the 1960s. Furnished with modern furniture, illustrating traditional craftsmanship.

Managed in association with the Paignton Heritage Society.

OPENING TIMES

See website for latest opening times

VISIT US

Direction: Located in Kirkham St, off Cecil Rd, Paignton

Train: Paignton ½ mile

Bus: Visit traveline.info for the latest bus timetables and routes

ACQ.1948

Caution: steep stairs.

MAP PAGE 303 (6F)
OS MAP 202, OL20/110: SX885610

MEMBERS' rewards

Don't forget to check out our **Members' Rewards** scheme. It gives you access to a variety of exclusive offers, discount deals, fantastic competitions and unforgettable experiences.

See p.300 for details.

DARTMOUTH CASTLE

—— DEVON – TQ6 0JN ——

In a lovely waterfront setting, Dartmouth Castle defended the busy port of Dartmouth against many enemies for over 550 years. Imaginative installations bring its history to life.

Begun in the 1380s by John Hawley, privateering mayor of Dartmouth, about a century later the castle became probably the very first fortification in Britain purpose-built to mount 'ship-sinking' heavy cannon. It was also equipped with a massive 250-metre-long iron chain spanning the Dart estuary, which could be drawn up to stop incoming enemy ships, making them an easy target for gunfire. An animated film explores how this feat of medieval engineering worked.

Installations bring the castle's story right up to its last call to action in the Second World War, and a dramatic audio and light display in the 19th-century gun battery shows a crew preparing to fire a heavy gun. Families can explore hands-on the weapons used to defend the fortress, trying on helmets and handling cannonballs. You're also introduced to characters from Dartmouth's history, and young history hunters can follow 'John Hawley's Explorer Trail', an activity trail throughout the castle.

Take the scenic boat trip to the castle (weather dependent) from the bustling town quay. The best views of the castle are from the water, so be sure to have your camera ready.

OPENING TIMES

Open daily 1 Apr-5 Nov

Open varying days 6 Nov-28 Mar

Site closed 24-26 Dec & 1 Jan

See website for latest opening times

Last entry 30 mins before closing

VISIT US

Direction: 1 mile SE of Dartmouth off B3205, narrow approach road. No coach access

Train: Kingswear Station on the Torbay & Paignton Railway and then catch the Dartmouth Lower Ferry or Passenger Ferry

Bus: Visit traveline.info for the latest bus timetables and routes

Ferry: The Dartmouth Castle Ferry operates from Dartmouth between Easter and end of October

Tel: 01803 834445

Local Tourist Information:
Dartmouth: 01803 834224

NON-MEMBERS

See website for entry prices

By being a Member, you save up to **£32.50** (price of a family ticket) when you visit **Dartmouth Castle**

ACQ 1909

Parking (not owned by English Heritage, charged).

Tearooms and toilets (not managed by English Heritage).

MAP PAGE 303 (6F)
OS MAP 202, OL20: SX887503

LYDFORD CASTLE, TOWN BANKS AND SAXON TOWN

DEVON – EX20 4BH

A Norman earthwork castle and a later Norman stone keep, built as a prison and notorious for harsh punishments. Beautifully sited on the fringe of Dartmoor, it stands within the defences of a Saxon fortified 'borough'.

Download a free audio tour from our website.

OPENING TIMES

Any reasonable daylight hours

VISIT US

Direction: In Lydford off A386; 8½ miles S of Okehampton

Bus: Visit traveline.info for the latest bus timetables and routes

ACQ.1934	Castle	ACQ.1965	North of Town Banks
ACQ.1968	South of Town Banks
ACQ.1972	Norman Fort

Parking (not owned by English Heritage).

Caution: steep slopes, steep stairs.

MAP PAGE 302 (5E)
OS MAP 191/201, OL28:
SX509848

OKEHAMPTON CASTLE

DEVON – EX20 IJA

The remains of the largest castle in Devon. Begun soon after the Norman Conquest, it was converted into a sumptuous residence in the 14th century by Hugh Courtenay, Earl of Devon. Riverside picnic area and woodland walks.

OPENING TIMES

Open daily 1 Apr-5 Nov

Site closed 6 Nov-28 Mar

See website for latest opening times

Last entry 30 mins before closing

VISIT US

Direction: Located ½ mile SW of Okehampton town centre (signposted). Turn into Castle Road by Post Office. Close to A30

Train: Okehampton 0.8 miles, regular service from Exeter

Bus: Visit traveline.info for the latest bus timetables and routes

Tel: 01837 52844

Local Tourist Information: Okehampton: 01837 52295

NON-MEMBERS

See website for entry prices

New guidebook.

Woodland Walk Guide available from kiosk.

MAP PAGE 302 (5E)
OS MAP 191, OL28/113:
SX583942

ROYAL CITADEL, PLYMOUTH

DEVON – PL1 2PD

Plymouth's most important historic building and one of Britain's finest 17th-century fortresses. Commissioned by Charles II in 1665 to counter a threatened Dutch invasion, it's still in military use today.

OPENING TIMES

Access by 2-hour guided tour only Apr-Oct. Security measures are in force as the site is a working military establishment. Photography is prohibited. Tickets must be booked online at least 24 hours in advance. Check website for further details

VISIT US

Direction: At E end of Plymouth Hoe

Train: Plymouth 1 mile

Bus: Visit traveline.info for the latest bus timetables and routes

ENTRY

Charge for tours

ROYAL CITADEL, PLYMOUTH

ACQ.1966

Parking on Plymouth Hoe. No large bags. Bags may be searched. No toilets on site.

Disabled access (some steep slopes).

Caution: unguarded drops, steep stairs.

MAP PAGE 302 (6E)
OS MAP 201, OL20/108:
SX480538

TOTNES CASTLE

DEVON – TQ9 5NU

Classic Norman motte-and-bailey castle, founded soon after the Conquest to overawe the Saxon town. A later shell keep crowns its steep mound, offering sweeping views across the rooftops to the River Dart.

OPENING TIMES

Open daily 1 Apr-5 Nov

Open varying days 6 Nov-28 Mar

Site closed 24-26 Dec & 1 Jan

See website for latest opening times

Last entry 30 mins before closing

VISIT US

Direction: In centre of Totnes, entrance on Castle Street. By car, follow signs for Historic Town Centre, turn onto Castle Street from Station Road (opposite train station). On foot from town centre, turn north off High Street (towards the train station)

Train: Totnes ¼ mile and South Devon Railway (Totnes Riverside) ½ mile

Bus: Visit traveline.info for the latest bus timetables and routes

Tel: 01803 864406

Local Tourist Information: Totnes: 01803 269190

NON-MEMBERS

See website for entry prices

ACQ.1947

Parking charged (not managed by English Heritage) 64 metre (210 feet) walk from castle, cars only, narrow approach roads.

Keep accessible only via steep steps.

New guidebook available summer 2023.

MAP PAGE 302 (6E)
OS MAP 202, OL20/110:
SX800605

Dartmoor National Park is home to historic sites dating right back to the Neolithic period. Discover this stunning landscape and sense how our ancestors lived on the wild moors and windswept hills.

Visit **english-heritage.org.uk/ dartmoor** to find out more.

GRIMSPOUND
DEVON – PL20 6TB

The best-known prehistoric Dartmoor settlement. Remains of 24 Bronze Age houses survive within a massive boundary wall.

Managed by the Dartmoor National Park Authority.

OPENING TIMES
Any reasonable daylight hours

VISIT US
Direction: 6 miles SW of Moretonhampstead, off B3212

Bus: Visit **traveline.info** for the latest bus timetables and routes

ACQ.1977 🎧 🐕 🐑 P ⚠

Parking in lay-by.

Caution: falling masonry.

MAP PAGE 302 (5E)
OS MAP 191, OL28: SX701809

HOUND TOR DESERTED MEDIEVAL VILLAGE
DEVON – TQ13 9XG

The remains of four 13th-century Dartmoor longhouses built of granite boulders, with their barns and garden plots. People lived at one end of the longhouse, their livestock at the other, divided by a passage. Set in an area originally farmed in the Bronze Age, this isolated moorland hamlet was probably abandoned in the early 14th century.

Managed by the Dartmoor National Park Authority.

OPENING TIMES
Any reasonable daylight hours

VISIT US
Direction: 2½ miles west of Haytor Vale on B3387, right turn to Hound Tor and Manaton, continue for 1½ miles

Bus: Visit **traveline.info** for the latest bus timetables and routes

ACQ.1972 🎧 🐕 🐑 P ⚠

Parking at Swallerton Gate (½ mile walk south-east across moor to monument).

Caution: falling masonry.

MAP PAGE 302 (5E)
OS MAP 191, OL28: SX746788

MERRIVALE PREHISTORIC SETTLEMENT
DEVON – PL20 6ST

Bronze Age settlement remains, along with ritual sites including Bronze Age cairns and cists, late Neolithic stone rows and a stone circle.

Managed by the Dartmoor National Park Authority.

OPENING TIMES
Any reasonable daylight hours

VISIT US
Direction: South of B3357 W of Princetown

Train: Gunnislake 10 miles

Bus: Visit **traveline.info** for the latest bus timetables and routes

ACQ.1973 🎧 🐕 🐑 P

Parking at Four Winds car park. Five minute walk west across moor.

MAP PAGE 302 (6E)
OS MAP 191, OL28: SX554748

UPPER PLYM VALLEY
DEVON – PL7 5EJ

These 6 square miles of Dartmoor are packed with Neolithic and Bronze Age monuments, plus medieval and later sites.

OPENING TIMES
Any reasonable daylight hours

VISIT US
Direction: 4 miles E of Yelverton

ACQ.1978 🎧 🐕 🐑 P

Parking – ½ mile walk to monuments. Limited parking at Trowlesworthy car park – OS map strongly advised.

MAP PAGE 302 (6E)
OS MAP 202, OL20/OL28: SX580660

ABBOTSBURY ABBEY REMAINS

DORSET – DT3 4JR

Part of a monastic building, perhaps the abbot's lodging, of the Benedictine Abbey of Abbotsbury. St Catherine's Chapel is within half a mile.

OPENING TIMES

Any reasonable daylight hours

VISIT US

Direction: Located in Abbotsbury, off B3157, near the churchyard

Train: Upwey 7½ miles

Bus: Visit **traveline.info** for the latest bus timetables and routes

Tel: 0370 333 1181

ACQ.1948

Parking charged (not English Heritage).

MAP PAGE 303 (5H)
OS MAP 194, OL15: SY578852

ABBOTSBURY, ST CATHERINE'S CHAPEL

DORSET – DT3 4JH

High on a hilltop overlooking Abbotsbury Abbey, this sturdily buttressed 14th-century chapel was built by the monks as a place of pilgrimage and retreat.

ABBOTSBURY, ST CATHERINE'S CHAPEL

OPENING TIMES

Any reasonable daylight hours

VISIT US

Direction: ½ mile S of Abbotsbury; by steep path from village, off B3157

Train: Upwey 7 miles

Bus: Visit **traveline.info**

Tel: 0370 333 1181

ACQ.1922

Parking charged (not English Heritage).

Caution: steep slopes.

Cattle and sheep may be grazing on the hill and footpaths leading to the chapel.

MAP PAGE 303 (5H)
OS MAP 194, OL15: SY573848

CHRISTCHURCH CASTLE AND NORMAN HOUSE

DORSET – BH23 1AS

Remains of Christchurch Castle, including parts of the keep and the 12th-century riverside 'Constable's House' – a very early example of domestic architecture with a rare Norman chimney. The important priory church is nearby.

OPENING TIMES

Any reasonable daylight hours

VISIT US

Direction: Located in Christchurch, near the Priory

Train: Christchurch ¾ mile

Bus: Visit **traveline.info**

Tel: 0370 333 1181

ACQ.1946

On-street parking.

Caution: falling masonry, deep water, steep slopes, steep stairs.

MAP PAGE 303 (5J)
OS MAP 195, OL22: SZ160927

FIDDLEFORD MANOR

DORSET – DT10 2BX

The principal parts of a small stone manor house, probably begun c. 1370 for William Latimer, Sheriff of Somerset and Dorset. The hall and solar chamber display outstanding timber roofs.

Please note: The adjoining building is a private residence and is not open to visitors.

OPENING TIMES

Open daily 1 Apr-28 Mar

Site closed 24-26, 31 Dec & 1 Jan

See website for latest opening times

VISIT US

Direction: 1 mile E of Sturminster Newton off A357

Bus: Visit **traveline.info** for the latest bus timetables and routes

ACQ.1961

Disabled access (ground floor only – with 1 step).

Free car park. Not suitable for large coaches.

Caution: deep water, steep stairs.

MAP PAGE 303 (4H)
OS MAP 194, 129: ST801136

JORDAN HILL ROMAN TEMPLE

DORSET – DT3 6PL

The foundations of a 4th-century AD Romano-British temple.

OPENING TIMES

Any reasonable daylight hours

VISIT US

Direction: Located 2 miles NE of Weymouth, off A353

Train: Upwey or Weymouth, 2 miles

Bus: Visit **traveline.info** for the latest bus timetables and routes

Tel: 0370 333 1181

ACQ.1933

On-street parking.

MAP PAGE 303 (5H)
OS MAP 194, OL15: SY699821

KINGSTON RUSSELL STONE CIRCLE
DORSET – DT3 4JX

A late Neolithic or early Bronze Age circle of 18 fallen stones, on a hilltop overlooking Abbotsbury and the sea.

OPENING TIMES
Any reasonable daylight hours

VISIT US
Direction: Turn left off Bishop's Road, approximately 1½ miles NE of Abbotsbury, immediately after the 90° right-hand bend

Train: Weymouth (1½ miles) or Dorchester South/West (8 miles)

Bus: Visit traveline.info for the latest bus timetables and routes

ACQ.1887 🐕 🐎 ⚠️

Limited parking on road verge at entrance to farm. Access to stone circle on foot only via public footpaths, approx. ½ mile. No off-road vehicle access.

Cattle and sheep may be grazing around footpaths to site.

> MAP PAGE 303 (5H)
> OS MAP 194, OL15: SY578878

KNOWLTON CHURCH AND EARTHWORKS
DORSET – BH21 5AE

A ruined medieval church stands at the centre of a large prehistoric henge, part of an important cluster of Neolithic and early Bronze Age monuments.

KNOWLTON CHURCH AND EARTHWORKS

OPENING TIMES
Any reasonable daylight hours

VISIT US
Direction: SW of Cranborne on Lumber Lane off B3078

Bus: Visit traveline.info for the latest bus timetables and routes

ACQ.1959 🐕 P ⚠️

Parking in lay-by limited.

Caution: steep slopes.

> MAP PAGE 303 (5J)
> OS MAP 195, 118: SU024103

MAIDEN CASTLE
DORSET – DT2 9PP

Among the largest Iron Age hillforts in Europe, Maiden Castle's huge multiple ramparts enclose an area equivalent to 50 football pitches. Excavations have revealed the site's 6,000-year history, from Neolithic ritual to late Roman times. Download the free audio experience, 'Echoscape', from our website.

OPENING TIMES
Any reasonable daylight hours

VISIT US
Direction: 2 miles S of Dorchester, off A354, N of bypass

Train: Dorchester South/West (2 miles)

MAIDEN CASTLE

Bus: Visit traveline.info for the latest bus timetables and routes

Tel: 0370 333 1181

ACQ.1908 🏠 🐕 🐎 ⚙️ P ⚠️

Caution: unguarded drops, steep slopes.

Sheep grazing on the monument.

> MAP PAGE 303 (5H)
> OS MAP 194, OL15: SY669884

THE NINE STONES
DORSET – DT2 9LX

Small late Neolithic circle of nine standing stones, now in a wooded glade. Winterbourne Poor Lot Barrows (p.104) are nearby.

Please note: Site not accessible at present. See website for re-opening date.

OPENING TIMES
Any reasonable daylight hours

VISIT US

ACQ.1895 ⚠️

Please note: permissive footpath to site parallel to A35 currently closed.

Caution: beware of traffic.

> MAP PAGE 303 (5H)
> OS MAP 194, OL15/117: SY611904

DON'T FORGET
Remember to take your membership card.

PORTLAND CASTLE

———— DORSET – DT5 1AZ ————

Overlooking and defending Portland harbour, this coastal artillery fortress was built by Henry VIII to counter threats from France and Spain. It retains its squat, rounded, seaward form, designed to deflect incoming cannon shot.

Much fought over during the Civil War, Portland Castle was taken and retaken several times by both Parliamentarians and Royalists. It later protected shipping against pirates, and vainly tried to control the local smuggling industry, before 'standing-to' again when Napoleonic invasion loomed.

Following a spell as a private home, it became a station for seaplanes flying anti-submarine patrols during the First World War. During the Second World War it served as an ordnance store and accommodation for British and American soldiers. In 1944 British and American forces carried out top-secret preliminary training for the D-Day landings in nearby bays.

Experience the fort's long and varied story through presentations, interactive exhibits and an audio tour. Be sure to visit the Tudor kitchen, armoury and gun decks. The Governor's Garden, designed by Christopher Bradley-Hole as part of the Contemporary Heritage Garden series, is a perfectly sheltered spot to enjoy the dramatic sea and harbour views.

Enjoy refreshments in the Captain's House Tearoom, including a range of home-made sandwiches, cakes and snacks made with locally sourced ingredients.

OPENING TIMES

Open daily 1 Apr–5 Nov

Site closed 6 Nov–28 Mar

See website for latest opening times

Last entry 30 mins before closing

Parts of the castle may be closed if an event is booked. Please call the site in advance or check website

VISIT US

Direction: Overlooking Portland Harbour in Castletown, Isle of Portland

Train: Weymouth 4½ miles

Bus: Visit traveline.info

Tel: 01305 820539

Local Tourist Information: Portland: 01305 821361

NON-MEMBERS

See website for entry prices

By being a Member, you save up to £28.50 (price of a family ticket) when you visit **Portland Castle**

Disabled access – Captain's House, parts of ground floor of castle (no lift available to other parts) and Governor's Garden.

Parking: charges apply to non-members, free for Members with valid English Heritage car sticker.

Captain's House Tearoom closes 1 hour before the castle.

MAP PAGE 303 (6H)
OS MAP 194, OL15: SY685744

SHERBORNE OLD CASTLE DORSET – DT9 3SA

Originally a fortified 12th-century bishop's palace, Sherborne Old Castle became the home of Sir Walter Ralegh. Later a powerful Royalist base, it saw fierce fighting during the Civil War. Look out for wildlife in the grounds. Refreshed interpretation panels.

OPENING TIMES

Please note that Sherborne Old Castle will be undergoing conservation/maintenance works. There may be restrictions to opening times and temporary access arrangements. Please check website for details

VISIT US

Direction: Situated at the end of Castleton Road, off B3145

Train: Sherborne ¾ mile

Bus: Visit traveline.info for the latest bus timetables and routes

NON-MEMBERS

See website for entry prices

By being a Member, you save up to £24.50 (price of a family ticket) when you visit **Sherborne Old Castle**

ACQ.1956 🚻 ♿ 🐕 ☕ 🅿 🎫 📷 ⚠ OVP

Refreshments available.

Parking: charges apply to non-members, free for Members with valid English Heritage car sticker.

Secure cycle parking available. National network route 26.

MAP PAGE 303 (4H)
OS MAP 183, 129: ST648168

WINTERBOURNE POOR LOT BARROWS
DORSET – DT2 9EB

A 'cemetery' of 44 Bronze Age burial mounds of varying types and sizes, by the A35 main road.

OPENING TIMES

Any reasonable daylight hours

VISIT US

Direction: 2 miles W of Winterbourne Abbas, S of junction of A35 with a minor road to Compton Valence. Access via Longlands Lane – 1 mile east of site south of A35

Train: Dorchester West or South, both 7 miles

Bus: Visit traveline.info for the latest bus timetables and routes

ACQ.1961 🐕 🐄 ⚠

Park on roadside approx. 1 mile south along Longlands Lane, follow public right of way, Jubilee Trail for 1 mile (approx.) west over farmland.

MAP PAGE 303 (5H)
OS MAP 194, OL15/117: SY590907

CHECK ONLINE

Pre-booking for visits to our staffed sites may be required, check our website for the latest guidance.

GLOUCESTERSHIRE

BELAS KNAP LONG BARROW
GLOUCESTERSHIRE – GL54 5AL

A particularly fine restored example of a Neolithic long barrow: remains of 31 people were found in the chambers.

Managed by Gloucestershire County Council.

OPENING TIMES
Any reasonable daylight hours

VISIT US
Direction: Near Charlton Abbots; ½ mile on Cotswold Way

Train: Cheltenham 9 miles

Bus: Visit traveline.info for the latest bus timetables and routes

ACQ 1928 [icons] P [icon]

Parking with ½ mile steep walk to monument.

Caution: unguarded drops.

MAP PAGE 303 (1J)
OS MAP 163, OL45: SP021254

CIRENCESTER AMPHITHEATRE
GLOUCESTERSHIRE – GL7 1XW

Earthwork remains of one of the largest Roman amphitheatres in Britain, serving the Roman city of Corinium (now Cirencester).

CIRENCESTER AMPHITHEATRE
Managed by Cirencester Town Council.

OPENING TIMES
Any reasonable daylight hours

VISIT US
Direction: Located W of Cirencester, next to the bypass. Access from the town, or along Chesterton Lane from the W end of the bypass, onto Cotswold Ave

Train: Kemble 4 miles

Bus: Visit traveline.info for the latest bus timetables and routes

ACQ 1973 [icons] P [icon]

Caution: steep slopes.

MAP PAGE 303 (2J)
OS MAP 163, OL45/169: SP020014

GLOUCESTER, BLACKFRIARS
GLOUCESTERSHIRE – GL1 2HS

Among the most complete surviving friaries of Dominican 'black friars' in England, finished in about 1270. After the Dissolution, it was converted into a Tudor mansion and cloth factory, but its medieval features are now visible again. There's a magnificent 13th-century scissor-braced timber roof over the former friars' library.

Managed by Gloucester City Council.

GLOUCESTER, BLACKFRIARS

OPENING TIMES
See website for latest opening times

VISIT US
Direction: In Blackfriars Lane, off Ladybellegate St, off Southgate St, Gloucester

Train: Gloucester ½ mile

Bus: Visit traveline.info for the latest bus timetables and routes

Tel: 01452 503050

ACQ 1955 [icons] P [icon]

Civil wedding ceremonies (through Gloucester City Council).

Parking adjacent. (Charge applies. Not managed by English Heritage).

Caution: steep stairs.

MAP PAGE 303 (1H)
OS MAP 162, 179: SO829184

GLOUCESTER, GREYFRIARS
GLOUCESTERSHIRE – GL1 1TS

Substantial remains of a medieval friary church of Franciscan 'grey friars', rebuilt in the early 16th century.

OPENING TIMES
Any reasonable daylight hours

VISIT US
Direction: On Greyfriars Walk

Train: Gloucester ½ mile

Bus: Visit traveline.info for the latest bus timetables and routes

ACQ 1969 [icons] [icon]

Caution: falling masonry.

MAP PAGE 303 (1H)
OS MAP 162, 179: SO832184

HAILES ABBEY

GLOUCESTERSHIRE – GL54 5PB

Set in lovely Cotswold countryside, Hailes Abbey was one of medieval England's most renowned pilgrim shrines. The strikingly presented museum displays the abbey's treasures and tells the intriguing story of the 'Holy Blood of Hailes'.

The Cistercian abbey was founded in 1246 by Richard, Earl of Cornwall, Henry III's younger brother and among the richest men in Europe. It became a major pilgrimage destination after 1270, when Richard's son Edmund presented it with a sensational relic – allegedly no less than a phial of Christ's own blood. Pilgrims flocked to its shrine and financed the rebuilding of the abbey on a magnificent scale. The ruins, picturesquely 'soft-capped' with turf for preservation, include cloister buildings and the footprint of the church, which was inspired by Westminster Abbey.

In the 1530s its relic was denounced as a fake, and the abbey was suppressed by Henry VIII and comprehensively looted. The outstanding museum helps you imagine it in all its glory. You can see lavish sculpture, heraldic floor tiles and even one of the oldest surviving medieval spectacle frames. More artefacts are displayed in a miniature glass 'cloister'.

Nearby, the delightful little parish church houses stained glass and tiles from the abbey, and outstanding medieval wall paintings.

Owned by the National Trust, managed and maintained by English Heritage.

OPENING TIMES

Open varying days 1 Apr-28 Mar

Site closed 24-26 Dec & 1 Jan

See website for latest opening times

Last entry 30 mins before closing

VISIT US

Direction: 2 miles NE of Winchcombe off B4632. On the Cotswold Way National Trail

Train: Cheltenham 10 miles. From March to October, Hayles Abbey Halt (600m from site) can be reached from Cheltenham, Winchcombe or Broadway by diesel railcar on the Gloucestershire and Warwickshire Steam Railway. See gwsr.com for timetables and prices

Bus: Visit traveline.info for the latest bus timetables and routes

Tel: 01242 602398

NON-MEMBERS

See website for entry prices

By being a Member, you save up to £28.50 (price of a family ticket) when you visit **Hailes Abbey**

National Trust members free, but charged for audio tour (£1) and special events

ACQ.1948 OVP

Disabled access (ramp to museum, disabled toilet).

Refreshments available.

MAP PAGE 303 (1J)
OS MAP 150/163, OL45: SP050300

GREAT WITCOMBE ROMAN VILLA

GLOUCESTERSHIRE – GL3 4TW

Remains of a large and luxurious Roman villa built c. AD 250, with a bath-house and possibly the shrine of a water spirit.

OPENING TIMES

Exterior:
Open daily 1 Apr-28 Mar

See website for latest opening times

There is no access to the buildings, which house the mosaics

VISIT US

Direction: Located 5 miles SE of Gloucester off Cirencester Road; 400 metres (440 yards) from Cotswold Way National Trail

Train: Gloucester 6 miles

Bus: Visit traveline.info

ACQ.1919

Parking: charges apply to non-members, free for Members with valid car sticker. No access for coaches. No parking anywhere on the access tracks. 300-metre walk to site.

Caution: steep slopes, unguarded drops, falling masonry.

MAP PAGE 303 (2J)
OS MAP 163, 179: SO899142

KINGSWOOD ABBEY GATEHOUSE

GLOUCESTERSHIRE – GL12 8RS

This 16th-century gatehouse, sole survivor of a Cistercian abbey, is one of the latest monastic buildings in England. Displays a richly sculpted window.

OPENING TIMES

Exterior: Reasonable daylight hours

See website for details of events and access to interior

VISIT US

Direction: In Kingswood, off B4060; 1 mile SW of Wotton-under-Edge

Train: Yate 8 miles

Bus: Visit traveline.info

ACQ.1950

On-street parking.

MAP PAGE 303 (2H)
OS MAP 162/172, 167: ST747920

NYMPSFIELD LONG BARROW

GLOUCESTERSHIRE – GL11 5AU

Large Neolithic burial mound with spectacular views over the Severn Valley. Its burial chambers are uncovered for viewing.

Managed by Gloucestershire County Council.

OPENING TIMES

Any reasonable daylight hours

VISIT US

Direction: Located 1 mile NW of Nympsfield on B4066

Train: Stroud 5 miles

Bus: Visit traveline.info for the latest bus timetables and routes

ACQ.1975

MAP PAGE 303 (2H)
OS MAP 162, 167/168: SO794013

ODDA'S CHAPEL

GLOUCESTERSHIRE – GL19 4BX

Among the most complete Saxon churches in England, built in 1056 by Earl Odda and rediscovered in 1865. Deerhurst's Saxon parish church is nearby.

OPENING TIMES

Open daily 1 Apr-28 Mar

Site closed 24-26, 31 Dec & 1 Jan

See website for latest opening times

VISIT US

Direction: Located in Deerhurst off B4213, at Abbots Court; SW of parish church

Train: Cheltenham 8 miles

Bus: Visit traveline.info for the latest bus timetables and routes

ACQ.1962

Parking (charges apply, not English Heritage).

MAP PAGE 303 (1J)
OS MAP 150, 179: SO869298

OFFA'S DYKE

GLOUCESTERSHIRE – NP16 7JR

Three-mile wooded section of the great 8th-century boundary dyke built by Offa, King of Mercia. Includes the Devil's Pulpit, with fine views of Tintern Abbey.

OPENING TIMES

Any reasonable daylight hours

VISIT US

Direction: Located 3 miles NE of Chepstow, off B4228. Via Tidenham Forestry Commission car park. 1 mile walk (waymarked) down to the Devil's Pulpit on Offa's Dyke

Train: Chepstow 7 miles

Bus: Visit traveline.info for the latest bus timetables and routes

ACQ.1973

Parking (not English Heritage).

Caution: steep slopes, unguarded drops, steep stairs.

Strong footwear is recommended.

MAP PAGE 303 (2H)
OS MAP 162, OL14/167
SO546011-ST549975

OVER BRIDGE

GLOUCESTERSHIRE – GL2 8BZ

A single-arch stone bridge spanning the River Severn, built in 1825-30 by the great engineer Thomas Telford.

OPENING TIMES

Any reasonable daylight hours

VISIT US

Direction: 1 mile NW of Gloucester, at junction of A40 (Ross) and A417 (Ledbury)

Train: Gloucester 2 miles

Bus: Visit traveline.info for the latest bus timetables and routes

ACQ.1978

Caution: deep water, steep slopes.

MAP PAGE 303 (1H)
OS MAP 162, 179: SO816196

ST BRIAVELS CASTLE
GLOUCESTERSHIRE – GL15 6RG

Well-preserved castle, former hunting lodge of King John, with fine gatehouse built by Edward I in 1292 and late Victorian restoration. Now a youth hostel.

OPENING TIMES
Exterior viewing only (moat area): Any reasonable daylight hours

Limited access to interior as working youth hostel (call in advance to check)

VISIT US
Direction: In St Briavels; 7 miles NE of Chepstow off B4228

Train: Lydney 6 miles; Chepstow 8 miles

Bus: Visit **traveline.info** for the latest bus timetables and routes

Tel: 01594 530272 (Youth Hostel)

ACQ.1982 🚶 ⛺ 🚫 P 🍴 ⚠

Caution: falling masonry.

Please do not climb on the walls.

MAP PAGE 303 (2H)
OS MAP 162, OL14: SO559046

ST MARY'S CHURCH, KEMPLEY
GLOUCESTERSHIRE – GL18 2AT

ST MARY'S CHURCH, KEMPLEY

Delightful Norman church, displaying one of the most complete sets of medieval wall paintings in England, dating from the 12th to 15th centuries (and recently conserved by our Members' wall paintings appeal).

Managed in association with the Friends of Kempley Church.

OPENING TIMES
Open daily 1 Apr-28 Mar

Site closed 24-26, 31 Dec & 1 Jan

See website for latest opening times

VISIT US
Direction: 1 mile N of Kempley off B4024; 6 miles NE of Ross-on-Wye

Train: Ledbury 8 miles

Bus: Visit **traveline.info** for the latest bus timetables and routes

Email: freetoenter.sites@english-heritage.org.uk for group bookings

ACQ.1979 ♿ 🚫 P

Audio tour available from website.

Parking (in lay-by). Disabled access (1 step).

MAP PAGE 303 (1H)
OS MAP 149, 189: SO670313

ULEY LONG BARROW (HETTY PEGLER'S TUMP)
GLOUCESTERSHIRE – GL11 5AR

Restored Neolithic chambered mound, 37 metres (121 feet) long, atmospherically sited overlooking the Severn Valley. The internal chambers are accessible through a very low entrance.

Managed by Gloucestershire County Council.

ULEY LONG BARROW

OPENING TIMES
Any reasonable daylight hours

VISIT US
Direction: Located 3½ miles NE of Dursley, on B4066. Take care crossing road

Train: Stroud 6 miles

Bus: Visit **traveline.info** for the latest bus timetables and routes

ACQ.1883 🚻 P ⚠

Parking (in lay-by).

Warning: cross road with care.

Caution: steep slopes.

Note: visitors are advised to bring a torch.

MAP PAGE 303 (2H)
OS MAP 162, 167/168: SO790000

WINDMILL TUMP LONG BARROW, RODMARTON
GLOUCESTERSHIRE – GL7 6PU

A Neolithic chambered tomb with an enigmatic 'false entrance'.

Managed by Gloucestershire County Council.

OPENING TIMES
Any reasonable daylight hours

VISIT US
Direction: 1 mile SW of Rodmarton on Oathill Lane

Train: Kemble 5 miles

Bus: Visit **traveline.info** for the latest bus timetables and routes

ACQ.1979 🚻 P

Parking in lay-by.

MAP PAGE 303 (2J)
OS MAP 163, 168: ST933973

CLEEVE ABBEY

SOMERSET – TA23 0PS

Gain a vivid insight into monastic life at Cleeve Abbey and admire its strikingly displayed tiled pavement.

Atmospheric Cleeve Abbey boasts the most impressively complete and unaltered set of monastic cloister buildings in England. Standing roofed and two storeys high, they include the gatehouse, the 15th-century refectory with its glorious angel roof, and an unusual 'painted chamber'. The great dormitory is one of the finest in the country. Beneath it are the vaulted warming room, and the sacristy with early 13th-century tilework and decoration.

Cleeve's crowning glory is the magnificent tiled floor of its earliest refectory. Decked from end to end with high-quality heraldic tiles dating from around 1270, it's the only large-scale survival of a decorated medieval monastic refectory floor in Britain. Its royal and baronial heraldry celebrates the abbey's wealthy patrons. Buried in the late 15th century and rediscovered in 1876, it had suffered from exposure to the elements. Now it's displayed within a purpose-built timber shelter, complete with seating and viewing platforms.

An exhibition and touchscreen virtual tour tell the story of abbey life. A story bag, 'Brother Cedric and the Missing Sheep', is a fun way for families to explore the abbey.

OPENING TIMES

Open varying days 1 Apr-5 Nov

Site closed 6 Nov-28 Mar

See website for latest opening times

Last entry 30 mins before closing

VISIT US

Direction: Located in Washford, ¼ mile S of A39

Train: Washford ½ mile (West Somerset Steam Railway)

Bus: Visit traveline.info for the latest bus timetables and routes

Tel: 01984 640377

Local Tourist Information: Watchet: 01984 632101

NON-MEMBERS

See website for entry prices

By being a Member, you save up to £28.50 (price of a family ticket) when you visit **Cleeve Abbey**

ACQ. 1951 ♿ 🚻 🎫 🖼 E 🧺 🖥 🧍 👥 P 🚗 📷
🚻♿ ⚠ OVP

Disabled access (grounds and ground floor only, plus toilet).

Dogs on leads (in grounds only).

Refreshments available.

MAP PAGE 303 (4F)
OS MAP 181, OL9: ST047407

DAW'S CASTLE

SOMERSET – TA23 0JP

Clifftop fortress begun by King Alfred to defend the people of Watchet against Viking attacks.

OPENING TIMES

Any reasonable daylight hours

VISIT US

Direction: ½ mile W of Watchet off B3191

Train: Watchet (West Somerset railway) ¾ mile

Bus: Visit **traveline.info** for the latest bus timetables and routes

ACQ. 1983

Parking in Watchet (paid, not English Heritage) and walk ½ mile via SW Coastal Path.

Caution: steep slopes.

> MAP PAGE 303 (4F)
> OS MAP 181, OL9: SS989432

DUNSTER, BUTTER CROSS

SOMERSET – TA24 6RT

The repositioned stump of a medieval stone cross, once a meeting place for butter sellers.

Managed by the National Trust on behalf of English Heritage.

OPENING TIMES

Any reasonable daylight hours

VISIT US

Direction: Beside minor road to Alcombe, 350 metres (400 yards) NW of Dunster parish church

Train: Dunster (West Somerset Railway) 1 mile

Bus: Visit **traveline.info** for the latest bus timetables and routes

ACQ. 1951

Parking in village (charged).

Caution: beware of traffic.

> MAP PAGE 303 (4F)
> OS MAP 181, OL9: ST823604

DUNSTER, GALLOX BRIDGE

SOMERSET – TA24 6SR

This ancient stone bridge – originally 'gallows bridge' – once carried packhorses bringing fleeces to Dunster market.

Managed by the National Trust on behalf of English Heritage.

OPENING TIMES

Any reasonable daylight hours

VISIT US

Direction: Located off A396 at the S end of Dunster village

Train: Dunster (West Somerset Railway) ¾ mile

Bus: Visit **traveline.info** for the latest bus timetables and routes

ACQ. 1951

Parking in village (charged).

Caution: deep water.

> MAP PAGE 303 (4F)
> OS MAP 181, OL9: SS989432

DUNSTER, YARN MARKET

SOMERSET – TA24 6SG

This fine 17th-century timber-framed octagonal market hall is a monument to Dunster's once-flourishing cloth trade.

Managed by the National Trust on behalf of English Heritage.

OPENING TIMES

Any reasonable daylight hours

VISIT US

Direction: In Dunster High St

Train: Dunster (West Somerset Railway) ½ mile

Bus: Visit **traveline.info** for the latest bus timetables and routes

ACQ. 1951

Parking in village (charged).

Caution: beware of traffic, falling masonry.

> MAP PAGE 303 (4F)
> OS MAP 181, OL9: SS992438

While in the region, why not visit **Stonehenge**, one of the wonders of the world and the best-known prehistoric monument in Europe. There's a world-class visitor centre, plus a spacious shop and café.

See **p.122** for details.

FARLEIGH HUNGERFORD CASTLE
SOMERSET – BA2 7RS

Sir Thomas Hungerford, Speaker of the Commons, began this fortified mansion in the 1370s. It was extended in the 15th century by his son Walter, Lord Hungerford, distinguished soldier and statesman. Remains include two tall corner towers and a complete chapel, displaying family monuments and wall paintings, some recently conserved. You can still see many Hungerford coffins in its crypt, some with 'death masks'.

The remarkable Hungerford family included two members executed during the Wars of the Roses and another – who imprisoned his wife here for four years – beheaded by Henry VIII. A Tudor Lady Hungerford burnt her murdered husband's body in the kitchen furnace.

Discover Farleigh's story through an audio tour and extensive displays in the Priests' House. There are family and educational facilities, and a base for schools.

🎬 The White Princess (2017).

OPENING TIMES

Open daily 1 Apr-5 Nov

Open varying days 6 Nov-28 Mar

Site closed 24-26 Dec & 1 Jan

See website for latest opening times

Last entry 30 mins before closing

VISIT US

Direction: In Farleigh Hungerford, 9 miles SE of Bath; 3½ miles W of Trowbridge on A366

Train: Avoncliffe 2 miles; Trowbridge 3½ miles

Bus: Visit traveline.info for the latest bus timetables and routes

Tel: 01225 754026

Local Tourist Information: Trowbridge: 01225 710535

NON-MEMBERS

See website for entry prices

By being a Member, you save up to **£24.50** (price of a family ticket) when you visit **Farleigh Hungerford Castle**

ACQ.1915 🎧 📶 🎯 🛒 E 🚿 📷 🚶
🚻 P 🚪 📷 ⚠ OVP

Dogs on leads are welcome in the grounds and the buildings.
Refreshments available.

MAP PAGE 303 (3H)
OS MAP 173, 143/156: ST801576

GLASTONBURY TRIBUNAL
SOMERSET – BA6 9DP

A fine 15th-century merchant's house and shop, probably built for Glastonbury Abbey, with an early Tudor facade, bay window and panelled interiors.

Managed by Glastonbury Antiquarian Society.

OPENING TIMES

See website for latest opening times

VISIT US

Direction: In Glastonbury High St

Bus: Visit traveline.info for the latest bus timetables and routes

NON-MEMBERS

Museum
See website for entry prices

ACQ.1932 📷 ❌ P ⚠

Disabled access (ground floor – 2 steps).

Parking (charged, not English Heritage).

Caution: steep stairs.

MAP PAGE 303 (4H)
OS MAP 182/183, 141: ST499389

SHARE THE FUN

Check our website for up-to-the-minute information on our year-long programme of events.

english-heritage.org.uk/events

MEARE FISH HOUSE

SOMERSET – BA6 9SP

A unique survivor both in function and design, this housed the keeper of medieval Glastonbury Abbey's (then) adjacent fishery lake.

OPENING TIMES

Any reasonable daylight hours

Key available from Manor House Farm

VISIT US

Direction: In Meare village, on B3151

Bus: Visit traveline.info for the latest bus timetables and routes

 ACQ.1911

Parking (in village on Muddy Lane).

MAP PAGE 303 (4G)
OS MAP 182, 141: ST458417

NUNNEY CASTLE

SOMERSET – BA11 4LW

A striking moated tower-house castle, built in the 1370s by Sir John de la Mere. Held by Royalists during the Civil War, it fell to Parliamentarian cannon, the damaged portion finally collapsing on Christmas Day 1910.

OPENING TIMES

Any reasonable daylight hours

VISIT US

Direction: Located in Nunney, 3½ miles SW of Frome, off A361 (no coach access)

Train: Frome 3½ miles

Bus: Visit traveline.info for the latest bus timetables and routes

ACQ.1926

Parking (not English Heritage).

Caution: deep water, steep slopes.

Please do not climb on the walls.

MAP PAGE 303 (4H)
OS MAP 183, 142: ST737457

MUCHELNEY ABBEY   SOMERSET – TA10 0DQ

There's a lot to enjoy at atmospheric Muchelney Abbey, set amid the Somerset Levels. Beside the foundations of this wealthy medieval Benedictine abbey (and its Anglo-Saxon predecessor) stands the abbots' lodgings, a complete early Tudor house. This includes a magnificent chamber with ornate fireplace and stained glass, rooms with wall paintings imitating cloth hangings, timber-roofed kitchens and parts of the richly decorated cloister walk. Don't miss the thatched two-storey monks' lavatory, unique in Britain.

New displays trace the abbey's history and highlight finds from the site. There's a touchscreen tour for visitors with mobility issues, and a new family trail.

The nearby parish church (with 17th-century painted ceiling) and medieval Priest's House are not managed by English Heritage.

OPENING TIMES

Open varying days 1 Apr–5 Nov

Site closed 6 Nov–28 Mar

See website for latest opening times

Last entry 30 mins before closing

VISIT US

Direction: In Muchelney, 2 miles S of Langport via Huish Episcopi

Bus: Visit traveline.info for the latest bus timetables and routes

Cycle: Sustrans: National Route 339

Tel: 01458 250664

Local Tourist Information: Langport: 01458 253527

NON-MEMBERS

See website for entry prices

By being a Member, you save up to **£28.50** (price of a family ticket) when you visit Muchelney Abbey

ACQ.1927 OVP

Disabled access (grounds and most of ground floor, adapted toilet).

Refreshments available.

MAP PAGE 303 (4G)
OS MAP 193, 129: ST429249

BRADFORD-ON-AVON TITHE BARN
WILTSHIRE – BA15 1LF

BRATTON CAMP AND WHITE HORSE
WILTSHIRE – BA13 4TA

CHISBURY CHAPEL
WILTSHIRE – SN8 3JA

A spectacular monastic stone barn, 51 metres (168 feet) long and 10 metres (33 feet) wide. Its magnificent timber-cruck roof supports a hundred tons of stone roof tiles.

Built in the early 14th century as part of a 'grange' or outlying farm belonging to Shaftesbury Abbey, the richest nunnery in England, it was in use until 1974.

Managed by Bradford-on-Avon Preservation Trust.

Bratton Camp is an Iron Age hillfort, which enclosed an earlier Neolithic long barrow and a Bronze Age burial mound as well as a 'town' of huts, stores and workshops. Below it stands the Westbury White Horse. Cut in 1778, this replaced an earlier horse, perhaps made in the late 1600s to commemorate King Alfred's decisive victory over the Vikings at 'Ethandun', probably fought nearby in AD 878.

An appealing thatched and flint-walled chapel, with the remains of fine windows and plasterwork and a 'consecration cross' within. It was built by the lord of Chisbury Manor in the 13th century, both as a symbol of his status and to save his tenants the inconvenient journey to Great Bedwyn parish church. In use until 1547, it later served as a barn. Set by the earthwork defences of Iron Age Chisbury Camp.

OPENING TIMES
See website for latest opening times

VISIT US
Direction: Located ½ mile S of town centre off B3109

Train: Bradford-on-Avon ½ mile

Bus: Visit traveline.info for the latest bus timetables and routes

ACQ.1939

Parking (adjacent, not managed by English Heritage – charge applies).

MAP PAGE 303 (3H)
OS MAP 173, 156: ST823604

OPENING TIMES
Any reasonable daylight hours

VISIT US
Direction: 2 miles E of Westbury off B3098, 1 mile SW of Bratton

Train: Westbury 3 miles

Bus: Visit traveline.info for the latest bus timetables and routes

ACQ.1930

Parking (not English Heritage).
Caution: steep slopes.

MAP PAGE 303 (3J)
OS MAP 184, 143: ST900516

OPENING TIMES
Any reasonable daylight hours

VISIT US
Direction: 300m walk off unclassified road, ¼ mile E of Chisbury, off A4; 6 miles E of Marlborough

Train: Bedwyn 1 mile

Bus: Visit traveline.info for the latest bus timetables and routes

ACQ.1982

Parking (in lay-by).

MAP PAGE 303 (3K)
OS MAP 174, 157: SU280660

HATFIELD EARTHWORKS (MARDEN HENGE)
WILTSHIRE – SN10 3RL

The earthworks of one of the largest Neolithic henges in Britain. The outer enclosure, raised in about 2500 BC, is formed on three sides by a bank and ditch, and on the other by a loop in the river Avon. Within is a second Neolithic henge, and the scanty remains of a monumental mound, once allegedly over 64 metres (210 feet) in diameter and a smaller version of Silbury Hill (p.119).

Excavations at the henge in 1969 and 2010 revealed evidence of Neolithic activity here. Ongoing research by the University of Reading is revealing more about this important site, and has recently suggested that the great sarsen stones used at Stonehenge were hauled through Marden on their way from the Marlborough Downs to Stonehenge, 10 miles away.

OPENING TIMES
Any reasonable daylight hours.
Note: Only a small section of henge accessible, marked with a fingerpost

VISIT US
Direction: 5½ miles SE of Devizes, off A342; NE of village of Marden. Look for the fingerpost

Train: Pewsey 5 miles

Bus: Visit **traveline.info** for the latest bus timetables and routes

ACQ.1972

Caution: steep slopes, beware of traffic.

MAP PAGE 303 (3J)
OS MAP 173, 130: SU092583

LUDGERSHALL CASTLE AND CROSS
WILTSHIRE – SP11 9QT

Ruins and extensive earthworks of a mainly 12th- to 14th-century royal castle, including a 'strong tower' probably built by King John and a hall and royal apartments added by Henry III. More a palatial hunting lodge than a fortress, Ludgershall was favoured by Plantagenet kings from Henry II to Edward III as a resting place on their travels to the west, and a base for hunting in Savernake Forest.

The remains of a market cross stand at the centre of the village, once an important medieval market town which elected two MPs.

OPENING TIMES
Any reasonable daylight hours

VISIT US
Direction: Located on the N side of Ludgershall, off A342

Train: Andover 7 miles

Bus: Visit **traveline.info** for the latest bus timetables and routes

ACQ.1915 Castle

ACQ.1952 Cross

Parking (limited).

Caution: steep slopes.

Please do not climb on the walls.

MAP PAGE 303 (3K)
OS MAP 184/185, 131: SU264512

NETHERAVON DOVECOTE
WILTSHIRE – SP4 9RH

A charming early 18th-century brick dovecote, with a pyramid roof and dormer windows. It still contains most of its 700 or more nesting boxes for doves or pigeons.

Dovecotes were 'living larders', providing fresh meat in winter as well as eggs and fertiliser, but their occupants ravaged surrounding crops, and until 1761 only important landowners could build them.

OPENING TIMES
Exterior viewing only from nearby Millenium Park, as there is no access across the field in which the dovecote is situated

VISIT US
Direction: In Netheravon, 4½ miles N of Amesbury on A345

Train: Pewsey 9 miles, Grateley 11 miles

Bus: Visit **traveline.info** for the latest bus timetables and routes

ACQ.1939

MAP PAGE 303 (3J)
OS MAP 184, 130: SU147484

DON'T FORGET
Remember to take your membership card.

OLD WARDOUR CASTLE

——— WILTSHIRE – SP3 6RR ———

Refreshed interpretation and an interactive family game help you explore the tumultuous story of Old Wardour Castle and its owners.

Beautifully sited beside a lake, the castle was built by John, Lord Lovel in the late 14th century as a lightly fortified but luxurious residence. A hexagonal tower house ranged round a central courtyard, its design is unique in England. It also pioneered the inclusion of self-contained suites for noble guests.

Modernised by the staunchly Roman Catholic Arundell family, the castle saw much fighting during the Civil War. In 1643 the 61-year-old Lady Arundell, with a garrison of just 25 soldiers, had to surrender it to 1,300 Parliamentarians after a five-day siege. But the Parliamentarians were almost immediately besieged in turn by Royalists led by her son, Henry, Lord Arundell. After an eventful three-month siege, they finally capitulated in March 1644.

'*Can you keep your castle?*', a family game, uses activities and challenges to follow the changing fortunes of the castle's owners.

The abandoned castle became a romantic ruin within the landscaped grounds of New Wardour Castle (not managed by English Heritage, no public access). Almost the last addition was the Georgian fantasy-Gothic Grotto, an artificial cave.

The castle is set in a Registered Landscape.

🎬 *Robin Hood: Prince of Thieves* (1991).

OPENING TIMES

Open daily 1 Apr-5 Nov

Open varying days 6 Nov-28 Mar

Site closed 24-26 Dec & 1 Jan

See website for latest opening times

Last entry 30 mins before closing

Parts of the castle may be closed if an event is booked. Please call site or check website for details

VISIT US

Direction: Located off A30 3½ miles SW of Tisbury. Also accessible from A350 (narrow rural roads). Coaches approach with care

Train: Tisbury 3½ miles

Bus: Visit traveline.info for the latest bus timetables and routes

Tel: 01747 870487

Local Tourist Information:
Shaftesbury: 01747 853514

NON-MEMBERS

See website for entry prices

By being a Member, you save up to **£24.50** (price of a family ticket) when you visit **Old Wardour Castle**

ACQ.1936 🔊 ♿ 🎒 🏪 🗡 🌱 🖼 🚶 ⚡ P 🏔
📷 ♿ ⚠ OVP

Disabled access (grounds and ground floor only), disabled toilet.

Refreshments available.

MAP PAGE 303 (4J)
OS MAP 184, 118: ST939263

OLD SARUM

—— WILTSHIRE – SP1 3SD ——

Explore the lost city of Old Sarum, crowning a ridge with sweeping views towards Salisbury. Iron Age people raised its mighty prehistoric earthworks in about 500 BC, and within them Saxons and, most importantly, the Normans later settled.

In 1086 William the Conqueror summoned all the great landowners of England here to swear an oath of loyalty. A Norman castle on the inner mound was soon joined by a royal palace. By the mid-12th century a bustling town occupied much of the great earthwork, complete with a noble new Norman cathedral. An original copy of Magna Carta was sent to the cathedral in 1215, and can still be seen in its successor, Salisbury Cathedral.

However, soldiers and priests quarrelled, and life on the almost waterless hilltop became intolerable, so the settlement migrated downhill to what became Salisbury, where a new cathedral was founded in 1220. Thereafter Old Sarum went into steep decline, with its cathedral demolished and its castle abandoned. Though largely uninhabited, it continued to 'elect' two MPs until 1832, becoming the most notorious of the corrupt 'Rotten Boroughs' swept away by the Reform Act.

Today, the remains of the prehistoric fortress and of the Norman palace, castle and cathedral evoke echoes of thousands of years of history.

OPENING TIMES

Open daily 1 Apr-28 Mar

Site closed 24-25 Dec

See website for latest opening times

Last entry 30 mins before closing

VISIT US

Direction: 2 miles N of Salisbury, off A345

Train: Salisbury 2 miles

Bus: Visit traveline.info for the latest bus timetables and routes; also Stonehenge Tour service. See thestonehengetour.info

Tel: 01722 335398

Local Tourist Information:
Salisbury: 01722 342860

NON-MEMBERS

See website for entry prices

By being a Member, you save up to £24.50 (price of a family ticket) when you visit **Old Sarum**

Disabled access (outer bailey and grounds only, disabled toilet).

Toilets located in the car park.

Parking: charges apply to non-members, free for Members with valid English Heritage car sticker.

Refreshments available.

MAP PAGE 303 (4J)
OS MAP 184, 130: SU138327

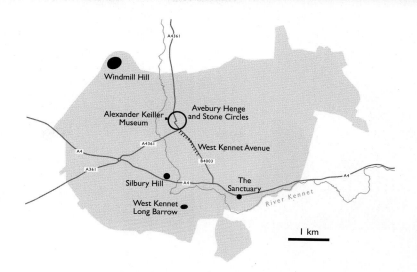

THE STONEHENGE, AVEBURY AND ASSOCIATED SITES WORLD HERITAGE SITE

Stonehenge and Avebury and their associated sites were inscribed onto the UNESCO World Heritage List in 1986. They stand alongside over 1,000 other outstanding sites across the world – such as the Great Wall of China and India's Taj Mahal – selected for their 'Outstanding Universal Value' to all people.

Stonehenge and Avebury were chosen for their extraordinary prehistoric monuments. These help us to understand the Neolithic and Bronze Age world, and demonstrate around 2,000 years of continuous use and monument building between 3700 and 1600 BC.

A management plan for both the Avebury and Stonehenge parts of the World Heritage Site brings a whole range of organisations and individuals together, working in partnership to manage the site and protect its Outstanding Universal Value.

Take time to visit both parts of the World Heritage Site and you will be well rewarded. At Stonehenge, displays in the spectacular visitor centre explore the evocative prehistoric landscape surrounding

this iconic monument. You can also view the rich collections in the Wiltshire Museum in Devizes and The Salisbury Museum, and learn more about the people who built the prehistoric monuments of the World Heritage Site. Experience a very different but equally rich visit to the Avebury area, with its many impressive prehistoric monuments and the Alexander Keiller Museum, displaying finds from the immediate region.

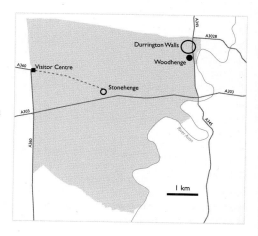

AVEBURY HENGE AND STONE CIRCLES
WILTSHIRE – SN8 1RF

AVEBURY, ALEXANDER KEILLER MUSEUM
WILTSHIRE – SN8 1RF

Opened in 1938, the museum was created by archaeologist and marmalade heir Alexander Keiller, who bought, saved, investigated and restored parts of Avebury stone circle and its nearby avenue. Many archaeological finds are presented in the original museum.

OPENING TIMES
Please see website for details

VISIT US
Direction: In Avebury, 7 miles W of Marlborough

Train: Pewsey 10 miles; Swindon 11 miles

Bus: Visit traveline.info for the latest bus timetables and routes

NON-MEMBERS
See website for entry prices

ACQ.1944 | ♿ E ⚹ ⚹ ✉ ✦ P OVP

Parking: National Trust car park S of Avebury off A4361. Free to English Heritage Members with a valid car sticker.

Parking (limited).

Shop and café not managed by English Heritage.

MAP PAGE 303 (3J)
OS MAP 173, 157: SU099700

Avebury henge and stone circles are among the greatest marvels of prehistoric Britain. Built and altered between 2600-2400 BC, the henge survives as a huge circular bank and ditch. Within it was a circle of originally about one hundred great sarsen stones, the largest circle in Britain. This enclosed two smaller stone circles, each enclosing a central stone setting.

Avebury is part of a much bigger complex of Neolithic and Bronze Age ceremonial sites, including West Kennet Avenue and The Sanctuary. Earlier West Kennet Long Barrow and Windmill Hill and later Silbury Hill are nearby. You can reach many of these sites by pleasant walks from Avebury village. This extraordinary assemblage of monuments seemingly formed a huge 'sacred landscape', whose purpose can still only be guessed at.

Avebury and its surroundings, with Stonehenge, are a World Heritage Site.

OPENING TIMES
Dawn to dusk

VISIT US
See Alexander Keiller Museum

ACQ.1944 | ♿ ✉ P

Parking (see Alexander Keiller Museum).

MAP PAGE 303 (3J)
OS MAP 173, 157: SU102700

DON'T FORGET
Remember to take your membership card.

DIG DEEPER INTO THE STORY OF STONEHENGE
Our two nearby partner museums give you even more insight into Stonehenge. See dazzling Bronze Age gold at **Wiltshire Museum** in Devizes, and learn about Stonehenge's place in the wider prehistoric world at the **The Salisbury Museum**. See p.288 for details.

USUAL FACILITIES MAY NOT BE AVAILABLE AROUND THE SUMMER SOLSTICE 20-22 JUNE

THE SANCTUARY NEAR AVEBURY, WILTSHIRE – SN8 1QF

Begun around 2500 BC, the Sanctuary was originally a setting of timber posts arranged in six concentric circles, together with two concentric circles of standing stones. Today concrete slabs and posts indicate these long-vanished components.

Various objects such as animal bones, pottery, flint tools and

even human remains were buried at the site, but its function remains a mystery. Like the similar monuments at Woodhenge and Durrington Walls, the Sanctuary complex was probably a free-standing ceremonial site rather than a building. Later, the West Kennet Avenue of standing stones was constructed to connect it with

Avebury henge, reinforcing the status of this enigmatic but clearly very important site. Part of the Avebury section of the World Heritage Site.

OPENING TIMES

Any reasonable daylight hours

VISIT US

Direction: ½ mile S of West Kennett, beside S side of A4

Train: Pewsey 9 miles, Bedwyn 12 miles

Bus: Visit traveline.info for the latest bus timetables and routes

ACQ.1944

Very limited parking in lay-by on S side of A4.

Caution: beware of traffic.

MAP PAGE 303 (3J)
OS MAP 173, 157: SU118680

SILBURY HILL NEAR AVEBURY, WILTSHIRE – SN8 1QH

Dramatically dominating the landscape around Avebury, mysterious Silbury Hill is the largest prehistoric artificial mound in Europe. Approximately 37 metres (120 feet) high and 500 metres (1,640 feet) in diameter, it compares in size with the roughly contemporary Egyptian pyramids.

The mound was built in a series of stages over perhaps 100 years around 2400 BC, starting with a small gravel mound. Antiquarians and archaeologists have dug three separate tunnels into its centre, but found no central burial. Though Silbury Hill's position near the source of the River Kennet was clearly important, its purpose and significance remain unknown. Part of the Avebury section of the World Heritage Site.

No access to the hill itself. This is to prevent erosion of archaeological deposits and rare chalk grassland (the hill is a Site of Special Scientific Interest).

OPENING TIMES

Viewing area during any reasonable daylight hours. Strictly no access to the hill itself

VISIT US

Direction: 1 mile W of West Kennett on A4

Train: Pewsey 9 miles, Swindon 13 miles

Bus: Visit traveline.info for the latest bus timetables and routes

ACQ.1883

Disabled access (viewing area).

Parking: charges apply to non-members, free for Members with valid car sticker.

MAP PAGE 303 (3J)
OS MAP 173, 157: SU100685

USUAL FACILITIES MAY NOT BE AVAILABLE AROUND THE SUMMER SOLSTICE 20-22 JUNE

WEST KENNET AVENUE

NEAR AVEBURY, WILTSHIRE – SN8 1RD

An avenue, originally of around 100 pairs of prehistoric standing stones, forming a winding 1½ mile link or pathway between the henge and stone circles of Avebury and the Sanctuary. The section nearest Avebury has been restored. Many of the pairs, set around 20-30 metres (approx. 80 feet) from the next pair and around 15 metres (50 feet) apart, seem to follow a set form, with a squat diamond-shaped stone matched with a slender straight-sided stone. Part of the Avebury section of the World Heritage Site.

OPENING TIMES

Any reasonable daylight hours

VISIT US

Direction: Runs alongside B4003

Train: Pewsey 9 miles, Swindon 12 miles

Bus: Visit traveline.info for the latest bus timetables and routes

ACQ.1944

Parking: please park at Avebury, Alexander Keiller Museum.

MAP PAGE 303 (3J)
OS MAP 173, 157: SU105695

WEST KENNET LONG BARROW

NEAR AVEBURY, WILTSHIRE – SN8 1QH

One of the largest, most impressive and most accessible Neolithic long barrow chambered tombs in Britain. It crowns a ridge above the River Kennet, with views across to Silbury Hill. Its grassed-over chalk mound, over 100 metres (328 feet) long and 3 metres (10 feet) high, is an oasis of wild flowers in summer. You can explore the five atmospheric burial chambers within, constructed of massive boulders and opening off a central passage fronted by a facade of huge sarsens.

Built around 3650 BC, it is among the oldest visible monuments in the Avebury landscape. The remains of at least 36 people were deposited here, over a short period of time and according to a system; children predominate in some chambers, adults in others. Part of the Avebury section of the World Heritage Site.

OPENING TIMES

Any reasonable daylight hours

VISIT US

Direction: ¾ mile SW of West Kennett, along footpath off A4

Train: Pewsey 9 miles, Swindon 13 miles

Bus: Visit traveline.info for the latest bus timetables and routes

ACQ.1883

Very limited parking in lay-by, S of A4 10-15 minutes uphill walk, on gravel and then grass track.

Caution: unguarded drops.

MAP PAGE 303 (3J)
OS MAP 173, 157: SU105677

USUAL FACILITIES MAY NOT BE AVAILABLE AROUND THE SUMMER SOLSTICE 20-22 JUNE

WINDMILL HILL

NEAR AVEBURY, WILTSHIRE
– SN4 9NW

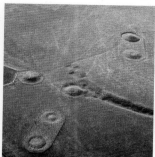

The classic Neolithic 'causewayed enclosure', constructed around 3675 BC and thus pre-dating the Avebury henge. Its three concentric but intermittent ditches cover an area of approximately 22 acres. Large quantities of animal bones, cereal crops, stone tools, artefacts and pottery were found here, suggesting the communal gathering of people to feast, trade and carry out ritual ceremonies. This site can be reached by a 40-50 minute walk from Avebury village, along footpaths. Part of the Avebury section of the World Heritage Site.

OPENING TIMES

Any reasonable daylight hours

VISIT US

Direction: 1¼ miles NW of Avebury

Train: Swindon 11 miles

Bus: Visit traveline.info for the latest bus timetables and routes

ACQ.1944

Sheep may be grazing on site.

MAP PAGE 303 (3J)
OS MAP 173, 157: SU087714

WOODHENGE AND DURRINGTON WALLS   WILTSHIRE – SP4 7AR

Woodhenge is a late Neolithic monument, where concrete markers now indicate the location of six concentric oval rings of timber posts. The timber structure is surrounded by a circular bank and ditch and is aligned north-east towards the summer solstice sunrise. A small central flint cairn marks the location of a child burial.

Nearby is Durrington Walls, a massive circular earthwork henge 500 metres (1,640 feet) in diameter, also built in the late Neolithic period, in about 2500 BC. Excavations here have revealed two concentric timber monuments, similar to Woodhenge, and the remains of many small buildings, possibly the houses where the builders or users of Stonehenge lived. At the Stonehenge visitor centre you can see replicas based on these buildings. Recent geophysical surveys suggest that the henge bank was built on the site of a circle of large timber posts, and that the whole complex was surrounded by a huge circuit of big pits or shafts, making Durrington a still more significant monument.

Part of the Stonehenge section of the World Heritage Site.

OPENING TIMES

Any reasonable daylight hours

VISIT US

Direction: 1½ miles N of Amesbury, signposted off A345, just S of Durrington

Train: Salisbury 9 miles

Bus: Visit traveline.info for the latest bus timetables and routes

ACQ.1971 Durrington Walls

ACQ.1932 Woodhenge

Limited car parking.

MAP PAGE 303 (4J)
OS MAP 184, 130: SU151434

Avebury Monuments: Ownership, Guardianship and Management

Avebury Henge and Stone Circles, the Alexander Keiller Museum, West Kennet Avenue and Windmill Hill are in the freehold ownership of the National Trust. The Sanctuary is in Department for Digital, Culture, Media and Sport (DCMS) ownership. Silbury Hill and West Kennet Long Barrow are in private ownership.

All the sites are in English Heritage guardianship, in the case of Alexander Keiller Museum on behalf of DCMS. The museum collection is on loan from DCMS.

Silbury Hill is directly managed by English Heritage. All other sites are managed by the National Trust on behalf of English Heritage, and the two organisations share the cost of managing and maintaining the properties.

USUAL FACILITIES MAY NOT BE AVAILABLE AROUND THE SUMMER SOLSTICE 20-22 JUNE

STONEHENGE

WILTSHIRE – SP4 7DE

Visiting Stonehenge is an unmissable experience. Follow in the footsteps of Neolithic and Bronze Age ancestors as you explore the iconic stone circle and its surrounding prehistoric monuments at this World Heritage Site. Discover more about the story of the circle and its people in our visitor centre exhibitions.

BUILDING STONEHENGE

The monument was begun in about 3000 BC, in the Neolithic period. First, a circular ditch was dug around a ring of pits, probably holding standing stones and into which many cremations were placed.

Some five hundred years later, the central stone settings were raised. It has recently been discovered that the larger 'sarsens', some weighing twenty tons or more, were brought from West Woods near Marlborough, 15 miles (24 kilometres) due north of Stonehenge. These were set up in an outer circle of 30 uprights, probably with a continuous circle of joining lintels. Within this were five trilithons (two upright stones capped by a horizontal lintel) arranged in a horseshoe shape.

Among the sarsens, the smaller bluestones, transported over 150 miles (240 kilometres) from the Preseli Hills in Pembrokeshire, were set in a double arc. Later, about 2300 BC, they were rearranged into an outer circle and an inner oval. At the centre was the sandstone Altar Stone. The enormous Heel Stone marks the position of the rising sun at midsummer.

The remains you see today are the final phase of this ancient monument, after 4,000 years of decay and destruction.

At any time of day or night, get a stunning real-time virtual experience of standing within the stone circle by visiting stonehengeskyscape.co.uk

Stonehenge is an astonishing testament to the engineering skills and communal effort of prehistoric people. Transporting the stones over long distances and raising them into position involved huge amounts of labour. Simple tools were used to smooth the stones and craft the joints linking the uprights with the horizontal lintels – a unique feature of Stonehenge.

There has long been debate about the meaning and function of Stonehenge. Archaeologists still advance new theories about why people built it. The orientation of the stones to the rising and setting of the sun at the solstices shows that these times were important for the people who built and used Stonehenge.

Stonehenge wasn't built in isolation. When it was begun, this area was already the focus of an early Neolithic monument complex, including long barrows and cursus monuments. Durrington Walls (p.121), site of a large Neolithic settlement, Woodhenge (p.121) and numerous other timber monuments were constructed as Stonehenge was being built. After major construction ended, many early Bronze Age round barrows were raised nearby.

Circles of Stone, the first ever Jōmon Japan exhibition in the UK, featuring objects never seen outside Japan. It tells the story of prehistoric Japan and its stone circles, the work of William Gowland, the 'father of Japanese archaeology', and also that of woodblock artist Yoshijirō Urushibara.

Celebrating the rich culture of Japan, this English Heritage exhibition highlights the surprising relationships between Stonehenge and ancient Jōmon Japan. Runs until August 2023.

VISITING THE STONES AND THEIR LANDSCAPE

The awe-inspiring stone circle will always be the focus of any visit. Reunited with its ancient processional approach, it is surrounded by a landscape rich in prehistoric monuments.

A shuttle bus runs every few minutes to the stones and back, or you can choose to walk the 1.3 miles along unmade paths through the surrounding landscape, which is owned and cared for by the National Trust.

To venture further into the landscape, pick up an orientation leaflet to see areas you can explore, and look out for panels explaining the features. Sturdy footwear, suitable clothes and sun protection are recommended.

The audio tour at Stonehenge is available to download onto your own device at **english-heritage.org.uk/stonehenge-audio-guides**

See Stonehenge close up with an unforgettable Stone Circle Experience outside usual opening times. There's limited availability, so you'll need to book in advance. Find out how at **english-heritage. org.uk/stonehenge-experience**

VISITOR CENTRE: EXHIBITIONS AND FACILITIES

At the visitor centre you'll find permanent and temporary exhibitions as well as spacious facilities to help you make the most of your day out at Stonehenge.

In the exhibition gallery, an immersive 360-degree introductory film gives you the experience of being inside the stone circle, and a widescreen presentation reveals how the Stonehenge landscape changed through prehistory. Showcases display an intriguing range of archaeological treasures excavated from Stonehenge and nearby sites. You'll discover tools used by the monument's builders, artefacts found at Durrington Walls and jewellery from surrounding burial mounds. Many of the artefacts have kindly been loaned by The Salisbury Museum and Wiltshire Museum.

To discover more about the people who lived at Stonehenge, visit the wonderful archaeology collections of our partners, The Salisbury Museum and Wiltshire Museum in Devizes (see p.288). English Heritage Members get 25% discount on entry.

Our café is a lovely spot for all ages to enjoy refreshments, and the next-door shop stocks a great range of products, many exclusive to Stonehenge.

Outside the visitor centre, discover examples of a sarsen and a bluestone, and see how the giant sarsens may have been moved. You can also wander among our strikingly reconstructed Neolithic houses, based on those discovered at Durrington Walls, to experience the lifestyles of the people who built and used Stonehenge. Our friendly and knowledgeable volunteers help you bring the houses and their inhabitants back to vivid life.

Pre-booking visits is recommended.

Please see the website for the latest information.

For details of how we're keeping you safe, please visit **english-heritage.org.uk/about-us/contact-us/visit-faqs**

🎬 *Transformers: The Last Knight* (2017).

OPENING TIMES

Open daily 1 Apr–28 Mar

Site closed 25 Dec

See website for latest opening times

Opening times on 20-22 Jun due to summer solstice and 22 Dec due to the winter solstice are subject to change. See website for details **english-heritage.org.uk/stonehenge**

Last entry 2 hours before closing

In bad weather visitors may not be able to use the walkway round the stone circle

Stone circle experience outside normal opening hours by advance booking only. Please book online at **english-heritage.org.uk/stonehenge-experience**

VISIT US

Address: Stonehenge Visitor Centre, nr Amesbury, Wiltshire SP4 7DE

Direction: satnav – use Stonehenge Visitor Centre and follow brown tourist signs. Off A360

Train: Salisbury 9½ miles

Bus: Wilts & Dorset Stonehenge Tour service. See thestonehengetour.info

Tel: 0370 333 1181 (Customer Services)

Local Tourist Information:
Amesbury Library: 01980 623491
and Salisbury: 01722 342860

NON-MEMBERS

See website for entry prices

Usually pre-booking is not required, although it is always recommended. Please check the website for the latest booking and visitor guidance

National Trust England members admitted free

Note: Tourist and education groups must be pre-booked

ACQ. 1918 | ♿ 🅿 | OVP

Stonehenge visitor centre and shuttle buses are wheelchair accessible but the grass path around the stones can get muddy.

Download an audio tour (12 languages) to your mobile device for free from the Apple App Store or Google Play Store. Free WiFi is available at the visitor centre.

Guidebooks (available to purchase in English, French, German, Italian, Japanese, Mandarin, Russian and Spanish).

Assistance dogs only. The National Trust has recently created dog-free zones in all fields that are grazed by sheep in the Stonehenge landscape where there is permissive access. Further details and map of where dogs are allowed can be found on the NT website. Please check website before bringing pets to Stonehenge.

Parking is free for Members with a valid English Heritage car sticker and advance ticket holders.

MAP PAGE 303 (4J)   OS MAP 184, 130: SU122422

SAVE TODAY By being a Member, you save up to **£86** (price of a family ticket) when you visit **Stonehenge**.

THE HERITAGE OF SCILLY

—————— ISLES OF SCILLY ——————

The stunningly beautiful Isles of Scilly hold vast arrays of archaeological riches both above and below sea level.

This compact archipelago of about 100 islands lies around 28 miles to the south-west of Land's End. None of them is any bigger than three miles across and only five are inhabited. Despite their landmass of only 6.18 square miles, these islands contain a remarkable number of historic sites. These range from traditional farmhouses and dwellings to ritual burial monuments, cist grave cemeteries and Romano-Celtic shrines. Early settlements provide evidence of a distinctively Scillonian prehistoric culture that thrived in the island group from around 4,500 years ago. At that time the sea level was lower, and much of Scilly formed a single landmass.

More recently, defensive monuments constructed during the Civil War and the Second World War stand as testament to the strategic importance of the islands.

The Gulf Stream keeps the climate warm, enabling exotic plants and wildlife to thrive in this designated Area of Outstanding Natural Beauty.

King Charles's Castle · St Martin's · Cromwell's Castle · Old Blockhouse · New Grimsby · Bryher · Tresco · Eastern Isles · Bant's Carn Burial Chamber · Innisidgen Burial Chambers · Samson · St Mary's · Harry's Walls · Porth Hellick Down · Garrison Walls · Hugh Town · Annet · Gugh · St Agnes · Western Isles

Travel details are available from Island Rover (who operate the round the island tour bus) on 01720 422131. Alternatively St Mary's Community Bus operates a similar route, but to a more frequent timetable. Contact Visit Isles of Scilly on 01720 424031 for details.

BANT'S CARN BURIAL CHAMBER AND HALANGY DOWN ANCIENT VILLAGE

ST MARY'S, ISLES OF SCILLY

The remains of a Romano-British village in a wonderfully scenic location. On the hill above stands a Neolithic or Bronze Age burial mound with entrance passage and inner chamber.

OPENING TIMES

Any reasonable daylight hours

VISIT US

Direction: 1 mile N of Hugh Town

ACQ.1950 🐕 ⚠ Caution: unguarded drops. Please do not climb on the monuments.

MAP PAGE 302 (5B)
OS MAP 203, 101: SV910123

CROMWELL'S CASTLE

TRESCO, ISLES OF SCILLY

Standing on a rocky promontory guarding the lovely anchorage between Bryher and Tresco, this round tower is one of the few surviving Cromwellian fortifications in Britain, built after the conquest of the Royalist Scillies in 1651.

OPENING TIMES

Any reasonable daylight hours

VISIT US

Direction: On the shoreline, approach with care, ¾ mile NW of New Grimsby

ACQ.1950 🐕 ⚠

Caution: deep water, steep stairs.

MAP PAGE 302 (4A)
OS MAP 203, 101: SV882159

GARRISON WALLS

ST MARY'S, ISLES OF SCILLY

You can enjoy a two-hour walk alongside the ramparts of these defensive walls and earthworks, dating from the 16th to 18th

GARRISON WALLS

centuries. Other remains include the Elizabethan Star Castle and the Powder House exhibition.

OPENING TIMES

Any reasonable daylight hours.
See website for latest Powder House opening times

VISIT US

Direction: Around the headland W of Hugh Town

ACQ.1973 🐕 ⚠

Caution: steep slopes, sheer drops.

MAP PAGE 302 (5B)
OS MAP 203, 101: SV898104

HARRY'S WALLS

ST MARY'S, ISLES OF SCILLY

An unfinished artillery fort, built above St Mary's Pool harbour in 1552-53.

OPENING TIMES

Any reasonable daylight hours

VISIT US

Direction: ¼ mile NE of Hugh Town

ACQ.1950 🐕 P ⚠

Caution: unguarded drops.

MAP PAGE 302 (5B)
OS MAP 203, 101: SV909109

INNISIDGEN LOWER AND UPPER BURIAL CHAMBERS

ST MARY'S, ISLES OF SCILLY

Two Neolithic or Bronze Age communal burial cairns of Scillonian type, with fine views. The upper cairn is the best preserved on the islands.

OPENING TIMES

Any reasonable daylight hours

VISIT US

Direction: 1¾ miles NE of Hugh Town

ACQ.1950 🐕

MAP PAGE 302 (5B)
OS MAP 203, 101: SV922127

KING CHARLES'S CASTLE

TRESCO, ISLES OF SCILLY

The ruins of a mid-16th-century coastal artillery fort, later garrisoned – hence the name – by Civil War Royalists. Reached from New Grimsby by footpath.

OPENING TIMES

Any reasonable daylight hours

VISIT US

Direction: Located ¾ mile NW of New Grimsby. Coastal location, approach with care

ACQ.1950 🐕 ⚠ Caution: sheer drops. Please do not climb on the walls.

MAP PAGE 302 (4A)
OS MAP 203, 101: SV882161

OLD BLOCKHOUSE

TRESCO, ISLES OF SCILLY

Substantial remains of a small 16th-century gun tower protecting Old Grimsby harbour, vigorously defended during the Civil War.

OPENING TIMES

Any reasonable daylight hours

VISIT US

Direction: On Blockhouse Point, at the S end of Old Grimsby harbour

ACQ.1950 🐕 ⚠ Caution: steep stairs.

MAP PAGE 302 (4B)
OS MAP 203, 101: SV897155

PORTH HELLICK DOWN BURIAL CHAMBER

ST MARY'S, ISLES OF SCILLY

A large and imposing Scillonian Bronze Age entrance grave, with kerb, inner passage and burial chamber all clearly visible.

OPENING TIMES

Any reasonable daylight hours

VISIT US

Direction: 1¾ miles E of Hugh Town

ACQ.1950 🐕 ⚠ Caution: steep slopes.

MAP PAGE 302 (5B)
OS MAP 203, 101: SV928108

WELCOME TO THE
EAST OF ENGLAND

Framlingham Castle, Suffolk

East of England

EAST OF ENGLAND

Head to the East of England for elegant country houses and eye-catching landscapes, from flower-filled formal gardens to intriguing hollows above a prehistoric flint mine.

See centuries of stunning garden design at **Wrest Park** (p.132), and taste life upstairs and downstairs at **Audley End House** (p.138), where you can wander through grand state apartments and fine formal gardens before exploring the recreated Service Wing, Victorian stables and organic Kitchen Garden.

Go underground to explore the Neolithic flint mines of **Grime's Graves** (p.152), and see how nature has reclaimed the scarred fields above. Towering over pretty market towns you'll find the keep of **Orford Castle** (p.158) and the mighty walls of **Framlingham Castle** (p.156), Ed Sheeran's 'Castle on the Hill' and the place where Mary Tudor was proclaimed queen in 1553.

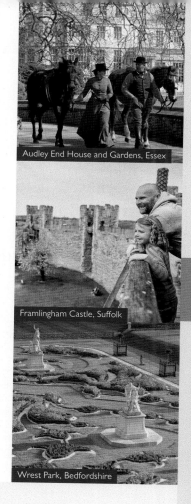

Audley End House and Gardens, Essex

Framlingham Castle, Suffolk

Wrest Park, Bedfordshire

WREST PARK

BEDFORDSHIRE – MK45 4HR

There's always something fresh to discover in Wrest Park's vast and infinitely varied gardens. From stately formal garden and lakes to secluded woodland paths, hidden surprises and a children's playground, there's a treat for everyone here.

Enlivened by charming follies and garden buildings, unexpected vistas and a wealth of statues, Wrest's 90-acre gardens reflect England's love affair with landscape. At the heart of the extensive waterside and woodland walks stands the iconic Archer Pavilion. A baroque showstopper built between 1709 and 1711, it was designed by fashionable architect Thomas Archer. Once the ultimate garden dining room, it still retains its outstanding interior decoration. Its breathtaking setting at the end of the Long Water makes it the most dramatic of the delightful set pieces for which Wrest's gardens are renowned.

Seek out Jemima, Marchioness Grey's enchanting Bath House, disguised in the Picturesque style as a thatched Classical ruin. Designed by Edward Stevens in 1769-71, it features a cold-water plunge pool and attached changing room with a pebble floor set with a pattern of deer vertebrae. We've restored its original surroundings, including the Cascade filling the Bath Pond. It's an ideal picnicking spot.

There's a lot more to see in these wonderful gardens. You can wander Capability Brown's pathways to the Chinese Bridge and Chinese Temple, its copper roof bedecked with sparkling golden bells. Nearby you'll find a memorial to Brown, one of many leading garden designers employed by the de Grey family to develop Wrest's grounds over three centuries.

And there's more. Strolling the intricate woodland paths of the Duke of Kent's 18th-century Great Garden, you'll discover a peaceful dogs' cemetery for de Grey family pets. Not far away are the secluded Ladies' Lake and ancient Graeco-Roman altars in a woodland clearing. Other walks lead you to the splendid 1830s Orangery. Nearer the great mansion, you can view the sculpture gallery in the Dairy, or step into the Rose Garden, the vibrantly planted Italian Garden, or the formal French Parterre.

All this remarkable garden history is being progressively brought to life in a 20-year-long restoration project. You'll find the gardeners happy to answer questions.

In addition to the gardens, you can visit parts of the ground floor of the French chateau-style mansion, designed and built by Thomas, Earl de Grey in 1834-39. Its unfurnished but opulently decorated staterooms include the Grand Staircase, the Library, the Drawing Room and the Dining Room. Countess Henrietta's Sitting Room, furnished as it appeared in the 1860s, looks through to a lofty conservatory. An exhibition reveals the history of the de Grey family, and you can admire family portraits.

DON'T
MISS

Wide-ranging new garden interpretation with interactive installations. 'Ghost building' viewers and reflective devices bring to life lost garden buildings and highlight views which inspired artists. Soundscapes in listening benches feature the voices of historical figures who designed and enjoyed the gardens. We help you identify the songs of our many garden birds, and an international planting display focuses on exotic plant species. You can now also play bowls near the original Bowling Green House.

STAY WITH US

You can now enjoy exclusive access to Wrest Park's gardens when staying at the **Gardener's House**. Set in the former walled kitchen garden, this holiday cottage provides spacious accommodation over three floors, and can sleep up to 8 people.

See p.13 for details on staying at Wrest Park and our other holiday cottages.

You can also combine a day out at Wrest Park with a guided journey through 2,000 years of history in the archaeological store, housing treasures from English Heritage sites around the country. Over 153,000 artefacts range from prehistoric antlers to Victorian dress fittings, 6,000 items from London houses and 1,000 historic wallpapers. Look out for guided tours throughout the year.

Within the Walled Garden, the spacious café offers a seasonal menu using locally sourced produce, and has indoor and outdoor seating overlooking a children's play area.

Please note: No flash photography or stiletto heels in the house.

Strictly Come Dancing (2015); *The Royals* (2015); *Death of Stalin* (2017); *The Crown* (2019); *Harlots* (2019); *The Great* (2020); *Belgravia* (2020); *The Serpent* (2020).

OPENING TIMES

Open daily 1 Apr-5 Nov

Open varying days 6 Nov-28 Mar

Site closed 24-25 Dec

See website for latest opening times

Last entry 1 hour before closing

If the staterooms are closed to visitors due to an event, the exhibition and Countess's Sitting Room will remain open. Last entry to the gardens may sometimes be earlier than the usual one hour before closing. Garden access for those already arrived will continue uninterrupted. Please call to check

VISIT US

Address: Wrest Park, Silsoe, Luton, Bedfordshire MK45 4HR

Direction: ¾ mile E of Silsoe off A6, 10 miles S of Bedford

Train: Flitwick 4 miles

Bus: Visit traveline.info

Tel: 0370 333 1181

NON-MEMBERS

See website for entry prices

Limited number of mobility scooters available. Pre-booking essential.

MAP PAGE 306 (5E)
OS MAP 153, 193: TL091355

SAVE TODAY

By being a Member, you save up to £52.50 (price of a family ticket) when you visit **Wrest Park**.

BUSHMEAD PRIORY
BEDFORDSHIRE – MK44 2LD

A rare survival of the complete refectory of a small priory of Augustinian 'black canons' – communities of priests living together like monks. Founded in 1195, Bushmead apparently housed only a prior and four canons.

The impressive refectory, where the canons ate together, is its only remaining building. It displays a fine original timber roof and notable early 14th-century wall paintings, including the Creation of Eve.

OPENING TIMES
See website for latest opening times. Pre-booked tours only on the first Sat of the month. Please call Wrest Park on 01525 860000 to book

VISIT US
Direction: Located off B660, 2 miles S of Bolnhurst

Train: St Neots 6 miles

Bus: Visit traveline.info for the latest bus timetables and routes

NON-MEMBERS
See website for entry prices

ACQ.1974

MAP PAGE 306 (4E)
OS MAP 153, 225: TL115607

DE GREY MAUSOLEUM, FLITTON
BEDFORDSHIRE – MK45 5EJ

Among the largest sepulchral chapels attached to any English church, this mausoleum houses a remarkable sequence of 17 monuments to the de Grey family of Wrest Park. They span nearly 250 years (1614-1859). Download the audio tour from our website before visiting.

OPENING TIMES
See website for latest opening times

VISIT US
Direction: Access via nave of St John the Baptist church in Flitton, on an unclassified road, 1½ miles W of A6 at Silsoe

Train: Flitwick 2 miles

Bus: Visit traveline.info for the latest bus timetables and routes

ACQ.1979

MAP PAGE 306 (5E)
OS MAP 153, 193: TL059359

HOUGHTON HOUSE
BEDFORDSHIRE – MK45 2EY

The shell of a large 17th-century mansion commanding impressive views, reputedly inspiration for the 'Palace Beautiful' in John Bunyan's *Pilgrim's Progress*. It was begun around 1615 for Mary Sidney Herbert, Dowager Countess of Pembroke, an accomplished poet, patron of the arts and pioneer scientist, as a focus for lavish entertaining. The architecture is an unusual mixture of the Jacobean and the new Classical styles: the ground floors of two Italianate loggias survive, possibly the work of Inigo Jones.

Audio tour available to download from our website.

OPENING TIMES
Daily 10am-6pm or dusk if earlier

VISIT US
Direction: 1 mile NE of Ampthill off B530, 8 miles S of Bedford

Train: Flitwick or Stewartby, both 3 miles

Bus: Visit traveline.info for the latest bus timetables and routes

ACQ.1938

Caution: falling masonry.

MAP PAGE 306 (5D)
OS MAP 153, 193: TL039395

DENNY ABBEY AND THE FARMLAND MUSEUM

CAMBRIDGESHIRE – CB25 9PQ

A fascinating building with an immensely varied history, Denny Abbey was in turn a Benedictine monastery, a home for elderly Knights Templar and a nunnery. When Henry VIII dissolved the nunnery in 1539, it became a farm, with the nuns' great refectory as its barn. It remained a working farm until the 1960s. All these changes produced an intriguing jigsaw puzzle of features, which graphic panels help you solve.

Alongside is the family-friendly Farmland Museum, telling the story of rural life in the Cambridgeshire Fens. It includes a fenman's hut, craftsmen's workshops and a 1940s village shop display.

Managed by the Farmland Museum. **dennyfarmlandmuseum.org.uk**

DENNY ABBEY AND THE FARMLAND MUSEUM

OPENING TIMES

See website for latest opening times

Last entry 30 mins before closing

VISIT US

Direction: Located 6 miles N of Cambridge on A10

Train: Waterbeach 3 miles

Bus: Visit traveline.info

Tel: 01223 860988

NON-MEMBERS

See website for entry prices

There will be a premium payable by all visitors, including Members, on special event days – please visit **dennyfarmlandmuseum.org.uk** for details

ACQ.1952

Disabled access (museum and abbey ground floor only).

Dogs on leads (restricted areas only).

Tearoom (now open during full opening times).

Caution: falling masonry.

MAP PAGE 307 (4F)
OS MAP 154, 226: TL492685

DUXFORD CHAPEL

CAMBRIDGESHIRE – CB22 4NL

A modest but complete and attractive 14th-century chantry chapel, perhaps originally a hospital.

DUXFORD CHAPEL

OPENING TIMES

Any reasonable daylight hours

VISIT US

Direction: Off A505 on Station Road, Whittlesford, between Whittlesford Station car park and the Red Lion Hotel

Train: Whittlesford, adjacent

Bus: Visit traveline.info for the latest bus timetables and routes

ACQ.1947

MAP PAGE 307 (4F)
OS MAP 154, 209: TL485473

ISLEHAM PRIORY CHURCH

CAMBRIDGESHIRE – CB7 5RX

The best example in England of a small Norman Benedictine priory church. It survives surprisingly unaltered, despite later conversion into a barn.

OPENING TIMES

Exterior: Any reasonable daylight hours. **Interior:** Key available summer 9am-6pm and winter 9am-4pm from Mrs R Burton, 72 West Street, Isleham CB7 5RA

VISIT US

Direction: Located in centre of Isleham, 16 miles NE of Cambridge on B1104

Train: Newmarket 8½ miles, Ely 9 miles

Bus: Visit traveline.info for the latest bus timetables and routes

ACQ.1944

Caution: falling masonry.

MAP PAGE 307 (3F)
OS MAP 143, 226: TL642743

LONGTHORPE TOWER

―――― CAMBRIDGESHIRE – PE3 6LU ――――

Modest little Longthorpe Tower houses a great treasure –
the most important set of medieval domestic wall paintings
in northern Europe. Imperilled by time and decay, they're
being expertly conserved as part of the Save Our Story
Members' Appeal.

Built both for defence and for show in about 1300, the tower was
an addition to the manor house of Robert Thorpe, an ambitious
lawyer and local landowner knighted for his service to King Edward II.
Between about 1320 and 1340 he commissioned the spectacular
wall paintings to adorn his inner sanctum, the first floor private
chamber. Covering almost every surface of its walls and ceiling,
they're designed to entertain, enlighten and impress, as well as
proclaiming Robert's educated taste and loyalty to the crown. They
offer an extraordinary insight into the medieval view of the world.

Kings, saints, angels and musicians mingle with naturalistic birds and
animals and fabulous mythical beasts – including the bonnacon,
notorious for its flaming excrement. On one wall, the Seven Ages
of Man traces life from babyhood to old age, and on another a rare
Wheel of the Five Senses symbolises taste, touch, smell, hearing and
sight as a monkey, spider's web, vulture, boar and cockerel. Royal
figures form a backdrop to the place where Robert would have sat,
and over all the vaulted ceiling represents the canopy of Heaven.

Rediscovered under layers of whitewash in 1945, these precious
paintings are severely endangered by cracking plaster, natural
environmental decay and well-meant but damaging earlier repairs.
In partnership with the Courtauld Institute, we've monitored them
using the latest investigative techniques, and are working on their
long-term conservation.

Managed by Nene Park Trust. nenepark.org.uk

OPENING TIMES

Visits by guided tour only –
pre-booking is recommended
to guarantee entry

See website for latest opening times

Last entry 3.30pm

Group and education visits outside
opening times by appointment

VISIT US

Direction: Located 2 miles W
of Peterborough on A47

Train: Peterborough 1½ miles

Bus: Visit traveline.info for the latest
bus timetables and routes

Tel: 01733 234193

NON-MEMBERS

See website for entry prices

ACQ.1947

Parking in car park at St Botolph's Church,
Thorpe Road, approximately 100 metres
from site.

No wheelchair access.

Caution: steep stairs.

MAP PAGE 306 (3E)
OS MAP 142, 227/235: TL162984

AUDLEY END HOUSE AND GARDENS

ESSEX – CB11 4JF

Whether you're exploring servants' domains and 'Mrs Crocombe's' kitchen, staterooms, fully working stables, the organic kitchen garden or the beautiful grounds, you'll find a warm welcome at Audley End. Costumed storytellers now reveal even more of its history.

BRINGING AUDLEY END TO LIFE

This noble Jacobean mansion in its landscaped setting is simply the best place in England to discover how a great mansion worked, both for servants and their masters. Throughout the summer, costumed interpreters in the Service Wing and working stables help you vividly experience Victorian servants' lives.

Audley End takes its name from Sir Thomas Audley, Henry VIII's Lord Chancellor. His grandson Thomas Howard, Earl of Suffolk, rebuilt the house on a palatial scale, making it one of the largest mansions in Jacobean England. Today, Audley End's interior largely represents the taste of the third Lord Braybrooke, who redecorated many of its rooms in the Jacobean style during the 1820s.

THE STATEROOMS

Make yourself at home in the staterooms – feel free to play the piano in the Library, admire the Georgian state bed or step into Lady Braybrooke's private apartments.

🎬 *The Crown* (2016); *Trust* (2018).

THE SERVICE WING

The Victorian Service Wing provides you with a unique insight into life 'below stairs' during the 1880s. The kitchens were once the domain of Mrs Avis Crocombe, Victorian cook and 21st-century YouTube celebrity. An adaptation of her original recipe book can be found in the shop. Kitchens, dairy, larder and laundries are fully equipped with original and reproduction Victorian fittings, and animated with lifelike sights and sounds. Costumed interpreters demonstrate traditional cooking and washing techniques on selected days. (Every weekend, May-September, excluding some event weekends, plus other days throughout the year.) You can also enjoy volunteer-led guided tours of the Adam Rooms, Service Wing and Butler's Pantry (on selected days).

THE NURSERY SUITE AND COAL GALLERY

The 1830s Nursery Suite uncovers the hidden world of the privileged Braybrooke children. You can try on period costumes, play with hands-on replicas of 1830s toys, and discover the personalities of the eight Braybrooke children. The sights and sounds within the Coal Gallery show you how servants provided warmth and hot water for the aristocratic family and their guests.

DON'T MISS

On selected dates, finding out more about Audley End from our costumed storytellers. Meet the Curious Collector in the house, showcasing the mysterious and imaginative artefacts the Braybrooke family collected over the years. Play along with our costumed Playing Card, telling stories of the parties when guests dressed as playing cards. Encounter the Garden Storyteller, revealing the secrets and significance of the plants and wildlife in the Walled Garden.

From a private collection, on loan to English Heritage at Audley End House and Gardens, Essex

STAY WITH US

Book a relaxing break in our *Cambridge Lodge*. Enjoy stunning views of the River Cam and the manicured lawns, and stroll through the grounds in private once the gates have closed to the public.

See p.13 for details on staying at Audley End and our other holiday cottages.

THE STABLES

Meet our resident horses in the lovely stables, which are set as they would have been in the 1880s. Discover the vital part horses played in the life of the mansion and estate, and enjoy regular riding displays, hands-on demonstrations of horse-care and other horsey activities throughout the day. Lively interactive displays 'virtually' introduce you to Audley End's Victorian outdoor staff, and you can even try dressing up as a period stable worker.

THE GARDENS

Remodelled by Capability Brown, Audley End's award-winning gardens offer many delights. Admire the Elysian Garden and Tea House Bridge; walk up to the Temple of Concord; visit the memorial to Second World War Polish resistance soldiers and enjoy the restored 19th-century formal garden. For practical gardeners, the organic Walled Kitchen Garden is a must. Nearby are the children's play area and Cart Yard Café.

Please note: Photography in the house is only permitted in the Nursery and Coal Gallery. No stiletto heels allowed in the house.

OPENING TIMES

Open daily 1 Apr-5 Nov

Open varying days 6 Nov-28 Mar

Site closed 24-25 Dec

See website for latest opening times

Last entry to the grounds is 1 hour before closing (last entry to house varies, please see website)

VISIT US

Address: Audley End House and Gardens, off London Road, Saffron Walden, Essex CB11 4JF

Direction: 1 mile W of Saffron Walden on B1383 (M11 exit 8 or 10)

Train: Audley End 1¼ miles. Note: Footpath is beside busy main road

Bus: Visit traveline.info for the latest bus timetables and routes

Tel: 0370 333 1181

SAVE TODAY

By being a Member, you save up to £76 (price of a family ticket) when you visit Audley End House and Gardens.

Local Tourist Information:
Saffron Walden: 01799 524002
Cambridge: 01223 791500

NON-MEMBERS

See website for entry prices

ACQ.1949

Disabled access (grounds, Great Hall, Stable Yard and Service Wing only. Please call for more information).

MAP PAGE 307 (5F)
OS MAP 154, 195: TL525382

COLCHESTER, BLUEBOTTLE GROVE

ESSEX – CO3 4DZ

First-century Iron Age earthworks, defending pre-Roman 'Camulodunum', capital of the British Catuvellauni tribe. Conquered by the Romans in AD 43, it later became Colchester.

Lexden Earthworks (below) are nearby.

Managed by Colchester Borough Council.

OPENING TIMES

Any reasonable daylight hours

VISIT US

Direction: 2 miles W of Colchester off A604. From Lexden Straight Road, turn left into Heath Road, left into Church Lane, right into Beech Hill and follow signs to site

Train: Colchester or Colchester Town, both 2½ miles

Bus: Visit traveline.info for the latest bus timetables and routes

Tel: 01206 282929

ACQ.1925

Caution: steep slopes.

MAP PAGE 307 (5H)
OS MAP 168, 184: TL965246

COLCHESTER, LEXDEN EARTHWORKS

ESSEX – CO3 9DD

Iron Age earthworks defending pre-Roman Colchester. Lexden Tumulus was the burial place of a wealthy British chieftain – perhaps a king. It contained both British and imported Roman treasures.

Bluebottle Grove (above) is nearby.

Managed by Colchester Borough Council.

OPENING TIMES

Any reasonable daylight hours

VISIT US

Direction: On Lexden Straight Road, 2 miles W of Colchester off A604

COLCHESTER, LEXDEN EARTHWORKS

Train: Colchester or Colchester Town, both 2½ miles

Bus: Visit traveline.info for the latest bus timetables and routes

Tel: 01206 282929

ACQ.1925

MAP PAGE 307 (5H)
OS MAP 168, 184: TL965246

COLCHESTER, ST BOTOLPH'S PRIORY

ESSEX – CO2 7EE

Remains of one of England's first Augustinian priories, founded c. 1100. An impressive example of early Norman architecture, the church has massive pillars and round arches and an elaborate west front.

Managed by Colchester Borough Council.

OPENING TIMES

See website for latest opening times

VISIT US

Direction: Nr Colchester Town station

Train: Colchester Town, adjacent

Bus: Visit traveline.info for the latest bus timetables and routes

Tel: 01206 282929

ACQ.1912

Caution: falling masonry.

MAP PAGE 307 (5H)
OS MAP 168, 184: TL999249

COLCHESTER, ST JOHN'S ABBEY GATE

ESSEX – CO2 7EZ

This elaborately decorated gatehouse is the sole survivor of the wealthy Benedictine abbey of St John. Built c. 1400 to strengthen the abbey's defences, it was stormed by Parliamentarian troops during the Civil War.

Managed by Colchester Borough Council.

OPENING TIMES

Exterior only: Any reasonable daylight hours

VISIT US

Direction: On St John's Green on southern side of central Colchester

Train: Colchester Town ¼ mile

Bus: Visit traveline.info for the latest bus timetables and routes

Tel: 01206 282929

ACQ.1983

Dogs on leads (exterior only).

Caution: falling masonry.

MAP PAGE 307 (5H)
OS MAP 168, 184: TL998248

OUR EVENTS

Check out our year-long programme of events.

english-heritage.org.uk/events

HILL HALL ESSEX – CM16 7QQ

Built in 1568-77 for the scholar, diplomat and politician Sir Thomas Smith, this splendid Elizabethan mansion is among the earliest Renaissance houses in England.

Its multi-columned Classical-style exterior imitates examples Smith had admired on his ambassadorial travels in France and Flanders. Its interior is adorned with very rare survivals of high-quality figurative wall paintings, among

the finest in English Heritage's collection. Now mainly visible to view in two rooms, they probably once extended throughout the house. One series depicts the Old Testament story of Hezekiah; the other the Classical legend of Cupid and Psyche. Expertly painted, they may be by Flemish artists, or English imitators: Sir Thomas himself may have overseen their design.

Hill Hall has now been divided into private houses, but parts remain open to the public by prior arrangement.

OPENING TIMES

See website for latest opening times.
Pre-booked guided tours only

To book please call 0370 333 1181
(Customer Services)

VISIT US

Direction: 3 miles SE of Epping. Entrance ½ mile N of Theydon Mount Church

Train: Epping or Theydon Bois 2½ miles

Bus: Visit traveline.info for the latest bus timetables and routes

NON-MEMBERS

See website for entry prices

MAP PAGE 307 (6F)
OS MAP 167/177, 174: TQ489995

PRIOR'S HALL BARN, WIDDINGTON ESSEX – CB11 3SB

Among the finest medieval barns in eastern England, probably built for New College, Oxford. Tree-ring dating showed that its timbers were felled in 1417-42. It was originally constructed of around 900 separate timber components, the product of some 400 oaks.

Clad with black weatherboarding in traditional Essex style, it contains a breathtaking aisled interior with a crown post roof, little altered over the centuries. The two huge porches allowed harvest carts to be wheeled in and unloaded under cover.

OPENING TIMES

Open Sat-Sun 1 Apr-30 Sep

Site closed 1 Oct-28 Mar

See website for latest opening times

VISIT US

Direction: In Widdington, on unclassified road 2 miles SE of Newport, off B1383

Train: Newport 2 miles

Bus: Visit traveline.info for the latest bus timetables and routes

ACQ.1976 Caution: trip hazards.

MAP PAGE 307 (5F)
OS MAP 167, 195: TL537318

HADLEIGH CASTLE
ESSEX – SS7 2AP

The romantic ruins of a royal castle, on a ridge overlooking the Essex marshes and the Thames Estuary. The first castle was begun in about 1215 by Hubert de Burgh, King John's powerful Justiciar, but it was extensively rebuilt by Edward III during the 1360s, to which date most of the surviving remains belong. Conveniently accessible from London by royal barge, the castle was probably a personal retreat, where Edward could stay in privacy and comfort.

After Edward's death in 1377, Hadleigh's tenancy passed to a series of absentee royal relations, including three of Henry VIII's queens. Eventually it was substantially demolished for building materials. Yet Edward III's two big eastern drum towers still remain, with the commanding south-east tower – allegedly used by Georgian revenue men looking out for smugglers – still standing three storeys high.

OPENING TIMES

Any reasonable daylight hours

VISIT US

Direction: ¾ mile S of A13 at Hadleigh

Train: Leigh-on-Sea 1½ miles by direct footpath

Bus: Visit traveline.info for the latest bus timetables and routes

ACQ 1948

Caution: steep slopes, falling masonry.

MAP PAGE 307 (6G)
OS MAP 178, 175: TQ810860

MISTLEY TOWERS
ESSEX – CO11 1HB

Two imposing Classical towers, which stood at each end of a highly unconventional Georgian church. One of only two churches designed by Robert Adam, it was built in about 1776. When the centre of the church was demolished in 1870, the columns from its porticos were added to the towers.

Managed by Mistley Thorn Residents' Association.

OPENING TIMES

Exterior: Any reasonable daylight hours

Interior: Key available from The Mistley Thorn Hotel, High Street, Mistley CO11 1HE, 100m to the right of the site, daily   10am-4pm

VISIT US

Direction: Located on B1352, 1½ miles E of A137 at Lawford, 9 miles E of Colchester

Train: Mistley ¼ mile

Bus: Visit traveline.info for the latest bus timetables and routes

ACQ 1958

Disabled access (exterior only).

Dogs on leads (exterior only).

Caution: falling masonry.

MAP PAGE 307 (5H)
OS MAP 168/169, 184/197:
TM116320

WALTHAM ABBEY GATEHOUSE AND BRIDGE
ESSEX – EN9 1XQ

Fine 14th-century gatehouse and other remains of the abbey refounded by Harold Godwinson, the last Saxon King of England. Famous for its miraculous 'Holy Cross', it became one of the greatest monasteries in medieval England. According to tradition, King Harold's body was secretly buried here after his death at the Battle of Hastings, and you can see the alleged site of his grave in the abbey grounds.

Managed by Lee Valley Regional Park Authority.

OPENING TIMES

Any reasonable daylight hours

VISIT US

Direction: In Waltham Abbey off A112

Train: Waltham Cross 1¼ miles

Bus: Visit traveline.info for the latest bus timetables and routes

Tel: 0845 677 0600

ACQ 1976

Parking (charges apply, not English Heritage).

Caution: falling masonry.

MAP PAGE 307 (6F)
OS MAP 166, 174
GATEHOUSE: TL381007
HAROLD'S BRIDGE: TL382009

TILBURY FORT

ESSEX – RM18 7NR

Tilbury Fort on the Thames Estuary defended London's seaward approach from Tudor times to the Second World War.

Henry VIII built the first permanent fort here, and Queen Elizabeth I famously delivered her Armada Speech at nearby Tilbury in 1588. King Charles II ordered his chief engineer, Sir Bernard de Gomme, to build the great artillery fort you can see today, with work beginning in 1670. It's the best example of a 17th-century bastioned fortress in England, with its complete circuit of moats and outworks still substantially surviving. Highland prisoners were held here after the Jacobite Rising of 1745, and much later the fort's guns helped shoot down a raiding Zeppelin in 1916.

As you enter the fort you'll pass through the magnificent Watergate, and you can also see the historic Landport gate. Visit the exhibition in the east gunpowder magazine to discover the fort's role in the defence of London and trace advances in military engineering. The atmospheric Victorian magazine tunnels in the north-east bastion give an insight into the life of a 19th-century gunner. Be sure to step onto the fort ramparts for impressive views of the Thames and the historic riverside town of Gravesend.

🎬 *Sharpe's Regiment* (1996); *The Brothers Grimsby* (2016); *Tulip Fever* (2017); *Wonder Woman* (2017); *Taboo* (2017); *SS-GB* (2017); *Peterloo* (2018).

OPENING TIMES

Open varying days 1 Apr-28 Mar

Site closed 24-26 Dec & 1 Jan

See website for latest opening times

Last entry 30 mins before closing

VISIT US

Direction: Off A13 and A1089, close to the Port of Tilbury. Beyond The Worlds End pub

Train: Tilbury Town 1½ miles

Bus: Visit traveline.info for the latest bus timetables and routes

Ferry: Gravesend – Tilbury Ferry, then ¼ mile walk

Tel: 01375 858489

NON-MEMBERS

See website for entry prices

By being a Member, you save up to **£28.50** (price of a family ticket) when you visit **Tilbury Fort**

ACQ.1948 🎧 ♿ 🐕 🍴 E 💧 🛏 🚶 🚻 P 🎁 📷 ⚠ OVP

Disabled access (exterior and Fort Parade Ground).

Dogs on leads (restricted areas).

Caution: trip hazards, steep drops, steep slopes.

MAP PAGE 307 (7G)
OS MAP 177/178, 162/163: TQ651753

english-heritage.org.uk

BERKHAMSTED CASTLE

HERTFORDSHIRE – HP4 1LJ

Substantial remains of a strong motte-and-bailey castle dating from the 11th to 15th centuries. Richard, Earl of Cornwall added a 13th-century palace complex. Managed by the Berkhamsted Castle Trust.

berkhamstedcastle.org.uk

OPENING TIMES

Open daily 1 Apr-28 Mar (times vary)

Site closed 25 Dec & 1 Jan

See website for latest opening times

VISIT US

Direction: Near Berkhamsted station

Train: Berkhamsted, adjacent

Bus: Visit traveline.info for the latest bus timetables and routes

ACQ.1929 🐎 ⚠️

Caution: deep water, steep slopes, steep stairs, falling masonry.

MAP PAGE 306 (6D)
OS MAP 165, 181: SP995082

OLD GORHAMBURY HOUSE

HERTFORDSHIRE – AL3 6AH

OLD GORHAMBURY HOUSE

Remains of an immense mansion built 1563-68 by Sir Nicholas Bacon, Queen Elizabeth's Lord Keeper, and visited by the queen at least four times. Its elaborate Classical two-storey porch and other elements survive.

OPENING TIMES

Any reasonable daylight hours but not earlier than 8am or later than 6pm (last access to drive at 5.30pm and gate is locked at 6pm)

Access is via the permissive path Gorhambury Drive. This is closed to the public on 1 Jun, most Sats and some weekdays from Sep to Jan, so it is not possible to visit the site on these days. Please check gorhamburyestate.co.uk for current closure details before you visit

The walk or cycle up Gorhambury Drive to the site is about 2 miles from the nearest parking. Closer access by car, followed by a ½ mile walk, is limited to Thu only, May-Sep 2pm-5pm

VISIT US

Direction: Just off A4147 on western outskirts of St Albans by the Roman Theatre of Verulamium (AL3 6AE). Walk or cycle 2 miles up permissive path Gorhambury Drive. Access by car is limited (see opening times)

Train: St Albans Abbey 3 miles, St Albans 3½ miles

Bus: Visit traveline.info for the latest bus timetables and routes

ACQ.1959 🎯 ⚠️

Caution: unguarded drops, falling masonry.

MAP PAGE 306 (6E)
OS MAP 166, 182: TL110076

ROMAN WALL, ST ALBANS

HERTFORDSHIRE – AL3 4AJ

Part of the 2-mile-long wall built AD 265-70 to defend the Roman city of Verulamium, including the foundations of towers and the London Gate.

OPENING TIMES

Any reasonable daylight hours

ROMAN WALL, ST ALBANS

VISIT US

Direction: Located in Verulamium Park on the S side of St Albans, ½ mile from the centre, off the A4147

Train: St Albans Abbey ½ mile, St Albans City 1¼ miles

Bus: Visit traveline.info for the latest bus timetables and routes

ACQ.1931 ♿🎯🌳⚠️ Steep slopes.

MAP PAGE 306 (6E)
OS MAP 166, 182: TL137066

BACONSTHORPE CASTLE

NORFOLK – NR25 6LL

Atmospherically sited moated ruins of a fortified manor house, chronicling the fortunes of the ambitious Heydon family. Begun during the Wars of the Roses, it was later given its turreted Elizabethan outer gatehouse, before the family went bankrupt.

Download a free audio tour from the English Heritage website before you visit.

OPENING TIMES

Any reasonable daylight hours

VISIT US

Direction: ¾ mile N of village of Baconsthorpe off unclassified road, 3 miles E of Holt

Train: Sheringham 4½ miles

Bus: Visit traveline.info

ACQ.1966 🎯 P ⚠️

Parking: charges apply to non-members, free for Members with valid car sticker.

Caution: deep water, falling masonry.

MAP PAGE 307 (1H)
OS MAP 133, 252: TG121382

BERNEY ARMS WINDMILL

NORFOLK – NR30 1SB

One of the tallest marsh mills in the Norfolk Broads, Berney Arms windmill stands over 70 feet (21 metres) high, visible for miles around. Probably built c. 1870 to grind a component of cement, it remained in use until 1948, ending its days powering a still-visible scoop wheel to drain surrounding marshes.

Supported by the RSPB.

OPENING TIMES

Currently closed for essential maintenance work. Please check website for current information

VISIT US

Direction: 3½ miles NE of Reedham on the N bank of River Yare. Accessible by hired boat, or by footpath from Halvergate (3½ miles)

Train: Berney Arms ¼ mile

Tel: 01493 857900

ACQ.1950 ⚠

Dogs on leads (exterior only). Assistance dogs allowed inside.

Caution: steep stairs.

> MAP PAGE 307 (2J)
> OS MAP 134, OL40: TG465049

BINHAM MARKET CROSS

NORFOLK – NR21 0DW

Tall shaft of a 15th-century cross, on the site of an annual fair held from the 1100s until the 1950s.

OPENING TIMES

Any reasonable daylight hours

VISIT US

Direction: Located on the Binham village green

Train: Wighton on the Wells & Walsingham Light Railway 3½ miles

Bus: Visit traveline.info for the latest bus timetables and routes

ACQ.1949

> MAP PAGE 307 (1H)
> OS MAP 132, 251: TF984396

BINHAM PRIORY

NORFOLK – NR21 0DQ

Among the most impressive monastic ruins in Norfolk. The virtually complete nave adjoining the ruins is now the parish church, with a striking 13th-century west front, tiers of Norman arches and painted screens.

Site finds display and children's activity area within the church.

Managed by Binham Parochial Church Council.

OPENING TIMES

Binham Priory (monastic ruins): Any reasonable daylight hours

---

BINHAM PRIORY

Priory Church:
Summer, daily	9am–6pm
Winter, daily	9am–4pm

VISIT US

Direction: ¼ mile NW of village of Binham on road off B1388

Train: Wighton on the Wells & Walsingham Light Railway 3½ miles

Bus: Visit traveline.info for the latest bus timetables and routes

Tel: 01328 830362

ACQ.1933 🅿 ⚠

Exhibition and toilets are in adjacent parish church.

Caution: unguarded drops, falling masonry.

> MAP PAGE 307 (1H)
> OS MAP 132, 251: TF982399

BLAKENEY GUILDHALL

NORFOLK – NR25 7NA

Remains of a 15th-century merchant's house with brick-vaulted undercroft, recalling Blakeney's medieval prosperity. Later the guildhall of local fish merchants.

Managed by Blakeney Parish Council.

OPENING TIMES

Adjacent to Blakeney Quay, the exterior can be viewed at any time. For access to the interior, see website for latest opening times

VISIT US

Direction: In Blakeney off A149

Train: Sheringham 9 miles

Bus: Visit traveline.info for the latest bus timetables and routes

Tel: 01263 741106

ACQ.1956 ⚠

Dogs on leads (exterior only). Assistance dogs allowed inside.

Caution: steep stairs.

> MAP PAGE 307 (1H)
> OS MAP 133, 251: TG028441

BURGH CASTLE ROMAN FORT

NORFOLK – NR31 9QB

The imposing towered walls of a Roman 'Saxon Shore' fort, with panoramic views over Breydon Water.

Owned and managed by Norfolk Archaeological Trust.

OPENING TIMES

Any reasonable daylight hours

VISIT US

Direction: At far W end of Breydon Water on unclassified road, 3 miles W of Great Yarmouth

Train: Great Yarmouth 5 miles

Bus: Visit **traveline.info** for the latest bus timetables and routes

ACQ.1929 🦽 🧺 **P** ⚠

Car park locked at 6pm.

There is a circular all-access route around the fort – see **norfarchtrust.org.uk** for further details.

Caution: steep slopes, steep stairs, falling masonry.

MAP PAGE 307 (2J)
OS MAP 134, OL40: TG475047

CAISTER ROMAN FORT NORFOLK – NR30 5JS

Excavated remains of a Roman 'Saxon Shore' fort, built around AD 200 and occupied until the late 4th century.

Managed by Great Yarmouth Borough Council.

OPENING TIMES

Any reasonable daylight hours

VISIT US

Direction: From Great Yarmouth, follow the A149 northbound and then the A149 Caister Bypass. Follow brown tourist signs for Caister Roman Fort. From other directions follow signs for Great Yarmouth and then brown tourist signs from the Caister Bypass roundabout. Parking and the entrance to the Fort are situated off a lay-by on Norwich Road ¼ mile from the roundabout

Train: Great Yarmouth 3 miles

Bus: Visit **traveline.info** for the latest bus timetables and routes

Tel: 01493 846534

ACQ.1954 🧺

On-street parking close by.

Step-free access to part of the monument.

MAP PAGE 307 (2J)
OS MAP 134, OL40: TG517123

CASTLE RISING CASTLE NORFOLK – PE31 6AH

One of the most complete and elaborately decorated Norman keeps in England, surrounded by stupendous earthworks. It was begun in 1138 by the ambitious lord William d'Albini for his wife Adeliza, beautiful widow of Henry I. In the 14th century it became the retirement home of Queen Isabella, widow (and alleged murderer) of Edward II.

Owned and managed by Lord Howard of Rising.

castlerising.co.uk

OPENING TIMES

See website for latest opening times

VISIT US

Direction: Located 4 miles NE of King's Lynn off A149

Train: King's Lynn 4½ miles

Bus: Visit traveline.info

Tel: 01553 631330

NON-MEMBERS

See website for entry prices

There will be a premium payable by all visitors, including Members, on special event days – please check **castlerising.co.uk** for details

ACQ.1958 🖼 🦽 🧺 🧍 🚻 **P** 📷 🛍 ⚠

Disabled access (exterior only, toilets).

Dogs allowed on leads (grounds only).

Caution: steep slopes, steep stairs, falling masonry.

MAP PAGE 307 (2G)
OS MAP 132, 250: TF666246

CASTLE ACRE
CASTLE AND BAILEY GATE

—— NORFOLK – PE32 2XB ——

The delightful village of Castle Acre boasts an extraordinary wealth of history.

Situated on the Peddars Way, a major trade and pilgrim route to Thetford, Bromholm Priory and Walsingham, it's a very rare and complete survival of a Norman planned settlement. It includes a castle, town, fine parish church and associated monastery. All this is the work of a powerful Norman baronial family, the Warennes, mainly during the 11th and 12th centuries.

The first William de Warenne founded the castle soon after the Conquest, probably as a stone 'country house'. But during the early 12th century more disturbed conditions prompted its conversion into a strong keep, further defended by stone walls and an immense system of colossal banks and ditches. It offers perhaps the finest medieval castle earthworks anywhere in England.

Meanwhile, the 'planned town' established outside the castle was also protected by earthwork defences with stone gates. The Bailey Gate of c.1200 survives, with the road into the village running between its towers.

You can trace the ancient street layout of this attractive village, lined with flint or brick houses, before exploring both the great castle earthworks and the extensive priory remains.

Pick up a family trail, available from Castle Acre Priory.

OPENING TIMES
Any reasonable daylight hours

VISIT US
Direction: Castle (PE32 2XB) located at SE edge of Castle Acre, 5 miles N of Swaffham. Parking in Pye's Lane. Bailey Gate (PE32 2AG) located in the centre of Castle Acre at the top of Bailey St

Bus: Visit traveline.info

[ACQ.1970] Castle [ACQ.1938] Bailey Gate

🍴 P ⚠ (Castle only)

Caution: Gate: beware of traffic. Castle: steep slopes, steep stairs, failing masonry.

MAP PAGE 307 (2G)
OS MAP 132, 236/238
BAILEY GATE: TF819152
CASTLE: TF819152

english-heritage.org.uk

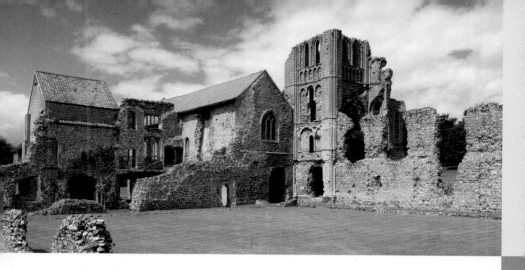

CASTLE ACRE PRIORY

NORFOLK – PE32 2XD

A family trail and fresh displays offer plenty for
you to enjoy at the priory.

Among the best preserved monastic sites in England,
the immense size and variety of Castle Acre Priory can't
fail to impress. Founded in about 1090 by William de
Warenne II, it reflected his family's devotion to the famous
French monastery of Cluny. You can see Cluny-style
architectural decoration displayed in the beautiful west
front of the great 12th-century priory church. Explore
beyond and discover the impressive remains of the
cloister and monks' living quarters, including a gigantic,
two-storey, 24-seater toilet block.

The west range is virtually complete and fully roofed.
Its flint-chequered porch and oriel-windowed prior's
lodging make a striking group with the church's west
front. A mansion in itself, the lodging includes a chamber
sumptuously revamped in early Tudor times, with a ceiling
painted with Tudor roses. The adjacent prior's chapel
displays intriguing traces of medieval wall paintings.

Be sure to leave time to explore the display of
archaeological site finds and take an audio tour featuring
a 15th-century chant from a Castle Acre songbook.

OPENING TIMES
Open daily 1 Apr-5 Nov
Open Sat-Sun, 6 Nov-28 Mar
Site closed 24-26 Dec & 1 Jan
See website for latest opening times
Last entry 30 mins before closing

VISIT US
Direction: ¼ mile W of village of Castle Acre,
5 miles N of Swaffham

Bus: Visit traveline.info

Tel: 01760 755394

NON-MEMBERS
See website for entry prices

By being a Member, you save up to £32.50
(price of a family ticket) when you visit
Castle Acre Priory

Disabled access (ground floor and grounds only).
Toilets (a short walk. 50 metres from entrance).

MAP PAGE 307 (2G)
OS MAP 132, 236/238: TF814148

COW TOWER, NORWICH
NORFOLK – NR1 4AA

Among the earliest purpose-built English artillery blockhouses, this brick tower of c. 1398-99 commands a strategic point in Norwich's defences.

External viewing only.

Managed by Norwich City Council.

OPENING TIMES
Exterior only: Any reasonable daylight hours

VISIT US
Direction: In Norwich, near cathedral (approx. ½ mile walk)

Train: Norwich ½ mile

Bus: Visit **traveline.info** for the latest bus timetables and routes

Tel: 01603 706229

> MAP PAGE 307 (2J)
> OS MAP 134, OL40/237: TG240092

CREAKE ABBEY
NORFOLK – NR21 9LF

CREAKE ABBEY

Set in tranquil countryside, the flint-walled ruins of this Augustinian abbey church tell a sad story of monastic disaster. After a devastating 15th-century fire, it was drastically reduced in size, with arches and windows blocked. Then plague struck, the last abbot died alone, and in 1506 the abbey closed.

Managed by Mr and Mrs A C Scott.

creakeabbey.co.uk

OPENING TIMES
Any reasonable daylight hours

VISIT US
Direction: N of North Creake off B1355

Bus: Visit **traveline.info** for the latest bus timetables and routes

ACQ.1950 ⚠ Caution: falling masonry.

> MAP PAGE 307 (1G)
> OS MAP 132, 251: TF856395

NORTH ELMHAM CHAPEL
NORFOLK – NR20 5JU

A small Norman chapel, probably on the site of the Saxon cathedral of East Anglia. Later converted into a 14th-century fortified mansion by Henry Despenser, warrior-Bishop of Norwich.

Managed by North Elmham Parish Council.

OPENING TIMES
Any reasonable daylight hours with a closing time of 8pm or dusk if earlier

NORTH ELMHAM CHAPEL

VISIT US
Direction: Located 6 miles N of East Dereham on B1110

Train: Wymondham 17 miles

Bus: Visit **traveline.info** for the latest bus timetables and routes

ACQ.1948

Disabled access to some of the site on gravel paths.

Caution: steep slopes.

> MAP PAGE 307 (2H)
> OS MAP 132, 238: TF988216

ST OLAVE'S PRIORY
NORFOLK – NR31 9HE

The wonderfully complete, 14th-century, brick-vaulted refectory undercroft – later a cottage occupied until 1902 – of a small Augustinian priory.

OPENING TIMES
Any reasonable daylight hours

VISIT US
Direction: Located 5½ miles SW of the town of Great Yarmouth on A143

Train: Haddiscoe 1¼ miles

Bus: Visit **traveline.info** for the latest bus timetables and routes

ACQ.1921

Disabled access (exterior only).

Dogs allowed on leads in the grounds only.

Caution: steep stairs.

> MAP PAGE 307 (3J)
> OS MAP 134, OL40: TM459996

GREAT YARMOUTH ROW HOUSES
AND GREYFRIARS' CLOISTERS

——— NORFOLK – NR30 2RG ———

These unique and vividly presented houses are rare survivors of Yarmouth's once-crowded 'Rows' – narrow alleyways linking the town's main thoroughfares.

Most 'Row houses' were destroyed by Second World War bombing or post-war clearances. These surviving examples are now presented at various stages in their history, leading you into centuries of fishing-port life. There are toys in the children's upstairs bedrooms.

Both Row 111 House and the Old Merchant's House were built in the early 17th century as wealthy merchants' residences, but later sub-divided into tenements. You'll find the Old Merchant's House, which has spectacular Jacobean plaster ceilings, appearing as it was in the 1850s, when fish merchant Simon Fleet occupied half the property, and in the 1890s when the other half housed Martha King's family. Adjacent Row 111 House is shown as in 1942 (just before it suffered a direct hit by an incendiary bomb).

Nearby stands Greyfriars' Cloisters, the remains of a medieval friary later converted into a number of Row dwellings. Traces of their interior features exist on the walls of the Cloister and church, which also display early 14th-century wall paintings.

OPENING TIMES
Due to essential conservation works, this site will be closed in 2023-24. Please see website for information about re-opening

VISIT US
Direction: Great Yarmouth, follow signs for Historic Quay

Train: Great Yarmouth ½ mile

Bus: Visit traveline.info for the latest bus timetables and routes

Tel: 01493 857900

NON-MEMBERS
See website for entry prices

By being a Member, you save up to £24.50 (price of a family ticket) when you visit Great Yarmouth Row Houses

Please see our website for guided tours of Greyfriars' Cloisters (may be closed for conservation)

ACQ.1950 🖐 🖵 Ⓜ ⊛ 📷 ⚠ OVP

MAP PAGE 307 (2J)
OS MAP 134, OL40
HOUSES: TG525072
CLOISTERS: TG524073

GRIME'S GRAVES
PREHISTORIC FLINT MINE

——— NORFOLK – IP26 5DE ———

New interpretation helps you explore Grime's Graves, the only Neolithic flint mine in Britain open to visitors.

A lunar landscape of over 400 shafts, quarries and spoil dumps, they were first named Grim's Graves by the Anglo-Saxons – meaning the pagan god Grim's quarries. Not until one was excavated in 1868-70 were they identified as flint mines dug over 5,000 years ago, during the later Neolithic and early Bronze Ages.

Digging with red deer antler picks, prehistoric miners sank shafts and dug radiating galleries following the seams of flint. Today, you can have the unforgettable experience of descending 9 metres (30 feet) by ladder into one excavated shaft.

Set amid the unique Breckland heath landscape, Grime's Graves is also a Site of Special Scientific Interest, the habitat of a variety of rare and distinctive plants and animals.

OPENING TIMES
Open Wed-Sun 1 Apr-5 Nov

Site closed 6 Nov-28 Mar

See website for latest opening times

Children must be seven and over to enter the mine shaft

Last entry 30 mins before closing

VISIT US
Direction: Located 7 miles NW of Thetford off A134

Train: Brandon 3½ miles

Tel: 01842 810656

NON-MEMBERS
See website for entry prices

By being a Member, you save up to **£28.50** (price of a family ticket) when you visit **Grime's Graves**

ACQ.1931 🔲 ⬛ E ⬛ 🔲 🔲 ⬛ P 🔲
⚠ OVP

Disabled access (exhibition area only; access track rough).

Dogs on leads (restricted areas).

Visitors intending to descend the shaft should wear flat shoes.

MAP PAGE 307 (3G)
OS MAP 144, 229: TL817899

NEW FOR 2023

From April 2023, many new features will transform the experience of visiting Grime's Graves. There'll be a new building, inspired by Neolithic dwellings, above accessible Peake's Pit, and a new immersive audiovisual experience in its main shaft. A new visitor centre exhibition includes Neolithic finds from the pits, replica objects to handle, and a film explaining how flint was worked. There's also an interactive virtual tour of the best-preserved mine, Greenwell's Pit, which isn't open to the public: accessible via a touchscreen in the exhibition or on your own device, it'll help you explore the mine and discover its history. New self-guided walking trails for adults and families lead you to the further reaches of the site.

THETFORD, CHURCH OF THE HOLY SEPULCHRE

NORFOLK – IP24 3PW

The only remains in England of a priory church of Canons of the Holy Sepulchre, later used as a barn.

OPENING TIMES

Currently closed for essential maintenance work. Please check website for current information

VISIT US

Direction: Located on the W side of Thetford on A134

Train: Thetford ¾ mile

Bus: Visit **traveline.info** for the latest bus timetables and routes

Tel: 01842 754038

 ACQ.1977 ☠ ⚠

Caution: falling masonry.

> MAP PAGE 307 (3G)
> OS MAP 144, 229: TL865831

THETFORD PRIORY

NORFOLK – IP24 1BB

Extensive remains of one of the most important East Anglian monasteries, the Cluniac Priory of Our Lady of Thetford. Founded in the early 12th century, it owed much of its prosperity to a miraculous appearance of the Virgin Mary. Her statue here was discovered to conceal relics of saints and became a magnet for pilgrims. Survivals include church and cloister walls, the impressive shell of the priors'

lodging and an almost complete 14th-century gatehouse. Burial place of the earls and dukes of Norfolk for 400 years, it enjoyed their powerful protection. It was almost the last English monastery to be suppressed, in 1540.

OPENING TIMES

Open daily 1 Apr-28 Mar (times vary)

Site closed 25 Dec

See website for latest opening times

VISIT US

Direction: Near Thetford station

Train: Thetford ¾ mile

Bus: Visit **traveline.info** for the latest bus timetables and routes

Tel: 01842 754038

ACQ.1932 ♿ ☠ ⚠

Disabled access to some areas on paths.

Limited free parking at the entrance to the priory.

Caution: falling masonry.

> MAP PAGE 307 (3G)
> OS MAP 144, 229: TL865831

THETFORD WARREN LODGE

NORFOLK – IP24 3NE

Probably built c. 1400 by the Prior of Thetford as a refuge from armed poachers. Much later used by local 'warreners', who harvested rabbits here.

OPENING TIMES

Exterior only: Any reasonable daylight hours

VISIT US

Direction: Located 2 miles W of Thetford off B1107

THETFORD WARREN LODGE

Train: Thetford 2½ miles

Bus: Visit **traveline.info** for the latest bus timetables and routes

 ACQ.1948 ☠ P

Parking (not English Heritage).

> MAP PAGE 307 (3G)
> OS MAP 144, 229: TL839984

WEETING CASTLE

NORFOLK – IP27 0RQ

The ruins of a substantial early medieval moated manor house, built in local flint.

OPENING TIMES

Any reasonable daylight hours. Access via steps

VISIT US

Direction: Located 2 miles N of Brandon off B1106

Train: Brandon 1½ miles

Bus: Visit **traveline.info** for the latest bus timetables and routes

ACQ.1926 ☠ ⚠

No wheelchair access.

Caution: deep water, falling masonry.

Please note: parts of the site are enclosed in fencing pending a conservation project.

> MAP PAGE 307 (3G)
> OS MAP 144, 229: TL778891

BURY ST EDMUNDS ABBEY
SUFFOLK – IP33 1UZ

Extensive remains of the wealthiest and most powerful English Benedictine monastery, shrine of St Edmund. Based on a recent digital reconstruction, striking new artwork panels and a refurbished 3-D model now help you to envisage the great abbey in its medieval heyday.

Managed by West Suffolk District Council.

OPENING TIMES
See website for latest opening times

VISIT US
Direction: E end of town centre

Train: Bury St Edmunds 1 mile

Bus: Visit traveline.info for the latest bus timetables and routes

Tel: 01284 764667

ACQ.1955

Caution: falling masonry.

New guidebook available via website.

MAP PAGE 307 (4G)
OS MAP 155, 211: TL857642

OUR EVENTS
Check out our year-long programme of events.

english-heritage.org.uk/events

LEISTON ABBEY
SUFFOLK – IP16 4TD

Among Suffolk's most impressive monastic ruins, the mainly 14th-century remains of an abbey of Premonstratensian canons.

Managed by Pro Corda Trust.

OPENING TIMES
Any reasonable daylight hours

VISIT US
Direction: N of Leiston off B1069

Train: Saxmundham 5 miles

Bus: Visit traveline.info for the latest bus timetables and routes

Tel: 01728 831354

ACQ.1964

Caution: steep stairs, falling masonry.

Please note: parts of the site are enclosed in fencing pending a conservation project.

MAP PAGE 307 (4J)
OS MAP 156, 212: TM445642

LINDSEY ST JAMES'S CHAPEL
SUFFOLK – IP7 6QA

A pretty, thatched, 13th-century chapel with lancet windows.

OPENING TIMES
Closed for essential maintenance. Please check website for information

VISIT US
Direction: Located on an unclassified road ½ mile E of Rose Green and 8 miles E of Sudbury

Train: Sudbury 8 miles

Bus: Visit traveline.info for the latest bus timetables and routes

ACQ.1930

Disabled access (single step).

MAP PAGE 307 (4H)
OS MAP 155, 196: TL9784444

MOULTON PACKHORSE BRIDGE
SUFFOLK – CB8 8SR

A pretty, four-arched, late medieval bridge spanning the River Kennet on the old route from Cambridge to Bury St Edmunds.

OPENING TIMES
Any reasonable daylight hours

VISIT US
Direction: In Moulton off B1085, 4 miles E of Newmarket

Train: Kennett 2 miles

Bus: Visit traveline.info for the latest bus timetables and routes

ACQ.1977

Caution: beware of traffic.

MAP PAGE 307 (4G)
OS MAP 154, 210/226: TL698645

CHECK ONLINE
Pre-booking for visits to our staffed sites may be required, check our website for the latest guidance.

LANDGUARD FORT

SUFFOLK – IP11 3TW

Landguard Fort defends the approach to Harwich Harbour, an important haven for shipping. The fort stands near a nature reserve and a busy container port.

An earlier fort here was the site of the last opposed seaborne invasion of England, when the Royal Marines (in their first land battle) repulsed a Dutch attack in 1667. The current polygonal fort was begun in the 18th century and updated in Victorian times, with emplacements for heavy guns and a fortified barrack block. Outside batteries were added in 1901, and in 1951 part of the fort became a Cold War control room.

Pre-booked guided tours of the fort are available, or a free audio-visual app can be downloaded, either during your visit or in advance, to a smartphone or tablet to guide you around the fort. A free standard audio tour is also available.

Managed by Landguard Fort Trust. landguard.com

The Felixstowe Museum is next to the fort, in a building once used for harbour defence and submarine mining. (For museum opening times and prices see felixstowemuseum.org or call 01394 674355. 20% discount for Members.)

OPENING TIMES

See website for latest opening times

Last entry 2 hours before closing. Pre-booked group and education visits are welcome and may be possible outside normal opening times

VISIT US

Direction: 1 mile S of Felixstowe town centre – follow signs to Landguard Point

Train: Felixstowe 2½ miles

Bus: Visit traveline.info

Bicycle: The fort lies on National Cycle Route 51 between Ipswich and Harwich

Tel: 01394 675900

NON-MEMBERS

See website for entry prices

There may be a premium payable by all visitors, including Members, on event days – please check landguard.com for details

ACQ.1975 🎧 ♿ 🐕 ♿ E 🏬 🗺 P 🚻 ♿ ⚠

Disabled access (to most of ground floor).

Caution: CCTV at site, steep stairs.

MAP PAGE 307 (5J)
OS MAP 169, 197: TM284319

FRAMLINGHAM CASTLE

SUFFOLK – IP13 9BP

One of medieval England's finest baronial fortresses, impressive Framlingham Castle offers you intriguing interpretation, hands-on children's activities and a spacious café in a historic setting. You'll discover the stories of medieval aristocrats, a Tudor queen and Georgian poorhouse children.

Framlingham Castle's spectacular walls are more than 10 metres (32 feet) high and 2 metres (6.5 feet) thick, and studded with 13 strong towers. Raised in the 1190s, they were among the first of their kind ever built in England. They proclaim the power and status of the earls and dukes of Norfolk, who owned the fortress for over four centuries.

You can follow the wall-top walk round them to view eight centuries of history from above, guided by a lively audio tour and panels which tell you about the castle's surroundings – the pretty market town, the parkland, the castle's outer earthworks and the Mere, the lake which mirrors the fortress walls. Don't forget to look up at the tall Tudor chimneys which crown every tower, each one decorated in a different brick design. There's a lift for easier access to our exhibition.

The exhibition, 'Power and Poverty', traces how the castle housed both the very richest and the very poorest over the centuries. You'll discover how successive dynasties of Framlingham's owners – the defiant Bigods, the mighty Mowbrays and the scheming Howards of Tudor times – wielded almost kingly power in East Anglia. Mary Tudor famously mustered her supporters here in 1553 before being crowned queen.

Later, in complete contrast, the castle walls sheltered a workhouse for the local poor, which operated until 1839.

The presentation includes Tudor and workhouse display costumes and interactive games, and you can try on hats from a Norman helmet to a workhouse pauper's cap. The 'Who Ate What' game helps you create plates of imitation foods and match them to the people – aristocrats, the very poor or 'everyone else' – who would have eaten them.

If this gives you an appetite, our revamped café serves delicious food and drink in a baronial setting with stone walls, round-arched windows and a huge fireplace.

There's plenty more to see and do at Framlingham. The Lanman Museum within the castle displays an intriguing variety of local objects, from kitchenware to a parish coffin. Outside the walls, you can explore the castle's outer defences, including the deep ditch and the grassy outer court between fortress and Mere. Leave time, too, to wander the picture-book market town and admire the impressive tombs of the Howard castle-owners, and that of Henry Fitzroy, Henry VIII's illegitimate son, in the parish church.

OPENING TIMES

Open daily 1 Apr-5 Nov

Open varying days 6 Nov-28 Mar

Site closed 24-25 Dec

See website for latest opening times

Last entry 30 mins before closing

VISIT US

Address: Framlingham Castle, Church Street, Framlingham, Suffolk

Direction: In Framlingham on B1116

Train: Wickham Market 6½ miles; Saxmundham 7 miles

Bus: Visit traveline.info for the latest bus timetables and routes

Tel: 0370 333 1181

SAVE TODAY By being a Member, you save up to **£47** (price of a family ticket) when you visit **Framlingham Castle.**

Local Tourist Information:
Woodbridge: 01394 382240

NON-MEMBERS

See website for entry prices

ACQ.1913

Disabled access (grounds and ground floor only) and first floor via a lift.

Parking: charges apply to non-members, free for Members with valid car sticker.

MAP PAGE 307 (4J)
OS MAP 156, 212: TM287637

Come and see how a vital £1m conservation programme has conserved Orford's keep, as well as recalling its original glory. Built of delicate local septaria or 'mudstone', the keep's external walls have been crumbling for centuries. After 13 years of research and trials, they've now been protected by a coating of lime render – there's evidence that this material was originally used to cover the keep's walls, so the render brings it closer to its medieval appearance. Parts of the grounds previously made hazardous by crumbling masonry are also accessible again.

ORFORD CASTLE

SUFFOLK – IP12 2ND

Discover the unique polygonal tower-keep of Orford Castle, set in a pretty Suffolk coastal town.

Built by Henry II between 1165 and 1177, the castle was intended to curtail the power of turbulent East Anglian barons such as Hugh Bigod of Framlingham Castle. An 18-sided drum with three square turrets, its keep was built to a revolutionary new design. From the roof you can enjoy magnificent views seaward to Orford Ness.

Both exterior and interior survive almost intact, allowing you to explore the basement, with its vital well, the lower and upper halls, and the maze of passages leading to the chapel, kitchen and other chambers. Displays, hands-on features and multimedia guides help you explore the castle, and a large model shows you how it appeared when newly built. Find out about the 'Wild Man of Orford', a mysterious being from the sea allegedly imprisoned here in the 12th century.

In the upper hall, take in the Orford Museum Trust's exhibition, featuring changing displays of local finds.

OPENING TIMES

Open daily 1 Apr-5 Nov

Open varying days 6 Nov-28 Mar

Site closed 24-26 Dec & 1 Jan

See website for latest opening times

Last entry 30 mins before closing

VISIT US

Direction: In Orford on B1084, 20 miles NE of Ipswich

Train: Wickham Market 8 miles

Bus: Visit traveline.info for the latest bus timetables and routes

Tel: 01394 450472

Local Tourist Information:
Woodbridge: 01394 382240

NON-MEMBERS

See website for entry prices

By being a Member, you save up to **£32.50** (price of a family ticket) when you visit **Orford Castle**

ACQ.1962

Toilets (close-by in Orford town).

Parking: charges apply to non-members, free for Members with valid English Heritage car sticker.

MAP PAGE 307 (4J)   OS MAP 169, 212: TM419499

SAXTEAD GREEN POST MILL

SUFFOLK – IP13 9QQ

Come and admire impressive Saxtead Green Post Mill, back in action with a new set of craftsman-built sails.

In an idyllic village green setting near Framlingham Castle, this striking four-sailed corn-grinding mill is a rare survivor of a post mill, whose whole body turns on its roundhouse base, propelled by wind on a 'fantail'. Originally raised in about 1796, it's been rebuilt three times. It ceased commercial milling in 1947, but remains one of only a handful of Suffolk mills still fully operational.

Its sails have a span of 18.2 metres, but were in poor condition. Working with Suffolk millwright Tim Whiting – one of the few practitioners of a critically endangered craft – we've given it a new set of sails, copied from 1930s photographs. We have installed a replacement structural staircase to the buck house and carried out repairs to the mill and the fantail at the rear of the windmill.

An audio experience enables you to dial up stories of the mill and its millers over the years – just call 0303 003 4000 to listen in.

OPENING TIMES

Open Fri-Sat (and bank holidays) 1 Apr-30 Sep

Site closed 1 Oct-28 Mar

See website for latest opening times

Last entry 30 mins before closing

VISIT US

Direction: 2½ miles NW of Framlingham on A1120

Train: Wickham Market 9 miles

Bus: Visit traveline.info for the latest bus timetables and routes

Tel: 01728 685789

NON-MEMBERS

See website for entry prices

By being a Member, you save up to **£21.50** (price of a family ticket) when you visit **Saxtead Green Post Mill**

ACQ 1951 ⬛ ⊗ ⬚ ⚠ OVP

MAP PAGE 307 (4J)
OS MAP 156, 212: TM253644

WELCOME TO THE

EAST MIDLANDS

East Midlands

Glossop

7

Buxton
Bakewell
Chesterfield
3
1
5
8 2
6 4
9

23
14
Gainsborough
Worksop
24
Mansfield

Market Rasen

Lincolnshire

15
Lincoln

13
Skegness
17
16
Boston

Nottinghamshire

Derbyshire

Derby

Nottingham

Grantham

Staffordshire

Spalding

10
Loughborough

Leicestershire

Oakham

12 11
Leicester

Rutland

Norfolk

25
21 18
Market
Harborough
22
Kettering
Corby
20

19

Northamptonshire

Cambridgeshire

West
Midlands

Daventry
Northampton

Bedfordshire

Essex

Warwickshire

Brackley

Buckinghamshire

Hertfordshire

Gloucestershire

Oxfordshire

West Yorkshire

East Riding

South Yorkshire

North Lincolnshire

North East
Lincolnshire

EAST MIDLANDS

Intriguing interiors and an idiosyncratic castle are among the historic gems in the towns and countryside of the East Midlands.

High on a hill overlooking the Derbyshire countryside, **Bolsover Castle** (p.166) contains a series of remarkable wall paintings that take you on a journey from earth to heaven. At **Gainsborough Old Hall** (p.172) you can trace centuries of changing tastes and fortunes – beginning life as a fine medieval mansion, it later housed a theatre and a pub. Its vast medieval kitchens remain a real highlight.

Kirby Hall (p.174) was once among the finest houses in Elizabethan England, and new interactive displays help you discover fascinating stories from its past. **Rushton Triangular Lodge** (p.176) is a puzzling folly with links to the Gunpowder Plot, while in the heart of the Peak District you'll find the dramatic remains of **Peveril Castle** (p.165).

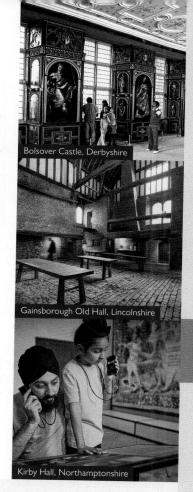

Bolsover Castle, Derbyshire

Gainsborough Old Hall, Lincolnshire

Kirby Hall, Northamptonshire

ARBOR LOW STONE CIRCLE AND GIB HILL BARROW

DERBYSHIRE – DE45 1JS

An important Neolithic henge atmospherically set amid moorland. Within an earthen bank, some fifty recumbent slabs surround a central stone 'cove'. Gib Hill is a burial mound.

Please note: Access charge of £1 per person to use path across private land to the stone circle.

Managed by Peak District National Park Authority.

OPENING TIMES

Any reasonable daylight hours

VISIT US

Direction: ½ mile E of A515, 2 miles S of Monyash

Train: Buxton 10 miles

Bus: Visit **traveline.info** for the latest bus timetables and routes

Tel: 01629 816200

Beware – cattle may be grazing.

Car park area (charged, not English Heritage).

MAP PAGE 308 (2E)
OS MAP 119, OL24: SK160636

BOLSOVER CUNDY HOUSE

DERBYSHIRE – S44 6BQ

This charming cottage-like 17th-century conduit house, with vaulted stone-slab roof, once supplied water to Bolsover Castle.

OPENING TIMES

Exterior only: Any reasonable daylight hours

VISIT US

Direction: Off M1 at junction 29A, follow signs for Bolsover Castle. Between junctions of Craggs Rd and Houfton Rd with Bolsover Hill, Bolsover, 6 miles E of Chesterfield on A362

Train: Chesterfield 6 miles or Langwith – Whaley Thorns 4½ miles

Bus: Visit **traveline.info** for the latest bus timetables and routes

Tel: 01246 822844 (Bolsover Castle)

ACQ.1945

MAP PAGE 309 (2F)
OS MAP 120, 269: SK471709

THE PERFECT GIFT

Give the gift of membership and you'll be giving friends and family the opportunity to enjoy the fantastic benefits of becoming a member of English Heritage.

Visit: **english-heritage.org.uk/join/the-gift-of-membership**

HOB HURST'S HOUSE

DERBYSHIRE – DE4 2NT

A square prehistoric burial mound with earthwork ditch and bank, amid remote moorland. Named after a local goblin.

Managed by Peak District National Park Authority.

OPENING TIMES

Any reasonable daylight hours

Access is across moorland with gates and stiles

VISIT US

Direction: On open moorland from unclassified road off B5057, 9 miles W of Chesterfield

Train: Chesterfield 9 miles

Bus: Visit **traveline.info** for the latest bus timetables and routes

Tel: 01629 816200

ACQ.1884

MAP PAGE 308 (2E)
OS MAP 119, OL24: SK287692

NINE LADIES STONE CIRCLE

DERBYSHIRE – DE4 2LS

A small Bronze Age stone circle, traditionally believed to represent nine ladies turned to stone.

Managed by Peak District National Park Authority.

OPENING TIMES

Any reasonable daylight hours

Access is through fields and woodland with gates and stiles

VISIT US

Direction: From an unclassified road off A6, 5 miles SE of Bakewell

Train: Matlock 4½ miles

Bus: Visit **traveline.info** for the latest bus timetables and routes

Tel: 01629 816200

ACQ.1883

MAP PAGE 308 (2E)
OS MAP 119, OL24: SK249635

HARDWICK OLD HALL

The 'bare bones' of a towering Elizabethan mansion, built by the formidable Bess of Hardwick on the site of her birthplace. Before it was finished, she began the even grander Hardwick Hall nearby.

Now roofless, it displays lavishly decorated plasterwork in former staterooms.

Managed by English Heritage and owned by the National Trust.

OPENING TIMES
A major conservation project is under way, so access will be limited. Please check the website for details

VISIT US
Direction: 8 miles SE of Chesterfield, off A6175 (J29 of M1)

Train: Chesterfield 8 miles

Bus: Visit traveline.info for the latest bus timetables and routes

Tel: 01246 850431

NON-MEMBERS
See website for entry prices

ACQ.1959 🎧🎁Ⓔ🖼👤👫🅿️📷
⚠️ OVP

MAP PAGE 309 (2F)
OS MAP 120, 269: SK462637

PEVERIL CASTLE

Towering high above the pretty Peak District market town of Castleton, Peveril is among the most spectacularly sited castles in England.

One of the first stone castles in England, it was begun soon after 1066 by William the Conqueror's trusted knight William Peverell, on a site naturally defended by sheer drops.

A century later, in the 1170s, Henry II further strengthened the castle, adding the hallmark keep on the hill summit, still rising almost to its original height. Its interior is now open again following repairs.

Breathtaking views over the Peak District are the great reward for venturing up to this wonderfully positioned castle.

🎬 *The Princess Bride* (1987).

OPENING TIMES
Open daily 1 Apr–5 Nov

Open varying days 6 Nov–28 Mar

Site closed 24-26 Dec & 1 Jan

See website for latest opening times

Last entry 45 mins before closing

VISIT US
Direction: Via the marketplace in Castleton; 15 miles W of Sheffield on A6187

Train: Hope 2½ miles

Bus: Visit traveline.info for the latest bus timetables and routes

Tel: 01433 620613

Local Tourist Information: 01433 620679

NON-MEMBERS
See website for entry prices

By being a Member, you save up to **£28.50** (price of a family ticket) when you visit **Peveril Castle**

ACQ.1932 👟🎁🚿🖼👤👫🅿️📷
⚠️ OVP

Wheelchair access to visitor centre only.

Parking (in town).

Caution: moderately challenging 10-15 mins uphill walk to castle from visitor centre.

MAP PAGE 308 (2E)
OS MAP 110, OL1: SK149826

SUTTON SCARSDALE HALL

The spectacular hilltop shell of Sutton Scarsdale Hall chronicles the rise and fall of a great mansion. Built in 1724-29 for the fourth Earl of Scarsdale, its immense cost almost bankrupted his heirs. In 1919 its lavish interiors were sold, mainly to America. Having narrowly escaped demolition, the impressive roofless shell is being conserved.

OPENING TIMES
Exterior only:
Open daily 1 Apr–28 Mar

Site closed 24-26 Dec & 1 Jan

See website for latest opening times

Due to a major conservation project, the hall is currently inaccessible. The grounds remain open. Please check the website for further details

VISIT US
Direction: Between Chesterfield and Bolsover, 1½ miles S of Arkwright Town

Train: Chesterfield 5 miles

Bus: Visit traveline.info

ACQ.1971 ♿🎁🅿️🖼⚠️

Caution: falling masonry.

MAP PAGE 309 (2F)
OS MAP 120, 269: SK442689

BOLSOVER CASTLE

DERBYSHIRE – S44 6PR

Exquisitely restored to recreate its past glories, Bolsover Castle was the fantasy hilltop pleasure palace of a horse-mad Cavalier playboy. This unique Stuart showpiece displays some of the most lavishly decorated rooms anywhere in England, a wonderfully recreated period garden, an astonishing riding school and amazing views. Be transported to a lost age of aristocratic extravagance, brought to life by fantastically costumed storytellers.

Our imaginative yet carefully researched re-presentation brings to life the golden days of the fairytale Stuart mansion and its larger-than-life creator, William Cavendish. You'll find there's plenty to see and do.

Bolsover Castle was always something special. Neither a fortress nor a conventional country house, it was designed purely to impress, entertain and intrigue visitors, particularly King Charles I and his court in 1634. Replacing a now-vanished medieval hilltop fortress, its site was carefully chosen both to dominate the landscape for many miles around and to astonish visitors with unrivalled panoramas.

Bolsover is again dazzling visitors. Explore the playfully pinnacled and battlemented 'Little Castle', the core of the mansion and focus of its magic. Begun by Sir Charles Cavendish in 1612, this Stuart plutocrat's fantasy was completed, decorated and furnished regardless of expense by his son William – playboy, poet, courtier and later Royalist general and Duke of Newcastle. There's a wealth of details to enjoy; the original exquisitely carved fireplaces, painted panelling and above all the astonishing array of dramatic murals (recently saved as part of our Members' wall paintings appeal). Absorb the atmosphere of the Star Chamber and Marble Closet with their striking replica tapestries, satin wall-hangings and red velvet upholstery. Interactive 'cabinets of curiosity' reveal how the rooms, including the extraordinary 'Elysium Closet' with its painted ceiling and frieze of naked Classical gods and goddesses, were used to intrigue and impress noble visitors. It's well worth exploring the whole building, from its top-floor bedchambers to its cavernous basement kitchen complex.

Outside you can stroll the wall walk around the Fountain Garden, where Stuart courtiers promenaded to see and be seen. Designed around a statue of a naked Venus – goddess of love and pleasure – emerging from her bath, the enchanting garden has been attentively recreated, with borders planted with over 5,000 flowers and plants fashionable in Bolsover's heyday. Investigate the secluded chamber set into the garden wall, once the scene of intimate banquets for the chosen few. Enjoy truly astonishing vistas over the surrounding countryside beyond.

english-heritage.org.uk

DON'T MISS

Immersing yourself in tales of Bolsover told by our fantastically costumed storytellers in the Little Castle. Meet the Storyteller, the castle personified, and encounter William and Margaret Cavendish, Stuart owners of the castle, whose extravagant outfits mirror their flamboyant lives and careers.

The easy-to-use handheld multimedia guide helps you experience Bolsover Castle at whatever level of detail you choose.

Narrated by actor Rupert Penry-Jones, the touchscreen guide lets you select from 'playlets', videos, reconstructions of room interiors and interviews with experts explaining how this captivating pleasure house operated. Don't miss exploring the dramatic roofless shell of the enormous Terrace Range, once the site of yet another set of sumptuous staterooms.

There's plenty more to discover at Bolsover. William Cavendish's passion for training horses is reflected in the vast indoor Riding House and the great Stables, where you'll find a stylish interactive exhibition (including a replica 17th-century saddle for children to try).

Children have their own entertainment too. A play area inspired by the castle's battlements and towers is ideally sited next to the tearoom's outdoor seating. In the Little Castle both children and adults can dress up in theatrical costumes and take the stage, echoing 'Love's Welcome at Bolsover', the masque performed here for Charles I and Queen Henrietta Maria at the zenith of the castle's now-revived glory.

Stop off at the tearoom, with indoor and outdoor seating and fantastic views towards the Riding House, for a refreshing break while exploring the site. Picnic benches are also available, or in fine weather you could spread out your picnic blanket on the grass.

OPENING TIMES

Open daily 1 Apr–5 Nov

Open varying days 6 Nov–28 Mar

Site closed 24–25 Dec

See website for latest opening times

Last entry 30 mins before closing

VISIT US

Address: Bolsover Castle, Castle Street, Bolsover, Derbyshire S44 6PR

Direction: In Bolsover, 6 miles E of Chesterfield on A632. Off M1 at junction 29A (signposted)

Train: Chesterfield 6 miles

Bus: Visit traveline.info for the latest bus timetables and routes

Tel: 01246 822844

Local Tourist Information: Chesterfield: 01246 345777

By being a Member, you save up to £52.50 (price of a family ticket) when you visit **Bolsover Castle**.

NON-MEMBERS

See website for entry prices

ACQ.1945

The coach drop-off point is in the council car park opposite.

There is good access to the grounds, but please note that the Little Castle is not accessible to wheelchairs.

MAP PAGE 309 (2F)
OS MAP 120, 269: SK470707

WINGFIELD MANOR
DERBYSHIRE – DE55 7NH

The vast ruins of a palatial medieval manor house, built in the 1440s for Ralph, Lord Cromwell, Treasurer of England.

Please note: Wingfield Manor is part of a working farm. Please respect the owner's privacy at all times. No public access.

OPENING TIMES

Currently no access during conservation project. Please check website for details

VISIT US

Direction: 17 miles N of Derby; 11 miles S of Chesterfield on B5035; ½ mile S of South Wingfield. From M1 junction 28, W on A38, A615 (Matlock Road) at Alfreton, 1½ miles and turn onto B5035

Train: Alfreton 4 miles

Bus: Visit traveline.info for the latest bus timetables and routes

Tel: 0370 333 1181 (for information)

NON-MEMBERS

See website for entry prices

ACQ.1960 🚫 ⚠️

Parking (none on site or in gateway).

MAP PAGE 309 (3F)
OS MAP 119, 269: SK374548

DON'T FORGET

Remember to take your membership card.

LEICESTERSHIRE

JEWRY WALL
LEICESTERSHIRE – LE1 4LB

Among the most massive survivals of Roman masonry in Britain, this wall of a town-centre Roman bath house complex still stands over 9 metres (30 feet) high. The baths were completed by about AD 160.

Managed by Leicester City Council.

OPENING TIMES

Access to the site is currently closed during refurbishment of the Jewry Wall Museum

Exterior viewable from adjacent footpath

VISIT US

Direction: In St Nicholas Street, W of Church of St Nicholas

Train: Leicester ¾ mile

Bus: Visit traveline.info for the latest bus timetables and routes

ACQ.1920 🚫 P

Parking (by museum, within St Nicholas Circle).

MAP PAGE 309 (4F)
OS MAP 140, 233: SK582045

KIRBY MUXLOE CASTLE LEICESTERSHIRE – LE9 2DH

The picturesque moated remains, including the fine gatehouse and a complete corner tower, of a largely brick-built fortified mansion. Begun in 1480 by Lord Hastings, a leading supporter and close friend of Edward IV, the 'castle' was constructed in the most up-to-date style in the fashionable new brick building material, and cosmetically equipped for artillery defence with gunports, some of them 'dummies'. But at a council meeting in 1483 the future king Richard III suddenly denounced his former ally Hastings as a traitor. He had Hastings immediately beheaded, and the showpiece mansion was never finished.

OPENING TIMES

Open varying days 1 Apr–5 Nov

Site closed 6 Nov–28 Mar

See website for latest opening times

Last entry 30 mins before closing

VISIT US

Direction: 4 miles W of Leicester off B5380; close to M1 junction 21A, northbound exit only

Train: Leicester 5 miles

Bus: Visit traveline.info for the latest bus timetables and routes

Tel: 0116 238 6886

NON-MEMBERS

See website for entry prices

By being a Member, you save up to £24.50 (price of a family ticket) when you visit **Kirby Muxloe Castle**

ACQ.1912 🚫 📷 P ⚠️ OVP

Small car park available on site.

Please note: this site is cash only and is unable to accept card payments.

MAP PAGE 309 (4F)
OS MAP 140, 233: SK524046

ASHBY DE LA ZOUCH CASTLE

———— LEICESTERSHIRE – LE65 1BR ————

Ashby de la Zouch Castle forms the backdrop to the famous jousting scenes in Sir Walter Scott's classic novel, *Ivanhoe*.

The castle began as a manor house in the 12th century, but achieved its greatest glory in the 15th century under Edward IV's friend and Lord Chamberlain, William, Lord Hastings (who also built Kirby Muxloe Castle). Between 1474 and his execution in 1483 by Richard Duke of Gloucester, later Richard III, Hastings added the chapel and the impressive keep-like Hastings Tower – a luxurious self-contained residence, and a castle within a castle.

Later, the castle hosted many royal visitors, including Henry VII, Mary Queen of Scots, James I and Charles I. A stubborn Royalist stronghold and raiding base during the Civil War, Ashby finally fell to Parliament after a long siege in 1646, and was later made unusable. Though the Hastings Tower was badly damaged, you can still climb 24 metres (78 feet) to the top for fine views. You can also explore an underground passage from the kitchen to the tower, probably created during the Civil War.

OPENING TIMES

Open daily 1 Apr–5 Nov

Open varying days 6 Nov–28 Mar

Site closed 24–26 Dec & 1 Jan

See website for latest opening times

Last entry 30 mins before closing

VISIT US

Direction: In Ashby de la Zouch, 12 miles S of Derby on A511

Train: Burton on Trent 9 miles

Bus: Visit traveline.info for the latest bus timetables and routes

Tel: 01530 413343

Local Tourist Information: 01530 411767

NON-MEMBERS

See website for entry prices

By being a Member, you save up to **£28.50** (price of a family ticket) when you visit **Ashby de la Zouch Castle**

Disabled access (grounds only).

Disabled only parking, please use the town centre car parks (charges apply).

MAP PAGE 309 (4F)   OS MAP 128, 245: SK361166

BOLINGBROKE CASTLE

LINCOLNSHIRE – PE23 4HH

Remains of a once-impressive, multi-towered 13th-century castle, begun in the 1220s by Ranulf, Earl of Chester and Lincoln. Famous as the birthplace in 1367 of Henry of Bolingbroke, the future King Henry IV. A Civil War Royalist base, it was besieged and taken in 1643 by Oliver Cromwell, and reduced to ruin.

Managed by Heritage Lincolnshire.

OPENING TIMES

Any reasonable daylight hours

VISIT US

Direction: In Old Bolingbroke, 16 miles N of Boston off A16

Train: Thorpe Culvert 9 miles

Bus: Visit traveline.info for the latest bus timetables and routes

Tel: 01529 461499

ACQ.1949 ⛺ ⛺ ⚠ Caution: deep water. Please take care around castle moat.

MAP PAGE 309 (2J)
OS MAP 122, 273: TF349650

SHARE THE FUN

Check our website for up-to-the-minute information on our year-long programme of events.

english-heritage.org.uk/events

SIBSEY TRADER WINDMILL

LINCOLNSHIRE – PE22 0SY

This six-storey Victorian mill has just undergone major conservation following storm damage. Repairs to the brick mill tower have been carried out, and a new cap, fantail and sails have been installed, bringing the mill back into working order. Please be sure to check our website before planning a visit.

sibseytraderwindmill.co.uk

OPENING TIMES

See website for latest opening times

VISIT US

Direction: ½ mile W of Sibsey off A16, 5 miles N of Boston

Train: Boston 5 miles

Bus: Visit traveline.info for the latest bus timetables and routes

Tel: 01205 460647/07718 320449

NON-MEMBERS

See website for entry prices

ACQ.1975 ♿ 🚹 🚻 ⊗ P 🅿 ⚠ OVP

Disabled access (exterior only).

Caution: steep stairs.

MAP PAGE 309 (3J)
OS MAP 122, 261: TF345510

TATTERSHALL COLLEGE

LINCOLNSHIRE – LN4 4LG

Remains of a grammar school for church choristers, founded in the mid-15th century by Ralph, Lord Cromwell, builder of Wingfield Manor (p.169) and nearby Tattershall Castle (National Trust).

Managed by Heritage Lincolnshire.

OPENING TIMES

Any reasonable daylight hours

VISIT US

Direction: In Tattershall, 14 miles NE of Sleaford on A153

Train: Ruskington 10 miles

Bus: Visit traveline.info for the latest bus timetables and routes

Tel: 01529 461499

ACQ.1972 ⛺

MAP PAGE 309 (2H)
OS MAP 122, 261: TF213578

GAINSBOROUGH OLD HALL

———— LINCOLNSHIRE – DN21 2NB ————

It's well worth venturing off the beaten track to Gainsborough Old Hall, one of the biggest and best-preserved yet least known medieval manor houses in England. Imaginative interpretation helps you trace its amazingly varied history during five and a half centuries at the core of Gainsborough's life.

Lavishly constructed in timber framing and fine brickwork, this imposing mansion was largely built during the later 15th century by Sir Thomas Burgh, the leading Lincolnshire Yorkist. Richard III stayed here in 1483, and Henry VIII and his ill-fated fifth wife, Catherine Howard, in 1541. Developed into a fashionable Jacobean residence by the wealthy and very Protestant Hickman family, it subsequently fell on hard times. Parts of it served as a theatre and preaching hall, crammed tenements for the poorest people, workshops and even a pub, before it became the hub of fashionable Victorian social life, eventually secured for the future by the people of Gainsborough.

There's a lot to see here, so allow plenty of time. Highlights include the magnificent medieval great hall – later a raucous Georgian theatre – and the finest medieval kitchen complex anywhere in England, with stupendous fireplaces and everything needed for the biggest of feasts. View bedchambers, lodgings for lords and paupers and the Victorian Assembly Rooms in the former great chamber. Climb the high brick tower for views over the town and the river Trent, explored by pictorial panels. Don't miss a stroll round the hall's impressive exterior, and take a break in the open-to-all tearoom, with indoor and outdoor seating.

🎬 *Peterloo* (2018).

OPENING TIMES

Open daily 1 Apr-5 Nov

Open varying days 6 Nov-28 Mar

Site closed 24-26 Dec & 1 Jan

See website for latest opening times

Last entry 30 mins before closing

VISIT US

Direction: In Parnell Road, Gainsborough, opposite the library

Train: Gainsborough Central ½ mile, Gainsborough Lea Road 1 mile

Bus: Visit traveline.info for the latest bus timetables and routes

Tel: 01427 677348

NON-MEMBERS

See website for entry prices

By being a Member, you save up to **£36.50** (price of a family ticket) when you visit **Gainsborough Old Hall**

Admission price payable by all visitors, including Members, on occasional special event days

15% discount on rates for groups of 11 or more paying a lump sum

ACQ.1969 🔊 ♿ 🍴 🎦 🖥 🚹 ♿ 👜 💷

Disabled access (most of ground floor).

Assistance dogs only within the house.
Dogs on leads permitted in tearoom and gift shop.

No dedicated parking at site. Free parking (max 1 hour) in surrounding streets, and longer-term paid parking at Riverside car park, 100 metres away.

MAP PAGE 309 (1G)
OS MAP 112/121, 280: SK813900

LINCOLN MEDIEVAL BISHOPS' PALACE

—— LINCOLNSHIRE – LN2 1PU ——

These intriguing remains of a medieval bishops' palace stand in the shadow of Lincoln Cathedral, at the heart of the ancient city.

Begun in about 1175 and continued by St Hugh of Lincoln and later bishops, it was the focus of a vast diocese stretching from the Humber to the Thames. Badly damaged during the Civil War and ruined ever since, it's now benefitting from a £2.5m sustainable conservation project.

NEW FOR 2023

Following years of closure or limited access, the palace re-opens in 2023. It's been conserved by an ambitious project combining the latest surveying technology with centuries old craft skills and techniques, including clearing walls of vegetation and soft-capping them to limit further damage, the use of lime mortar and painstaking masonry repairs. Where stonework was beyond repair, replacement limestone from Lincoln Cathedral's quarry was used, and the tooled detailing created by the original masons was reproduced.

OPENING TIMES
See website for latest opening times

VISIT US

Direction: On the south side of Lincoln Cathedral. From Exchequer Gate, follow the wall to your right to the doorway directly opposite cathedral south porch, then take Chesney Gate tunnelled walkway. Entrance to the left down the pathway

Train: Lincoln 1 mile

Bus: Visit traveline.info

NON-MEMBERS
See website for entry prices

By being a Member, you save up to £28.50 (price of a family ticket) when you visit **Lincoln Medieval Bishops' Palace**

ACQ.1954

MAP PAGE 309 (2H)
OS MAP 121, 272: SK978717

KIRBY HALL

NORTHAMPTONSHIRE – NN17 3EN

Magnificent Kirby Hall is one of England's greatest Elizabethan and 17th-century houses. Imaginative interactive displays help you trace its rise, fall and rescue through 450 years – and experience a royal visit.

Standing in splendid isolation amid rolling countryside, Kirby Hall offers visitors an unforgettable experience, not to be missed. For though its finest staterooms survive impressively complete, much of this vast mansion is now a dramatic roofless shell, intriguing to explore. Its rich decoration and ambitious architecture set successive owners at the forefront of new ideas about design and aristocratic lifestyle.

Begun in 1570 for local landowner Sir Humphrey Stafford, Kirby's inner courtyard displays the pioneering use of Classical-style features never previously seen in English mansions. Soon afterwards the house was bought by Sir Christopher Hatton, who first attracted Queen Elizabeth I's favour by his dancing and eventually became her Lord Chancellor. He added an outer forecourt and a wing of lavishly regal staterooms, lit by noble double-height bow windows. The third Sir Christopher Hatton modernised the mansion during the 1630s, and a fourth Sir Christopher added the great garden, now strikingly recreated as it appeared in the late 17th century.

Displays in the staterooms trace the story of Kirby's rise and fall, from its foundation to its abandonment in the 19th century and eventual rescue after 1930, when it became the first major mansion taken into state care. There's also an intriguing array of site finds, along with examples of the panelling, wallpapers and other decorative features which once graced Kirby's interiors. You'll find out about the mansion's people across the centuries, including the black servant James Chappell, who heroically rescued the fourth Sir Christopher and his daughters from disaster before apparently becoming landlord of the local pub.

You can also experience a royal visit. Though the first Sir Christopher waited in vain to welcome Queen Elizabeth on one of her 'progresses', King James I visited his successors no fewer than nine times. A tapestry trail draws you into the excitement of a regal stay, and interactives let you discover what you look like in aristocratic 17th-century clothes and judge who 'takes the chair' as the most important person present. In the best bedchamber you can even try out a theatrical recreation of a grand royal bed, inspired by one recorded here in 1619.

The comprehensive audio tour enhances your visit, and there's a family activity trail featuring Edmund, one of Kirby Hall's famous resident peacocks.

Owned by the Earl of Winchilsea and managed by English Heritage.

APETHORPE PALACE NORTHAMPTONSHIRE – PE8 5DJ

OPENING TIMES

Open Wed-Sun 1 Apr-5 Nov

Open varying days 6 Nov-28 Mar

Site closed 24-26 Dec

See website for latest opening times

Last entry 30 mins before closing

VISIT US

Direction: On an unclassified road off A43, 4 miles NE of Corby

Train: Corby 4 miles; Kettering 11 miles

Bus: Visit traveline.info for the latest bus timetables and routes

Tel: 01536 203230

NON-MEMBERS

See website for entry prices

By being a Member, you save up to **£36.50** (price of a family ticket) when you visit **Kirby Hall**

ACQ.1930 🎧 ♿ 🐾 E ❄ 💻 🧍

🧍 P 🎪 📷 ⚠

Disabled access (grounds, gardens and ground floor only).

Dogs on leads (restricted areas only).

Please note: there is no tearoom at Kirby Hall, but plenty of places to picnic.

MAP PAGE 309 (5G)
OS MAP 141, 224: SP926927

🎬 *Mansfield Park* (1999).

Visitors have a unique opportunity to discover stately Apethorpe Palace, owned by Elizabeth I and favourite royal residence of James I and Charles I.

Among England's greatest stately homes, Apethorpe Palace holds a particularly important place in history because of its ownership by, and role in entertaining, Tudor and Stuart monarchs.

Elizabeth I once owned the building, which she had inherited from Henry VIII. For a period, Apethorpe was a royal palace lived in regularly by James I and Charles I.

James I so loved Apethorpe that he personally contributed to its extension, to make it more suitable for his 'princely recreation' and 'commodious entertainment', particularly for hunting in the nearby royal forest of Rockingham. The resulting series of staterooms, including the King's Bedchamber and the impressive long gallery, is one of the most complete to survive from the Jacobean period.

Apethorpe Palace has a private owner who is committed to opening the gardens and the staterooms to the public.

Please note: There are lots of stairs, and no resting/seating points available. Children under 16 must be accompanied by an adult. We are unable to admit children under 12.

OPENING TIMES

Open by pre-booked guided tour only (charge applies). See website for dates and booking information

VISIT US

Direction: Located off the A43 towards King's Cliffe. If entering Apethorpe via King's Cliffe Road, advance to Laundry Lane, not the High Street. If entering via Bridge St, pass the stone cross and turn left into Laundry Lane

Train: 14 miles from Peterborough. Trains via Kings Cross to Peterborough (approx. 45 mins)

Bus: Visit traveline.info for the latest bus timetables and routes

Tel: 0370 333 1181

NON-MEMBERS

See website for entry prices

ACQ.2004 P

Access via narrow residential lane – please observe 10mph speed limit at all times.

MAP PAGE 309 (5H)
OS MAP 141, 224/234: TL023954

CHICHELE COLLEGE

NORTHAMPTONSHIRE – NN10 8DX

The remains of a residence for priests serving the parish church, founded by locally born Henry Chichele, Archbishop of Canterbury 1414-43. Often exhibits local artists' work.

Managed by Higham Ferrers Tourism, Business and Community Partnership.

OPENING TIMES

Garden: Any reasonable daylight hours

Interior: Open during events and exhibitions – please check website for details

VISIT US

Direction: College Street, Higham Ferrers

Train: Wellingborough 5 miles

Bus: Visit traveline.info for the latest bus timetables and routes

ACQ.1949

Dogs on leads (grounds only).

Caution: falling masonry.

MAP PAGE 309 (5H)
OS MAP 153, 224: SP960687

ELEANOR CROSS, GEDDINGTON

NORTHAMPTONSHIRE – NN14 1AD

This stately triangular cross is the finest survivor of the 'Eleanor Crosses', which marked the places where the body of Eleanor of Castile, wife of Edward I, rested on its way to Westminster Abbey.

OPENING TIMES

Viewing from adjacent highway. Any reasonable daylight hours

VISIT US

Direction: In Geddington, off A43 between Kettering and Corby

Train: Kettering 4 miles

Bus: Visit traveline.info

ACQ.1915   Caution: beware of traffic.

MAP PAGE 309 (5G)
OS MAP 141, 224: SP894830

RUSHTON TRIANGULAR LODGE

NORTHAMPTONSHIRE – NN14 1RP

The extraordinary creation of an extraordinary Elizabethan, this intriguing triangular folly was built in 1593-97 by Sir Thomas Tresham, father of one of the Gunpowder Plotters.

Tresham was a staunch Roman Catholic, often fined or imprisoned for his faith. His lodge testifies to his defiant Catholicism, but also to his obsession with individualistic buildings, symbolism and numbers – particularly three. All its features come in threes, symbolising the Holy Trinity. There are three floors, trefoil windows and three sides each 33⅓-feet-long, with three triangular gables. Inscribed over the door is 'Tres Testimonium Dant' ('there are three that bear witness'), a Biblical reference to the Trinity. It's also a pun on Tresham's name; his wife called him 'Good Tres', so the inscription could also mean 'Tres bears witness'.

OPENING TIMES

Entrance by pre-booked guided tour on select days only (charge applies). See website for details

VISIT US

Direction: 1 mile W of Rushton, on unclassified road; 1 mile from Desborough on A6

Train: Kettering 5 miles

Bus: Visit traveline.info for the latest bus timetables and routes

Tel: 01536 710761

NON-MEMBERS

See website for entry prices

ACQ.1951   OVP

Dogs on leads (restricted areas only).

Parking in lay-by on opposite side of road to entrance.

MAP PAGE 309 (5G)
OS MAP 141, 224: SP830831

NOTTINGHAMSHIRE

MATTERSEY PRIORY

NOTTINGHAMSHIRE – DN10 5HN

Remote remains (mainly the refectory) of a tiny priory housing just six Gilbertine canons – the only wholly English monastic order. Sculpted panels from here are now in the village church.

OPENING TIMES

See website for latest opening times

VISIT US

Direction: Approx. 1 mile from Mattersey village. Park in village, then walk from church along Abbey Road (bridleway). Access is by landowner's permission through private land.
Please note: no vehicular access to site

Train: Retford 7 miles

Bus: Visit traveline.info

Tel: 01604 735464

ACQ.1913

Access to the site is over a stile and there may be animals grazing.

MAP PAGE 309 (1G)
OS MAP 112/120, 280: SK703896

RUFFORD ABBEY

NOTTINGHAMSHIRE – NG22 9DF

England's best-preserved remains of a Cistercian abbey west cloister range, dating from c. 1170. Incorporated into part of a 17th-century and later mansion, in Rufford Country Park.

Owned by Nottinghamshire County Council and managed by Parkwood Outdoors.

OPENING TIMES

Due to a conservation project, external viewing only of abbey ruins. See **parkwoodoutdoors.co.uk/ centre/rufford-abbey** for full details

Site closed 25 Dec

VISIT US

Direction: 2 miles S of Ollerton off A614

Train: Mansfield 8 miles

Bus: Visit **traveline.info** for the latest bus timetables and routes

Tel: 01623 821338

ACQ.1959

Parking (charge applies – not managed by English Heritage).

Shops in Stable Block.

Caution: falling masonry.

MAP PAGE 309 (2G)
OS MAP 120, 270: SK646648W

LYDDINGTON BEDE HOUSE
RUTLAND – LE15 9LZ

Set beside the church in a picturesque ironstone-built village, Lyddington Bede House originated as the late medieval wing of a palace of the Bishops of Lincoln.

By 1600 it had passed to Sir Thomas Cecil, son of Queen Elizabeth's chief minister. He converted it into an almshouse for twelve poor 'bedesmen' over 30 years old and two women (who had to be over 45), all guaranteed free of lunacy, leprosy or the French pox. It continued as an almshouse until the 1930s.

You can explore the bedesmen's rooms, with their tiny windows and fireplaces, view a fine timbered roof, and admire the bishops' great chamber on the first floor, with its beautiful carved Tudor cornice. Interpretation includes audio boxes where you can hear letters read by the bedesmen. A bedesman's and a bedeswoman's room have been recreated as they appeared in Victorian times.

OPENING TIMES

Open Wed-Sun 1 Apr-5 Nov

Site closed 6 Nov-28 Mar

See website for latest opening times

Last entry 30 mins before closing

VISIT US

Direction: In Lyddington, 6 miles N of Corby; 1 mile E of A6003, next to the church

Train: Oakham 7 miles

Bus: Visit **traveline.info**

Tel: 01572 822438

NON-MEMBERS

See website for entry prices

By being a Member, you save up to £28.50 (price of a family ticket) when you visit **Lyddington Bede House**

ACQ.1952   OVP

Dogs on leads (restricted areas only).

MAP PAGE 309 (4G)
OS MAP 141, 234: SP876870

Kenilworth Castle and Elizabethan Garden, Warwickshire

WELCOME TO THE

WEST
MIDLANDS

WALES

Merseyside

Greater
Manchester

South Yorkshire

Cheshire

Derbyshire

Stoke-on-Trent

.23

Staffordshire

18
Oswestry

Shropshire

17

Burton upon Trent

Stafford

12

15

Shrewsbury

22

Telford

8

24

10

9

13

21

Tamworth

Leicestershire

7

Wolverhampton

16

14

20

Nuneaton

Bishop's Castle

27 Birmingham

26

West
Midlands

Coventry

11

19

Kidderminster

25

Rugby

Ludlow

Worcestershire

Warwickshire

6

29

Leominster

Warwick

2

28 Worcester

Herefordshire

Stratford-upon-Avon

Great Malvern

1

Evesham

Hereford

5

4

Ross-on-Wye

3

Gloucestershire

Oxfordshire

West
Midlands

South
Gloucestershire

Wiltshire

Berkshire

Bristol

North
Somerset

Bath &
N.E. Somerset

WEST MIDLANDS

From Romans and royals to the Industrial Revolution, there are so many stories to explore in the West Midlands.

Boscobel House and The Royal Oak, Shropshire

Roam the ruins of **Wroxeter** (p.194) to discover what life was like in one of Roman Britain's biggest cities, or play hide and seek at **Boscobel House and The Royal Oak** (p.186), where Charles II hid in a priest hole and in the branches of a tree – a descendant of which can still be seen today. More royal tales played out at **Kenilworth Castle and Elizabeth Garden** (p.196), which was transformed by Robert Dudley to impress Elizabeth I.

Elsewhere, lost echoes of glamour and grandeur haunt the ruins of **Witley Court** (p.200), while the world's first **Iron Bridge** (p.189) is the centrepiece of a UNESCO World Heritage Site. Head to **Goodrich Castle** (p.182) to explore a formidable stronghold or visit charming **Stokesay Castle** (p.192) for a glimpse of medieval country house living.

Goodrich Castle, Herefordshire

Kenilworth Castle and Elizabethan Garden, Warwickshire

GOODRICH CASTLE

HEREFORDSHIRE – HR9 6HY

Goodrich is the perfect medieval castle. Lively interpretation and a fun family game offer you even more reasons to visit this strikingly well-preserved baronial fortress.

Set in beautiful wooded country, Goodrich Castle guarded a strategic crossing of the River Wye. The earliest fortress here – 'Godric's Castle' – was begun in the late 11th century by an English landowner called Godric. A generation later, the de Clare family added the well-preserved little Norman keep which still stands at the core of the castle. Then, after ownership by William the Marshal (renowned as 'the Greatest Knight'), the castle was rebuilt in the most up-to-date style by King Edward I's uncle William de Valence, Earl of Pembroke.

This late 13th-century castle is revealed as you walk up the gentle slope from the ticket office. Still almost completely walled, it has massive round towers reinforced by distinctive 'spur buttresses', the latest fashion in castle building. It's surrounded by a rock-cut ditch, which you'll cross by a once-fortified bridge modelled on one at the Tower of London – another symbol of William's almost-royal status. Passing through the heavily defended gatehouse, you'll find the courtyard crowded with buildings.

Goodrich, in fact, boasts one of the most complete sets of medieval living quarters surviving in any English castle. From rare surviving records, we know a lot about how these were used by William's widow Countess Joan. She often stayed here, packing nearly 200 servants, staff and guests into the castle.

Pick up the family game from the ticket office and you can join her household as you explore the castle. The game features nine cartoon characters ranging from Countess Joan herself to the baker's assistant. You can choose how they might have answered questions – or make up your own cheeky replies. Adventurous (and reasonably fit) visitors can venture into the pitch-dark dungeon, or climb the steep narrow stairway to the keep top for breathtaking views over the castle and its surroundings. Don't miss the chapel, with its two striking modern stained-glass windows.

In the courtyard you'll also meet 'Roaring Meg', the only surviving Civil War mortar in England. During Goodrich's greatest crisis, the two-month siege of 1646, it lobbed deadly exploding 'bombs' into the Royalist-held castle, eventually forcing its surrender. One struck and buried the well, where excavations have produced a fascinating array of finds, from Civil War weapons to everyday household objects. You'll find some displayed in the ticket office exhibition.

Before returning for a break in the tearoom (which has indoor and outdoor seating), it's worth walking right round the castle's dry moat. It's a great place to picnic, and the frowning walls above you are a reminder of how strong Goodrich was. Look out for the garderobe tower, which housed multiple medieval loos – spot the aperture at its base, which allowed the 'gong farmer' to clear the cesspit.

OPENING TIMES

Open daily 1 Apr–5 Nov

Open varying days 6 Nov–28 Mar

Site closed 24–26 Dec & 1 Jan

See website for latest opening times

Last entry 30 mins before closing

VISIT US

Address: Goodrich Castle,
Castle Lane, Goodrich, Ross-on-Wye,
Herefordshire HR9 6HY

Direction: 5 miles S of
Ross-on-Wye off A40

Bus: Visit traveline.info

Tel: 01600 890538

NON-MEMBERS

See website for entry prices

By being a Member, you save up to **£36.50** (price of a family ticket) when you visit **Goodrich Castle**.

ACQ.1920

Disabled access (limited, please call for details or ask the Visitor Centre on arrival). No disabled access to the castle.

Caution: the stairs to the keep top are steep, dark and narrow.

The tearoom will close 30 minutes before the site closes.

Parking: charges apply to non-members, free for Members with valid car sticker.

MAP PAGE 308 (7C)
OS MAP 162, OL14: SO577200

ARTHUR'S STONE

HEREFORDSHIRE – HR3 6AX

Ridge-top Neolithic chambered tomb made of great stone slabs, with spectacular views over the Golden Valley.

According to legend, King Arthur killed a giant here; certainly Charles I picnicked here in 1645.

OPENING TIMES

Any reasonable daylight hours

VISIT US

Direction: 7 miles E of Hay-on-Wye via B4348, signposted from Dorstone off steep minor road to Bredwardine

Train: Hereford 16 miles

Bus: Visit **traveline.info** for the latest bus timetables and routes

ACQ.1909 🐕 P ⚠

Parking in village of Dorstone. Very limited parking on site.

Please do not climb on the stones. Walk from Dorstone village approx. 1km.

Caution: unguarded drops.

> MAP PAGE 308 (6B)
> OS MAP 148/161, OL13/201: SO319431

EDVIN LOACH OLD CHURCH

HEREFORDSHIRE – HR7 4PW

Ruins of a small early Norman church, displaying striking herringbone work masonry. Stands within the earthworks of a motte-and-bailey castle, with a pretty Victorian church beside it.

OPENING TIMES

Any reasonable daylight hours

VISIT US

Direction: 4 miles N of Bromyard via B4203, then narrow lanes signposted Edvin Loach. Look for EH sign after Steeples Farm. WARNING: track to church is very uneven, drive with care

Bus: Visit **traveline.info** for the latest bus timetables and routes

ACQ.1980 🐕 P

> MAP PAGE 308 (6C)
> OS MAP 149, 202: SO663584

LONGTOWN CASTLE

HEREFORDSHIRE – HR2 0LE

A powerful 12th-century round keep on a steep mound dominates this Welsh Border castle, whose outer defences probably originated as a Roman fort. Set in the beautiful Olchon Valley, with the Black Mountains as a backdrop. See **longtowncastles.com** for recent discoveries here.

Managed in association with Longtown Village Pride.

OPENING TIMES

Any reasonable daylight hours

VISIT US

Direction: In Longtown village, accessible by minor roads from Hay-on-Wye

Bus: Visit **traveline.info** for the latest bus timetables and routes

ACQ.1973 🐕 P 🏕 ⚠

Parking on roadside.

Garden available for picnics.

Caution: steep stairs.

> MAP PAGE 308 (7B)
> OS MAP 161, OL13: SO321291

ROTHERWAS CHAPEL

HEREFORDSHIRE – HR2 6LD

The family chapel of the Roman Catholic Bodenham family. The originally simple medieval building has a fine Elizabethan timber roof, a rebuilt 18th-century tower, and striking Victorian interior decoration and furnishings by the Pugins.

ROTHERWAS CHAPEL

Managed in association with the Friends of Rotherwas Chapel.

OPENING TIMES

See website for latest opening times

Key available from the Herefordshire Archive and Records Centre. herefordshire.gov.uk/archives Tel: 01432 260750

VISIT US

Direction: 1½ miles SE of Hereford on B4399, left into Chapel Road

Train: Hereford 3½ miles

Bus: Visit **traveline.info** for the latest bus timetables and routes

ACQ.1928 ♿ 🚫 ⚠

Parking at Herefordshire Archive & Records Centre, 800m away.

Disabled access (ground floor only – one step).

Caution: steep stairs.

> MAP PAGE 308 (6C)
> OS MAP 149, 189: SO536383

WIGMORE CASTLE

HEREFORDSHIRE – HR6 9UB

Among the most unusual ruins in England, this stronghold of the turbulent medieval Mortimer family is now maintained as a romantic ruin and conserved for its wildlife habitats. Many of its part-buried fortifications survive, including its towering keep-mound.

OPENING TIMES

Any reasonable daylight hours

WIGMORE CASTLE

VISIT US

Direction: Located 8 miles W of Ludlow on A4110. Accessible via footpath ¾ mile from the village on Mortimer Way

Train: Bucknell 6 miles, Ludlow 10 miles

Bus: Visit traveline.info for the latest bus timetables and routes

ACQ.1995 🐕 P ⚠

Parking at Wigmore Village Hall. Toilets in the village hall are open from Easter to October half-term, inclusive. There is a disabled toilet with ramp access.

Caution: the site contains steep steps, which are hazardous in icy and wet conditions. Children must stay under close control. Please do not climb on the walls or banks. Strong footwear is recommended.

MAP PAGE 308 (5B)
OS MAP 137/148, 203: SO408693

SHROPSHIRE

ACTON BURNELL CASTLE

SHROPSHIRE – SY5 7PF

The dramatic battlemented red sandstone shell of one of the earliest medieval English fortified mansions, in an atmospheric wooded setting by an attractive Shropshire village. Begun after 1284 by Bishop Robert Burnell, a local man who rose to prominence as King Edward I's Lord Chancellor, its large windows demonstrate that it was designed for show rather than defence. It once contained the lavish private apartments at the core of a much larger house, where King Edward stayed in 1283, holding a famous Parliament nearby. Bishop Burnell's impressive church stands beside it.

OPENING TIMES

Any reasonable daylight hours

VISIT US

Direction: Located in Acton Burnell, signposted from A49, 8 miles S of Shrewsbury

Train: Shrewsbury or Church Stretton, both 8 miles

Bus: Visit traveline.info for the latest bus timetables and routes

ACQ.1930 ♿ 🐕 P ⚠

Please do not climb on the walls.

Car park is closed at dusk.

MAP PAGE 308 (4C)
OS MAP 126, 241: SJ534019

BUILDWAS ABBEY

SHROPSHIRE – TF8 7BW

Impressive ruins of a Cistercian abbey, including its unusually unaltered 12th-century church, beautiful vaulted chapter house and crypt chapel.

In a wooded Severn-side setting, near the Iron Bridge (p.189) and Wenlock Priory (p.191).

OPENING TIMES

Open daily 1 Apr-28 Mar

Site closed 24-26, 31 Dec & 1 Jan

See website for latest opening times

BUILDWAS ABBEY

VISIT US

Direction: On S bank of River Severn on A4169, 2 miles W of Ironbridge

Train: Telford Central 6 miles

Bus: Visit traveline.info for the latest bus timetables and routes

ACQ.1925 ♿ 🐕 📷 P ⚠

Disabled access is limited.

Parking: charges apply to non-members, free for Members with valid car sticker.

Caution: unguarded drops, falling masonry. Please do not climb on the walls.

MAP PAGE 308 (4C)
OS MAP 127, 242: SJ643043

CANTLOP BRIDGE

SHROPSHIRE – SY5 7DD

A single-span, cast-iron road bridge over the Cound Brook. Possibly designed and certainly approved by the great engineer Thomas Telford, who was instrumental in shaping industrial Shropshire and the West Midlands.

OPENING TIMES

Any reasonable daylight hours

VISIT US

Direction: ¾ mile SW of Berrington on an unclassified road off A458

Train: Shrewsbury 5 miles

Bus: Visit traveline.info for the latest bus timetables and routes

ACQ.1977 ♿ 🐕 P ⚠

Parking in lay-by.

Caution: deep water, sheer drop into water.

MAP PAGE 308 (4C)
OS MAP 126, 241: SJ517062

BOSCOBEL HOUSE AND THE ROYAL OAK

SHROPSHIRE – ST19 9AR

Boscobel House and its Royal Oak tree played a starring role in English history, hiding the young Charles II from his Cromwellian pursuers. Our family-friendly 'Hide and Seek' representation transforms visits to the house and its surroundings. It brings to life both the king's hairsbreadth escape and Boscobel's later life as a busy Victorian farm.

Originally surrounded by dense woodland, Boscobel House was ostensibly a hunting lodge, but also a secret hiding place for persecuted Catholics. So it was an ideal refuge for the 21-year-old Charles II, fleeing for his life from Cromwellian troopers after his Civil War defeat at Worcester in 1651.

Imaginative interactive interpretation in the house – backed up on selected days by storytellers in period costume – leads you through the king's 'Hide and Seek' visit. Pick up an electronic candle, which conjures up sights and sounds as you explore the rooms. You'll discover how he hid for 14 hours in the 'Royal Oak' tree before spending a cramped night in a still-visible priest's hole in the house. Interactives help families to seek the king's hiding place and puzzle out the crucial choices faced by ordinary men and women during the turbulent Civil War period.

You'll also find the house's extensive surroundings looking more as they did when Charles took refuge here. Following a contemporary illustration, we've strikingly revived the 1651 style of the gardens, complete with period box hedging and flowers and the recreated 'pretty arbour upon a

mount' where Charles briefly relaxed. From here you can see dozens of young oak trees recently planted near the veteran Royal Oak, beginning to restore its original woodland setting.

More features tempt children to play historical hide-and-seek. There's a winding willow tunnel to explore near the gardens, and the tree-themed playground includes a tunnel, aerial walkway, slide, basket swing and willow pod. It's conveniently sited near the tearoom in a former stable, with indoor and outdoor seating.

There are farm animals to meet, too, helping to vividly revive Boscobel's later life as a Victorian farm. You can also discover the stables, barn, smithy, earth closet privies and other atmospheric farm buildings. Models and audios suggest how they were used, and who used them.

QR codes around the site help you to delve deeper into its history.

The descendant of the original Royal Oak stands near the house, and a pretty 20-minute country walk takes you to White Ladies Priory (p.190), another of Charles II's hiding places.

DON'T MISS

Meeting real rare breed farm animals, recalling those which lived at Victorian Boscobel farm. There are chickens, ducks, charming Tamworth pigs and Shropshire and Coloured Ryeland sheep. Younger children won't want to miss the imaginative tree-themed Hide and Seek playground.

OPENING TIMES

Open daily 1 Apr-5 Nov

Open varying days 6 Nov-28 Mar

Site closed 24-26 Dec & 1 Jan

See website for latest opening times

Last entry 1 hour before closing

VISIT US

Address: Brewood, Bishop's Wood, Shropshire ST19 9AR

Direction: 8 miles NW of Wolverhampton. On minor road off A41 Whitchurch road, north of M54 Junction 3. Turn right at Bell Inn, then after 3 miles right again at Bishop's Wood Village Hall

Train: Cosford 3 miles

Bus: Visit traveline.info for the latest bus timetables and routes

Tel: 01902 850295

NON-MEMBERS

See website for entry prices

By being a Member, you save up to £41.50 (price of a family ticket) when you visit **Boscobel House and The Royal Oak.**

ACQ 1954

Dogs on leads (grounds only).

Parking (coaches welcome but must book with site in advance).

Disabled access limited. For visitors with mobility issues, free tablets available at the shop offer a virtual tour of the house.

MAP PAGE 308 (4D)
OS MAP 127, 242: SJ838082

CLUN CASTLE

SHROPSHIRE – SY7 8JT

Dramatic riverside ruins and earthworks of a Welsh Border castle, its tall 13th-century keep unusually set on the side of its mound. Panels tell the story of the castle and adjacent town.

OPENING TIMES

Any reasonable daylight hours

VISIT US

Direction: In Clun, off A488, 18 miles W of Ludlow

Train: Hopton Heath 6½ miles; Knighton 6½ miles

Bus: Visit traveline.info for the latest bus timetables and routes

ACQ.1991

Toilets available in car park (not managed by English Heritage).

Caution: steep slopes, sheer drop into water.

MAP PAGE 308 (5B)
OS MAP 137, 201: SO299809

LANGLEY CHAPEL

SHROPSHIRE – SY5 7HU

LANGLEY CHAPEL

Experience what churches looked like before the Victorians. This uniquely unaltered chapel, amid remote countryside, has a perfect set of rustic Jacobean furnishings, including gentry box pews, canopied pulpit and musicians' pew.

OPENING TIMES

See website for latest opening times

VISIT US

Direction: 9½ miles S of Shrewsbury and 1½ miles S of Acton Burnell, on an unclassified narrow road. Signposted from Acton Burnell

Train: Shrewsbury 7½ miles

Bus: Visit traveline.info for the latest bus timetables and routes

ACQ.1914

Very limited parking (2 cars).

MAP PAGE 308 (4C)
OS MAP 126/127/138, 217/241: SJ538001

HAUGHMOND ABBEY SHROPSHIRE – SY4 4RW

Extensive remains of an Augustinian abbey, including its abbots' quarters and cloister. The chapter house displays rich 12th- and 14th-century carving and a fine timber roof.

LILLESHALL ABBEY

SHROPSHIRE – TF10 9HW

Extensive Augustinian abbey ruins, in a deeply rural setting. Much of the church survives, unusually viewable from gallery level, along with an elaborate processional doorway.

OPENING TIMES

Open daily 1 Apr-28 Mar

Site closed 24-26, 31 Dec & 1 Jan

See website for latest opening times

VISIT US

Direction: On an unclassified road off A518, 4 miles N of Oakengates

Train: Oakengates 4½ miles

Bus: Visit traveline.info for the latest bus timetables and routes

ACQ.1950

Disabled access (kissing gate only).

Guidebook available from online shop.

1 Nov-31 Mar, parking on roadside only with access via kissing gate.

Caution: steep stairs.

Please do not climb on the walls.

MAP PAGE 308 (4C)
OS MAP 127, 242: SJ738142

OPENING TIMES

Open daily 1 Apr-28 Mar

Site closed 24-26, 31 Dec & 1 Jan

See website for latest opening times

VISIT US

Direction: Located 3 miles NE of Shrewsbury off B5062

Train: Shrewsbury 3½ miles

Bus: Visit traveline.info

ACQ.1931

Disabled access is limited.

Guidebook available from online shop.

Please do not climb on the walls.

MAP PAGE 308 (4C)
OS MAP 126, 241: SJ542152

IRON BRIDGE

— SHROPSHIRE – TF8 7JP —

This famous structure is the world's very first iron bridge, an iconic symbol of the Industrial Revolution. Our £3.6m conservation project has safeguarded the bridge for future generations.

Britain's best-known industrial monument was erected over the River Severn in 1779. It gave its name to spectacular wooded Ironbridge Gorge, once an industrial powerhouse and the cradle of the Industrial Revolution. Ironbridge Gorge is now a World Heritage Site.

In the early 18th century, Abraham Darby I pioneered the process of using coke made from local coal to smelt iron ore. Expansion was hampered by the lack of a bridge over the Severn here, and any bridge had to be a single span to allow barge traffic. Abraham Darby III cast the bridge in his Coalbrookdale foundry, using 378 tons of iron, at a cost of over £6,000. A crucial turning point in design and engineering, this testament to the achievements of Shropshire ironmasters remained in use by traffic until 1934.

Over the 240 years since it was built, the bridge suffered many stresses, some dating from its original construction. Ground movement in the surrounding gorge, countless floods and even an earthquake in 1896 had left the historic structure under threat, placing stresses on the ironwork and leading to cracking. Our major conservation project has repaired and protected the bridge for the future. Among changes is the colour of the bridge, restored to its original dark red-brown after samples of the earliest historic paintwork were discovered as part of the project.

For more information about the conservation project, visit english-heritage.org.uk/visit/places/iron-bridge/project-iron-bridge/

OPENING TIMES
Any reasonable daylight hours

VISIT US
Direction: Adjacent to A4169

Train: Telford Central 5 miles

Bus: Visit **traveline.info** for the latest bus timetables and routes

ACQ 1975 ♿ ♖ Ｐ

Parking (charge applies). Car park not managed by English Heritage.

MAP PAGE 308 (4C)
OS MAP 127, 242: SJ672034

MITCHELL'S FOLD STONE CIRCLE

SHROPSHIRE – SY15 6DE

Neolithic stone circle, the focus of many legends, set amid dramatic moorland. It once consisted of some 30 stones – 15 are still visible.

OPENING TIMES

Any reasonable daylight hours

VISIT US

Direction: 16 miles SW of Shrewsbury, on unclassified road off A488

Train: Welshpool 10 miles

Bus: Visit traveline.info for the latest bus timetables and routes

ACQ. 1915

Parking in lay-by at end of track – no vehicular access onto the moor.

MAP PAGE 308 (4B)
OS MAP 137, 216: SO304984

CHECK ONLINE

Pre-booking for visits to our staffed sites may be required, check our website for the latest guidance.

MORETON CORBET CASTLE

SHROPSHIRE – SY4 4DW

Ruins of the castle and Tudor mansion of the Corbets, dominated by the theatrical shell of an Elizabethan wing, devastated during the Civil War.

OPENING TIMES

Any reasonable daylight hours

VISIT US

Direction: In Moreton Corbet off B5063 (a turning off A49), 7 miles NE of Shrewsbury

Train: Yorton 4 miles

Bus: Visit traveline.info for the latest bus timetables and routes

ACQ. 1939

Disabled access is limited.

Guidebook available from online shop.

Caution: hidden drops.

Please do not climb on the walls.

MAP PAGE 308 (4C)
OS MAP 126, 241: SJ561231

OLD OSWESTRY HILLFORT

SHROPSHIRE – SY11 1DR

Among the most hugely impressive Iron Age hillforts on the Welsh Borders, covering 40 acres, with formidable multiple ramparts.

OPENING TIMES

Any reasonable daylight hours

VISIT US

Direction: 1 mile N of Oswestry, off an unclassified road off A483

OLD OSWESTRY HILLFORT

Train: Gobowen 2 miles

Bus: Visit traveline.info for the latest bus timetables and routes

ACQ. 1946

Parking at top of Gateacre Ave.

Dogs on leads (restricted areas only).

Caution: steep slopes.

MAP PAGE 308 (3B)
OS MAP 126, 240/258: SJ295310

WHITE LADIES PRIORY

SHROPSHIRE – WV8 1QZ

Ruined Norman church of a nunnery of 'white ladies', later part of a vanished mansion. Charles II rested here in 1651 before seeking refuge at nearby Boscobel House (p.186).

Best reached via a footpath from Boscobel House (approximately 20 minutes' walk).

OPENING TIMES

Any reasonable daylight hours

VISIT US

Direction: Located 1 mile SW of Boscobel House off an unclassified road between A41 and A5; 8 miles NW of Wolverhampton

Train: Cosford 2½ miles

Bus: Visit traveline.info for the latest bus timetables and routes

ACQ. 1938

Toilet facilities, café and shop available at Boscobel House.

Very limited roadside parking. Other parking at Boscobel House.

Caution: CCTV at site.

MAP PAGE 308 (4D)
OS MAP 217, 242: SJ826076

WENLOCK PRIORY

SHROPSHIRE – TF13 6HS

The tranquil ruins of Wenlock Priory are picturesquely sited on the fringe of Much Wenlock.

An Anglo-Saxon monastery was founded here by King Merewalh of Mercia, whose abbess daughter Milburga became a saint. Her relics were miraculously rediscovered here in 1101, attracting both pilgrims and prosperity.

By then Wenlock had been refounded as a Norman Cluniac priory. Its impressive remains reflect everywhere the Cluniac love of elaborate decoration. Parts of the great 13th-century church still stand high; and there is a replica of an unusual monks' washing fountain with 12th-century carvings. The priory's greatest glory is the extravagantly decorated chapter house, its walls bedecked with interlocking round arches on multiple carved columns.

Set in a topiary-filled garden, against the backdrop of the monastic infirmary wing, later converted into a mansion and still a private residence.

OPENING TIMES

Open daily 1 Apr-5 Nov

Open varying days 6 Nov-28 Mar

Site closed 24-26 Dec & 1 Jan

See website for latest opening times

Last entry 30 mins before closing

VISIT US

Direction: In Much Wenlock

Train: Telford Central 9 miles

Bus: Visit traveline.info for the latest bus timetables and routes

Tel: 01952 727466

NON-MEMBERS

See website for entry prices

ACQ.1964

Parking: charges apply to non-members, free for Members with valid English Heritage car sticker.

MAP PAGE 308 (4C)
OS MAP 127/138, 217/242: SJ625001

STOKESAY CASTLE

SHROPSHIRE – SY7 9AH

Stokesay Castle is the finest and best-preserved fortified medieval manor house in England. Unobtrusive interpretation and a children's riddle quest help you to explore the history and legends of this atmospherically unaltered survival from the Middle Ages.

A treasure bypassed by time, the moated manor, timber-framed gatehouse and parish church make an unforgettably picturesque group. Though 'builded like a castle', Stokesay was really a lightly defended mansion, designed for comfort and show as well as security. Lawrence of Ludlow, the wealthiest wool merchant in England, began rebuilding it in about 1285. Tree-ring dating proves that work was completed by 1291, with the same team of carpenters used throughout. Amazingly, the dating also revealed that Stokesay has changed very little since; there are few places in England where you can see so much unaltered medieval timberwork.

So that you can discover Stokesay's story while still experiencing its unspoiled atmosphere, we've discreetly installed information panels into period-style features, showing how the rooms were used. There's also an absorbing audio tour. Families can follow an intriguing puzzle quest, inspired by the legend of two giants who lived on wooded hills flanking the castle. Riddles and clues tucked away throughout the castle help you track down the giants' lost key.

There's plenty to see here. In the magnificent open-hearthed great hall you can admire a fine timber roof and shuttered gable windows, and even climb an original 13th-century staircase with treads cut from whole tree trunks. This leads to

the three-storey north tower, featuring a room with a medieval tiled floor and a spacious second-floor guest chamber. On the other side of the hall is a 'solar' (private apartment) block and the tall south tower – the most defensible and castle-like part of the house – offering wonderful views when you climb via tiers of rooms to its battlements.

The solar block includes one of the few later additions to Stokesay, a magnificent panelled chamber. It's dominated by a fireplace with a richly carved overmantel, where you can just trace original painting in five colours. This was created in about 1641, at the same time as the delightful castle gatehouse, timber-framed and embellished in the lavish Welsh Marches style. Look out for the 'Stokesay dragons' and charming carvings of Adam and Eve.

Outside, you can enjoy the courtyard garden, replanted in the Edwardian cottage garden style of 1908. Don't miss a walk round the dry moat for impressive exterior views of the castle walls and the north tower's overhanging timber-framed 'jetty', and look into the adjacent parish church with its unusually unchanged 17th-century interior (not managed by English Heritage). Just outside the castle, the attractive cottage tearoom is open to all and is dog friendly. It has an outdoor play space and additional outdoor seating with views of the surrounding Welsh Border hills.

FILM STAR

Stokesay Castle plays a starring role in a new film, *Catherine, called Birdy*, released in September 2022. Written and directed by Lena Dunham, it stars Andrew Scott and Billie Piper as the parents of Catherine (played by Bella Ramsey of *Game of Thrones*), a medieval teenager struggling to avoid an arranged marriage and live a life of her own. It's set in 1290, almost exactly the year when Stokesay Castle was completed, so there couldn't be a better place to film it.

OPENING TIMES

Open daily 1 Apr-5 Nov

Open varying days 6 Nov-28 Mar

Site closed 24-26 Dec & 1 Jan

See website for latest opening times

Last entry 30 mins before closing

VISIT US

Address: Stokesay Castle, Nr Craven Arms, Shropshire SY7 9AH

Direction: 7 miles NW of Ludlow off A49

Train: Craven Arms 1 mile

Bus: Visit traveline.info for the latest bus timetables and routes

Tel: 01588 672544

Local Tourist Information:
Ludlow: 01584 875053

NON-MEMBERS

See website for entry prices

ACQ.1986

SAVE TODAY By being a Member, you save up to £36.50 (price of a family ticket) when you visit **Stokesay Castle**.

Disabled access (call site for details).

Dogs allowed within the grounds on a lead but not allowed within the castle.

Entrance to the courtyard is through a historic gate. Unsuitable for motorised scooters and unassisted wheelchair users. Cottage tearoom fully accessible.

Cottage tearoom is outside the castle and open to all. It closes 30 minutes before castle.

Parking: charges apply to non-members, free for Members with valid car sticker.

Caution: some steep unlit staircases within the castle, especially in the south tower.

MAP PAGE 308 (5B)
OS MAP 137/148, 203: SO436815

WROXETER ROMAN CITY

SHROPSHIRE – SY5 6PJ

Journey back through the centuries to encounter the wonders of Wroxeter's glorious past, its buildings, its people and the Wroxeter Roman way of life.

Equal in size to Pompeii, Wroxeter (or Viriconium), was once among the largest cities in Roman Britain. Today you can explore the remains of the heart of the city and its most important public buildings, forming the bath house complex: the bathing suite, the market ('macellum') and bath house basilica. Here people came to exercise, but also to seek cures for ailments and curses, as well as beauty treatments and hairstyling. You can also see a recreation of a Roman town house, built for the Channel 4 series *Rome Wasn't Built in a Day*.

🎬 *Rome Wasn't Built in a Day* (2011); *I am Patrick* (2020)

NEW SUMMER 2023

Major new interpretation focuses on Wroxeter's prosperous heyday in the 2nd to 3rd centuries, when many wealthy people lived here in large town houses and a specifically Romano-British town life developed. A redisplayed museum highlights many site-finds never displayed before. Personal possessions, jewellery and specialist equipment reveal the daily lives of 'Wroxeter Romans' – a cast of characters including an elite couple, a market trader, a witch and a doctor. Graphic panels feature new reconstruction illustrations. There are family-friendly interactives and a refreshed audio tour.

OPENING TIMES

Open daily 1 Apr-5 Nov

Open varying days 6 Nov-28 Mar

Site closed 24-26 Dec & 1 Jan

See website for latest opening times

Last entry 30 mins before closing

VISIT US

Direction: 5 miles SE of Shrewsbury, on a minor road signposted from the B4380

Train: Shrewsbury 5½ miles; Wellington Telford West 6 miles

Bus: Visit traveline.info for the latest bus timetables and routes

Tel: 01743 761330

NON-MEMBERS

See website for entry prices

By being a Member, you save up to **£32.50** (price of a family ticket) when you visit **Wroxeter Roman City**

An education room is available for schools.

Light refreshments are available.

MAP PAGE 308 (4C)
OS MAP 126, 241: SJ565087

CROXDEN ABBEY
STAFFORDSHIRE – ST14 5JG

OPENING TIMES
Open daily 1 Apr-28 Mar

Site closed 24-26, 31 Dec & 1 Jan

See website for latest opening times

VISIT US
Direction: 5 miles NW of Uttoxeter off A522

Train: Uttoxeter 6 miles

Bus: Visit **traveline.info** for the latest bus timetables and routes

ACQ.1936

Limited parking.

Caution: unguarded drops.

Please do not climb on the walls.

MAP PAGE 308 (3E)
OS MAP 128, 259: SK066397

The impressive ruins of an abbey of Cistercian 'white monks', once prosperous from sheep farming. They include the towering west walls and tall lancet windows of its 13th-century church, its infirmary and 14th-century abbot's lodging. Information panels and a decorative stonework display tell the story of Croxden's spectacular architecture.

WALL ROMAN SITE (LETOCETUM)
STAFFORDSHIRE – WS14 0AW

OPENING TIMES
Open Air Site
Any reasonable daylight hours

Museum
See website for latest opening times

VISIT US
Direction: Off Eastbound A5 at Wall, near Lichfield

Train: Shenstone 1½ miles

Bus: Visit traveline.info

ACQ.1949

Parking (not English Heritage).

Toilet facilities are available during museum opening hours.

New guidebook.

Caution: beware of traffic.

Please do not climb on the walls.

MAP PAGE 308 (4E)
OS MAP 139, 244: SK098066

An important staging post on Watling Street, the Roman military road to North Wales, Wall provided overnight accommodation for travelling Roman officials and imperial messengers. It displays foundations of an inn and bath house, with excavated finds in the on-site museum.

Managed by English Heritage for the National Trust, with thanks to the Friends of Letocetum.

KENILWORTH CASTLE AND ELIZABETHAN GARDEN

WARWICKSHIRE – CV8 1NG

Spend a royal day out at spectacular Kenilworth Castle. Hear tales of the castle from our costumed storytellers, climb to lofty viewing platforms for a 'queen's-eye view' of the castle and enjoy playful new viewfinders in the famous Elizabethan Garden.

A vast medieval fortress, which endured an epic siege and later became an Elizabethan palace, Kenilworth Castle is among Britain's biggest historic sites. Extensive developments highlight Kenilworth's famous associations with Queen Elizabeth I and her favourite, Robert Dudley.

Spanning more than nine centuries, Kenilworth's varied buildings reflect its long connection with English monarchs. Henry I's treasurer began the massive Norman keep in the 1120s, Henry II made Kenilworth a royal castle and King John greatly strengthened it. Thus it could withstand the longest siege in medieval English history in 1266, when rebellious barons held out here for six months. In the impressively timbered Tudor stables, which also house the tearoom, you can see trebuchet balls from the siege in the interactive display of the castle's history.

John of Gaunt, Duke of Lancaster, rebuilt Kenilworth's inner court, beginning the castle's transition into a favoured residence of the Lancastrian and early Tudor kings. You can still admire the shell of Gaunt's 14th-century Great Hall. By Henry VIII's time it was already renowned for its 'many fair chambers'. The scene was set for Kenilworth's greatest period of fame.

This began when Queen Elizabeth I's childhood friend, Robert Dudley, Earl of Leicester, took possession of the castle in 1563. He then lavished fortunes on converting it into a great showpiece mansion, designed to receive the queen and her court on their ceremonial 'progresses' around England. You can see striking evidence of his transformation everywhere at Kenilworth, including the tall, mansion-sized 'Leicester's Building' designed specifically for the queen's use.

Viewing platforms within Leicester's Building allow you to climb 18 metres (59 feet) to the level of the queen's apartments. Here you can admire fantastic views over the castle and surrounding countryside, once enjoyed only by Elizabeth and her highest-ranking courtiers. Interpretation helps you imagine this miniature palace in its heyday.

Leicester's Gatehouse is the imposing entrance to his transformed 'wonder-house'. Discover its lower floor chambers recreated as they might have appeared in the 1930s. On its top floor, take in an exhibition telling the story of Elizabeth I's relationship with Dudley and her four visits to his castle.

DON'T
MISS

Playful new viewfinders exploring Queen Elizabeth's 1575 visit and the pageant Robert Dudley mounted to impress her. You can imagine what happened in five locations within the castle grounds, and then view specially commissioned illustrations revealing scenes from the queen's arrival to flamboyant pageant displays.

On selected days, you can also hear tales of Kenilworth Castle from our costumed storytellers. Encounter an Elizabethan lady-in-waiting and learn about the queen's visit. Speak to our friendly Jester and Storyteller and hear stories of the foundation of the castle, the great siege of 1266, and the work of the mighty John of Gaunt. Or meet the Bear with Ragged Staff in the Elizabethan garden, find out why the garden was made for Elizabeth I and discover more about her relationship with Robert Dudley.

THE ELIZABETHAN GARDEN

On the most famous of these visits, in July 1575, Elizabeth stayed for 19 days. Dudley not only entertained her royally throughout, he also created a fabulous garden especially for her visit. This garden was lost for centuries, but in 2009 we brought it back to life, basing our meticulous recreation on careful archaeological research and the survival of an eye-witness description by a courtier, who sneaked a visit while the queen was out hunting. It presents the most complete evocation of an Elizabethan garden anywhere in the world and opens a window on the period's most enduring love story – that of Elizabeth I and her favourite, Robert Dudley.

Among the glories of the garden you'll discover a Renaissance aviary, plant beds full of scent, colour and fruit, and an imposing fountain carved from Carrara marble. The rejuvenated garden features refreshed paths, flower beds and woodwork, and a garden gate. Families can play Tudor garden games, and new viewfinders in five locations help you recreate the queen's most famous visit.

The 'Speed and Power' exhibition in the gatehouse celebrates Coventry-based motoring and aviation pioneer John Siddeley, first Baron Kenilworth, who gave the castle to the nation in 1938. Exhibits celebrate his cars and planes, and there's a family room where families can play together.

OPENING TIMES

Open daily 1 Apr–5 Nov

Open varying days 6 Nov–28 Mar

Site closed 24-25 Dec

See website for latest opening times

Last entry 30 mins before closing

VISIT US

Address: Kenilworth Castle, Castle Green, off Castle Road, Kenilworth, Warwickshire CV8 1NG

Direction: In Kenilworth off A46. Clearly signposted from the town centre, off B4103

Train: Kenilworth 1 mile

Bus: Visit traveline.info for the latest bus timetables and routes

Tel: 01926 852078

Local Tourist Information:
Kenilworth: 0300 555 8171

SAVE TODAY By being a Member, you save up to £52.50 (price of a family ticket) when you visit **Kenilworth Castle and Elizabethan Garden.**

NON-MEMBERS

See website for entry prices

ACQ 1938

Audio tours available (English, French, German and a children's version). Audio tours not available on special event days.

Tearoom open as per site, closing 30 minutes before the site closes.

Parking: charges apply to non-members, free for Members with valid car sticker.

MAP PAGE 308 (5E)
OS MAP 140, 221: SP278723

J.W. EVANS SILVER FACTORY
BIRMINGHAM – B1 3EA

One of the most complete surviving historic factories in Birmingham's Jewellery Quarter, established in 1881. Behind the frontage of terraced houses, the workshops retain their dies for silverware manufacture, working equipment, stock and business records. English Heritage rescued the factory in 2008. Pre-booked guided tours only.

OPENING TIMES
Pre-booked tours only. For dates and booking please go to our website

VISIT US
Direction: 54-57 Albion Street, ½ mile from city centre

Train: Birmingham New Street or Birmingham Snow Hill ½ mile

Bus: Visit traveline.info

Tel: 0370 333 1181

ACQ.2008

MAP PAGE 308 (5E)
OS MAP 139, 220: SP062870

HALESOWEN ABBEY
WEST MIDLANDS – B62 8RJ

Remains of an abbey founded by King John in the 13th century.

OPENING TIMES
Open to view from the public footpath only

VISIT US
Direction: Off A456, ½ mile W of J3, M5

Train: Old Hill 2½ miles

Bus: Visit traveline.info

ACQ.1976

MAP PAGE 308 (5D)
OS MAP 139, 219: SO975828

WORCESTERSHIRE

LEIGH COURT BARN
WORCESTERSHIRE – WR6 5LB

An outstanding display of medieval carpentry, this huge 14th-century timber-framed barn is the largest cruck-framed structure in Britain, 46 metres (150 feet) long.

OPENING TIMES
See website for latest opening times

VISIT US
Direction: 5 miles west of Worcester, on minor road signposted from A4103 at Bransford roundabout. Footpath to barn signposted at gateway to Leigh Court (private), next to church

Train: Worcester Foregate Street 5 miles

Bus: Visit traveline.info

ACQ.1990   ♿ ⊗

Very limited parking on roadside verges near church.

Access via kissing gate.

MAP PAGE 308 (6D)
OS MAP 150, 204: SO783535

WITLEY COURT AND GARDENS

WORCESTERSHIRE – WR6 6JT

Inspire the whole family with a day out at Witley Court. Guided by new interpretation, explore the Victorian mansion amid vast and beautiful grounds. Experience the legendary Perseus and Andromeda fountain, admire the colourful formal gardens, wander enchanted woodland walks and try out the imaginative wilderness play area.

In its late-Victorian heyday Witley Court was staffed by over a hundred servants. It hosted lavish house parties attended by the Prince of Wales – later Edward VII – and his opulent friends, while at Christmas the ballroom's tree was hung with jewellery for female guests. The house fell into decline after the First World War and was accidentally burnt to a roofless shell in 1937. Wander through its dramatic Italianate ruins and you can still conjure up images of its glamorous past.

We've recreated the mansion's colourful formal gardens, originally laid out from the 1850s by leading landscape designer William Andrews Nesfield. The East Parterre, with its Flora Fountain, imitates embroidery, while the elegant South Parterre focuses on the astonishing Perseus and Andromeda fountain.

One of Europe's greatest fountains, this dramatically depicts the legendary Greek hero Perseus swooping down on his winged horse Pegasus to rescue the beautiful Andromeda, chained to a rock as a sacrifice to a sea monster. Its central jet reaches a height of up to 30 metres, complemented by nearly 30 more jets hidden among shells, sea nymphs and dolphins. Fully restored to working order, between April and October it fires on the hour from 11am until an hour before closing – a sight and sound not to be missed.

Wend your way up to the mansion through Witley's paradise of wild gardens, with their winding paths, rustic bridges, surprise lake vistas, trees and flowering shrubs from all over the world. Enchanting woodland walks are signposted for you, including a lakeside path to the Victorian boathouse: they offer glimpses of the park's abundant wildlife. Near the visitor centre is an 'organic' wilderness play area for children. With lots of exciting activities for different age groups, it's sure to fire their imaginations. The centrepiece is a tree house, reached by a wobbly bridge. A section for younger children includes a nest-like basket swing and wooden animal rides. There's also an adventure area with a scramble net and rope walks. However many visits they make, children will have a different experience every time they come.

Leave time to visit Great Witley Church, attached to the mansion, with its golden dome and gleaming gilded baroque interior. There's a tearoom near the church. (Please note: church and tearoom not managed by English Heritage.)

Stay in our *Pool House* holiday cottage (see p.13).

NEW FOR 2023

We've developed new interpretation to help you explore and enjoy Witley Court and its wonderful gardens. There's a new audio guide and family trail, and new information panels reflecting the latest research on the mansion and estate.

You can also see a specially commissioned installation by contemporary artist Keith Harrison. It's inspired by Witley Court's relationship with the coal, iron and steel industries of the Black Country – which funded the opulent lifestyle of the Earl of Dudley, owner of the mansion at the peak of its grandeur.

OPENING TIMES

Open daily 1 Apr–5 Nov

Open varying days 6 Nov–28 Mar

Site closed 24–26 Dec & 1 Jan

See website for latest opening times

Last entry 1 hour before closing

VISIT US

Address: Witley Court, Worcester Road, Great Witley, Worcestershire WR6 6JT

Direction: 10 miles NW of Worcester on A443

Train: Droitwich Spa 8½ miles

Bus: Visit traveline.info for the latest bus timetables and routes

Tel: 01299 896636

Local Tourist Information: Worcester: 01905 726311

By being a Member, you save up to £36.50 (price of a family ticket) when you visit **Witley Court.**

NON-MEMBERS

See website for entry prices

ACQ 1972

Disabled access (exterior and grounds only). A terrain guide is available on the website.

Tearoom (seasonal): 1 Apr–end of Oct (not managed by English Heritage).

Parking: charges apply to non-members, free for Members with valid car sticker.

MAP PAGE 308 (6D)
OS MAP 138/150, 204: SO769649

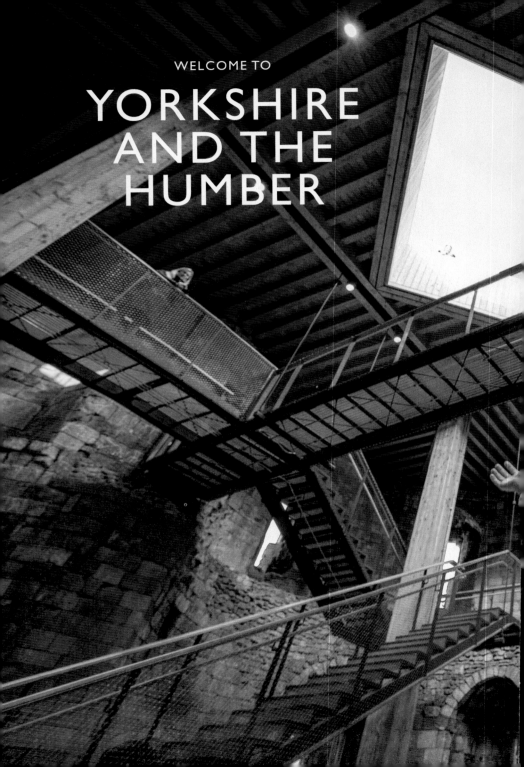

WELCOME TO

YORKSHIRE
AND THE
HUMBER

Clifford's Tower, York, North Yorkshire

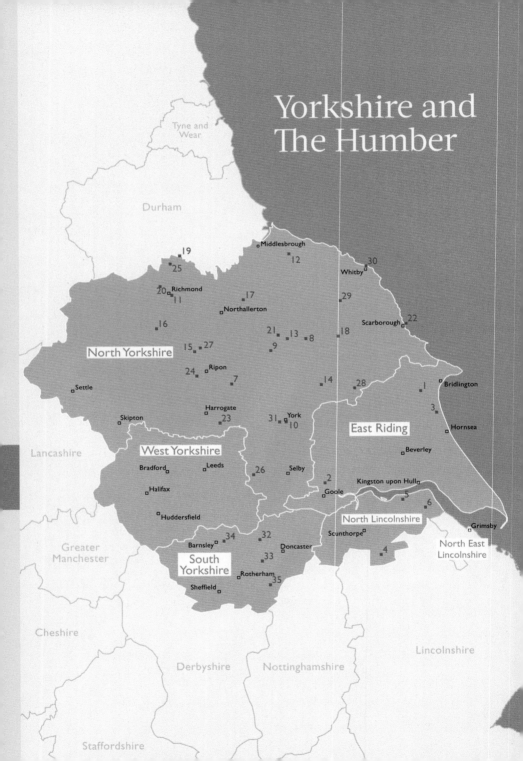

YORKSHIRE AND THE HUMBER

There are a host of heritage highlights across Yorkshire.

At **Brodsworth Hall** (p.230) you can trace the fortunes of a family and explore acres of award-winning Victorian gardens. Head to the North York Moors to visit the soaring ruins of **Rievaulx Abbey** (p.222) or **Mount Grace Priory** (p.218), where you can discover beautiful Arts and Crafts gardens and the remains of cells which once housed hermit-like monks of the austere Carthusian order. On the coast, **Whitby Abbey** (p.226) has inspired saints and writers over the centuries, including St Hild and the creator of *Dracula*.

We care for eight castles in the region, including **Scarborough** (p.224), **Richmond** (p.220), **Middleham** (p.217), **Conisbrough** (p.229), **Helmsley** (p.214) and York, where a major project has transformed the experience of visiting **Clifford's Tower** (p.210). Elsewhere in the city, **York's Cold War Bunker** (p.228) shines a light on our more recent past.

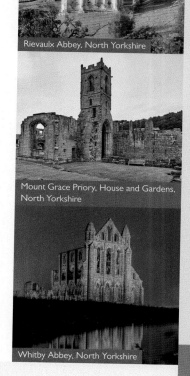

Rievaulx Abbey, North Yorkshire

Mount Grace Priory, House and Gardens, North Yorkshire

Whitby Abbey, North Yorkshire

BURTON AGNES MANOR HOUSE

EAST RIDING OF YORKSHIRE
– YO25 4NB

A medieval manor house interior, with an atmospheric vaulted Norman undercroft and a 15th-century roof. Encased in brick walls in the 18th century, when it became a laundry.

OPENING TIMES

See website for latest opening times

The nearby Burton Agnes Hall and Gardens are privately owned and are not managed by English Heritage. Entrance to the Manor House remains free but access is via the Hall and Gardens: please tell Hall staff that you are visiting the Manor House

VISIT US

Direction: In Burton Agnes village, 5 miles SW of Bridlington on A166

Train: Nafferton 5 miles

Bus: Visit traveline.info for the latest bus timetables and routes

ACQ.1948 🐕 🚶 ♿ 🅿 ⛺ 🍴 📷 ⚠

Parking (in Hall and Gardens car park).

Caution: steep stairs.

MAP PAGE 311 (3J)
OS MAP 101, 295: TA102632

HOWDEN MINSTER

EAST RIDING OF YORKSHIRE
– DN14 7BS

HOWDEN MINSTER

The ruins of an elaborately decorated 14th-century chancel and chapter house (exterior viewing only), attached to the working 'minster' parish church of Howden.

OPENING TIMES

Any reasonable daylight hours

Site closed 24-26, 31 Dec & 1 Jan

VISIT US

Direction: In Howden, 23 miles W of Kingston Upon Hull, 25 miles SE of York, near the junction of A63 and A614

Train: Howden 1½ miles

Bus: Visit traveline.info for the latest bus timetables and routes

ACQ.1971 🐕 🅿

Parking (on-street parking nearby – pay and display).

MAP PAGE 311 (4H)
OS MAP 105/106, 291: SE748283

SKIPSEA CASTLE

EAST RIDING OF YORKSHIRE
– YO25 8TH

Impressive earthworks of a huge Norman motte-and-bailey castle and settlement, perhaps dating from the 1070s and among the first built in Yorkshire. It's been controversially suggested, however, that the immense motte – 85 metres in diameter and 13 metres tall – is actually a reused Iron Age burial mound. If so, it would be unique in Britain.

OPENING TIMES

Any reasonable daylight hours

VISIT US

Direction: Located 8 miles S of Bridlington, W of Skipsea village

Train: Bridlington 9 miles

SKIPSEA CASTLE

Bus: Visit traveline.info for the latest bus timetables and routes

ACQ.1911 🐕 🐄 ⚠

Dogs on leads (restricted areas only).

Waterproof footwear recommended.

Caution: steep slopes.

Beware – cattle may be grazing on site.

MAP PAGE 311 (3J)
OS MAP 107, 295: TA162551

GAINSTHORPE MEDIEVAL VILLAGE

NORTH LINCOLNSHIRE – DN21 4JH

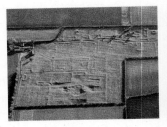

One of the best-preserved deserted medieval villages in England, clearly visible as a complex of grassy humps. According to legend, the village was inhabited by thieves and was demolished by locals who could tolerate them no more.

OPENING TIMES

Any reasonable daylight hours

VISIT US

Direction: Located on minor road W of A15 – towards Cleatham; S of Hibaldstow; 5 miles SW of Brigg

Train: Kirton Lindsey 3 miles

Bus: Visit traveline.info for the latest bus timetables and routes

ACQ.1974 🐄 🐄 ⚠

Access via grazing field.

Beware – livestock may be grazing on site.

MAP PAGE 311 (5H)
OS MAP 112, 281: SE954011

THORNTON ABBEY
& GATEHOUSE

—— NORTH LINCOLNSHIRE – DN39 6TU ——

Among the most extraordinary medieval buildings in England, Thornton Abbey's ornate gatehouse is worth travelling a long way to see.

This largest and most magnificent of all English monastic gatehouses was raised around the 1380s. An early example of large-scale English building in brick, it's bedecked with an extravaganza of turrets, sculpture and carved figures. Within the entrance arch, look out for the original 14th-century doors and medieval graffiti of sailing ships.

Though it's also lavishly equipped with arrow loops and other castle-like features, the gatehouse was built principally for show rather than defence. It proclaimed the wool-trade-based wealth and power of one of the richest Augustinian monasteries in England.

You can explore the gatehouse's intriguing interior, with its two floors of passageways and stairways, 'garderobe' toilets, tiny chambers and two big rooms, one probably housing the abbot's law courts. Now this 'great chamber' displays a wealth of carvings from the ruins, along with an exhibition tracing Thornton Abbey's history, including Henry VIII's visit, the abbey's brief rebirth as a Tudor 'college', and its role in huge Victorian temperance rallies. There's a further display of site finds and tactile features in the small ground-level visitor centre.

Don't miss the tranquil remains of the abbey itself, notably two beautifully decorated walls of the octagonal chapter house of 1282-1308. Full of fascinating features to discover, they're also an ideal place to picnic and relax.

St Peter's Church, Barton-upon-Humber (see p.208) is nearby.

OPENING TIMES
Major conservation works are planned. Please check the website prior to visit

VISIT US
Direction: 18 miles NE of Scunthorpe, on a road N of A160; 7 miles SE of the Humber Bridge, on a road E of A1077

Train: Thornton Abbey ¼ mile

Bus: Visit traveline.info

Tel: 01469 541445

NON-MEMBERS
See website for entry prices

By being a Member, you save up to **£28.50** (price of a family ticket) when you visit **Thornton Abbey & Gatehouse**

Disabled access (except gatehouse interior and part of ruins).

Caution: steep narrow stairs within gatehouse. No dogs allowed as livestock may be grazing around ruins.

MAP PAGE 311 (4J)
OS MAP 113, 284: TA118189

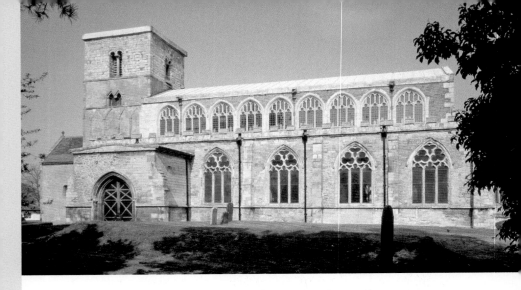

ST PETER'S CHURCH

BARTON-UPON-HUMBER

──── NORTH LINCOLNSHIRE – DN18 5EX ────

An archaeological as well as an architectural treasure, this famous Anglo-Saxon church reveals a thousand fascinating years of the 'Buried Lives' of its people.

The oldest parts of the church, its striking Anglo-Saxon tower and adjacent baptistery, were built in the early 11th century. Look out for the tower's characteristically Saxon triangular-headed windows and decoration with thin stone strips – a feature echoing Saxon timber buildings. In medieval times the church was progressively enlarged, eventually reaching six times its original size: its upper tier of big 15th-century windows fills it with light.

Declared redundant in 1972, the church and churchyard were comprehensively excavated. The remains of nearly 3,000 people were recovered, as well as perfectly preserved medieval coffins. Well preserved by waterlogged ground, they span the thousand years between Anglo-Saxon and Victorian times. Research on them is vividly presented in the Buried Lives display, where you can trace the effects of historic disease, diet and surgery, witness family tragedies and the sometimes mysterious objects buried with bodies, and discover how and why medieval children and adults grew at differing rates from their modern descendants.

Thornton Abbey and Gatehouse (see p.207) is not far away.

OPENING TIMES

Open varying days 1 Apr-5 Nov

Site closed 6 Nov-28 Mar

See website for latest opening times

Last entry 30 mins before closing

VISIT US

Direction: Off Beck Hill, near Barton-upon-Humber town centre

Train: Barton-upon-Humber ½ mile

Bus: Visit traveline.info for the latest bus timetables and routes

Tel: 01652 632516
Thornton Abbey: 01469 541445

NON-MEMBERS

See website for entry prices

By being a Member, you save up to **£21.50** (price of a family ticket) when you visit St Peter's Church

ACQ.1923 Limited parking in adjacent street.

MAP PAGE 311 (4J)
OS MAP 107, 112, 281: TA035219

ALDBOROUGH ROMAN TOWN

NORTH YORKSHIRE – YO51 9ES

Beneath the picturesque village of Aldborough lies the Roman town of Isurium Brigantum,

administrative capital of the Brigantes, the largest tribal confederation in Britain. Remains of its defences are visible amid towering pine trees in a Victorian garden, and two fine Roman mosaics – evidence of the town's prosperity – are displayed within charming period buildings. The refreshed site museum displays an outstanding collection of Roman finds tracing three centuries of archaeology at Isurium, including important recent discoveries. Updated information panels help to guide you round the site.

OPENING TIMES

Open varying days 1 Apr-5 Nov

Site closed 6 Nov-28 Mar

See website for latest opening times

Last entry 30 mins before closing

Please check website for details of Friends of Roman Aldborough tours

VISIT US

Direction: In Aldborough, ¾ mile SE of Boroughbridge on a minor road off B6265; within 1 mile of junction of A1 and A6055

Train: Cattal 7½ miles

Bus: Visit traveline.info for the latest bus timetables and routes

Tel: 01423 322768

NON-MEMBERS

See website for entry prices

Dogs on leads (restricted areas only).

Limited parking on adjacent street.

MAP PAGE 311 (3F)
OS MAP 299, 99: SE405662

BYLAND ABBEY NORTH YORKSHIRE – YO61 4BD

Admire the stately ruins of Byland Abbey, one of Yorkshire's greatest Cistercian monasteries.

Set against a backdrop of wooded hills, Byland was planned to the grandest of designs. The immense church, which today dominates the ruins, was the most ambitious Cistercian church in 12th-century Europe, and helped to pioneer the new

Gothic style of architecture in northern England. You can trace the transition today in the combination of round Norman and pointed Gothic arches, and the towering west front. Decorative tiled floors still adorn many parts of the church.

You can also explore the remains of the monastic buildings, which originally housed some 300

monks and lay brothers, later reduced to just 14 by plague and Scots raiders.

OPENING TIMES

Grounds:
Any reasonable daylight hours

Museum:
Opened by volunteers

See website for latest opening times

VISIT US

Direction: 2 miles S of A170, between Thirsk and Helmsley; near Coxwold village

Train: Thirsk 10 miles

Bus: Visit traveline.info

Parking (adjacent to Abbey Inn).

Toilets and restaurant at Abbey Inn.

Caution: falling masonry.

MAP PAGE 311 (2G)
OS MAP 100, OL26/299: SE549789

CLIFFORD'S TOWER, YORK

NORTH YORKSHIRE – YO1 9SA

Crowning a Norman motte, Clifford's Tower is the largest remaining building of York Castle, northern England's greatest medieval royal fortress. Today, it offers unrivalled views over the ancient city. Our multisensory experience makes the tower's history and interior more accessible than they've been for centuries, bringing its dramatic and sometimes tragic story to life as never before.

At the base of the motte, a visitor welcome area includes a large-scale timeline and a tactile map of the castle and city. To make climbing the steep tower steps easier, there are three well-spaced resting places. For visitors unable to access the tower, a new virtual tour is available via the English Heritage website.

As York Castle's keep, Clifford's Tower was commissioned by King Henry III in 1244. Its elaborate four-lobed plan is unique in England. The tower proclaimed royal power over the city from the 13th century until its interior was gutted by a (supposedly) accidental fire and explosion in 1684.

Reflecting its four-lobed plan, multisensory interpretation within the tower explores four key periods of its history. You'll discover how William the Conqueror devastated the city during his brutal Harrying of the North, and how York's Jewish community tragically committed mass suicide in the tower's timber predecessor in 1190, to escape massacre by a mob. Then learn how the present tower was rebuilt in stone, becoming the focus of royal government during the long Anglo-Scottish wars. In Tudor times, Robert Aske, leader of the 'Pilgrimage of Grace', was hung in chains from the tower; during the Civil War Siege of York in 1644 it became a platform for heavy guns, before the 1684 fire destroyed the interior. Later, the tower became a romantic ruin, concealed for a century behind prison walls.

All text information is available in audio and can be downloaded to a smartphone: it's accessible in a number of languages, available via QR codes. Information in Braille is also available. On the sound-looped benches, hear tales of York Castle and Clifford's Tower told by fictional characters from its history and voiced by York actors, and immerse yourself in the ambient historic soundscape.

A spectacular system of new internal stairs and suspended walkways allows you to explore the first-floor level. There you can view features inaccessible since the 17th century, including the ingeniously flushed royal 'garderobe' medieval lavatory and the remains of the medieval royal chapel, tucked away off a spiral staircase.

At the top of the tower the timber deck viewing platform offers safe access to 360-degree panoramas over the city of York and beyond. Illustrated panels help you identify significant landmarks and buildings, and reveal how these related to Clifford's Tower through nearly a thousand years of history.

english-heritage.org.uk

DON'T
MISS

Experiencing the astonishing 360-degree panoramas of York from the tower-top viewing platform. You won't find better views of the ancient city anywhere. Its minster, parish churches and buildings spanning ten centuries are identified for you by clear interpretation panels. They're an ideal introduction to historic York, and well worth the climb.

OPENING TIMES

Open daily 1 Apr-28 Mar

Site closed 24-25 Dec

See website for latest opening times

Last entry 30 mins before closing

VISIT US

Address: Tower Street, York, North Yorkshire YO1 9SA

Direction: Tower St, York

Train: York 1 mile

Bus: Visit traveline.info for the latest bus timetables and routes

Tel: 01904 646940

SAVE TODAY By being a Member, you save up to **£32.50** (price of a family ticket) when you visit **Clifford's Tower, York.**

NON-MEMBERS

See website for entry prices

| ACQ.1915 | ✱ | ▢ | ✈ | P | ⚠ | OVP |

Parking (charged, not managed by English Heritage).

Caution: access via steep steps.

Please do not attempt to climb the steep slopes of the tower mound. It's very dangerous, and will damage the historic mound and the wildflowers growing on it.

MAP PAGE 311 (3G)
OS MAP 105, 290: SE605515

BEADLAM ROMAN VILLA
NORTH YORKSHIRE – YO62 7TD

A small number of bookable guided tours of Beadlam Roman Villa will be available. Set in a riverside meadow below the southern fringe of the North York Moors, Beadlam is one of the most northerly Roman villas in Britain which can be seen above ground. Low walls of the north range of a villa complex are visible. This contained eight domestic rooms, some heated by hypocausts, and was fronted by a veranda. Remains of the east and west ranges (which included a bath suite) exist below ground. Though possibly begun earlier, the villa was mainly in use during the third and fourth centuries AD. A mosaic from the villa is in Helmsley Archaeology Store (p.214).

OPENING TIMES
Pre-booked tours only. Please see website for details

VISIT US
Direction: Between Helmsley and Beadlam, off A170: full directions provided on booking

ACQ.1972

No parking near villa. No facilities at site. No access except on pre-booked tours.

Beware – livestock may be grazing on site.

MAP PAGE 311 (2G)
OS MAP 100, OL26: SE634841

DON'T FORGET
Remember to take your membership card.

EASBY ABBEY
NORTH YORKSHIRE – DL10 7EU

Impressive ruins of a Premonstratensian abbey, set by the River Swale. They include a lavishly appointed refectory of c. 1300 and extensive monastic buildings. The neighbouring parish church displays outstanding 13th-century wall paintings.

Easby can also be reached via a pleasant walk from Richmond Castle (p.220).

OPENING TIMES
See website for latest opening times

VISIT US
Direction: 1 mile SE of Richmond, off B6271

Bus: Visit traveline.info for the latest bus timetables and routes

ACQ.1930

Caution: unguarded drops.

MAP PAGE 311 (2F)
OS MAP 92, 304: NZ185003

GISBOROUGH PRIORY
NORTH YORKSHIRE – TS14 6HG

The ruins of an Augustinian priory founded in 1119 by the Bruce family, afterwards Kings of Scotland. The dramatic east end wall of the church is one of the finest examples of late 13th-century architecture in England. Substantial pier bases, a knight's grave slab and the remains of the 12th-century gatehouse hint at the priory's former grandeur.

We are grateful to the Gisborough Priory Project, who manage the site and the adjoining historic woodland gardens. For more details see gisboroughprioryproject.org.uk

OPENING TIMES
Open Wed-Sun (and bank holidays)
1 Apr-28 Mar

Site closed 6 Nov-29 Feb

See website for latest opening times

VISIT US
Direction: Church Street Guisborough, next to the parish church

Train: Marske 4½ miles

Bus: Visit traveline.info for the latest bus timetables and routes

Tel: 07391 351757
The number is manned by volunteers but any messages left will be responded to as soon as possible

ACQ.1932

Parking and toilets in town.

MAP PAGE 311 (1G)
OS MAP 94, OL26/306: NZ617160

KIRKHAM PRIORY

———— NORTH YORKSHIRE – YO60 7JS ————

The picturesque ruins of Kirkham Priory stand in an idyllic setting beside the river Derwent. They played an important part in rehearsals for the D-Day landings.

This priory of Augustinian canons was founded during the 1120s by Walter Espec of Helmsley Castle, who later also founded Rievaulx Abbey. The heraldry of the lords of Helmsley Castle bedecks the richly embellished priory gatehouse, along with worn figures of St George and the Dragon and David and Goliath.

Ranged across a riverside slope, the priory's extensive ruins testify to its medieval size and wealth. Remains of a tall east end window recall the vanished magnificence of its church, but much more survives of the cloister buildings. Look out for the finely carved 13th-century 'laver', where the canons washed before entering their refectory through an elaborately sculpted 12th-century doorway.

During the Second World War the site was a focus of training for the D-Day invasion. Tanks due to land on the Normandy beaches tested their waterproofing in the Derwent and a pool created between ruins and river, while troops tried out scrambling nets hung on the priory walls. Winston Churchill and King George VI paid a top-secret visit to Kirkham to view the preparations.

OPENING TIMES

Open varying days 1 Apr-5 Nov

Site closed 6 Nov-28 Mar

See website for latest opening times

Last entry 30 mins before closing

VISIT US

Direction: 5 miles SW of Malton, on a minor road off A64

Train: Malton 6 miles

Bus: Visit traveline.info

Tel: 01653 618768

NON-MEMBERS

See website for entry prices

By being a Member, you save up to £21.50 (price of a family ticket) when you visit **Kirkham Priory**

MAP PAGE 311 (3H)
OS MAP 100, 300: SE736658

HELMSLEY CASTLE

NORTH YORKSHIRE – YO62 5AB

Set beside an attractive market town, Helmsley Castle was in turn a formidable medieval fortress, an Elizabethan mansion, a besieged stronghold and a romantic ruin. Discover how life was lived here in war and peace.

The spectacular double banks and ditches surrounding the castle were created in the mid-1100s for its founder Walter Espec, a Norman baron of 'immense stature… with a voice like a trumpet'. Renowned for piety as well as soldiering, he also founded Kirkham Priory (p.213) and nearby Rievaulx Abbey (p.222).

Walter's successors, the de Roos family, raised the castle's impressive stonework defences between the late 12th and 14th centuries. They include the strong south barbican through which you enter the castle and the tall, keep-like east tower which still dominates Helmsley town, as it was always intended to do. Later the medieval west range was converted into a luxurious Elizabethan mansion by the Manners family; you can admire some of its fine timber panelling and elaborate plasterwork (look out for mermaids and dolphins) within its upper storey.

Yet Helmsley remained a powerful stronghold. In 1644, during its first and last military challenge, the castle's garrison of 200 Royalists held out for three months against a stronger force of cannon-armed Parliamentarians, marching out with the honours of war only when starved into surrender. Thereafter its defences were systematically made unusable, though the mansion remained intact: you can still see rubble from the part-demolished east tower lying in the castle ditch. Finally abandoned as a residence in the early 18th century, the castle

became a romantic 'eye-catcher' ruin in the designed landscape of nearby Duncombe Park.

Extensive displays of site-finds in the mansion – from a Civil War mortar bomb to tableware and a 17th-century aristocratic chamber pot – combine with models and interactives to explore life in the castle through five centuries of war and peace. Don't miss a walk along the embankment between the castle ditches (accessible from the north barbican). This offers fine views of the fortress exterior, the adjacent parkland and the restored Helmsley Walled Garden (not managed by English Heritage), as well as the chance in season to spot some of the castle's abundant wild flowers and wildlife.

From April-October, you can also book a free monthly expert-guided tour of Helmsley Archaeology Store, housing fascinating artefacts from English Heritage's sites in northern England. See english-heritage.org.uk/visit/places/helmsley-castle/helmsley-archaeology-store or call 0370 333 1181 for information.

Rievaulx (p.222) and Byland (p.209) abbeys are both nearby. Rievaulx can be reached on foot via the well-signposted Cleveland Way National Trail. Approx. 2 hours 15 minutes (3½ miles) each way. Some gradients and steep steps: strong footwear required.

OPENING TIMES

Open daily 1 Apr-5 Nov

Open varying days 6 Nov-28 Mar

Site closed 24-26 Dec & 1 Jan

See website for latest opening times

Last entry 30 mins before closing

Helmsley Archaeology Store Tours
For tour dates and times, please
check our Helmsley Archaeology
Store web page. Booking is essential

Tours are free for Members and
non-members and are led by
members of the curatorial team

VISIT US

Address: Helmsley Castle,
Castlegate, Helmsley,
North Yorkshire YO62 5AB

Direction: Near the town centre;
follow brown signs to long stay
car park

SAVE TODAY By being a
Member, you
save up to
£32.50 (price
of a family ticket) when you
visit **Helmsley Castle.**

Bus: Visit **traveline.info** for the latest
bus timetables and routes

Tel: 01439 770442

NON-MEMBERS

See website for entry prices

ACQ.1923

Audio tours.

Parking: large car park adjacent to castle
entrance. Charge payable by all visitors
(not managed by English Heritage).

Toilets (in car park and town centre).

MAP PAGE 311 (2G)
OS MAP 100, OL26: SE611836

MARMION TOWER

NORTH YORKSHIRE – HG4 5JQ

Fine 15th-century riverside fortified gatehouse-tower, with a beautiful oriel window. Monuments of the Marmion family owners grace the adjacent church.

OPENING TIMES

See website for latest opening times

VISIT US

Direction: On A6108 in West Tanfield

Train: Thirsk 10 miles

Bus: Visit traveline.info for the latest bus timetables and routes

ACQ.1976

MAP PAGE 311 (2F)
OS MAP 99, 298: SE268787

PIERCEBRIDGE ROMAN BRIDGE

NORTH YORKSHIRE – DL2 3SW

Stonework foundations of a bridge, now marooned in a field, which once led to Piercebridge Roman Fort.

OPENING TIMES

Any reasonable daylight hours

VISIT US

Direction: At Piercebridge; 4 miles W of Darlington, on B6275

Train: Darlington 5 miles

Bus: Visit traveline.info for the latest bus timetables and routes

ACQ.1975

Parking available at nearby George Hotel. May infrequently be restricted when hosting large functions. Not managed by English Heritage.

MAP PAGE 311 (1F)
OS MAP 93, 304: NZ214155

PICKERING CASTLE

NORTH YORKSHIRE – YO18 7AX

Impressive ruins of a medieval royal castle, on the fringe of an attractive moors-edge market town. A classic example of how early earth-and-timber castles were progressively rebuilt in stone, its core is a high and steep-sided Norman 'motte' mound surrounded by a ditch. Among the earliest in northern England, this was raised by William the Conqueror during his devastating Harrying of the North in 1069-70. It was later crowned by a stone shell keep, and you can climb the motte stairway for panoramic views over the surrounding countryside. During the 13th and 14th centuries the castle's timber outer defences were replaced by stone curtain walls. Three of their imposing towers stand almost to full height: the Mill Tower housed a prison. Discover more about the castle's story in the chapel exhibition, and look out for its abundant wildlife – kestrels sometimes nest here.

OPENING TIMES

Open daily 1 Apr-5 Nov

Site closed 6 Nov-28 Mar

See website for latest opening times

Last entry 30 mins before closing

PICKERING CASTLE

VISIT US

Direction: In Pickering; 15 miles SW of Scarborough

Train: Malton (9 miles) or Pickering (North Yorkshire Moors Railway) ¼ mile

Bus: Visit traveline.info for the latest bus timetables and routes

Tel: 01751 474989

NON-MEMBERS

See website for entry prices

ACQ.1926

Disabled access (except motte).
Caution: steep drops.

MAP PAGE 311 (2H)
OS MAP 100, OL27: SE799845

ST MARY'S CHURCH, STUDLEY ROYAL

NORTH YORKSHIRE – HG4 3DY

Magnificent High Victorian Anglican church, designed in the 1870s by the flamboyant architect William Burges. Its extravagantly decorated interior survives unaltered.

Owned by English Heritage and managed by the National Trust as part of the Fountains Abbey and Studley Royal Estate (see p.291).

OPENING TIMES

See website for latest opening times

VISIT US

Direction: Located 2½ miles W of Ripon, off B6265; in the grounds of the Studley Royal Estate

Bus: Visit traveline.info for the latest bus timetables and routes

Tel: 01765 608888

ACQ.1975

Parking (at visitor centre or Studley Royal).

MAP PAGE 311 (3F)
OS MAP 99, 298/299: SE275693

MIDDLEHAM CASTLE

NORTH YORKSHIRE – DL8 4QG

One of Yorkshire's most impressive medieval fortresses, Middleham Castle became the northern power base of King Richard III. It stands in an attractive Wensleydale market town.

The castle's core is the immense Norman keep, among the biggest in England. Three storeys high, it was probably built during the 1170s. Around this keep the powerful Neville family, Earls of Westmorland and of Warwick, progressively constructed three ranges of luxurious lodgings. By the mid-15th century the castle had turned into a fortified palace – 'the Windsor of the North'. Though roofless, most of the castle's buildings survive, including a multi-storey latrine tower and the remains of a later horse-powered mill, making Middleham a rewarding place to explore.

Though there is no firm evidence that Richard III lived here as a child, he may have visited as a teenager in the guardianship of 'Warwick the Kingmaker'. But in the 1470s Richard certainly made Middleham the focus of his growing power in the north, taking over the castle after Warwick's death and marrying his daughter Anne. The couple's only son, Edward of Middleham, was born and died here, aged no more than 10.

Enjoy views over Wensleydale from the keep's viewing platform. In a small exhibition about the castle's past you'll see a replica of the famous Middleham Jewel, a 15th-century gold and sapphire pendant found nearby. Engraved with religious images and magic words, it may have belonged to Richard's mother-in-law, Anne Beauchamp.

Children's games are available for the family to enjoy.

OPENING TIMES
Open daily 1 Apr-5 Nov

Open varying days 6 Nov-28 Mar

Site closed 24-26 Dec & 1 Jan

See website for latest opening times

Last entry 30 mins before closing

VISIT US
Direction: Located at Middleham, 2 miles S of Leyburn on A6108

Train: Leyburn (Wensleydale Railway) 2 miles

Bus: Visit traveline.info for the latest bus timetables and routes

Tel: 01969 623899

Local Tourist Information: Leyburn: 01969 623069

NON-MEMBERS
See website for entry prices

By being a Member, you save up to £28.50 (price of a family ticket) when you visit **Middleham Castle**

ACQ 1926

Disabled access (except keep).

MAP PAGE 311 (2F)

OS MAP 99, OL30: SE127876

MOUNT GRACE PRIORY, HOUSE AND GARDENS

NORTH YORKSHIRE – DL6 3JG

There's something for everyone to enjoy on a day out at Mount Grace. You'll find the Arts and Crafts gardens maturing beautifully and wilder spaces to wander, as well as an Arts and Crafts mansion and the most strikingly unusual of all our medieval monasteries.

Picturesquely set against the wooded Cleveland Hills, Mount Grace Priory was the last of the great Yorkshire monasteries, founded in 1398. Five centuries later, its ruins were bought by wealthy industrialist Sir Lowthian Bell, patron of the Arts and Crafts movement. Following the movement's principles of craftsmanship, natural materials and simplicity, he refurbished a 17th-century mansion adapted from the priory's guest house, fronting it with terraced gardens.

Masterminded by celebrity garden designer Chris Beardshaw, these award-winning Arts and Crafts gardens are now maturing. You can wander the terraces with their richly planted herbaceous borders, cross a bridge to the Moat Island, and walk through a wildflower meadow to the Monks' Pond. Individual pamphlets for each season highlight garden and wildlife changes throughout the year. The Orchard Café, open to all, is set by an orchard recreated with local varieties of fruit trees.

Within the mansion, you'll see how Sir Lowthian sensitively combined 17th-century features with Arts and Crafts remodelling. Rooms have been dressed as they might have appeared in 1901. Don't miss the attics, which were nurseries for the Bell children in the 1920s and 30s.

Sir Lowthian's granddaughter Gertrude Bell, the famous adventurer, archaeologist and Middle East diplomat, knew and loved Mount Grace.

The mansion also houses a fascinating display about medieval Mount Grace Priory, best preserved of the few English Carthusian monasteries. Stepping into its extensive ruins, you'll notice how they differ radically from conventional monasteries. Unlike other monks who lived and worshipped communally, the austere and much-respected Carthusians were semi-hermits. Each monk lived in solitude in one of the cottage-like cells ranged round the immense Great Cloister.

One of these two-storeyed cells – a private monastery in itself – is recreated as it appeared in the 15th century. It contains a living room, study and bedroom-chapel and workshop. An L-shaped hatch allowed servants to pass in the monk's frugal meat-free meals without seeing him. The monk's walled garden has a toilet, flushed by an ingenious plumbing system which channelled water to each cell. The garden has been replanted, and you'll discover which plants the hermit-monks grew for food, healing and contemplation.

Owned by the National Trust, maintained and managed by English Heritage.

DON'T MISS

2023 marks the 625th anniversary of the foundation of Mount Grace Priory in 1398. Join us for a year of celebrations of this momentous date.

Visit our website to find out more about what will be happening.

STAY WITH US

Prior's Lodge sleeps four, with views over the mansion's garden in one direction, the monastic ruins in the other.

See p.13 for details on staying at **Mount Grace** and our other holiday cottages.

See p.13 for details on staying at **Mount Grace** and our other holiday cottages.

OPENING TIMES

Open daily 1 Apr-5 Nov

Open varying days 6 Nov-28 Mar

Site closed 24-26 Dec & 1 Jan

See website for latest opening times

Last entry 30 mins before closing

During the winter, the attics may close early due to low light levels

VISIT US

Address: Staddlebridge, Northallerton, North Yorkshire DL6 3JG

Direction: 12 miles N of Thirsk, and 6 miles NE of Northallerton, signposted from A19

Train: Northallerton 6 miles

Tel: 01609 883494

Local Tourist Information:
Thirsk: 01845 522755

SAVE TODAY By being a Member, you save up to £41.50 (price of a family ticket) when you visit **Mount Grace Priory, House and Gardens.**

NON-MEMBERS

See website for entry prices

National Trust members admitted free, except on event days

ACQ.1955

Parking: charges apply to non-members, free for Members with valid car sticker. Parking fee applies to National Trust members.

Dogs on leads (grounds only).

MAP PAGE 311 (2G)
OS MAP 99, OL26: SE449985

RICHMOND CASTLE

—— NORTH YORKSHIRE – DL10 4QW ——

Dominating a picturesque Dales market town, impressive Richmond Castle is among the oldest Norman stone fortresses in England. An extensive exhibition and imaginative interactives help you enjoy your visit.

Colourful displays highlight the many intriguing characters who made the castle's long story, from its 11th-century founder Count Alan the Red to the Conscientious Objectors who suffered here for refusing to fight in the First World War. You'll discover how generations of aristocrats, knights, soldiers and servants defended and lived in the castle. Find out how it inspired myths and legends, try your hand at designing heraldry, and enjoy the children's dressing-up box.

The Non-Combatant Corps was based here in 1916. You can hear the voices of those who wouldn't carry weapons, and the 'absolutists' who refused all war work – including the 'Richmond 16', sent to France and threatened with execution. A touchscreen presentation explores the poignant graffiti they left on their cell walls, proclaiming their pacifist beliefs and remembering loved ones.

Interactive displays and challenges tempt families to explore the great fortress, ranged round a vast grassy space. Don't miss the impressive ruins of Scolland's Hall and tiny St Nicholas's Chapel, among the oldest Norman domestic buildings in England. Try out the fun 'Seats of Power' feature inside the towering 100ft (30 metre) high 12th-century keep, and climb to the roof for amazing panoramic vistas over the castle, the ancient town and the Yorkshire Dales. Our orientation toposcopes help you explore the views.

OPENING TIMES

Open daily 1 Apr–5 Nov

Open varying days 6 Nov–28 Mar

Site closed 24–26 Dec & 1 Jan

See website for latest opening times

Last entry 30 mins before closing

VISIT US

Direction: In Richmond, just off the market place

Bus: Visit traveline.info for the latest bus timetables and routes

Tel: 01748 822493

NON-MEMBERS

See website for entry prices

By being a Member, you save up to £28.50 (price of a family ticket) when you visit **Richmond Castle**

ACQ.1916 ▮▮▮▮▮▮▮▮ E ▮▮
▮▮▮▮▮▮ OVP

Disc parking (2 hours free in market place – not managed by English Heritage).

Disabled parking available at site on request, or in market place.

MAP PAGE 311 (2F)
OS MAP 92, 304: NZ172007

SPOFFORTH CASTLE
NORTH YORKSHIRE – HG3 1DA

The ruined hall and chamber of a fortified medieval manor house of the powerful Percy family, rebuilt in the 15th century. Its undercroft is cut into a rocky outcrop.

Managed by Spofforth-with-Stockeld Parish Council.

OPENING TIMES
See website for latest opening times

VISIT US
Direction: 3½ miles SE of Harrogate, off A661 at Spofforth

Train: Pannal 4 miles

Bus: Visit traveline.info for the latest bus timetables and routes

ACQ.1924

Dogs on leads (restricted areas only).

MAP PAGE 311 (3F)
OS MAP 104, 289: SE360511

STANWICK IRON AGE FORTIFICATIONS
NORTH YORKSHIRE – DL11 7RU

A reconstructed portion of the ramparts of the huge Iron Age power centre of the Brigantes, the most important tribe in pre-Roman northern Britain. Its defences were once some 4 miles long. The Brigantian capital later moved to Aldborough Roman Town (see p.209).

STANWICK IRON AGE FORTIFICATIONS

OPENING TIMES
Any reasonable daylight hours

VISIT US
Direction: Located on a minor road off A6274, at Forcett Village

Train: Darlington 10 miles

Bus: Visit traveline.info for the latest bus timetables and routes

ACQ.1953

Dogs on leads (restricted areas only).
Caution: deep water, steep slopes.

MAP PAGE 311 (1F)
OS MAP 92, 304: NZ179124

STEETON HALL GATEWAY
NORTH YORKSHIRE – LS25 5PD

A fine example of a small, well-preserved manorial gatehouse dating from the 14th century.

OPENING TIMES
Exterior only: Any reasonable daylight hours

VISIT US
Direction: Located 4 miles NE of Castleford, on a minor road off A162 at South Milford

Train: South Milford 1 mile

Bus: Visit traveline.info for the latest bus timetables and routes

ACQ.1948

Dogs on leads (restricted areas only).

MAP PAGE 311 (4G)
OS MAP 105, 290: SE484314

THORNBOROUGH HENGES
NORTH YORKSHIRE – DL8 2RA

Thornborough Henges are the most striking and important prehistoric monument in northern England. Dating from around 2500 BC in the late Neolithic era, the three impressive earthwork henges form part of a much wider ritual landscape, significant over a long period and comparable with the prehistoric landscapes around Avebury and Stonehenge. Unique in size, form and layout, each henge is around 240 metres in diameter, and almost perfectly circular, with paired entrances aligned to midwinter sunrise; their banks once stood up to 5 metres high. They're aligned approximately north-west – south-east, with a dogleg in their mile-long alignment, which may mirror the three stars of Orion's Belt in the prominent Orion constellation.

Now in the care of English Heritage, the central and southern henges have planned repairs, so access may be restricted. Please see website for further information.

OPENING TIMES
Any reasonable daylight hours

See website for latest details as parts of the site may be closed for repair

VISIT US
Direction: Located between West Tanfield and Thornborough, on a minor road off the A6108 at West Tanfield

Train: Thirsk 9 miles

Bus: Visit traveline.info for the latest bus timetables and routes

ACQ.2023

Dogs on short leads (restricted areas only).
Caution: uneven surfaces.

MAP PAGE 311 (2F)
OS MAP 99, 298, 299: SE286793

RIEVAULX ABBEY

NORTH YORKSHIRE – YO62 5LB

Rievaulx Abbey offers a host of exciting discoveries. Set in a tranquil wooded valley, the stately ruins are enhanced by many attractions. A welcoming café, site museum and audio tour trail help visitors of all ages enjoy the most impressive and extensive monastic remains in Britain.

'High hills surround the valley, clothed by trees and encircling it like a crown'; this 12th-century description of Rievaulx's setting still applies today. Here, in 1132, just 12 monks of the new Cistercian order, which was revolutionising monasticism in western Europe, founded an abbey, 'far from the haunts of men'. It became one of the wealthiest monasteries in medieval England. By the 1160s a peak of around 640 monks were living here, attracted by the holiness of Abbot Aelred. After his death the monks successfully sought his canonisation, rebuilding the east end of the church in the new Early English style of Gothic architecture to house his shrine.

Surviving almost to its full height, the east end of this church still serenely dominates the ruins. You can also explore the maze of monastic buildings where the white-robed Cistercian choir monks and their brown-clad lay brothers lived, worked and cared for their sick. The audio tour and pictorial interpretation panels help you find the site's highlights, like the refectory – the finest example in Britain – where the monks ate their largely vegetarian meals. You can also seek out intriguing features like the warming house sink where the monks did their laundry, the monks' toilets, and the tannery where they prepared leather in vats of urine.

Discover lots more about life at Rievaulx in the must-see museum. Here a wonderful display of artefacts ranges from beautifully carved stonework (including a tiger hunt using a mirror to distract the prey), via building tools, writing equipment and a 'scourge' whip for monastic penance, to everyday items like 'patten' footwear for muddy weather. A screen presentation illustrates major chapters in Rievaulx's story, including its suppression by Henry VIII in 1538. The 'Shattered Remains' display recalls the wholesale destruction at this time, before Rievaulx's later rebirth as a supremely romantic ruin, a delight to visit.

You can take a break from exploring in the imaginatively designed café. Soak up views of the abbey as you sample a wide range of Yorkshire dishes. There's indoor and outdoor seating, picnic tables, and a big shop offering local products, so allow plenty of time for your visit to Rievaulx Abbey, one of England's most fascinating and atmospheric monastic ruins.

You can also reach Rievaulx from Helmsley Castle (p.214) on foot, via the Cleveland Way National Trail. Approx. 2 hours 15 minutes (3.5 miles) each way. Some gradients and steep steps: strong footwear required. Byland Abbey (p.209), another great Yorkshire Cistercian monastery, is within easy driving distance.

Stay in our *Refectory Cottage*, see p.13 for details.

english-heritage.org.uk

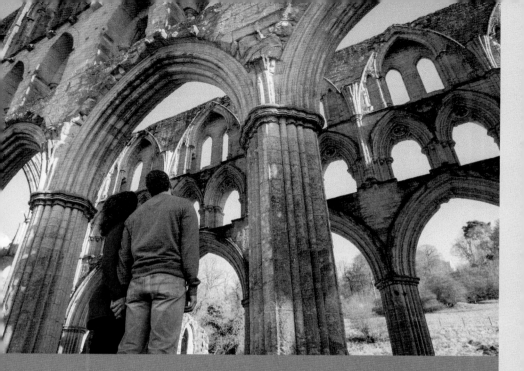

DON'T MISS

The intriguing Rye Valley Abbey exhibition, exploring how the monks harnessed the valley's natural water supply, using it to supply water for a diversity of practical, spiritual and industrial purposes.

The exhibition gallery features an array of water-related medieval monastic artefacts, many displayed for the first time.

A trail of interpretation panels helps you discover how fresh water was brought to the abbey and channelled round the monastery.

Mounted in partnership with the Ryevitalise Landscape Project.

OPENING TIMES

Open daily 1 Apr-5 Nov

Open varying days 6 Nov-28 Mar

Site closed 24-25 Dec

See website for latest opening times

Last entry 30 mins before closing

Café open to abbey closing time

VISIT US

Address: Rievaulx Abbey, Rievaulx, Nr Helmsley, N. Yorks YO62 5LB

Direction: In Rievaulx; 2¼ miles N of Helmsley, on minor road off B1257

Bus: Visit traveline.info for the latest bus timetables and routes

Tel: 01439 798228

SAVE TODAY By being a Member, you save up to £41.50 (price of a family ticket) when you visit **Rievaulx Abbey**.

NON-MEMBERS

See website for entry prices

Parking: charges apply to non-members, free for Members with valid English Heritage car sticker.

MAP PAGE 311 (2G)
OS MAP 100, OL26: SE577850

SCARBOROUGH CASTLE

NORTH YORKSHIRE – YO11 1HY

Battered by siege and attack but still majestic, Scarborough Castle crowns a spectacular headland with a 3,000 year story, amazing views – and 16 acres of history to explore.

Soaring between the two bays of the famous seaside resort, with steep drops on three sides, the headland is a natural stronghold, reachable only by a slender neck of land. It attracted prehistoric, Roman, Saxon and perhaps Viking settlers, and the medieval castle made it almost impregnable. As you approach the castle via the strongly fortified barbican and narrow bridge, the only way in, you'll soon see why it was so hard to attack, defying medieval barons, Tudor rebels and Civil War besiegers. Dominating the fortress stands Henry II's 12th-century Great Tower keep, with one side sheered away by Parliamentarian heavy cannon in 1645. But even then the besiegers couldn't get in, and the garrison had to be starved out.

In the Master Gunner's House museum, you can trace the headland's long history through site-finds, from a replica Bronze Age sword via Civil War cannonballs to the nose-cap of a shell fired at Scarborough in 1914 during a bombardment by audacious German warships, which shocked the whole nation.

Leave plenty of time to explore the vast grassy headland – bigger than 12 football pitches – and discover its many historic features. It is maintained as a gigantic wildflower meadow, where in high summer you may even spot orchids. On the cliff edge furthest from the keep you'll find the remains of a Roman signal station, one of a chain of beacon towers which gave warning of Saxon coastal raids in the 4th century AD. An Anglo-Saxon church

built on its site may have stood here when the Viking King Harald Hardrada seized the headland in 1066, hurling down blazing timbers to fire the town below.

You can follow the long and many-towered curtain wall, which King John built to guard the slope facing towards the harbour. Scarborough was among the busiest east-coast ports in medieval England, making the castle which protected it one of the most important in Yorkshire. Within the ditched Inner Bailey, the heart of the castle, a lofty viewing platform offers you amazing views over the town, the harbour, and the great sweep of South Bay. You'll also get wonderful views – over the narrow castle approach and North Bay – from the platform within the Great Tower, with its tiers of round-topped Norman windows. Dominating the castle and the landscape for miles around, it's one of the finest keeps raised by the champion royal castle-builder King Henry II.

With the finest coastal views in Yorkshire, so much history and such a vast area to explore or play in, Scarborough Castle offers the ideal family day out. Take a break from exploring at our Coffee Shed, serving barista coffee.

Guided tours with staff or volunteers are available most weekends throughout the year and on some summer weekdays, at no additional charge. Please call site in advance for confirmation.

Scarborough (2019).

A striking new sculpture in Scarborough Castle's grounds, focussing on the threat of climate change. Created by artist Ryan Gander, it's inspired by a 'dolos', a concrete wave-breaker set on shorelines to limit coastal erosion, and called *'We are only human (Incomplete sculpture for Scarborough to be finished by snow)'*. So it will be seen completed – if ever – only after a heavy snowfall, something made increasingly rare in Scarborough by global warming. The thought-provoking artwork is made of ultra-low carbon concrete, incorporating recycled glass and limestone, and also serves as a seat and a viewing point for clifftop wildlife and panoramic sea views. It's part of the long-term 'Wild Eye' art and nature project for the North Yorkshire coast, a collaboration between English Heritage, Yorkshire Wildlife Trust and Invisible Dust.

DON'T MISS

OPENING TIMES

Open daily 1 Apr–5 Nov

Open varying days 6 Nov–28 Mar

Site closed 24–25 Dec

See website for latest opening times

Last entry 30 mins before closing

Please note: coffee shop closes 30 mins before castle. During winter, opening times of coffee shop may vary

VISIT US

Address: Castle Road, Scarborough, North Yorkshire YO11 1HY

Direction: Castle Road, E of the town centre

Train: Scarborough 1 mile

Bus: Visit traveline.info for the latest bus timetables and routes

SAVE TODAY

By being a Member, you save up to **£32.50** (price of a family ticket) when you visit **Scarborough Castle**.

Tel: 01723 372451

Local Tourist Information: Scarborough: 01723 383636

NON-MEMBERS

See website for entry prices

No public parking (very limited parking for Blue Badge holders only, please enquire in advance of visit, especially on event days).

MAP PAGE 311 (2J)
OS MAP 101, 301: TA050892

WHITBY ABBEY

NORTH YORKSHIRE – YO22 4JT

Crowned by the hauntingly spectacular Gothic ruins of Whitby Abbey, the headland towering above the picturesque fishing port has been inspiring visitors and artists for 1,500 years. Our imaginative presentation helps you experience this iconic place in fresh ways – including an audio guide downloadable to your smartphone.

Hosting in turn St Hild's Anglo-Saxon monastery, a great medieval abbey and a 17th-century seat of power, the headland is the focus of many stories and legends. Here the cowherd-poet Caedmon was miraculously inspired, and here a visit by Victorian novelist Bram Stoker spawned the notorious fictional vampire, Count Dracula.

On the vast grassy headland loom the ruins of the great abbey church, built in the Early English Gothic style in the 13th century. The pinnacled east end and north transept still stand high, richly carved with characteristic 'dog's tooth' embellishment and naturally etched with intricate patterns by centuries of wind and rain. Battered by time, weather and war, they're still immensely impressive and atmospheric. Our unique Ammonite Quest helps families and groups of friends explore the headland together. Collect an ammonite device and a lanyard information swatch from the visitor centre. Flashing coloured lights and pulses reveal where key artefacts in the museum were originally found, and when you're walking over the sites of now-vanished abbey buildings.

The visitor centre is sited in Abbey House, the 17th-century mansion of the Cholmley family. Imaginatively themed and dramatically lit, its first-floor museum introduces you to the headland, its people and their stories, from prehistory to the present day. It houses a treasury of original artefacts, from Anglo-Saxon crosses and magic charms to elaborate medieval carvings and Victorian paintings. The displays trace how the Anglo-Saxon monastery, famous for holiness and learning, was destroyed by Vikings, refounded soon after the Norman Conquest and eventually superseded by a great mansion. Adult and child-level listening posts, peep-holes and animations tell the headland's many stories: how Hild turned snakes to stone 'ammonites', how Caedmon became a poet, how the lost abbey bells are still heard beneath the waves, and how a real shipwreck at Whitby helped spark off the Dracula tale. There's even a first edition of the famous novel, signed by Bram Stoker himself.

The spacious shop offers an amazing range of products, from folklore and history books to vampire blood cordials and Goth-style bat-patterned parasols.

There's never been a better time to visit Whitby Abbey.

Please note: from the Whitby harbour area, you can reach the abbey directly on foot via the famous 199 'church steps'. Alternatively, a well-signposted road leads from the town outskirts to the abbey.

🖼 *Dracula* (2020).

RECORD-BREAKING VAMPIRES

At 9pm on Thursday 26 May 2022, Whitby Abbey broke the world record for the largest number of people dressed as vampires ever gathered in one place. No fewer than 1,369 'vampires' from all over the world assembled here, beating the previous total of 1,039 gathered in 2011 in the USA. Vampires wore a set costume and, of course, fangs. The world-beating gathering celebrated the 125th anniversary of the publication of Bram Stoker's best-selling novel *Dracula*.

OPENING TIMES

Open daily 1 Apr-5 Nov

Open varying days 6 Nov-28 Mar

Site closed 24-25 Dec

See website for latest opening times

Last entry 30 mins before closing

Café open until site closing time

VISIT US

Address: Whitby Abbey, Abbey Lane, Whitby, North Yorkshire YO22 4JT

Direction: On cliff top, E of Whitby

Train: Whitby ½ mile

Bus: Visit traveline.info for the latest bus timetables and routes

Tel: 01947 603568

Local Tourist Information: Whitby: 01723 383636

SAVE TODAY By being a Member, you save up to **£41.50** (price of a family ticket) when you visit **Whitby Abbey**.

NON-MEMBERS

See website for entry prices

ACQ.1920

Disabled access (south entrance parking, charged).

Parking not managed by English Heritage (charge payable).

Toilets situated in the car park are not operated by English Heritage (charge payable).

Tearooms not managed by English Heritage.

MAP PAGE 311 (1H)

OS MAP 94, OL27: NZ903112

WHARRAM PERCY DESERTED MEDIEVAL VILLAGE

NORTH YORKSHIRE – YO17 9TN

Europe's best-known deserted medieval village, in a remote Wolds valley. Continuously occupied for six centuries, Wharram was abandoned by c. 1527. Above the substantial church ruins and mill pond, the outlines of many houses are traceable on a grassy plateau. Graphic panels recreate their original appearance.

Download a free audio tour from our website.

OPENING TIMES

Any reasonable daylight hours

VISIT US

Direction: 6 miles SE of Malton, on minor road from B1248; ½ mile S of Wharram-le-Street. Park in car park, then ¾ mile walk via uneven track, steep in places. Site also accessible on foot via Wolds Way footpath. Sturdy and waterproof footwear required. Parts of site slope steeply, and farm livestock likely to be present on site and access path

Train: Malton 8 miles

Bus: Visit traveline.info for the latest bus timetables and routes

Please note: site is hazardous in snowy conditions.

Beware – cattle may be grazing.

Parking: charges apply to non-members, free for Members with valid car sticker.

Caution: deep water, steep slopes, falling masonry.

> MAP PAGE 311 (3H)
> OS MAP 100, 300: SE859644

WHEELDALE ROMAN ROAD

NORTH YORKSHIRE –YO22 5AP

An enigmatic mile-long stretch of stone trackway amid wild and beautiful moorland. Usually identified as a Roman road, it may actually be medieval, or even a prehistoric boundary marker.

OPENING TIMES

Any reasonable daylight hours

VISIT US

Direction: Approximately 4 miles SW of Goathland via moorland roads (Wheeldale Road). 7 miles SW of Whitby

YORK COLD WAR BUNKER

NORTH YORKSHIRE – YO24 4HT

For 30 years the volunteers of the Royal Observer Corps watched for nuclear Armageddon here. At a time of crisis 60 men and women would be entombed within 'No 20 Group Control', ready to plot nuclear explosions and radioactive fallout across Yorkshire. Within the brutal concrete exterior is a chilling Cold War time capsule, where original monitoring and communications equipment sits alongside the necessities of life; a canteen, a dormitory and support systems designed to last just 30 days.

Visits are by guided tour, enhanced by a striking 10-minute film (PG rated) telling the story of the Cold War.

WHEELDALE ROMAN ROAD

Train: Goathland (North Yorkshire Moors Rly) (4 miles) or Newtondale Halt (then 3 mile forest walk)

Bus: Visit traveline.info for the latest bus timetables and routes

Local Tourist Information:
Pickering: 01751 473791

Parking on roadside.

Stout footwear essential if walking track.

Livestock may be present.

> MAP PAGE 311 (2H)
> OS MAP 94/100, OL27: SE806977

OPENING TIMES

Open varying days 1 Apr-28 Mar

Site closed 24-26 Dec & 1 Jan

See website for latest opening times

Please visit the website to book your tour. Tours last approximately 1 hour

VISIT US

Direction: Monument Close, off Acomb Road (B1224), turning opposite Hobgate, approx. 2 miles from York city centre

Train: York 1¼ miles

Bus: Visit traveline.info for the latest bus timetables and routes

Tel: 01904 797935

Local Tourist Information:
York: 01904 555670

NON-MEMBERS

See website for entry prices

> MAP PAGE 311 (3G)
> OS MAP 105, 290: SE580515

CONISBROUGH CASTLE

SOUTH YORKSHIRE – DN12 3BX

Step into the inspirational setting of Walter Scott's *Ivanhoe* novel. This most unusual medieval fortress has been brought to life by a spectacular and highly imaginative makeover funded by the Heritage Lottery Fund.

The design of Conisbrough Castle's tall cylindrical keep, ringed with six great turret buttresses, is unique in Britain. Probably begun in the 1170s, it was later reinforced by a turreted outer wall. It proclaims the ambition, power and wealth of its builders: Hamelin Plantagenet, illegitimate half-brother of King Henry II, and his wife, the formidable Lady Isabel de Warenne, heiress of Conisbrough.

You can explore the whole fully roofed and floored keep, with its three big chambers and lovely miniature chapel, guided by larger-than-life wall-projected figures of Hamelin, Isabel and their steward. Climbing to the roof, you'll find wonderful all-round vistas over the surrounding countryside.

Graphic novel style interpretation, featuring builders, servants, ladies-in-waiting and squires from the castle's history, offers vivid guidance around the whole fortress. Don't miss the fascinating introductory exhibition, including many excavated site finds. It traces Conisbrough's history from its beginnings to the present day. A striking cutaway model, with moving figures, offers a virtual tour of the keep if you don't wish to ascend its stairways.

OPENING TIMES

Open daily 1 Apr–5 Nov

Open varying days 6 Nov–28 Mar

Site closed 24–26 Dec & 1 Jan

See website for latest opening times

Last entry 30 mins before closing

VISIT US

Direction: Located NE of Conisbrough town centre off A630; 4½ miles SW of Doncaster

Train: Conisbrough ½ mile

Bus: Visit **traveline.info** for the latest bus timetables and routes

Tel: 01709 863329

NON-MEMBERS

See website for entry prices

By being a Member, you save up to **£28.50** (price of a family ticket) when you visit **Conisbrough Castle**

ACQ.1950 ♿ 🐕 ▮ 🛡 E 🚶 ♂ 📷 ⚠ OVP

Dogs on leads (in grounds only).

Disabled parking available outside the visitor centre.

No disabled access to or within the keep, due to steep stairways.

An interactive device is available for visitors unable to access the keep, allowing them to explore the building and meet characters.

Access limited to some areas.

MAP PAGE 311 (5G)
OS MAP 111, 279: SK515989

BRODSWORTH HALL AND GARDENS

SOUTH YORKSHIRE – DN5 7XJ

Few places in England can match Brodsworth Hall. In this grand yet gently time-worn Victorian mansion you can experience life in a country house as it really was. Now we've revived even more of its delightful Victorian garden features.

'Conserved as found' when English Heritage took over, Brodsworth still reflects its original opulence, but also reveals how its owners and servants weathered the changes and challenges of the 20th century. It's a house full of surprises.

Brodsworth Hall was built in the 1860s by the fabulously wealthy Charles Sabine Augustus Thellusson, and occupied by his family for over 120 years. The grand rooms on the ground floor recall the house's Victorian heyday, with glittering chandeliers and marble statues.

As you look closer, you can see the changes wrought by time. The last resident, the indomitable Sylvia Grant-Dalton, fought a losing battle against subsidence and leaking roofs. Following her death in 1988, we took the bold decision to conserve the interiors as they were found, rather than restoring them. The house remains as she used it, making do and mending with dwindling funds and ever fewer servants. Some of the bedrooms were modernised over the years, and contain furnishings dating from the 1860s to the 1980s. Other rooms fell out of use, though most of the Victorian servants' furnishings have survived.

Downstairs, the cavernous kitchen with its stupendous cooking range was deserted for a cosier room with an Aga range cooker. Beside the Aga rests the battered armchair of the last cook-housekeeper, Emily Chester. Displays reveal more about the Thellusson family, their servants, and how they lived together.

THE AWARD-WINNING GARDENS

Brodsworth's extensive gardens have been restored to their original splendour as 'a collection of grand gardens in miniature'. Romantic views from the restored summerhouse take in both the formal gardens and the pleasure grounds. Stroll through the statue walks, the fern dell grotto and the beautiful wild rose dell.

In spring, snowdrops, daffodils and bluebells put on a fantastic show. In summer, colourful formal bedding and roses contrast strikingly with the sculptural topiary and ferns. After the brilliant autumn colours fade, you can admire the extensive collection of Victorian hollies throughout the winter. On summer Sunday afternoons, enjoy the best of Yorkshire's brass bands from the garden terraces.

english-heritage.org.uk

MORE REVIVED GARDEN FEATURES

We've been progressively reviving forgotten features of Brodsworth's gardens, including the charming 1864 garden 'privy' toilet and the rare survival of a Victorian game larder. We've strikingly restored the Target Range to its Edwardian glory as a mosaic of brilliantly planted beds and intricate paving. Now we've also restored the Eyecatcher, a ruined Classical-style structure designed to draw the eye along the Target Range, and the Target House, a picturesque chalet-roofed summerhouse where the family rested from archery, which displays new interpretation.

A FAMILY-FRIENDLY PROPERTY

The hall and gardens are welcoming whatever your age. There's an outdoor play area, and families can make the most of events and activities in the garden. Everyone can enjoy the tearoom in the Servants' Wing, or watch the local croquet club in action. Inside the hall, friendly and knowledgeable volunteer room stewards will share stories from Brodsworth's past.

> *Darkest Hour* (2017); *Testament of Youth* (2014); *The Thirteenth Tale* (2013); ITV series *Victoria*.

OPENING TIMES

House and Servants' Wing
Open daily 1 Apr–5 Nov

Closed 6 Nov–28 Mar*

*Servants' Wing open weekends and school holidays during this period

No flash photography allowed

Garden and Tearooms
Open daily 1 Apr–5 Nov

Open varying days 6 Nov–28 Mar

Site closed 24–25 Dec

See website for latest opening times

Last entry 30 mins before closing

Mobility Around the Site
Prams and back carriers for babies are not allowed in the hall, small padded pushchairs are available instead. For visitors with mobility needs, an electric buggy operates a shuttle service from the car park. Benches throughout the gardens, although steps and steep slopes limit access to some areas. The hall has ramps and seats, and a lift to the first floor

VISIT US

Address: Brodsworth Hall and Gardens, Brodsworth, Doncaster, South Yorkshire DN5 7XJ
Please note: some satellite navigation systems give multiple locations for the postcode. To avoid confusion, please follow the brown signs in the local area

SAVE TODAY

By being a Member, you save up to £52.50 (price of a family ticket) when you visit **Brodsworth Hall and Gardens.**

Direction: In Brodsworth, 5 miles NW of Doncaster off A635 Barnsley Road; from junction 37 of A1(M)

Train: South Elmsall 4 miles; Moorthorpe 4½ miles; Doncaster 5½ miles; Adwick Le Street 3 miles

Bus: Visit traveline.info for the latest bus timetables and routes

Tel: 01302 722598

Local Tourist Information:
Doncaster: 01302 734309

NON-MEMBERS

See website for entry prices

ACQ.1990

MAP PAGE 311 (5G)
OS MAP 111, 279: SE506070

MONK BRETTON PRIORY SOUTH YORKSHIRE – S71 5QD

OPENING TIMES

Open daily 1 Apr-28 Mar
(managed by a key keeper)

Site closed 24-26, 31 Dec & 1 Jan

See website for latest opening times

VISIT US

Direction: Located 1 mile E of
Barnsley town centre, off A633

Train: Barnsley 2½ miles

Bus: Visit traveline.info for the latest
bus timetables and routes

NON-MEMBERS

Charges may apply on event days

ACQ.1932 🐕 P 🚻 ⚠

Caution: CCTV at site.

MAP PAGE 311 (5F)
OS MAP 110/111, 278: SE373065

The substantial ruins of a Cluniac monastery, later absorbed into the Benedictine order, with an unusually well-marked ground plan, almost complete west range and 15th-century gatehouse.

ROCHE ABBEY SOUTH YORKSHIRE – S66 8NW

OPENING TIMES

Open daily 1 Apr-5 Nov

Site closed 6 Nov-28 Mar

See website for latest opening times

Last entry 30 mins before closing

VISIT US

Direction: 1½ miles S of Maltby,
off A634

Train: Conisbrough 7 miles

Bus: Visit traveline.info for the latest
bus timetables and routes

Tel: 01709 812739

NON-MEMBERS

See website for entry prices

By being a Member, you save up to
£21.50 (price of a family ticket) when
you visit **Roche Abbey**

ACQ.1921 ♿ 🐕 🖼 🏪 🛍 👨 🚹 P 🚻
📷 ⚠ OVP

MAP PAGE 311 (5G)
OS MAP 111/120, 279: SK544898

The extensive remains of a small Cistercian abbey, in a beautiful setting. The soaring early Gothic transepts of its church were preserved as a 'Romantic eye-catcher' when Capability Brown drastically landscaped their surroundings from the 1760s, covering up other parts of the ruins. These now reveal one of the most complete ground plans of any English Cistercian monastery.

Beeston Castle and Woodland Park, Cheshire

WELCOME TO THE

NORTH WEST

North West

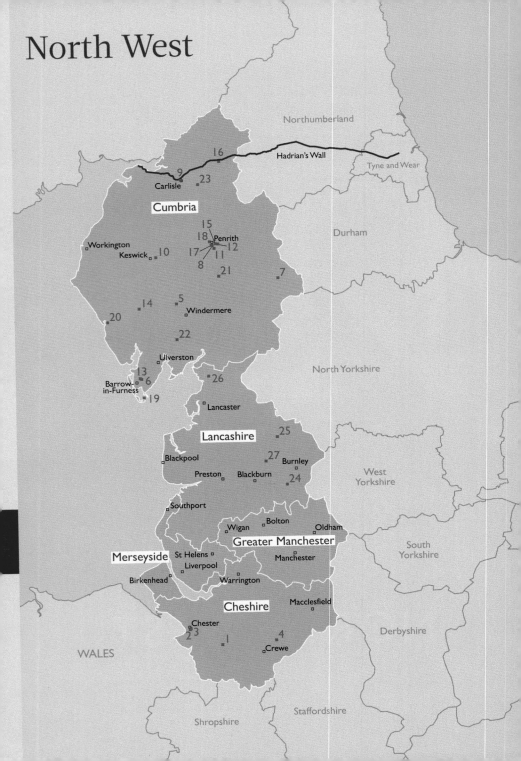

Northumberland

Hadrian's Wall

Tyne and Wear

16

9
Carlisle

23

Cumbria

Durham

15
18 Penrith
Workington   17   12
Keswick   10   11
8
21
7
20
14   5
Windermere
22

North Yorkshire

Ulverston

13
6   26
Barrow-
in-Furness   19
Lancaster

Lancashire   25

Blackpool   27   Burnley
Preston   Blackburn   24

West
Yorkshire

Southport

Wigan   Bolton   Oldham

Greater Manchester

South
Yorkshire

Merseyside   St Helens
Liverpool   Manchester

Birkenhead   Warrington

Cheshire   Macclesfield

Derbyshire

Chester
2 3   1   4
Crewe

WALES

Shropshire   Staffordshire

NORTH WEST

Visit the North West for spectacular sites with fascinating stories.

At the top of **Beeston Castle** (p.238) you'll enjoy far-reaching views across eight counties and tales of lost medieval treasure, while below you can wander through a wildlife-rich woodland park and see a recreated Bronze Age roundhouse. On the tranquil shores of Lake Windermere **Stott Park Bobbin Mill** (p.248) is a rather noisy reminder of our industrial past – you can hear the clatter of old-fashioned machinery and watch bobbins being made on selected days.

Elsewhere, the castles at **Brougham** (p.241) and **Carlisle** (p.242) are monuments to centuries of bitter border wars between English and Scots (Carlisle was also where Mary Queen of Scots was imprisoned in 1568). **Furness Abbey** (p.244) is a haven of tranquillity in a beautiful wooded valley; and **Castlerigg Stone Circle** (p.241) is among England's most picturesque prehistoric sites.

Just half a mile from **Hadrian's Wall**, **Lanercost Priory** (p.246) is one of the North West's best-preserved monasteries.

Beeston Castle and Woodland Park, Cheshire

Castlerigg Stone Circle, Cumbria

Stott Park Bobbin Mill, Cumbria

BEESTON CASTLE AND WOODLAND PARK

CHESHIRE – CW6 9TX

Crowning a sandstone crag towering above the Cheshire Plain, Beeston Castle is among the most dramatically sited fortresses in England, offering some of the best views in the country. Long before the castle was built, the crag was a busy hive of human activity. Our recreated Bronze Age roundhouse brings its prehistoric past strikingly to life.

Based on Bronze Age houses discovered here on the site, the roundhouse was meticulously reconstructed by a team of over 60 volunteers with help from expert advisers. Using only tools and techniques available in the Bronze Age, they crafted the thatched house from Beeston crag oaks and local ash and hazel. The recreation also drew on evidence from across Europe, including Must Farm in the Cambridgeshire Fens, where archaeologists recently found evidence of not only the ground plans but also the roof structures and even the contents of Bronze Age houses. By no means a primitive shack – with a ground area of over 50 square metres, it's bigger than some modern homes – the roundhouse offers education groups immersive learning experiences in prehistoric crafts and building techniques. And for all visitors, it's a vivid evocation of life at Beeston 4,000 years ago.

Much later, in the 1220s, the 'Castle of the Rock' was begun here by Ranulf, Earl of Chester, one of the greatest barons in Henry III's England. It's approached via a ruined gatehouse in a multi-towered outer wall, defining a huge outer bailey climbing steadily up the hill to the castle's crowning glory, the inner bailey. Defended by a rock-cut ditch and a mighty double-towered gatehouse, this offers you truly astounding views across eight counties, from the Welsh Mountains to the Pennines. It also contains the famous castle well, over 100 metres (328 feet) deep and among the deepest in any English castle. According to legend, it's the hiding place of Richard II's treasure, allegedly guarded by demons.

Set in 40 acres of woodland, Beeston Castle is a paradise for walkers, nature lovers and adventurous children. A circular woodland walk winds around the base of the crag, through wildlife-thronged woods and past Beeston's sandstone caves (external viewing only). You can also reach the caves directly from the visitor centre, where the 'Castle of the Rock' display retells Beeston's 4,000-year story, including a famous Civil War siege.

The Sandstone Café offers hot and cold snacks and drinks. No indoor seating, but picnic tables are available outside.

OPENING TIMES

Open daily 1 Apr-5 Nov

Open varying days 6 Nov-28 Mar

Site closed 24-25 Dec

See website for latest opening times

Last entry 30 mins before closing

VISIT US

Address: Beeston Castle, Chapel Lane, Beeston, Cheshire CW6 9TX

Direction: Located 11 miles SE of Chester, on minor road off A49

Train: Chester 11 miles or Crewe 15 miles

Bus: Visit traveline.info for the latest bus timetables and routes

Tel: 01829 260464

Local Tourist Information: Chester: 01244 402111

By being a Member, you save up to £36.50 (price of a family ticket) when you visit **Beeston Castle and Woodland Park.**

NON-MEMBERS

See website for entry prices

ACQ.1959 🖼 🍴 🏛 👕 📧 ✋ 🛍
💻 🚹 👶 🌳 P 📷 🎧 ☕ ♿
⚠ OVP

Caution: steep ascent to inner bailey (no disabled access to the top of the hill). Steps and rough path to roundhouse. Boots or sturdy footwear recommended for woodland walk.

Parking: charges apply to non-members, free for Members with valid car sticker.

MAP PAGE 310 (6D)
OS MAP 117, 257/258: SJ537593

CHESTER CASTLE: AGRICOLA TOWER AND CASTLE WALLS

CHESHIRE – CH1 2DN

The original gateway to Chester Castle, this 12th-century tower houses a chapel with traces of wall paintings of c.1220, rediscovered in the 1980s.

OPENING TIMES

See website for latest opening times and events

VISIT US

Direction: Access via Assizes Court car park on Grosvenor St

Train: Chester 1 mile

Bus: Visit traveline.info for the latest bus timetables and routes

ACQ.1912

Caution: steep stairs.

> MAP PAGE 310 (6C)
> OS MAP 117, 266: SJ405657

CHESTER ROMAN AMPHITHEATRE

CHESHIRE – CH1 1RE

The largest Roman amphitheatre in Britain, used by the 20th Legion, based at the fortress of 'Deva' (Chester). Excavations revealed two successive stone-built amphitheatres with wooden seating. The two buildings differed from all other British amphitheatres, underlining the importance of Roman Chester.

Managed by Cheshire West and Chester Council.

CHESTER ROMAN AMPHITHEATRE

OPENING TIMES

Any reasonable daylight hours

VISIT US

Direction: On Vicar's Lane, beyond Newgate, Chester

Train: Chester ¾ mile

Bus: Visit traveline.info for the latest bus timetables and routes

ACQ.1964

Disabled access (no access to amphitheatre floor).

Caution: unguarded drops.

> MAP PAGE 310 (6C)
> OS MAP 117, 266: SJ408662

SANDBACH CROSSES

CHESHIRE – CW11 1AT

Dominating Sandbach market square, these are among the finest surviving Anglo-Saxon high crosses. Probably dating from the 9th century, and originally painted as well as elaborately carved.

OPENING TIMES

Any reasonable daylight hours

VISIT US

Direction: Market Sq, Sandbach

Train: Sandbach 1½ miles

Bus: Visit traveline.info for the latest bus timetables and routes

ACQ.1937

> MAP PAGE 310 (6D)
> OS MAP 118, 268: SJ759608

CUMBRIA

AMBLESIDE ROMAN FORT

CUMBRIA – LA22 0EN

Foundations of a 2nd- to 4th-century Roman fort, in a meadow beside Windermere. Possibly a supply base for Lake District patrols.

Managed by the National Trust.

OPENING TIMES

Any reasonable daylight hours

VISIT US

Direction: In Borrans Field, beside A5075 on south-western outskirts of Ambleside. 182 metres W of Waterhead car park

Train: Windermere 5 miles

Bus: Visit traveline.info for the latest bus timetables and routes

ACQ.1978

Beware – cattle may be grazing.

No parking at site. Stout footwear advised.

Caution: unguarded drops.

> MAP PAGE 312 (6D)
> OS MAP 90, OL7: NY372034

BOW BRIDGE

CUMBRIA– LA13 0PL

This narrow 15th-century stone bridge across Mill Beck carried an old packhorse route to nearby Furness Abbey (see p.244).

OPENING TIMES

Any reasonable daylight hours

VISIT US

Direction: Located ½ mile N of Barrow-in-Furness, on minor road off A590; near Furness Abbey

Train: Barrow-in-Furness 1½ miles

Bus: Visit traveline.info for the latest bus timetables and routes

ACQ.1950

Beware – livestock may be grazing on site.

Caution: sheer drop into water.

> MAP PAGE 312 (7D)
> OS MAP 96, OL6: SD224715

BROUGH CASTLE

CUMBRIA – CA17 4EJ

On a ridge commanding Stainmore Pass. Frequently the target of Scots raids, its towering keep dates from c. 1200. Like many other castles hereabouts, Brough was restored in the 17th century by Lady Anne Clifford, whose additions are still visible.

OPENING TIMES

See website for latest opening times

VISIT US

Direction: 8 miles SE of Appleby

Train: Kirkby Stephen 10 miles

Bus: Visit traveline.info

Please note: approach may be muddy, stout footwear recommended.

Limited parking nearby. Please do not park on farm's access road.

Beware – livestock may be grazing on site.

New guidebook.

Caution: steep slopes.

MAP PAGE 310 (1D)
OS MAP 91, OL19: NY791141

CASTLERIGG STONE CIRCLE   CUMBRIA – CA12 4RN

Among the most dramatically sited prehistoric stone circles in Britain, surrounded by a panorama of Lakeland fells. It's also one of the earliest circles, probably raised around 3000 BC. Thirty-three of its close-set stones still stand. Managed by the National Trust.

OPENING TIMES

Any reasonable daylight hours

VISIT US

Direction: 1½ miles E of Keswick. Signposted from A66 and A591

Train: Penrith 16 miles

Bus: Visit traveline.info

Limited parking in lay-by.

Beware – livestock may be grazing on site.

Sturdy footwear is recommended.

MAP PAGE 312 (5D)
OS MAP 89/90, OL4: NY291236

BROUGHAM CASTLE   CUMBRIA – CA10 2AA

In a picturesque setting beside the River Eamont, near the site of a Roman fort, red sandstone Brougham Castle was founded in the early 13th century by Robert de Vieuxpont. His tall keep largely survives amid many later buildings added by the powerful Clifford family. These include the unusual double gatehouse and impressive 'Tower of League'. A formidable barrier against Scots invaders and a proclamation of baronial splendour, the castle welcomed Edward I in 1300. Falling into decay after James I's visit in 1617, Brougham was restored by the indomitable Lady Anne Clifford. She often visited with her travelling 'court', and died here in 1676.

There's a lot to explore at Brougham, and you can climb the spiral stairs to the keep top for panoramic views over the Eden Valley.

While in the area, don't forget to visit the Countess Pillar (see p.245).

OPENING TIMES

Open daily 1 Apr-5 Nov

Open varying days 6 Nov-28 Mar

Site closed 24-26 Dec & 1 Jan

See website for latest opening times

Last entry 30 mins before closing

VISIT US

Direction: 1½ miles SE of Penrith, off A66

Train: Penrith 2 miles

Bus: Visit traveline.info for the latest bus timetables and routes

Tel: 01768 862488

Local Tourist Information:
Penrith: 01768 867466
Rheged: 01768 860034

NON-MEMBERS

See website for entry prices

By being a Member, you save up to £24.50 (price of a family ticket) when you visit **Brougham Castle**

Please note: car parking limited, in 'no through road' opposite castle entrance.

There is good wheelchair access to most of the site (excluding the keep).

New guidebook.

MAP PAGE 312 (5E)
OS MAP 90, OL5: NY537290

CARLISLE CASTLE

CUMBRIA – CA3 8UR

The storm-centre of many famous sieges, Carlisle Castle was for centuries the flashpoint of frontier warfare, as well as a notorious prison. Trace its long and sometimes grim history as you view our vivid displays and explore the powerful and newly conserved keep.

Carlisle Castle remains a dominating presence in the city it has watched over for nine centuries. You can witness its rich and varied story in a vivid exhibition celebrating Carlisle's fame as the most besieged town in Britain.

The medieval castle was built on the site of an important Roman fortress. The commanding keep was begun during the 12th century by King Henry I of England and completed by King David I of Scotland. It's a reminder that Carlisle Castle was for centuries a disputed frontier fortress, guarding the especially turbulent western end of the Anglo-Scottish border. It triumphantly repelled a siege by King Robert Bruce of Scotland in 1315, after a great Scots siege engine got stuck fast in mud.

The castle's violent history also included skirmishes with Elizabethan Border Reivers, a Civil War siege – the longest siege of a town in English history – and Bonnie Prince Charlie's Jacobite Rising of 1745-46. Carlisle was then the very last English fortress ever to suffer a siege. Overwhelmed by the Duke of Cumberland's Hanoverian army, its Jacobite defenders were imprisoned in the keep's dank basement. Today you can see the legendary 'licking stones', which they supposedly licked for moisture. The unique and fantastic carvings on the keep's second floor were probably cut in about 1480, and have recently been extensively conserved.

By the time Mary Queen of Scots was imprisoned here in 1568, Henry VIII's updating for heavy artillery had left its mark on the fortress, including the Half Moon Battery defending the Captain's Tower gatehouse. You can explore both the Tudor Battery and the 12th-century gatehouse, one of the best preserved in England.

Discover more highlights in 'Besieged', a display which includes examples of the weapons used during Carlisle's many sieges, a reconstruction graphic of the keep, a retelling of the daring rescue of a Border Reiver, and a 360-degree virtual tour of the castle.

Unusually, the medieval castle remained an operational fortress well into the 20th century. From 1873 to 1959 it was the regimental headquarters of the Border Regiment, and today it hosts Cumbria's Museum of Military Life, which explores the regiment's 300-year history. English Heritage Members get free entry to the museum. There's a café in the museum, which also hosts a programme of temporary exhibitions. Separate opening times apply. Please visit **cumbriasmuseumofmilitarylife.org** for details.

Outlander (2014).

DON'T MISS

Seeking out the extraordinary carvings on the keep's second floor. More than just casual graffiti, they include the boar badge of the future King Richard III, a mermaid, a crucifixion and fantastic birds and beasts. Probably dating from around 1480, they may have been carved by prisoners, garrison members, a bored priest or prison guard. Long threatened by water seeping into the sandstone walls, they've been newly conserved as part of a recently completed major project to repair the keep's roof, masonry, pointing and drainage.

OPENING TIMES

Open daily 1 Apr-5 Nov

Open varying days 6 Nov-28 Mar

Site closed 24-26 Dec & 1 Jan

See website for latest opening times

Last entry 30 mins before closing

VISIT US

Address: Carlisle Castle, Castle Way, Carlisle, Cumbria CA3 8UR

Direction: In Carlisle city centre. Follow Castle Street, past Carlisle Cathedral on left. At main road, take underpass to the castle

Train: Carlisle ½ mile

Bus: Visit traveline.info for the latest bus timetables and routes

Tel: 01228 591922

Local Tourist Information:
Carlisle: 01228 598596

NON-MEMBERS

See website for entry prices

By being a Member, you save up to **£47** (price of a family ticket) when you visit **Carlisle Castle**.

Ticket price includes entry to Cumbria's Museum of Military Life

ACQ.1963

Disabled access (limited).

Dogs on leads (restricted areas only).

Guided tours available to pre-book at a small extra charge.

Parking (disabled only, but signposted city centre car parks nearby).

Cumbria's Museum of Military Life café not managed by English Heritage.

MAP PAGE 312 (4D)
OS MAP 85, 315: NY396562

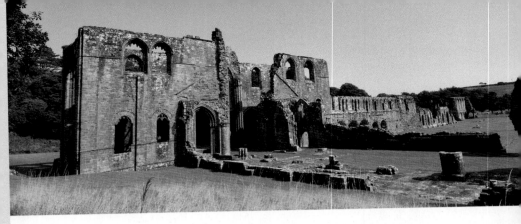

FURNESS ABBEY

―――― CUMBRIA – LA13 0PJ ――――

Among the North West's finest sights, the imposing remains of Furness Abbey are cradled in a lovely wooded valley. These grand ruins inspired the painter Turner and the poet Wordsworth. Thanks to a major conservation programme, there's now more to explore here.

Founded by Stephen, later King of England, Furness became the second richest Cistercian abbey in England. Its extensive red sandstone ruins proclaim its prosperity. Dating principally from the 12th and 13th centuries, they include the western tower and east end of the great church, with its presbytery – now accessible again after many years. You can also explore the chapter house, with its fine carved decoration, and almost the entire cloister east range. Follow the footpath up to the viewing platform for fantastic vistas over the abbey ruins.

The visitor centre exhibition features a large collection of sculpture from the ruins, including striking effigies of knights, and the rare silver-gilt 12th-century 'Furness Crozier' and gemstone ring from an abbot's grave.

We're very grateful to the Furness Abbey Fellowship for their support furnessabbeyfellowship.org/

OPENING TIMES

Open daily 1 Apr-5 Nov

Open varying days 6 Nov-28 Mar

Site closed 24-26 Dec & 1 Jan

See website for latest opening times

Last entry 30 mins before closing

VISIT US

Direction: Located 1½ miles N of Barrow-in-Furness. Signposted off A590 via Abbey Road

Train: Dalton and Roose 2 miles; Barrow-in-Furness 2 miles

Bus: Visit traveline.info for the latest bus timetables and routes

Tel: 01229 823420

NON-MEMBERS

See website for entry prices

By being a Member, you save up to **£28.50** (price of a family ticket) when you visit **Furness Abbey**

Dogs on leads (restricted areas only).

MAP PAGE 312 (7D)
OS MAP 96, OL6: SD218717

NEW FOR 2023

Thanks to funding from the FCC Communities Foundation, we're making improvements at Furness. They'll include enhancing access across the site for wheelchairs and pushchairs, and orienting visitors as they explore the abbey.

english-heritage.org.uk

CLIFTON HALL

CUMBRIA – CA10 2EA

The well preserved early Tudor tower of an otherwise vanished manor house, now surrounded by a busy working farmyard. Graphic panels reveal its history, and you can climb the spiral stairs to look into the kitchen and private chambers it contained, with a fine king-post roof.

OPENING TIMES

Any reasonable daylight hours

Site closed 24-26 Dec & 1 Jan

VISIT US

Direction: In Clifton, 2 miles S of Penrith; signposted from A6 in village

Train: Penrith 2½ miles

Bus: Visit traveline.info

 ACQ.1973

No vehicular access. Please park in the village and walk to the site.

Beware – livestock may be grazing on site.

Farmyard may be muddy: stout footwear recommended.

Caution: steep stairs.

> MAP PAGE 312 (5E)
> OS MAP 90, OL5: NY530271

COUNTESS PILLAR, BROUGHAM

CUMBRIA – CA10 2AB

A monument erected in 1656 by Lady Anne Clifford of nearby Brougham Castle, to commemorate her final parting here from her mother, 40 years earlier. Sundials are carved on three faces, and on the low stone beside it money was given to the poor on each anniversary of their parting.

OPENING TIMES

Any reasonable daylight hours

VISIT US

Direction: ¼ mile E of Brougham. An access route has also been created, which runs from the B6262

COUNTESS PILLAR, BROUGHAM

(to Brougham) and starts near the junction with the A66

Train: Penrith 2½ miles

Bus: Visit traveline.info

ACQ.1977

Caution: site on a very busy main road. Parking on B6262, close to the junction with A66. Safe access by footpath.

> MAP PAGE 312 (5E)
> OS MAP 90, OL5: NY546289

HARDKNOTT ROMAN FORT   CUMBRIA – CA19 1TH

Among the remotest and most spectacularly sited Roman forts in England, guarding a Roman road across the high fells. Its complete perimeter walls, headquarters building and nearby bath house and 'sauna' are clearly visible.

Managed by the National Trust.

OPENING TIMES

Any reasonable daylight hours

VISIT US

Direction: 9 miles NE of Ravenglass; at W end of Hardknott Pass, via short uphill path from unclassified road

Train: Dalegarth (Ravenglass & Eskdale) 3 miles or Ravenglass 10 miles

Bus: Visit traveline.info

ACQ.1949 P

Very limited parking in lay-by. More parking at Jubilee Bridge, ½ mile to west. Access hazardous in winter months or bad weather. Stout footwear essential.

Beware – livestock may be grazing on site.

Visitors are strongly advised to approach from the western (Eskdale) direction: the road from Ambleside over the Wrynose and Hardknott passes is hazardous in poor weather, with hairpin bends and 1-in-3 gradients. Not accessible by coaches.

Caution: steep slopes.

> MAP PAGE 312 (6D)
> OS MAP 89/90, OL6: NY218015

KING ARTHUR'S ROUND TABLE

CUMBRIA – CA10 2BX

Grassy banks of a late Neolithic earthwork henge, dating from c. 2000-1000 BC, but much later believed to be King Arthur's jousting arena. Mayburgh Henge is nearby.

OPENING TIMES

Any reasonable daylight hours

VISIT US

Direction: At Eamont Bridge, 1 mile S of Penrith. Signposted from A6 at S end of village

Train: Penrith 1½ miles

Bus: Visit traveline.info

ACQ.1884

No parking at site. Park at Mayburgh Henge (400 metres away).

Strictly no dogs when cattle are on site. Dogs on leads at other times.

Beware – cattle may be grazing.

> MAP PAGE 312 (5E)
> OS MAP 90, OL5: NY523284

MAYBURGH HENGE

CUMBRIA – CA10 2BX

Among the biggest and most impressive prehistoric henges in northern England, dating from the late Neolithic period. Its enormous circular bank still stands over 3 metres (10 feet) high. King Arthur's Round Table is nearby.

OPENING TIMES

Any reasonable daylight hours

VISIT US

Direction: At Eamont Bridge, 1 mile S of Penrith. Signposted from A6 at S end of village

Train: Penrith 1½ miles

Bus: Visit traveline.info

ACQ.1884

Limited parking (roadside only).

Strictly no dogs when cattle are on site. Dogs on leads at other times.

Beware – cattle may be grazing.

Caution: steep slopes.

Sturdy and waterproof footwear required.

> MAP PAGE 312 (5E)
> OS MAP 90, OL5: NY519284

LANERCOST PRIORY

—— CUMBRIA – CA8 2HQ ——

The tranquil setting of Augustinian Lanercost Priory belies an often troubled history.

Less than half a mile from Hadrian's Wall, it suffered frequent attacks during the long Anglo-Scottish wars. The mortally sick King Edward I rested here for five months in 1306-07, shortly before his death on his final campaign.

There is still a great deal for you to see in one of Cumbria's best-preserved monasteries. The east end of the noble 13th-century church survives to its full height and you can admire some recently conserved monuments within its dramatic triple tier of arches. The nave, with its lofty west front, is still in full use as the parish church.

Lanercost's cloisters include a beautiful vaulted 13th-century refectory undercroft. Converted into the Tudor mansion of the Dacre family, they also include the Dacre Tower, adapted from the monastic kitchen, and the Dacre Hall (used as the village hall, so not often open to the public). The Dacre Hall displays fragments of 16th-century wall painting and a splendid Jacobean chimneypiece, recently returned here.

Set beside an ancient vicarage and 'vicar's pele tower' (exterior viewing only), Lanercost Priory's extensive remains offer an unforgettable visit.

Nearby farm buildings have been converted into a tearoom. The parish church, Dacre Hall, tearoom and visitor centre are not managed by English Heritage.

When you're in the area, visit Hadrian's Wall (p.250).

OPENING TIMES

Open daily 1 Apr-5 Nov

Open varying days 6 Nov-28 Mar

Site closed 24-26 Dec & 1 Jan

See website for latest opening times

Last entry 30 mins before closing

VISIT US

Direction: Off the minor road through Lanercost, next to the church; 2½ miles NE of Brampton

Train: Brampton 3 miles

Bus: Visit traveline.info for the latest bus timetables

Tel: 01697 73030

NON-MEMBERS

See website for entry prices

By being a Member, you save up to **£24.50** (price of a family ticket) when you visit **Lanercost Priory**

[ACQ.1930] 🍴 P 📷 ⚠ OVP

Please note: no toilet facilties available at site.

Lanercost tearoom is open every day except 25 and 26 Dec. Tel: 01697 741267 cafelanercost.co.uk (not managed by English Heritage).

MAP PAGE 312 (4E)
OS MAP 86, 315: NY556637

PENRITH CASTLE

CUMBRIA – CA11 7EA

Begun in the later 14th century and subsequently transformed into a luxurious residence by Richard, Duke of Gloucester (afterwards Richard III). Surviving in places to its full height.

OPENING TIMES

Any reasonable daylight hours

VISIT US

Direction: Opposite Penrith railway station

Train: Penrith (adjacent)

Bus: Visit traveline.info for the latest bus timetables and routes

ACQ.1913

Caution: steep slopes.

MAP PAGE 312 (5E)
OS MAP 90, OL5: NY513299

PIEL CASTLE

CUMBRIA – LA13 0QN

PIEL CASTLE

An exciting place to visit, the massive keep of Piel Castle dominates a little island in Barrow harbour; it's accessible only by small boat ferry. It was built in the 14th century by Furness Abbey (p.244) as a refuge from pirates and seaborne Scots raiders.

OPENING TIMES

Any reasonable daylight hours. Seasonal access by ferry boat not managed by English Heritage

VISIT US

Direction: Via ferry from Roa Island, accessible by road 3¼ miles SE of Barrow-in-Furness

By Small Boat: Piel Castle can only be accessed by boat, please check website for latest ferry information

Train: Barrow-in-Furness 4 miles

Bus: Visit traveline.info for the latest bus timetables and routes

ACQ.1973

Public house for refreshments (not managed by English Heritage).

Caution: deep water, steep slopes.

MAP PAGE 312 (7D)
OS MAP 96, OL6: SD233636

RAVENGLASS ROMAN BATH HOUSE

CUMBRIA – CA18 1SR

Among the tallest surviving Roman structures in northern Britain, the walls of this bath house stand up to 4 metres (13 feet) high, complete with remains of plasterwork and · elegant niches for statues. It served Ravenglass Roman fort, which guarded a useful harbour and was garrisoned by troops from Hadrian's fleet.

OPENING TIMES

Any reasonable daylight hours

Parts of the site may be cordoned off due to conservation works

RAVENGLASS ROMAN BATH HOUSE

VISIT US

Direction: ½ mile SE of Ravenglass station, via signposted footpath from village car park and then private road. No vehicular access or parking at site

Train: Ravenglass (adjacent)

Bus: Visit traveline.info for the latest bus timetables and routes

ACQ.1980

Caution: falling masonry.

MAP PAGE 312 (6C)
OS MAP 96, OL6: SD088959

SHAP ABBEY

CUMBRIA – CA10 3NB

The impressive full height 15th-century tower and other remains of a remote abbey of Premonstratensian 'white canons'. Information panels guide you round the abbey and illustrate daily monastic life.

OPENING TIMES

Any reasonable daylight hours

VISIT US

Direction: 1½ miles W of Shap, on the bank of the River Lowther

Train: Penrith 10 miles

Bus: Visit traveline.info

ACQ.1948

Disabled access (limited views from outside the site).

Steep access road may be hazardous in wintry weather.

Parking: charges apply to non-members, free for Members with valid car sticker.

Caution: sheer drop into water.

MAP PAGE 312 (5E)
OS MAP 90, OL5: NY548152

STOTT PARK BOBBIN MILL

—————— CUMBRIA – LA12 8AX ——————

Experience the Industrial Revolution first-hand at unique Stott Park Bobbin Mill. Let demonstrations lead you to a bygone era, then enhance your visit with a seasonal woodland walk.

Fully working Stott Park is an unmissable one-off. In a lovely woodland setting near Lake Windermere, it's the very last survivor of the hundred-odd Lake District mills which produced wooden bobbins for the Lancashire cotton industry. 'Bobbin boys' aged from 10 to 14 worked 16 hours a day here to produce up to 250,000 bobbins a week. Packed with clattering belt-driven machinery, it's presented just as it was in about 1880.

Still fully operational, the mill's pulsating line shaft and pulley wheels were powered first by water and then by a magnificent original steam engine. The refurbished cross-tubed boiler, providing steam for the engine, was reinstalled in 2019. It's powered up on bank holidays and special event days throughout the year.

Displays tell the stories of Stott Park's people, and a hands-on family trail with children's dressing-up clothes helps you imagine what it was like to work here. You can also explore the mill's woodland surroundings. A timber footbridge handmade by local craftsmen crosses the stream, leading to a 200 metre-long footpath through two acres of woodland, where trees were coppiced to provide wood for bobbins. It's carpeted with bluebells in late April and early May.

Demonstrations of the mill machinery, showing you how a raw piece of coppiced timber is transformed into a bobbin, take place throughout the day.

Please visit our website or call the site for details of special events throughout the year.

OPENING TIMES
Open varying days 1 Apr-5 Nov

Site closed 6 Nov-28 Mar

See website for latest opening times

Last entry 1 hour before closing

Please call for details of steam days

VISIT US
Direction: Located 1½ miles N of Newby Bridge, off A590

Train: Grange-over-Sands 8 miles; Lakeside Station (Lakeside & Haverthwaite railway) ¾ mile

Bus: Visit traveline.info for the latest bus timetables and routes

Boat: Windermere Lake Cruises from Ambleside or Bowness to Lakeside, then ¾ mile walk

Tel: 01539 531087

Local Tourist Information: Hawkshead: 01539 436946

NON-MEMBERS
See website for entry prices

By being a Member, you save up to £36.50 (price of a family ticket) when you visit **Stott Park Bobbin Mill**

ACQ.1974 🅰️ OVP

Disabled access (ground floor only. Specific interpretation for visually impaired visitors).

Dogs are not allowed in the mill itself but are welcome around the grounds.

Lower car park for disabled parking (short downhill path to mill). Upper car park for general parking.

Disabled visitors can be dropped off at the mill entrance (with level access to site) before cars are parked. Please phone site in advance to arrange.

Parking: charges apply to non-members, free for Members with valid English Heritage car sticker.

MAP PAGE 312 (6D)
OS MAP 96/97, OL7: SD372881

WETHERAL PRIORY GATEHOUSE

CUMBRIA – CA4 8ES

Well preserved early 16th-century gatehouse, the sole survivor of a small Benedictine priory. A miniature 'pele tower' containing two storeys of comfortable rooms, it later became a fortified vicarage, a defence against border raiders.

OPENING TIMES

See website for latest opening times

VISIT US

Direction: Near Wetheral village; 6 miles E of Carlisle, on B6263

Train: Wetheral ½ mile

Bus: Visit traveline.info

 ACQ.1978 Caution: steep stairs.

MAP PAGE 312 (4D)
OS MAP 86, 315: NY468541

LANCASHIRE

GOODSHAW CHAPEL

LANCASHIRE – BB4 8QB

English Heritage's only Nonconformist place of worship, this atmospheric Baptist chapel displays a complete set of Georgian box pews, galleries and pulpit.

OPENING TIMES

Please call the key keeper for details
Tel: 01706 227333

VISIT US

Direction: In Crawshawbooth, 2 miles N of Rawtenstall via A682 (in Goodshaw Ave – turning off A682 opp. Alderson & Horan). Chapel approx. 1½ miles from main road

Train: Burnley Manchester Road 4½ miles

GOODSHAW CHAPEL

Bus: Visit traveline.info for the latest bus timetables and routes

ACQ.1976 Caution: steep stairs.

MAP PAGE 310 (4D)
OS MAP 103, OL21: SD814261

SAWLEY ABBEY

LANCASHIRE – BB7 4NH

Riverside remains of a Cistercian abbey founded in 1148. Its monks briefly returned during the Pilgrimage of Grace, but the insurrection collapsed and their abbot was executed.

OPENING TIMES

See website for latest opening times

VISIT US

Direction: Located at Sawley; 3½ miles N of Clitheroe, off A59

Train: Clitheroe 4 miles

Bus: Visit traveline.info for the latest bus timetables and routes

ACQ.1951 Caution: falling masonry.

MAP PAGE 310 (3D)
OS MAP 103, OL41: SD777464

WARTON OLD RECTORY

LANCASHIRE – LA5 9PH

A rare survival of a large 14th-century stone house with great hall and chambers. It served as a residence and courthouse for the wealthy and powerful rectors of Warton.

WARTON OLD RECTORY

OPENING TIMES

See website for latest opening times

VISIT US

Direction: At Warton; 1 mile N of Carnforth, on minor road off A6

Train: Carnforth 1 mile

Bus: Visit traveline.info for the latest bus timetables and routes

ACQ.1969

MAP PAGE 310 (3C)
OS MAP 97, OL7: SD499723

WHALLEY ABBEY GATEHOUSE

LANCASHIRE – BB7 9TN

The 14th-century gatehouse of the nearby Cistercian abbey, the second wealthiest monastery in Lancashire, beside the River Calder. The first floor was probably a chapel.

OPENING TIMES

Any reasonable daylight hours. External viewing only

VISIT US

Direction: In Whalley; 6 miles NE of Blackburn, on minor road off A59

Train: Whalley ¼ mile

Bus: Visit traveline.info for the latest bus timetables and routes

ACQ.1971

MAP PAGE 310 (4D)
OS MAP 103, 287: SD729362

WELCOME TO

HADRIAN'S WALL

HADRIAN'S WALL

Started just over 1,900 years ago, Hadrian's Wall is an incredible feat of ancient engineering. The northern frontier of the mighty Roman empire, Hadrian's Wall crosses wild countryside and climbs high crags for 73 miles from coast to coast, and much of it survives to this day.

Among the most important of the forts guarding the frontier was **Housesteads** (p.256), which today offers panoramic views and is the most complete example of a Roman fort anywhere in Britain. **Birdoswald Roman Fort** (p.254) features award-winning displays and interactives to bring the past to life for visitors of all ages, while fascinating artefacts shine a light on Roman life at **Chesters Roman Fort** (p.258) and **Corbridge Roman Town** (p.260).

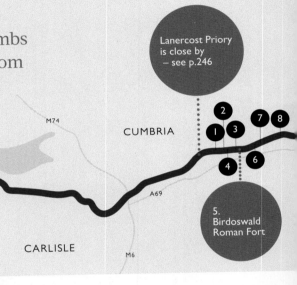

Lanercost Priory is close by — see p.246

CUMBRIA

M74

A69

CARLISLE

M6

5. Birdoswald Roman Fort

Use this map to discover more of the Wall and make the most of your day

5 ···· 12
- 12.5 miles*
- 🚗 25 mins
- 🚶 4 hrs
- 🚲 1 hr 15 mins

12 ···· 16
- 8 miles*
- 🚗 10 mins
- 🚶 2 hrs 45 mins
- 🚲 42 mins

16 ···· 20
- 8 miles*
- 🚗 15 mins
- 🚶 2 hrs 30 mins
- 🚲 45 mins

Hadrian's Wall
73 miles

Main Roads

National Cycle Network route number

*All distances between sites are using most direct routes.

english-heritage.org.uk

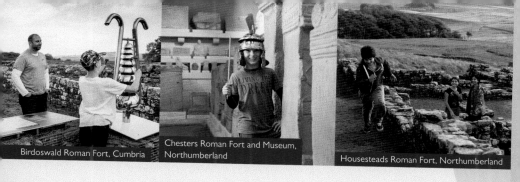

Birdoswald Roman Fort, Cumbria

Chesters Roman Fort and Museum, Northumberland

Housesteads Roman Fort, Northumberland

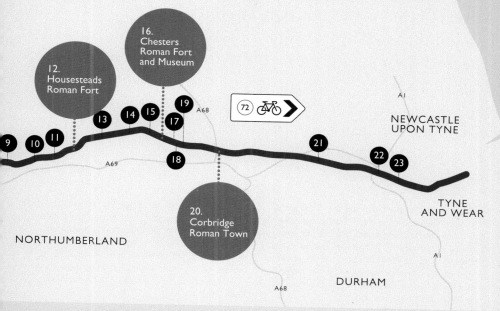

16.
Chesters Roman Fort and Museum

12.
Housesteads Roman Fort

9 10 11 13 14 15 17 18 19 A68

72

NEWCASTLE UPON TYNE

A1

21 22 23

A69

20.
Corbridge Roman Town

NORTHUMBERLAND

TYNE AND WEAR

A1

A68

DURHAM

A68

Caring for the Hadrian's Wall World Heritage Site and National Trail

When planning your holiday or visit, please remember to observe 'Every Footstep Counts' – the World Heritage Site's own country code. As you will appreciate, Hadrian's Wall is a fragile environment and the archaeology is easily damaged.

You can help us to protect this great Wonder of the World by ensuring you:

- Never walk on the Wall, as this may cause it to collapse.
- Always keep to the signed paths.
- Keep dogs on a lead and under close control.
- Use public transport whenever you can.

- Note that Hadrian's Wall Path National Trail is a footpath only. Please cycle on legal routes only, i.e. bridleways, byways, roads and cyclepaths.
- Visit the organised paying sites, which are more robust and can accommodate visitors. Also please avoid walking alongside the Wall when the ground is very wet. The buried archaeology underfoot is particularly vulnerable to damage in the wet winter months between November and April.
- Avoid walking in a single file.
- Respect livestock and land.

BIRDOSWALD ROMAN FORT ⑤

CUMBRIA – CA8 7DD

A great place for a family day out, Birdoswald is an ideal base for discovering the Wall. Our award-winning displays – packed with interactives, family-friendly features and original artefacts – allow people of all ages to engage and explore together. They show you how and why the Wall was built, how it was used and defended, and what kind of people once lived here.

Among the most important Hadrian's Wall forts, Birdoswald was one of 16 major bases along the Wall. It has the best-preserved defences of any Wall fort. Known to the Romans as 'Banna', it was garrisoned by up to 1,000 Roman auxiliary soldiers – for most of its history a unit of Dacians, originally raised in what's now Romania, later joined by troops from northern Holland.

Just outside the fort, you'll find the longest continuous stretch of Hadrian's Wall visible today, a truly impressive sight. Once inside, imaginative displays introduce you not just to the Wall, but to the whole story of Roman Britain. You can create a model of the Wall with Lego bricks, use a crane to assemble an arch, take a digital quiz to discover what kind of Wall dweller you are, learn about signalling techniques and try out a periscope to get a soldier's-eye view over the original 5-metre (16.5-feet) height of the Wall. You'll also find out about the people who lived here for over three centuries; memorials and burial urns excavated near the site reveal the stories of soldiers and their wives and children. A great experience for children and adults alike, the displays are a must if you want to discover the full history of the Wall.

Innovative features also guide you round the whole of the fort. 'Viewfinders' help you explore vistas within and beyond the defences, and you can play Roman games and listen in to gossip from the commandant's house. Clues and puzzles lead families on the hunt for a spy, taking in the three main gates and the view over the ravine of the River Irthing.

You'll also discover another unique feature of Birdoswald; how it was continuously occupied for 16 centuries after the collapse of Roman rule – by local post-Roman warlords, medieval and Elizabethan Borderers and the Victorian farmers who built the present picturesque turreted farmhouse.

Birdoswald is a family-friendly site. There's a generously sized room where visitors with younger children can park buggies, wash, hang coats and boots, play Wall-related games, get into a Roman tent and even try on a Roman toga.

Offering a café and an education room, Birdoswald also makes an ideal base for exploring the wild and beautiful surrounding countryside. The fort stands on the Hadrian's Wall Path National Trail, making it a perfect stopping place for ramblers and cyclists.

Archaeology Live: 12 Jun-7 Jul 2023

This is the third instalment of a major five-year archaeological excavation at Birdoswald Roman Fort. A collaboration between Historic England and Newcastle University, it continues to examine links between the fort and its adjacent settlements, its relationship with the Wall and the successive turf and stone Walls. Guided tours will provide fascinating insights, as more World Heritage Site secrets are unearthed. See website for details.

STAY WITH US

Go to bed and wake up in a Roman Fort. *The Bunkhouse* at Birdoswald is perfect for residential educational visits and large groups, sleeping up to 36 persons in 7 bedrooms.

See Birdoswald web pages for details.

OPENING TIMES

Open daily 1 Apr-5 Nov

Open varying days 6 Nov-28 Mar

Site closed 24-25 Dec

See website for latest opening times

Last entry 30 mins before closing

Café closes 4.30pm (summer) and 3.30pm (winter)

VISIT US

Address: Gilsland, Brampton, Cumbria CA8 7DD

Direction: 4 miles west of Greenhead off B6318. Signposted from A69 Carlisle – Hexham road at Brampton roundabout

Train: Haltwhistle 7 miles

Bus: Visit traveline.info for the latest bus timetables and routes

Tel: 01697 747602

Local Tourist Information:
Haltwhistle: 01434 321863

SAVE TODAY By being a Member, you save up to £36.50 (price of a family ticket) when you visit **Birdoswald Roman Fort.**

NON-MEMBERS

See website for entry prices

ACQ.1946

Please note: short uphill walk from car park to fort.

Disabled access (to visitor centre, toilets, shop, tearoom and part of site. Disabled parking on site).

Parking: charges apply to non-members, free for Members with valid English Heritage car sticker.

MAP PAGE 312 (4E)
OS MAP 86, OL43: NY615663

HOUSESTEADS (12) ROMAN FORT

NORTHUMBERLAND – NE47 6NN

Set high on a hilltop with panoramic views, spectacularly sited Housesteads is the most complete example of a Roman fort anywhere in Britain – a must-see for all visitors to the Wall. Discover the stories of the fort and its people in the interactive exhibition, and find out how soldiers and their families lived on this wild northern frontier of the Roman Empire.

Among the most popular sites on Hadrian's Wall, this famous fort stands on the Whin Sill escarpment, flanked by dramatic stretches of the Wall. Hadrian's Wall Path runs just above it. The site museum houses an outstanding exhibition, vividly interpreting life here on the northern edge of the Roman Empire.

Begun in about AD 124 as one of 16 permanent forts supporting Hadrian's frontier system, Housesteads was known as Vercovicium. It was garrisoned by around 1,000 infantry from a unit originally raised in what's now eastern Belgium, and later reinforced by cavalry. The 5-acre fort displays the remains of gateways and a turreted wall: within are a host of clearly traceable buildings, including the commandant's house, hospital and the renowned multi-seater communal lavatories.

The Roman south gate was much later adapted into a 'bastle' farmhouse, fortified against the 'rank robbers hereabouts': the Border Reivers. Outside the fort wall are the excavated foundations of the Roman civilian settlement. One of the houses here produced evidence of a gruesome Roman double murder.

Visit the museum to witness the story of Housesteads and its people retold in a multimedia display. A short film traces the history of the fort and recreates its original appearance. Every aspect of Roman life here – what the soldiers wore, the tools and weapons they used, how they were cared for when sick, and deities they worshipped, including 'Hooded Gods' – is illuminated by displays. These feature many fascinating objects from the fort, most strikingly a winged Victory statue. Children can enjoy a dressing-up 'Discovery Box', and touchable replicas of Roman objects set at child-height, explained by Felix the Roman soldier. You can also follow Felix in the panels that guide you round the fort.

The fort and museum stand uphill from the car park (via a fairly strenuous 10-minute walk). The National Trust visitor centre by the car park offers a welcome and introduction to the site and an indoor café with outdoor seating for warm days.

Owned by the National Trust and managed by English Heritage.

OPENING TIMES

Open daily 1 Apr-28 Mar

Site closed 24-25 Dec

See website for latest opening times

Last entry 45 mins before closing

VISIT US

Address: Housesteads Roman Fort, Haydon Bridge, Hexham, Northumberland NE47 6NN

Direction: Bardon Mill 4 miles

Bus: Visit traveline.info for the latest bus timetables and routes

Tel: 01434 344363

Local Tourist Information:
Hexham: 01670 620450

NON-MEMBERS

See website for entry prices

Free to National Trust members

SAVE TODAY By being a Member, you save up to £36.50 (price of a family ticket) when you visit **Housesteads Roman Fort.**

Disabled access to the museum (companion recommended). Limited access to site. 750-metre walk up a steep gradient. Disabled parking available at the top of the hill. Please enquire at the visitor centre in the roadside car park to arrange disabled parking. Assistance dogs only in the museum.

Car park not operated by English Heritage (charge payable to Northumberland National Park).

MAP PAGE 313 (4F)
OS MAP 86/87, OL43: NY790688

CHESTERS ROMAN FORT AND MUSEUM ⑯

NORTHUMBERLAND – NE46 4EU

Set in the beautiful valley of the River Tyne, Chesters is the best-preserved Roman cavalry fort in Britain, with the finest surviving Roman bath-house complex and a unique Victorian-style museum.

Imaginative interpretation throughout the site, including a family trail, helps you explore the fort and its links with John Clayton, 'Saviour of the Wall'.

Known as Cilurnum, Chesters was positioned to defend the vulnerable section of Hadrian's Wall where it crossed the river. Around five hundred cavalry troops – the elite of the Roman auxiliary forces – were based here. From the late 2nd century the garrison was a regiment originating from Asturias in northern Spain.

Pictorial panels guide you round the many clearly marked features of the fort, including its four gates, a barrack block, which cavalrymen shared with their horses, the headquarters building with its underground strongroom and the commanding officer's mansion with its private baths.

Children can seek out the 'rubbing stones' concealed among the buildings, collecting tips to help them in their chosen roles of commander, trooper, guard, messenger, musician or commander's dog. Two viewfinders reveal how parts of the fort once appeared.

Between the fort and the river, the garrison's bath house survives to above head-height; the finest example of a military bath house in Britain. It's easy to imagine how the soldiers enjoyed this 'spa' complex of cold, warm and hot sauna baths,

together with a big changing-room-cum-clubhouse, still equipped with niches, which probably housed bathers' clothes.

All this was rediscovered by John Clayton, the wealthy Victorian landowner whose mansion stands within sight of the west gate. His groundbreaking excavations here, and lifelong fascination with the Wall – sections of which he bought and safeguarded – played a crucial role in saving Hadrian's great frontier system for us to enjoy today.

His single-minded vision – and the help he got from family, friends and staff – is celebrated in the unique Clayton Museum, an absolute must-see for all visitors to Chesters. Packed with hundreds of fascinating finds from the central section of the Wall, it preserves its traditional Victorian layout and atmosphere. Sensitive reordering and creative storytelling, including Kindles disguised as Victorian books, help visitors to explore museum treasures – from statues of gods to a tiny dog figurine – at their chosen level of detail.

Take a break from your journey of discovery in the Chesters Tearoom with its indoor and outdoor seating. Check the website for details of an active events programme which runs throughout the summer.

OPENING TIMES

Open daily 1 Apr–5 Nov

Open varying days 6 Nov–28 Mar

Site closed 24-25 Dec

See website for latest opening times

Last entry 30 mins before closing

VISIT US

Address: Chollerford, Hexham, Northumberland NE46 4EU

Direction: ¼ mile W of Chollerford, on B6318

Train: Hexham 5½ miles

Bus: Visit traveline.info for the latest bus timetables and routes

Tel: 01434 681379

Local Tourist Information: Hexham: 01670 620450

SAVE TODAY

By being a Member, you save up to **£36.50** (price of a family ticket) when you visit **Chesters Roman Fort and Museum.**

NON-MEMBERS

See website for entry prices

ACQ.1954 ♿ 🐕 ✋ 🖼 🧍 🧍 ✉ **P**
🪑 🛍 ☕ WC ⚠ OVP

Disabled access (companion recommended). Disabled parking and toilets.

Dogs on leads (restricted areas only).

Tearoom.

Parking: charges apply to non-members, free for Members with valid car sticker.

MAP PAGE 313 (4F)
OS MAP 87, OL43: NY912702

20

CORBRIDGE ROMAN TOWN

——— NORTHUMBERLAND – NE45 5NT ———

For a really in-depth look at how people lived, worked and worshipped near Hadrian's Wall, Corbridge is the place to visit. Our extensive site museum offers you unique insights into Roman social life at Corbridge – the only place in Britain where you can walk the high street of a Roman town.

Beginning as a series of forts, Corbridge was founded well before Hadrian began his Wall, 2½ miles away. It developed into a prosperous town, the most northerly in the whole Roman Empire, providing goods and services for the Wall garrisons. You can still walk the original surface of its Roman main street, flanked by the impressive remains of granaries, mansions, markets and workshops.

Our museum showcases the most fascinating of our internationally important collection of site-finds, illuminating as never before the social and working life of a Roman town. You'll discover how Corbridge's people originated from all over the Roman Empire; thematically displayed weapons, jewellery and personal possessions mingle with grave finds and images of the town's many gods. A pictorial timeline traces Corbridge's development from its foundation until the collapse of Roman rule and the move to the site of the present town, clearly visible from the ruins.

Don't miss the Corbridge Lion sculpture, the poignant monuments to Corbridge's Roman children, or the intriguing Corbridge Hoard, one of the most important finds from Roman Britain.

OPENING TIMES

Open daily 1 Apr-5 Nov

Open varying days 6 Nov-28 Mar

Site closed 24-26 Dec & 1 Jan

See website for latest opening times

Last entry 30 mins before closing

VISIT US

Direction: ½ mile NW of Corbridge, on minor road, then signposted

Train: Corbridge 1¼ miles

Bus: Visit traveline.info for the latest bus timetables and routes

Tel: 01434 632349

Local Tourist Information:
Corbridge: 01434 632815

NON-MEMBERS

See website for entry prices

By being a Member, you save up to **£36.50** (price of a family ticket) when you visit **Corbridge Roman Town**

ACQ.1933

Dogs on leads (restricted areas only).

Disabled access (parking, toilet, audio tour, access to the museum and perimeter of site).

Please note: we don't have a tearoom, but you'll find plenty of refreshment spots in Corbridge.

MAP PAGE 313 (4F)
OS MAP 87, OL43: NY982648

1 HARE HILL

A short length of Wall still stands 2.7 metres (8ft 10in) high.

VISIT US

Direction: ¾ mile NE of Lanercost

ACQ.1972

OS MAP 86, 43: NY564646

2 BANKS EAST TURRET

Imposing and well-preserved turret with adjoining stretches of Hadrian's Wall.

VISIT US

Direction: On minor road E of Banks village; 3½ miles NE of Brampton

ACQ.1934

Parking: charges apply to non-members, free for Members with valid car sticker.

OS MAP 86, 315: NY575647

3 PIKE HILL SIGNAL TOWER

The remains of one of a network of signal towers predating Hadrian's Wall, Pike Hill was later joined to the Wall at an angle of 45 degrees.

VISIT US

Direction: On minor road E of Banks village

ACQ.1971

Caution: steep slopes, unguarded drops.

OS MAP 86, 315: NY577648

4 LEAHILL TURRET & PIPER SIKE TURRET

Turrets west of Birdoswald: Piper Sike has a cooking-hearth.

VISIT US

Direction: On minor road 2 miles W of Birdoswald Fort

ACQ.1952

OS MAP 86, OL43/315: NY586652

5 BIRDOSWALD ROMAN FORT
See feature on p.254

6 HARROW'S SCAR MILECASTLE & WALL

A mile-long section of the Wall, rebuilt in stone later in Hadrian's reign. It's linked to Birdoswald Roman Fort (see p.254).

VISIT US

Direction: ¼ mile E of Birdoswald, on minor road off B6318

ACQ.1946

Parking at Birdoswald.

OS MAP 86, OL43: NY620664

DON'T FORGET
Remember to take your membership card.

7 WILLOWFORD WALL, TURRETS AND BRIDGE

A fine 914-metre (2,999-foot) stretch of Wall, including two turrets and impressive bridge remains beside the River Irthing. Linked by a bridge to Birdoswald Roman Fort (see p.254).

VISIT US

Direction: W of minor road, ¾ mile W of Gilsland

ACQ.1946

Beware – livestock may be grazing on site.
Caution: deep water, steep slopes.

OS MAP 86, OL43: NY627664

8 POLTROSS BURN MILECASTLE

One of the best-preserved milecastles on Hadrian's Wall, Poltross includes an oven, a stair to the rampart walk, and the remains of its north gateway. Known locally as 'the King's Stables'.

VISIT US

Direction: On minor road E of Banks village. Immediately SW of Gilsland village, by old railway station

ACQ.1938

Parking (follow brown signs).
Caution: deep water.

OS MAP 86, OL43: NY634662

FOR UPDATES ON HADRIAN'S WALL, DON'T FORGET TO FOLLOW US ON FACEBOOK AND TWITTER.

9 WALLTOWN CRAGS

One of the best places of all to see the Wall, dramatically snaking and diving along the crags of the Whin Sill.

VISIT US

Direction: 1 mile NE of Greenhead, off B6318

ACQ.1939 🐕 🐄 **P** ⚠

Parking not operated by English Heritage. Parking charge applies (payable to Northumberland National Park).

Caution: steep slopes, unguarded drops.

OS MAP 86/87, 43: NY674663

10 CAWFIELDS MILECASTLE

A fine stretch of Hadrian's Wall on a steep slope, with turrets and an impressive milecastle, probably built by the Second Legion.

VISIT US

Direction: 1¼ miles N of Haltwhistle, off B6318

ACQ.1960 🐕 🐄 🚶 👶 **P** ⚠

Parking not operated by English Heritage. Parking charge applies (payable to Northumberland National Park).

Caution: unguarded drops.

OS MAP 86/87, OL43: NY716667

See Hadrian's Wall by bus with the AD122 service (subject to change, see **traveline.info** for details).

11 WINSHIELDS WALL

The highest point on the Wall, in rugged country with spectacular views.

VISIT US

Direction: W of Steel Rigg car park; on minor road off B6318

ACQ.1937 🐕 🐄 ⚠

Caution: unguarded drops.

OS MAP 86/87, 43: NY742676

12 HOUSESTEADS ROMAN FORT
See feature on p.256

13 SEWINGSHIELDS WALL

A length of Wall with milecastle remains, impressively sited along the Whin Sill. It commands fine views of many prehistoric and later earthworks to the north.

VISIT US

Direction: N of B6318; 1½ miles E of Housesteads Fort

ACQ.1946 🐕 ⚠

Caution: steep slopes.

OS MAP 86/87, OL43: NY805702

14 CARRAWBURGH ROMAN FORT AND TEMPLE OF MITHRAS

Built around AD 122, the fort housed a garrison of about 500 soldiers – first from France, later from Belgium – responsible for defending the frontier of the Roman Empire. It occupies an area of 3.5 acres on a natural terrace, overlooking the Northumberland National Park. Just below the fort hides a little stone temple to the eastern soldiers' god Mithras, with facsimiles of altars found during excavation.

VISIT US

Direction: 3¾ miles W of Chollerford, on B6318

ACQ.2020 Carrawburgh Roman Fort
ACQ.1953 Temple of Mithras 🐕 🐄 **P**

Parking not operated by English Heritage. Parking charge applies (payable to Northumberland National Park).

OS MAP 87, 43: NY859711

15 BLACK CARTS TURRET

A 460-metre (1,509-foot) length of Hadrian's Wall including one turret.

VISIT US

Direction: On Hadrian's Wall National Trail, about 20 minutes signposted walk from Chesters Roman Fort

ACQ.1970 ♿ 🐕 🐄 ⚠

Please note: no visitor parking available. Parking at Chesters Roman Fort (20 minute walk).

OS MAP 86, 315: NY575647

16 CHESTERS ROMAN FORT AND MUSEUM
See feature on p.258

17 CHESTERS BRIDGE ABUTMENT

Close to Chesters Roman Fort are the remains of a bridge which carried Hadrian's Wall across the North Tyne. Visible on both river banks, but best viewed from the Roman fort.

VISIT US
Direction: ½ mile S of Low Brunton, on A6079

ACQ.1946

Site is liable to flooding.

Caution: deep water, steep slopes.

OS MAP 87, 43: NY914701

18 BRUNTON TURRET

Wall section and a surviving piece of turret 2.5 metres (8ft 2in) high, built by men of the Twentieth Legion.

VISIT US
Direction: ¼ mile S of Low Brunton, off A6079

ACQ.1947

OS MAP 87, OL43: NY922698

19 PLANETREES ROMAN WALL

A 15-metre (49-foot) length of narrow Wall on broad foundations, reflecting a change of policy concerning the thickness of the Wall during construction.

VISIT US
Direction: 1 mile SE of Chollerford on B6318

ACQ.1945

OS MAP 87, OL43: NY929696

20 CORBRIDGE ROMAN TOWN
See feature on p.260

21 HEDDON-ON-THE-WALL

A consolidated stretch of Wall, up to 2 metres (6ft 6in) thick in places.

VISIT US
Direction: Immediately E of Heddon village, S of A69

ACQ.1935

OS MAP 88, 316: NZ137669

OUR EVENTS

Check out our year-long programme of events.

english-heritage.org.uk/events

22 DENTON HALL TURRET

The foundations of a turret and a 65-metre (213-foot) length of Wall.

VISIT US
Direction: 4 miles W of Newcastle upon Tyne city centre, located immediately SE of A69

ACQ.1934

OS MAP 88, 316: NZ198655

23 BENWELL ROMAN TEMPLE

The remains of a small temple to the native god 'Antenociticus', in the 'vicus' (civilian settlement), which stood outside Benwell Fort.

VISIT US
Direction: Temple located immediately SE of A69, at Benwell in Broomridge Ave; Vallum Crossing in Denhill Park

ACQ.1936

OS MAP 88, 316: NZ217647

BENWELL VALLUM CROSSING

A stone-built causeway, where the road from the south crossed the Vallum earthwork on its way to Benwell Fort.

ACQ.1934

Viewing only – no access to the Vallum.

OS MAP 88, 316: NZ216646

FOR UPDATES ON HADRIAN'S WALL, DON'T FORGET TO FOLLOW US ON FACEBOOK AND TWITTER.

WELCOME TO THE

NORTH EAST

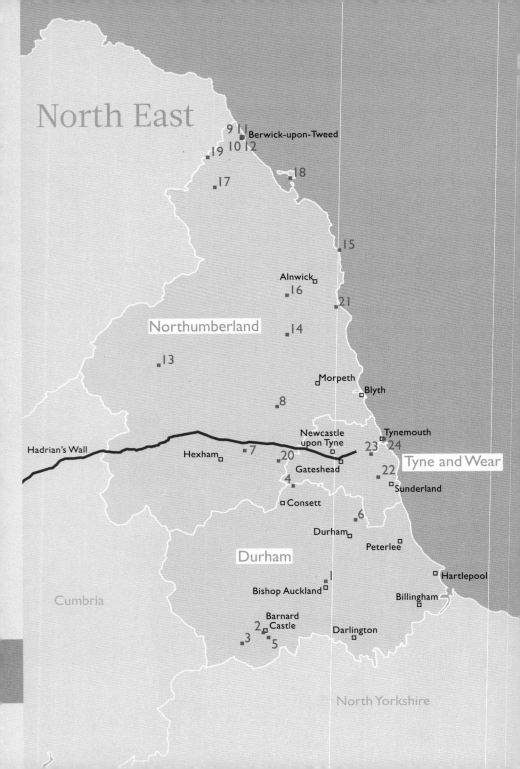

North East

Berwick-upon-Tweed

9 11
19 10 12
17
18

15

Alnwick
16
Northumberland
14
13
Morpeth
8
Blyth
Newcastle
upon Tyne
Tynemouth
Hadrian's Wall
Hexham 7 23 24
20
Gateshead
Tyne and Wear
4 22
Consett Sunderland

6
Durham
Peterlee
Durham
Hartlepool
1
Bishop Auckland
Billingham
Barnard
Castle
2
3 5
Darlington

Cumbria

North Yorkshire

NORTH EAST

From invasions to innovative architecture, our sites in the North East tell stories of raids, border battles and – at times – peaceful religious life.

At **Belsay** (p.272) you can see a medieval castle in the beautiful grounds of a Greek Revival hall, and from this year there'll be more to see and do here than ever before. Some of our finest castles can be found elsewhere in the region, including **Warkworth Castle** (p.278), which was home to the powerful Percy family and has just been refreshed with new displays and family activities. The stunning remains of **Dunstanburgh Castle** (p.274) are sited on a remote and wild headland, while **Norham Castle** (p.275) was besieged at least 13 times by Scottish armies.

Lindisfarne Priory (p.276) is one of the country's best-known monastic sites, famed for its holy men, tranquil atmosphere and world-renowned Anglo-Saxon Gospels.

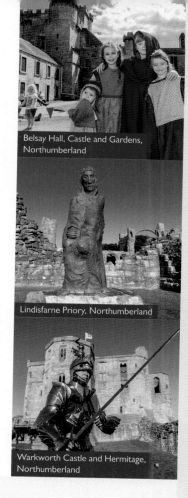

Belsay Hall, Castle and Gardens, Northumberland

Lindisfarne Priory, Northumberland

Warkworth Castle and Hermitage, Northumberland

AUCKLAND CASTLE DEER HOUSE

DURHAM – DL14 7QJ

A Gothic Revival 'eye-catcher' of 1760. A deer shelter with facilities for picnics and enjoying the view.

Managed by The Auckland Project.

OPENING TIMES

See website for latest opening times

VISIT US

Direction: Located in Auckland Park, Bishop Auckland; N of town centre on A68

Train: Bishop Auckland 1 mile

Bus: Visit traveline.info for the latest bus timetables and routes

Parking (pay and display in town centre).

MAP PAGE 313 (5G)
OS MAP 93, 305: NZ216304

BARNARD CASTLE

DURHAM – DL12 8PR

Spectacularly set high above the River Tees, on the fringe of an attractive market town, this imposing fortress takes its name from its 12th-century founder, Bernard de Balliol. Later developed by Richard III, whose boar emblem is carved above a window in the inner ward, the castle's chief strength: here loyalist forces were besieged during the 1569 Northern Rising against Elizabeth I, before surrendering to 5,000 rebels. There are fine views over the Tees gorge.

OPENING TIMES

Open daily 1 Apr-5 Nov

Open varying days 6 Nov-28 Mar

Site closed 24-26 Dec & 1 Jan (possibly)

See website for latest opening times

Last entry 30 mins before closing

VISIT US

Direction: In Barnard Castle town

Bus: Visit traveline.info for the latest bus timetables and routes

Tel: 01833 638212

NON-MEMBERS

See website for entry prices

Parking (pay and display in town centre).

MAP PAGE 313 (5F)
OS MAP 92, OL31: NZ049165

BOWES CASTLE

DURHAM – DL12 9LG

Impressive ruins of Henry II's 12th-century keep, on the site of a Roman fort guarding strategic Stainmore Pass over the Pennines.

OPENING TIMES

Any reasonable daylight hours

VISIT US

Direction: In Bowes Village off A66; 4 miles W of Barnard Castle town

Bus: Visit traveline.info for the latest bus timetables and routes

Caution: steep slopes.

MAP PAGE 313 (6F)
OS MAP 92, OL30/31: NY992135

DERWENTCOTE STEEL FURNACE

DURHAM – NE17 7RS

Built in the 1730s, Derwentcote is the last surviving cementation steel-making furnace in Britain. It produced high-grade steel for springs and cutting tools.

A circular walk through the Derwent Valley starts and finishes in the site car park. For more about the mill's surroundings, see landofoakandiron.org.uk

OPENING TIMES

Any reasonable daylight hours Grounds only – no access to furnace except for guided tours

See website for tours and latest opening times

DERWENTCOTE STEEL FURNACE

Woodland walk from site (stout footwear recommended). Please see English Heritage website and landofoakandiron.org.uk for up-to-date information about tours and events

VISIT US

Direction: 10 miles SW of Newcastle, on A694; between Rowland's Gill and Hamsterley

Train: MetroCentre, Gateshead, 7 miles

Bus: Visit traveline.info for the latest bus timetables and routes

ACQ.1985 ⛔🅿️⚠️

Dogs on leads (restricted areas only).

Parking across main road from site.

Caution: deep water, steep slopes.

> MAP PAGE 313 (4G)
> OS MAP 88, 307: NZ130566

EGGLESTONE ABBEY
DURHAM – DL12 9TN

Ruins of a Premonstratensian monastery, picturesquely sited by the River Tees. Remains include parts of the 13th-century church and living quarters.

Egglestone Abbey can be reached by a short walk from Barnard Castle (p.268).

OPENING TIMES

Open daily 1 Apr-28 Mar

Site closed 24-26, 31 Dec & 1 Jan

See website for latest opening times

VISIT US

Direction: 1 mile S of Barnard Castle, on a minor road off B6277

Bus: Visit traveline.info for the latest bus timetables and routes

ACQ.1925 ♿⛔🅿️🏞️

Parking: charges apply to non-members, free for Members with valid car sticker.

> MAP PAGE 313 (5G)
> OS MAP 92, OL31: NZ062151

FINCHALE PRIORY   DURHAM – DH1 5SH

Extensive ruins of a 13th-century priory, on the site of the hermitage of retired merchant adventurer St Godric. Beautifully positioned by the River Wear, with riverside walks nearby.

OPENING TIMES

Open daily 1 Apr-28 Mar

Site closed 24-26, 31 Dec & 1 Jan

See website for latest opening times

VISIT US

Direction: 3 miles NE of Durham; on minor road off A167

Train: Durham 5 miles

Bus: Visit traveline.info for the latest bus timetables and routes

ACQ.1916 ⛔🅿️⚠️

Car park (£4 charge, not English Heritage).

Caution: falling masonry, hidden drops.

Please do not climb on the walls.

> MAP PAGE 313 (4G)
> OS MAP 88, 308: NZ296471

NORTHUMBERLAND

AYDON CASTLE   NORTHUMBERLAND – NE45 5PJ

An outstandingly complete defensible medieval manor house in a secluded and beautiful woodland setting, very near Hadrian's Wall. By 1315 Aydon had been fortified against the Scots. The 'castle' served as a farmhouse until 1966, yet remains remarkably unchanged. Explore the fully roofed hall and chambers, mount the battlements and picnic in the orchard.

A short drive from Corbridge Roman Town (p.260) and Chesters Roman Fort (p.258), and under a mile from Hadrian's Wall Trail.

🎬 *Ivanhoe* (1997); *Elizabeth* (1998).

OPENING TIMES

Open varying days 1 Apr-5 Nov

Site closed 6 Nov-28 Mar

See website for latest opening times

Last entry 30 mins before closing

VISIT US

Direction: 3 mile NE of Corbridge, on minor road off B6321 or A68

Train: Corbridge 4 miles

Bus: Visit traveline.info for the latest bus timetables and routes

Tel: 01434 632450

NON-MEMBERS

See website for entry prices

ACQ.1966 ♿⛔🅿️🏞️ ⚠️ OVP

Disabled access (ground floor only).

Dogs on leads (restricted areas only).

Short walk from car park.

Accessible parking outside castle gate.

Parking: charges apply to non-members, free for Members with valid car sticker.

> MAP PAGE 313 (4F)
> OS MAP 87, 316: NZ001663

The northernmost town in England, strongly fortified Berwick-upon-Tweed was the key to the long-disputed Anglo-Scottish border. Our sites here trace many centuries of conflict and crisis.

BERWICK-UPON-TWEED BARRACKS NORTHUMBERLAND – TD15 1DF

Begun in 1717, Ravensdowne Barracks were among the first purpose-built English barracks. Look out for the 'candle smoke drawings', doodled by soldiers in the 1720s-60s.

They house an exhibition about the life of the British infantryman from the Civil War to 1914-18, plus the King's Own Scottish Borderers Regimental Museum and Berwick Museum and Art Gallery (opening times for museums and gallery may vary from rest of site).

OPENING TIMES

Open varying days 1 Apr-5 Nov

Site closed 6 Nov-28 Mar

See website for latest opening times

Last entry 30 mins before closing

VISIT US

Direction: On the Parade, off Church Street in town centre

Train: Berwick-upon-Tweed ¼ mile

Bus: Visit traveline.info for the latest bus timetables and routes

Tel: 01289 304493

NON-MEMBERS

See website for entry prices

By being a Member, you save up to **£24.50** (price of a family ticket) when you visit **Berwick-upon-Tweed Barracks**

ACQ.1981 ♿ ☂ ▣ E ❀ ▣ ♟ ♨
☒ ◫ ⬚ OVP

The barrack square is accessible to wheelchairs, but the museums are not.

Parking: pay and display in town.

MAP PAGE 313 (1F)
OS MAP 75, 346: NU001531

BERWICK-UPON-TWEED CASTLE
NORTHUMBERLAND – TD15 1DF

Riverside ruins of a medieval castle rebuilt by Edward I in 1296-98. Crucial in border warfare, this once-important castle changed hands between English and Scots several times before being superseded by the Ramparts.

OPENING TIMES

Any reasonable daylight hours

VISIT US

Direction: Accessible from riverside near Berwick-upon-Tweed railway station

Train: Berwick-upon-Tweed (adjacent)

Bus: Visit traveline.info for the latest bus timetables and routes

ACQ.1931 ♿ ☂ ⚠ Caution: deep water.

Parking: pay and display in town.

Please do not climb on the walls.

MAP PAGE 313 (1F)
OS MAP 75, 346: NT993534

BERWICK-UPON-TWEED MAIN GUARD
NORTHUMBERLAND – TD15 1HN

Georgian military guardhouse, displaying permanent and changing exhibitions about Berwick's history.

Managed by Berwick-upon-Tweed Civic Society.

OPENING TIMES

See website for latest opening times

VISIT US

Direction: Adjacent to Ramparts in Palace Street

Train: Berwick-upon-Tweed ¼ mile

Bus: Visit traveline.info for the latest bus timetables and routes

ACQ.1981 ▣ E ☒

Two steps to entrance.

Parking: pay and display in town.

MAP PAGE 313 (1F)
OS MAP 75, 346: NU000525

BERWICK-UPON-TWEED RAMPARTS
NORTHUMBERLAND – TD15 1DF

Surviving largely intact, Berwick's immensely impressive artillery ramparts make it one of the most important fortified towns in Europe. Begun in 1558 and updated to counter later threats, they surround the whole historic town, and you can walk their entire circuit.

A leaflet and map is available locally, or on our website.

OPENING TIMES

Any reasonable daylight hours
Please note: Dangerous after dark

VISIT US

Direction: the ramparts surround the town (accessed at various points)

Train: Berwick-upon-Tweed (adjacent)

Bus: Visit traveline.info for the latest bus timetables and routes

ACQ.1931

Caution: dangerous steep hidden and unguarded drops. Proceed with great care. Please closely supervise children and keep dogs on leads.

Parking: pay and display in town.

MAP PAGE 313 (1F)
OS MAP 75, 346: NU003530

BLACK MIDDENS BASTLE HOUSE

NORTHUMBERLAND – NE48 1NE

A fortified farmhouse with thick walls and living quarters only accessible at first-floor level. Characteristic of the troubled 16th-century Anglo-Scottish borders.

OPENING TIMES

Any reasonable daylight hours

VISIT US

Direction: 180 metres N of minor road, 7 miles NW of Bellingham; or along a minor road from A68

Bus: Visit traveline.info for the latest bus timetables and routes

ACQ.1978

Caution: unguarded drops.

MAP PAGE 313 (3F)
OS MAP 80, OL42: NY773900

BRINKBURN PRIORY NORTHUMBERLAND – NE65 8AR

The beautiful church of Augustinian Brinkburn Priory, built in the Early English style, survives as completely roofed and restored in Victorian times. The church and adjoining Manor House are picturesquely set by the River Coquet, and reached by a scenic 10-minute walk from the car park.

OPENING TIMES

Open varying days 1 Apr-5 Nov

Site closed 6 Nov-28 Mar

See website for latest opening times

Last entry 30 mins before closing

VISIT US

Direction: 4½ miles SE of Rothbury, off B6344

Train: Morpeth 12 miles, Acklington 10 miles

Bus: Visit traveline.info for the latest bus timetables and routes

Tel: 01665 570628

NON-MEMBERS

See website for entry prices

By being a Member, you save up to **£24.50** (price of a family ticket) when you visit **Brinkburn Priory**

ACQ.1965 P OVP

MAP PAGE 313 (3G)
OS MAP 92, 325: NZ116983

BELSAY HALL, CASTLE AND GARDENS

NORTHUMBERLAND – NE20 0DX

Come and see how the major 'Belsay Awakes' project has transformed a place with something for everyone. Twenty acres of reinvigorated gardens make a wonderful setting for a succession of fascinating buildings: a freshly interpreted medieval castle, enlarged into a Jacobean mansion, and the elegant and newly conserved Greek Revival-style house that succeeded it.

The whole ensemble is the creation of the Middleton family over more than seven centuries. The castle, dominated by its massive 14th-century 'pele tower', was mainly built for defence, but also to impress. Later a Jacobean mansion wing was added, where the family lived until they moved into Belsay Hall.

Belsay Hall is an elegant Classical Greek Revival villa. Begun in 1807, it was designed by Sir Charles Monck (formerly Middleton), a man inspired by Ancient Greece and the buildings he'd seen on his honeymoon in Athens. Despite its austere facade, it had a comfortable interior, arranged round an amazing central 'Pillar Hall'. It's displayed without furnishings, so you can admire the fine craftsmanship of its construction.

The vast gardens provide a magnificent backdrop for the castle and hall. Grade I listed as among the best preserved examples of the 'Picturesque' style of gardens in Britain, they're also largely Sir Charles's work. Explore his romantic Quarry Garden, created where stone was cut for his hall, with ravines and sheer rock faces inspired by the quarries of Syracuse in Sicily. His grandson Sir Arthur Middleton, likewise a pioneering plantsman, further embellished the quarry with exotic species, now in full maturity.

BELSAY AWAKES

Due for completion in summer 2023, the transformative Belsay Awakes project has been made possible by a £3.4 million grant from the National Lottery Heritage Fund. Among the finishing touches will be an imaginative new play area, themed around the Wild Man, the heraldic emblem of the Middleton family. There'll also be magical new interpretation in the castle, children's story trails and wildlife trails in the grounds, and a bright and welcoming café in the former coach house.

In the biggest Conservation in Action project ever undertaken by English Heritage, we've already completely replaced the roof of the hall and safeguarded its architectural features. The gardens have been reinvigorated to the plans of renowned garden designer Dan Pearson, with new views and the wilder parts of the grounds opened up. The whole site has been made more accessible for all, with new resources and facilities for schools, groups and individuals with a variety of needs.

OPENING TIMES

Open daily 1 Apr–5 Nov

Open varying days 6 Nov–28 Mar

Site closed 24–25 Dec

See website for latest opening times

Last entry 45 mins before closing

VISIT US

Address: Belsay Hall,
Castle & Gardens, Belsay,
Northumberland NE20 0DX

Direction: In Belsay; 14 miles NW
of Newcastle, on A696

Train: Morpeth 10 miles

Bus: Visit traveline.info for the latest
bus timetables and routes

Tel: 01661 881636

Local Tourist Information:
Morpeth: 01670 500700

SAVE TODAY
By being a Member, you save up to **£47** (price of a family ticket) when you visit **Belsay Hall, Castle and Gardens.**

NON-MEMBERS

See website for entry prices

ACQ.1980 ⬛⬛⬛⬛⬛⬛⬛ E
⬛⬛⬛⬛⬛⬛⬛ P ⬛⬛
⬛⬛ ⚠ OVP

Disabled access (grounds, tearoom and ground floor of hall and castle; toilets).

Dogs on leads (grounds only).

New guidebook.

Tearoom (open daily Apr–Oct, weekends Nov–Mar).

MAP PAGE 313 (3G)
OS MAP 88, 316: NZ086785

DUNSTANBURGH CASTLE

NORTHUMBERLAND – NE66 3TW

Take a bracing coastal walk to Dunstanburgh Castle, one of the most dramatically sited fortresses in England.

Defending a headland jutting from the rugged Northumberland coast, the castle was begun in 1313 by Earl Thomas of Lancaster, cousin and leading baronial enemy of Edward II. He built on a grand scale, perhaps to underline his rivalry with the Crown. The castle's most striking feature is the great double-towered gatehouse. It imitated the new royal castles – such as Harlech – built in Wales.

When his rebellion faltered in 1322, Lancaster may have hoped to take refuge in his remote fortress. But before reaching it, he was defeated, captured and beheaded. Later the castle was inherited by John of Gaunt, Richard II's powerful but unpopular uncle. Gaunt strengthened it against Scots attacks during the 1380s, converting the gatehouse into a strong keep.

Dunstanburgh's strength made it a target for both sides during the Wars of the Roses, when it saw fierce fighting. It changed hands at least three times, once after a siege by 10,000 Yorkists in 1462.

Today it's a peaceful place, though still remote and reachable only on foot. You can explore its circuit of walls and strong towers, and look into the rocky cove it protected. This is a famous place for seabirds. Kittiwakes, fulmars and razorbills all nest on the cliffs in the spring and summer, and the grassland is home to ground-nesting birds like skylarks.

Owned by the National Trust, maintained and managed by English Heritage.

OPENING TIMES

Open daily 1 Apr-5 Nov

Open varying days 6 Nov-28 Mar

Site closed 24-25 Dec

See website for latest opening times

Last entry 1 hour before closing

VISIT US

Direction: 8 miles NE of Alnwick; on footpaths from Craster or Embleton – stunning 1½ mile coastal walk. **Please note:** Satnav NE66 3TW directs to Craster car park. If parking at Craster, please allow at least 3-4 hours overall for visit and walk to and from castle

Train: Alnmouth, 7 miles from Craster; Chathill (not Sun), 5 miles from Embleton; 7 miles from Castle

Bus: Visit traveline.info for the latest bus timetables and routes

Tel: 01665 576231

Local Tourist Information: Craster: 01665 576007

NON-MEMBERS

See website for entry prices

Free to National Trust members

ACQ.1929 🐾 ▢ ▣ ◻ ⚠ OVP

Parking (in Craster village; approx. 1½ mile walk. A charge is payable – not English Heritage).

MAP PAGE 313 (2G)
OS MAP 75, 332: NU257219

EDLINGHAM CASTLE
NORTHUMBERLAND – NE66 2BW

The tower and other remains of a fortified medieval manor house, in a remote and beautiful setting.

OPENING TIMES
Any reasonable daylight hours

VISIT US
Direction: Accessible via a short path from Edlingham church, on a minor road off B6341; 6 miles SW of Alnwick

Train: Alnmouth 9 miles

Bus: Visit traveline.info for the latest bus timetables and routes

ACQ.1975

Waterproof footwear recommended. Guide pamphlet available in church.

MAP PAGE 313 (2G)
OS MAP 81, 332: NU116092

NORHAM CASTLE
NORTHUMBERLAND – TD15 2JY

Besieged at least 13 times by the Scots, this important medieval border castle was called 'the most dangerous place in the country'.

Recaptured after falling to James IV in 1513, it was rebuilt as an artillery fortress.

NORHAM CASTLE

Download a free audio tour from the English Heritage website.

OPENING TIMES
Open daily 1 Apr-30 Oct

Open varying days 31 Oct-28 Mar

Site closed 24-26, 31 Dec & 1 Jan

See website for latest opening times

VISIT US
Direction: In Norham village; 6 miles SW of Berwick-upon-Tweed, on minor road off B6470 (from A698)

Train: Berwick-upon-Tweed 7½ miles

Bus: Visit traveline.info for the latest bus timetables and routes

ACQ.1923

Disabled access (excluding keep).

Caution: steep slopes, unguarded drops.

MAP PAGE 313 (1F)
OS MAP 74/75, 335: NT906476

ETAL CASTLE NORTHUMBERLAND – TD12 4TN

Etal Castle was begun in the early 14th century as a tower house, in a strategic position by a ford on the Anglo-Scottish border. Vulnerable to raiders, it was soon reinforced by a curtain wall with corner towers and a gatehouse.

In 1513 the castle was suddenly thrust into the forefront of history, when King James IV of Scotland invaded with the largest Scots army ever to attack England. He quickly captured Etal Castle, but was soon afterwards defeated at the nearby Battle of Flodden, the greatest-ever English victory over the Scots. King James was killed along with nine Scots earls, fourteen lords, and thousands of his men.

You can also visit the nearby Flodden battlefield.

OPENING TIMES
Open Wed-Sun 1 Apr-5 Nov

Site closed 6 Nov-28 Mar

See website for latest opening times

Last entry 30 mins before closing

VISIT US
Direction: In Etal village, 10 miles SW of Berwick-upon-Tweed

Train: Berwick-upon-Tweed 10½ miles

Bus: Visit traveline.info for the latest bus timetables and routes

Tel: 01890 820332

NON-MEMBERS
See website for entry prices

ACQ.1975   OVP

Toilets (in car park). Car park free but not managed by English Heritage.

MAP PAGE 313 (1F)
OS MAP 74/75, 339: NT925393

LINDISFARNE PRIORY

NORTHUMBERLAND – TD15 2RX

You'll never forget a visit to the serene and remote Holy Island of Lindisfarne. It's been drawing visitors for over thirteen centuries, and still evokes powerful memories of the monks and saints of Anglo-Saxon and medieval Northumbria. Now brand-new museum displays and new information panels around the site help you explore Lindisfarne's stories. You can also enjoy the island's wildlife and wonderful coastal views.

Founded by the Irish monk St Aidan in AD 635 and still a place of pilgrimage today, Lindisfarne Priory was one of the most important centres of early Christianity in Anglo-Saxon England. The dramatic approach to the island across the causeway only emphasises the tranquil appeal of this supremely atmospheric place.

St Cuthbert is the most celebrated of the priory's many holy men. After ten years seeking peace as a hermit on lonely Inner Farne Island, he reluctantly became bishop before retiring to die on Inner Farne in 687. Eleven years after his burial, his coffin was opened and his body found to be undecayed – a sure sign of sanctity. His remains were then transferred to a pilgrim shrine in the abbey church, where miracles were soon being reported.

But the rich and isolated monastery was easy prey for sea-raiders, suffering a devastating attack by Vikings in 793 – the first significant Viking raid in British history. In 875 the monks left, carrying Cuthbert's remains, which after long wanderings were enshrined in Durham Cathedral in 1104, where they still rest. Only after that time did

Durham monks re-establish a priory on Lindisfarne. Today you can see the evocative ruins of the richly decorated priory church they completed in about 1150, with the famous 'rainbow arch' – a vault-rib of the now-vanished crossing tower.

The priory is also renowned for the Lindisfarne Gospels, among England's greatest artistic and religious treasures. They were produced here in the late 7th or early 8th century by Bishop Eadfrith.

The same Lindisfarne artists may well have produced the extraordinary 'name stones' discovered around the site. Visit the site museum's extensive and now re-invigorated displays to explore these rare survivals of 8th-century craftsmanship, unique links with the vanished Saxon monastery.

To enhance the wider experience of visiting Lindisfarne, be sure not to miss the beautiful parish church of St Mary the Virgin.

Stay in our *Coastguard's Cottage*, see p.13 for details.

NEW FOR 2023

There's lots more to see and do at Lindisfarne Priory in 2023. A new museum presentation includes the island's internationally significant Anglo-Saxon artefacts and finds from recent excavations, with specially commissioned poems and artworks. The new family museum trail is inspired by the Lindisfarne Gospels. New information panels help you explore the whole site, and there's a new monument to St Cuthbert. There are improvements to the visitor welcome, together with resources supporting school visits.

OPENING TIMES

Open daily 1 Apr–5 Nov

Open varying days 6 Nov–28 Mar

Site closed 24-26 Dec & 1 Jan

See website for latest opening times

Last entry 30 mins before closing. Opening times vary depending on the tides – please check website before visiting

The causeway floods at high tide so it is very important to check the tide times before crossing

VISIT US

Address: Lindisfarne Priory, Holy Island, Berwick-upon-Tweed, Northumberland TD15 2RX

Direction: On Holy Island, only reached at low tide across causeway; tide tables at each end, or from Tourist Information Centre

Train: Berwick-upon-Tweed 14 miles, via causeway

Bus: Visit traveline.info for the latest bus timetables and routes

SAVE TODAY

By being a Member, you save up to **£32.50** (price of a family ticket) when you visit **Lindisfarne Priory.**

Tel: 01289 389200

Tourist Information Centre: 01289 330733

NON-MEMBERS

See website for entry prices

[ACQ. 1913] [icons]

Parking and toilets in the village. Parking pay and display operated by Northumberland County Council.

Disabled access (limited in some areas of priory grounds).

New guidebook.

MAP PAGE 313 (1G)
OS MAP 75, 340: NU126417

WARKWORTH CASTLE AND HERMITAGE

NORTHUMBERLAND – NE65 0UJ

Among the biggest, strongest and most impressive medieval fortresses in northern England, Warkworth Castle was the favourite home of the powerful and turbulent Percy family, Earls of Northumberland. Aided by imaginative new interpretation, you can explore its almost complete Great Tower and elaborate defences, and venture out to the atmospheric riverside hermitage.

Warkworth Castle straddles the neck of a tight loop in the River Coquet, guarding an attractive stone-built town. Its still-complete circuit of towered walls, including the powerful gatehouse and formidable Grey Mare's Tail Tower, took shape during the 13th century, and the fortress repelled a Scots siege in 1327.

But Warkworth attained its greatest glory under the Percy family, who wielded almost kingly power in the North during the later Middle Ages. The Percy lion badge proudly adorns the Great Tower, the castle's most outstandingly distinctive feature. Built on top of an earlier mound, this ingeniously planned 'keep' houses everything a medieval baron could desire. Ground-floor wine cellars; first-floor kitchens, great hall, chapel and great chamber and second-floor bedchambers are interconnected by completely separate systems of passages and stairways for servants and masters, so food and wine could appear in the lord's staterooms, without being seen on their way.

Cleverly lit by a central light well, this masterpiece of medieval design for gracious living is an intriguing place to explore. On selected days you can also view the second-floor 'Duke's Rooms', restored in the 1850s and equipped with antique-style Victorian furniture (please phone the site for latest opening times).

The Great Tower was built after 1377 for the first Percy Earl of Northumberland, who along with his famous son Harry 'Hotspur' – hero of many Border ballads – helped depose Richard II and set Henry IV on the throne, only to rebel against him in turn. Both were killed in battle, as were the second and third earls. Then the fourth earl remodelled Warkworth's courtyard, adding a complete new set of staterooms – entered via the still-impressive Lion Tower, bedecked with Percy heraldry – before himself being murdered by an angry mob in 1489.

A delightful riverside walk and a rowing boat ferry take you to a contrastingly tranquil feature of Warkworth, the supremely atmospheric 'Hermitage' hewn into a sandstone cliff (open selected days). Here a priest said prayers for the Percy family's souls. Within its tiny unlit chapel you can still trace worn carvings of a Nativity scene. Even tinier 'closets' provided views of the altar for worshippers, and yew trees grow amid the ruins of the priest's house. Take time to quietly experience this extraordinary survival from medieval England.

OPENING TIMES

Castle

Open daily 1 Apr–5 Nov

Open varying days 6 Nov–28 Mar

Site closed 24-25 Dec

Please see website for opening times of the Duke's Rooms

Hermitage

Open varying days 1 Apr–5 Nov

Hermitage closed 6 Nov–28 Mar

See website for latest opening times

Last entry 30 mins before closing

VISIT US

Address: Castle Terrace, Warkworth, Northumberland NE65 0UJ

Direction: In Warkworth; 7½ miles S of Alnwick, on A1068. Access to Hermitage is via an approx. 15-minute riverside walk from the castle, including some slopes, and rowing boat ferry (included in entry charge). Staff will give directions. The Hermitage is reached by uneven steps, and unlit within

SAVE TODAY By being a Member, you save up to £47 (price of a family ticket) when you visit **Warkworth Castle and Hermitage.**

Train: Alnmouth 3½ miles

Bus: Visit **traveline.info** for the latest bus timetables and routes

Tel: 01665 711423

NON-MEMBERS

See website for entry prices

ACQ.1922

Disabled access: limited access in castle (steps to and within Great Tower). Disabled access to Hermitage is difficult.

Dogs on leads welcome in most areas.

Parking: charges apply to non-members, free for Members with valid car sticker.

MAP PAGE 313 (2G)
OS MAP 81, 332: NU247058

PRUDHOE CASTLE NORTHUMBERLAND – NE42 6NA

Guarding a strategic crossing of the River Tyne, impressive Prudhoe Castle was a vital bastion against Scots invaders. After resisting two Scots sieges during the 1170s – when King William the Lion of Scotland lamented 'as long as Prudhoe stands, we shall never have peace' – it was given its tall keep, and later reinforced by towered walls. In the late 14th century it became a stronghold of the locally all-powerful Percy family, Earls of Northumberland.

You'll witness Prudhoe's great strength as you approach via the barbican, passing the picturesque mill pond and crossing the inner ditch to the formidable gatehouse. You can climb the steps to the atmospheric gatehouse chapel, explore the inner and outer baileys and look up at the towering keep. There's also a fine 'Regency Gothic' mansion within the walls, built by the Percys in the early 1800s as a 'gentleman's residence' for their land agent. Its elegant unfurnished rooms house family-friendly displays tracing the long history of this crucial fortress, continuously occupied for over nine centuries.

There's an array of site finds and a children's activity room with games.

Hadrian's Wall is a short drive away.

OPENING TIMES

Open varying days 1 Apr-5 Nov

Site closed 6 Nov-28 Mar

See website for latest opening times

Last entry 30 mins before closing

VISIT US

Direction: In Prudhoe, on minor road off A695

Train: Prudhoe ¼ mile

Bus: Visit traveline.info for the latest bus timetables and routes

Tel: 01661 833459

NON-MEMBERS

See website for entry prices

By being a Member, you save up to **£28.50** (price of a family ticket) when you visit **Prudhoe Castle**

Dogs on leads (restricted areas only).

Toilets with disabled access on site.

MAP PAGE 313 (4G)
OS MAP 88, 316: NZ091634

HYLTON CASTLE

TYNE AND WEAR – SR5 3PA

The gatehouse-tower of a castle built by Sir William Hylton c. 1400. Supported by the National Lottery Heritage Fund, Hylton Castle Trust and Sunderland City Council have transformed the castle shell into a visitor attraction. Find out more at hyltoncastle.org.uk

OPENING TIMES

Please see website hyltoncastle.org.uk

VISIT US

Direction: 3¾ miles W of Sunderland

Metro: Seaburn (2½ miles)

Bus: Visit traveline.info

Caution: CCTV at site.

MAP PAGE 313 (4H)
OS MAP 88, 308: NZ358588

ST PAUL'S MONASTERY, JARROW

TYNE AND WEAR – NE32 3DY

Home of the Venerable Bede, chronicler of early English Christianity. The Anglo-Saxon church, founded AD 685, partly survives.

OPENING TIMES

Monastery ruins: any reasonable daylight hours

VISIT US

Direction: In Jarrow, on minor road N of A185; follow signs for Bede's World

Metro: Bede ¾ miles

Bus: Visit traveline.info

Tel: 0191 489 7052

Caution: steep slopes.

MAP PAGE 313 (4G)
OS MAP 88, 316: NZ339652

TYNEMOUTH PRIORY AND CASTLE

TYNE AND WEAR – NE30 4BZ

Dramatic Tynemouth Priory and Castle is one of our most fascinating and varied coastal sites. Uniquely combining a medieval monastery and fortifications with 20th-century gun batteries and all-round seaward views, it crowns a rocky headland commanding the entrance to the River Tyne, the gateway to Newcastle.

A natural stronghold, the steep-sided headland housed an important Anglo-Saxon monastery, burial place of the sainted King Oswine of Northumbria. After this was destroyed by Vikings, a medieval monastery was founded on the site. It was later fortified against the Scots and became one of the largest defended areas in England.

You enter it through the powerful 14th-century monastic gatehouse, a miniature castle. Take in the displays, where characters from Tynemouth's long and varied history help you explore the headland. The voice of Arthur Lloyd, a Second World War gunner, describes air raids, sinking ships and the primitive living conditions.

The spectacular ruins of the great 11th- to 13th-century monastic church, dominating the site, rise amid intriguing tombstones of Tynemouth mariners and artillerymen. At the east end is the priory's greatest treasure, the tiny 15th-century 'Percy Chantry' chapel, with its rose window and elaborately vaulted roof crowded with carved saints.

The fortress headland continued to guard the Tyne entrance right up until 1956. To experience life here during the two World Wars, venture down to explore the underground gun batteries, topped by a real long-range gun.

OPENING TIMES

Open daily 1 Apr-5 Nov

Open varying days 6 Nov-28 Mar

Site closed 24-26 Dec & 1 Jan

See website for latest opening times

Last entry 45 mins before closing

VISIT US

Direction: In Tynemouth, near North Pier

Metro: Tynemouth ½ mile

Bus: Visit traveline.info for the latest bus timetables and routes

Tel: 0191 257 1090

NON-MEMBERS

See website for entry prices

By being a Member, you save up to **£28.50** (price of a family ticket) when you visit **Tynemouth Priory and Castle**

ACQ.1969

Disabled access (priory only). Toilets with disabled access on site. Limited disabled parking available.

MAP PAGE 313 (4H)
OS MAP 88, 316: NZ373694

King Gary (2021).

Associated attractions in England

As well as free, unlimited entry to the hundreds of sites in our care, English Heritage membership also gives you free or discounted access to many associated attractions in England.

Visit **english-heritage.org.uk/ associated-attractions** for the full list of discounts as well as terms and conditions.

Cutty Sark
GREENWICH,
LONDON – SE10 9HT

25% DISCOUNT*

Visit the award-winning *Cutty Sark* and delve into the extraordinary history of this iconic sailing ship. Climb the mast, explore the decks, meet characters from the past and discover what life was like on board the fastest ship of its day.

*Redemption by phone or online: rmg.co.uk/EnglishHeritage.

rmg.co.uk/cuttysark **/** 020 8312 6608

Foundling Museum
CAMDEN, LONDON
– WC1N 1AZ

50% DISCOUNT*

Explore the history of the Foundling Hospital, the UK's first children's charity and first public art gallery. Discover how we use our art and objects to unravel the past and keep the Foundling story alive.

*Tickets must be booked in advance online with code EH50. Image © GG Archard.

foundlingmuseum.org.uk **/** 020 7841 3600

Strawberry Hill House & Garden
TWICKENHAM, LONDON – TW1 4ST

10% DISCOUNT*

Strawberry Hill House & Garden, created by Horace Walpole in the 18th century, is internationally famous as Britain's finest example of Georgian Gothic revival architecture and home to an increasingly important collection of paintings and objects.

*Offer can be redeemed online or on arrival.

strawberryhillhouse.org.uk **/** 020 8744 1241

Please note: coloured square denotes Associated Attraction region

Anne of Cleves House Museum

LEWES, EAST SUSSEX – BN7 1JA

Discover how the Tudors and the Elizabethans lived, worked and relaxed. This 15th-century Wealden hall-house features authentically furnished rooms, traditional planted gardens and a museum.

*Offer can be redeemed on arrival.

▦ sussexpast.co.uk/attraction/anne-of-cleves-house-museum / 01273 474610

50% DISCOUNT*

Bletchley Park

BLETCHLEY, BUCKINGHAMSHIRE – MK3 6EB

Bletchley Park, once the top-secret home of the World War Two Codebreakers, is now a vibrant heritage attraction, open every day to visitors. Step back in time to experience the stories of the extraordinary achievements of the men and women who worked here.

*Valid on general admission tickets. Free for under 12s. Book online or redeem on arrival.

▦ bletchleypark.org.uk / 01908 640404

20% DISCOUNT*

Butser Ancient Farm

HAMPSHIRE – PO8 0BG

Explore life in the past. Visit homes of the Stone Age, Bronze Age, Iron Age, Roman and Saxon periods, recreated as an experimental archaeology project in the beautiful South Downs.

*Pre-booking essential. Use discount code EH25 to book tickets online.

▦ butserancientfarm.co.uk / 023 9259 8838

25% DISCOUNT*

Canterbury Cathedral

CANTERBURY, KENT – CT1 2EH

Founded by St Augustine in AD 597, Canterbury Cathedral is integral to England's story. Discover beautiful stonework, stained glass, Becket's Martyrdom, the Black Prince's tomb, and much more at this iconic World Heritage Site.

*Discount applies to tickets bought on the door at the Cathedral's Visitor Centre only.

▦ canterbury-cathedral.org / 01227 762862

20% DISCOUNT*

Cogges Manor Farm

2 for 1 ENTRY*

WITNEY, OXFORDSHIRE – OX28 3LA

A unique historic farmstead in the heart of Witney, Oxfordshire, with a beautiful 13th-century Manor House, enchanting walled garden, orchard, woodland adventure play areas and friendly animal residents.

*Offer can be redeemed on arrival.

☰ cogges.org.uk / 01993 772602

Fishbourne Roman Palace

50% DISCOUNT*

FISHBOURNE, WEST SUSSEX – PO19 3QR

Welcome to the largest Roman home in Britain. Stroll around the recreated Roman gardens – the earliest gardens found anywhere in the country – and enjoy the largest collection of in situ mosaics in the UK.

*Offer can be redeemed on arrival.

☰ sussexpast.co.uk/fishbourne / 01243 785859

Gilbert White's House & Gardens

2 for 1 ENTRY*

SELBORNE, HAMPSHIRE – GU34 3JH

Home to the 18th-century naturalist and writer Gilbert White. A historic house and gardens, with galleries dedicated to Lawrence Oates, who was part of Scott's 1912 Terra Nova expedition.

*Please purchase your ticket on arrival.

☰ gilbertwhiteshouse.org.uk / 01420 511275

Lewes Castle and Museum

50% DISCOUNT*

LEWES, EAST SUSSEX – BN7 1YE

Climb the zig-zag steps to the top of this early Norman castle for stunning panoramic views across Sussex, from the Downs to the coast. The adjoining Museum of Sussex Archaeology contains artefacts from prehistoric to medieval Sussex.

*Offer can be redeemed on arrival.

☰ sussexpast.co.uk/attraction/lewes-castle / 01273 486290

USE YOUR MEMBERSHIP TO GET DISCOUNTED ENTRY AT OVER 50 ATTRACTIONS.
PLEASE REMEMBER TO SHOW YOUR CARD AS PROOF OF MEMBERSHIP.

Terms and conditions may apply, so make sure you check the details on our website or call the individual property for more information.

Michelham Priory House & Gardens

EAST SUSSEX – BN27 3QS

This picturesque island boasts a Tudor house and 14th-century medieval gatehouse with activities and displays of furniture and artefacts. Rooms include an interactive Victorian kitchen, Second World War evacuee's bedroom, Tudor kitchen, prior's room and undercroft.

*Offer can be redeemed on arrival.

sussexpast.co.uk/michelham / 01323 844224

50% DISCOUNT*

Powell–Cotton Museum

BIRCHINGTON-ON-SEA, KENT – CT7 0BH

The Powell-Cotton Museum offers an exciting day out for all. Encounter extraordinary animals in our world-famous dioramas and celebrate wonderful world cultures, displayed across seven galleries. For a more gentle pace, visit Quex House or explore our gardens and woodland.

*Offer can be redeemed on arrival only.

powell-cottonmuseum.org / 01843 842168

20% DISCOUNT*

The Royal Pavilion

BRIGHTON, EAST SUSSEX – BN1 1EE

Discover the magnificent seaside residence of King George IV. The Indian architecture contrasts with interiors inspired by China. Regency garden and gift shop.

*Offer can be redeemed on arrival or by telephone.

brightonmuseums.org.uk / 0300 029 0900

20% DISCOUNT*

Rycote Chapel

OXFORDSHIRE – OX9 2PE

15th-century chapel with original furniture, including exquisitely carved and painted woodwork. Also restored Capability Brown ice house. Managed by the Rycote Buildings Charitable Foundation.

*Offer can be redeemed on arrival.

rycotepark.com / 01844 210210

50% DISCOUNT*

Please note: coloured square denotes Associated Attraction region

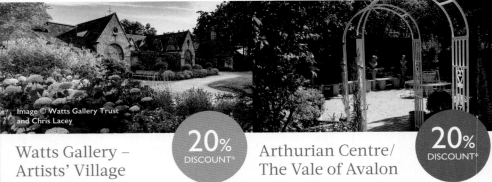

Image © Watts Gallery Trust and Chris Lacey

Watts Gallery – Artists' Village

20% DISCOUNT*

SURREY – GU3 1DQ

Founded by artists George Frederic Watts and Mary Seton Watts in the 1890s. See artworks, a magical chapel, beautiful woodlands and the artists' home. The founders' ethos of 'Art for all by all' remains at the heart of this unique place.

*Offer can be redeemed online in advance or in person on the day. On the website, select the ticket option 'English Heritage Member Admission' in order to redeem discount.

■ ⊞ 👪6   wattsgallery.org.uk / 01483 810235

Arthurian Centre/ The Vale of Avalon

20% DISCOUNT*

CAMELFORD, CORNWALL – PL32 9TT

Beautiful walks through historic landscape – King Arthur's legendary last battlefield, 6th-century scheduled monument, 13th-century longhouse, 18th-century garden and 'Muse' gardens, orchard, exhibition, tearoom, gifts. Five miles from Tintagel Castle.

*Offer can be redeemed on arrival.

■ ⊞ 👪4   thevaleofavalon.co.uk / 01840 213947

BITTON

Arundells

50% DISCOUNT*

SALISBURY, WILTSHIRE – SP1 2EN

A beautiful Grade II listed house with 2 acres of garden in the heart of Salisbury. The former home of Sir Edward Heath.

*No pre-booking required. Offer valid Thu-Mon.

■ ⊞ 👪6   arundells.org / 01722 326546

Avon Valley Railway

2 for 1 ENTRY*

BITTON, SOUTH GLOUCESTERSHIRE – BS30 6HD

Three-mile heritage railway, located between the historic cities of Bristol and Bath. Enjoy a fifty minute steam or diesel-hauled train ride. Visit avonvalleyrailway.org to find out more.

*Pre-book your tickets online to guarantee your seats and enter the code EH241. Or, simply show your EH membership card at the booking office when you arrive.

■ ⊞   avonvalleyrailway.org / 0117 932 5538

USE YOUR MEMBERSHIP TO GET DISCOUNTED ENTRY AT OVER 50 ATTRACTIONS.
PLEASE REMEMBER TO SHOW YOUR CARD AS PROOF OF MEMBERSHIP.

Terms and conditions may apply, so make sure you check the details on our website or call the individual property for more information.

Bowood House & Gardens

20% DISCOUNT*

WILTSHIRE – SN11 0LZ

Bowood House & Gardens is situated in 2,000 acres of 'Capability' Brown parkland. Visit the spectacular garden and grounds, children's adventure playground and Bowood House.

*Discount on Day Ticket Admission only when visiting Bowood House & Gardens between 1 Apr-30 Jun 2023. Pre-book tickets at bowood.org/tickets using code EH20.

 bowood.org/bowood-house-gardens / 01249 812102

Dartington Hall Gardens

2 for 1 ENTRY*

DEVON – TQ9 6EL

Visit Dartington's historic gardens, with 26 acres of formal grounds and natural wilderness to explore. Plus a children's activity trail, shops, barn cinema, gallery, playground, restaurant and cafés. Accommodation available.

*Redeem offer on arrival at the Welcome Centre.

dartington.org/gardens / 01803 847150

Glastonbury Abbey

20% DISCOUNT*

GLASTONBURY, SOMERSET – BA6 9EL

Once the richest abbey in England, Glastonbury Abbey is set in 36 acres of stunning grounds. Visit the museum, tour the ruins with a living history guide or explore at your own pace.

*Discounted entry can be booked online at glastonburyabbey.com using the discount code EH202320 or by producing your membership card upon arrival.

glastonburyabbey.com / 01458 832267

Pencarrow House & Gardens

2 for 1 ENTRY*

CORNWALL – PL30 3AG

Beautiful Georgian house and gardens, owned and loved by the Molesworth-St Aubyn family for the last 500 years. Café, children's play area, gift and plant shop, free parking. Dogs welcome in the gardens.

*Offer can be redeemed on arrival only.

pencarrow.co.uk / 01208 841369

The Salisbury Museum

25% DISCOUNT*

SALISBURY, WILTSHIRE – SP1 2EN

Nationally important collections relating to Stonehenge and local archaeology. The museum is housed in a Grade I listed building in the Cathedral Close, where King James I stayed in 1610 and 1613.

***Offer can be redeemed on arrival.**

⊞ ⅰⅱ 4 salisburymuseum.org.uk / 01722 332151

Sherborne Castle & Gardens

£1.50 DISCOUNT*

DORSET – DT9 5NR

Built by Sir Walter Raleigh in 1594 and home to the Digby family since 1617. The castle displays magnificent staterooms and collections, Raleigh's kitchen and a museum. Breathtaking landscape gardens by Capability Brown.

***Offer can be redeemed on arrival.**

⊞ ⅰⅱ 4 sherbornecastle.com / 01935 813182

Wiltshire Museum

25% DISCOUNT*

DEVIZES, WILTSHIRE – SN10 1NS

See gold from the time of Stonehenge in our award-winning Prehistory galleries – a 'must see' when visiting Stonehenge and Avebury. Tells the story of Wiltshire across 13 galleries.

***Offer can be redeemed on arrival.**

⊞ wiltshiremuseum.org.uk / 01380 727369

Stow Maries Great War Aerodrome

2 for 1 ENTRY*

ESSEX – CM3 6RN

The last remaining functioning WWI aerodrome in Europe, featuring award-winning exhibitions, aircraft, a period café and lots more. Find us using What3words at ///passports.glorious.mulled.

***Advanced booking is required on event days, check the attraction website for details.**

⊞ stowmaries.org.uk

USE YOUR MEMBERSHIP TO GET DISCOUNTED ENTRY AT OVER 50 ATTRACTIONS.
PLEASE REMEMBER TO SHOW YOUR CARD AS PROOF OF MEMBERSHIP.

Terms and conditions may apply, so make sure you check the details on our website or call the individual property for more information.

The National Holocaust Centre and Museum

2 for 1 ENTRY*

NOTTINGHAMSHIRE – NG22 0PA

Britain's first-ever place of Holocaust remembrance and learning. We welcome families to visit 'The Journey' exhibition. Please see our website for age appropriate guidance.

*Offer can be redeemed on arrival only.

holocaust.org.uk / 01623 836627

National Civil War Centre

30% DISCOUNT*

NOTTINGHAMSHIRE – NG24 1JY

Explore one of the most fascinating times in UK history, a remarkable story of superstitions, serious sibling rivalry and seismic change which has affected the country we live in today.

*Tickets can be booked online at nationalcivilwarcentre.com/visit. Advance booking is not required and tickets can also be purchased in person on arrival.

nationalcivilwarcentre.com / 01636 655765

British Motor Museum

£2 DISCOUNT*

WARWICKSHIRE – CV35 0BJ

Discover the world's largest collection of historic British cars. Experience the sights, sounds and stories of our motor industry. A great day out with the family.

*Offer can be redeemed online or on arrival. Use discount code EH-BMM-VDE21 when purchasing tickets online.

4 britishmotormuseum.co.uk/ / 01926 895300

Hawkstone Park Follies

25% DISCOUNT*

SHROPSHIRE – SY4 5JY

Set in 100 acres of parkland, the Follies are a range of dramatic and rugged natural sandstone hills that were developed to include gullies, caves, towers and bridges, becoming one of the most visited landscapes in Britain during the 19th century.

*Discount only available for pay on day, not pre-booked.

6 hawkstoneparkfollies.co.uk / 01948 841777

The Ironbridge Gorge Museums

COALBROOKDALE, SHROPSHIRE – TF8 7DQ

15% DISCOUNT*

Open your mind and unleash your imagination. With fascinating places to explore, space to unwind and experiments to try, a visit will transform the way you see the world.

*This discount is only available in-person at any of the Museum sites.

▦ ▦4 ironbridge.org.uk / 01952 433424

Warwick Castle

WARWICKSHIRE – CV34 4QU

50% DISCOUNT*

Witness 1,100 years of history come vividly to life. Spectacular shows and attractions, spellbinding storytelling and exhilarating experiences make Warwick Castle one of the most exciting historic locations in Europe.

*Tickets must be booked in advance. To book, please visit warwick-castle.com/?keyword=Heritage

▦ ▦4 warwick-castle.com / 01926 406663

Barley Hall

YORK, YORKSHIRE – YO1 8AR

15% DISCOUNT*

Barley Hall is a hidden medieval gem, tucked away down one of York's oldest streets. Now lovingly restored to its original 15th-century splendour with high ceilings, exposed timber frames, and possibly the only horn window in England.

*Apply the discount when you pre-book online by selecting the 'English Heritage' option, by calling 01904 615505 or when you buy a ticket on admission.

▦ ▦6 barleyhall.co.uk / 01904 615505

Bolton Castle

NORTH YORKSHIRE – DL8 4ET

10% DISCOUNT*

Bolton Castle, one of the country's best-preserved late medieval castles, gives visitors a taste of what life was really like during medieval times and during Mary Queen of Scots' stay. With falconry, archery displays and wild boar feeding.

*Offer can be redeemed on arrival.

▦ boltoncastle.co.uk / 01969 623981

USE YOUR MEMBERSHIP TO GET DISCOUNTED ENTRY AT OVER 50 ATTRACTIONS.
PLEASE REMEMBER TO SHOW YOUR CARD AS PROOF OF MEMBERSHIP.

Terms and conditions may apply, so make sure you check the details on our website or call the individual property for more information.

DIG:
An Archaeological
Adventure

YORK, YORKSHIRE – YO1 8NN

2 for 1 ENTRY*

From the creators of JORVIK Viking Centre, a hands-on archaeological experience giving kids the chance to become trainee diggers for the day! This is one of a kind so... DIG IT! SHAKE IT! FEEL IT!

*You can apply the discount when you pre-book by calling 01904 615505 or when you buy a ticket on admission.

[#] [††6] digyork.com / 01904 615505

Fountains Abbey
& Studley Royal
Water Garden

NORTH YORKSHIRE – HG4 3DY

FREE ENTRY*

Spectacular World Heritage Site including 12th-century abbey ruins and stunning Georgian water garden.

*Offer can be redeemed on arrival.

[#] [††6] nationaltrust.org.uk/fountainsabbey / 01765 608888

The Green
Howards Museum

RICHMOND, NORTH YORKSHIRE – DL10 4QN

2 for 1 ENTRY*

Friendship and adventure, service and sacrifice. We tell the 300-year history of this illustrious regiment with the stories of the soldiers who served.

*Offer can be redeemed online or on arrival.

[#] [††6] greenhowards.org.uk / 01748 826561

Harewood House

WEST YORKSHIRE – LS17 9LG

50% DISCOUNT*

Harewood sits in the heart of Yorkshire and is one of England's Treasure Houses. Visitors can explore a range of exhibitions, bird garden, farm and over 100 acres of gardens.

*To redeem, book online at harewood.org and use EHMEMBER.
Image © Harewood House Trust and Lee Beel.

[#] [††5] harewood.org / 0113 218 1010

Please note: coloured square denotes Associated Attraction region

JORVIK Viking Centre

YORK, YORKSHIRE – YO1 9WT

15% DISCOUNT*

Visit the award-winning JORVIK Viking Centre to discover York's fascinating legacy! Climb aboard a time capsule to 10th-century York, discover some of the most significant Viking-age artefacts in the UK and chat to friendly Vikings.

*You can apply the discount when you pre-book online by selecting the 'English Heritage' option, by calling 01904 615505 or when you buy a ticket on admission.

⊞ 👪6 jorvikvikingcentre.co.uk / 01904 615505

Lotherton

WEST YORKSHIRE – LS25 3EB

10% DISCOUNT*

A beautiful Edwardian estate with historic hall, extensive grounds, traditional gardens, Wildlife World and red deer park.

*Pre-booking essential. Please book via the website and enter code EHMEMBER10.

⊞ 👪3 lotherton.leeds.gov.uk / 0113 378 2959

Merchant Adventurers' Hall

YORK, NORTH YORKSHIRE – YO1 9XD

50% DISCOUNT

Discover the Merchant Adventurers' Hall, built in 1357; one of the finest medieval guildhalls in the world. Home to York's entrepreneurs for over 665 years – and counting.

*Offer can be redeemed on arrival.

⊞ 👪6 merchantshallyork.org / 01904 654818

Temple Newsam

WEST YORKSHIRE – LS15 0AE

10% DISCOUNT*

An impressive country estate set on the outskirts of Leeds, with a historic mansion, rare-breed farm and extensive parks, woodland and gardens.

*Pre-booking essential. Please book via the website and enter code EHMEMBER10.

⊞ 👪3 museumsandgalleries.leeds.gov.uk/ temple-newsam / 0113 336 7460

USE YOUR MEMBERSHIP TO GET DISCOUNTED ENTRY AT OVER 50 ATTRACTIONS.
PLEASE REMEMBER TO SHOW YOUR CARD AS PROOF OF MEMBERSHIP.

Terms and conditions may apply, so make sure you check the details on our website or call the individual property for more information.

York Mansion House

YORK, NORTH YORKSHIRE – YO1 9QL

Discover the home of the Lord Mayor of York! With secrets to explore, gold and silver to marvel at and Georgian cooking demonstrations to watch, there is something for everyone.

*Offer can be redeemed on arrival.

mansionhouseyork.com / 01904 553663

25% DISCOUNT*

Western Approaches

LIVERPOOL, MERSEYSIDE – L2 8SZ

Walk through hidden rooms and discover the stories locked in the Second World War bunker that protected the secrets of the British armed forces, plotting to strengthen the Western Approaches and aid the Allied victory.

*Bookings can be made on the day or booked in advance on the website using code EnglishHeritage go to liverpoolwarmuseum.co.uk

liverpoolwarmuseum.co.uk / 0151 227 2008

10% DISCOUNT*

Alnwick Castle

ALNWICK, NORTHUMBERLAND – NE66 1NQ

Alnwick Castle, home to the Percy family for 700 years, has a fascinating history, rich with drama and intrigue. Medieval architecture houses spectacular Italianate interiors and world-class art. A popular film location, best known for *Harry Potter and the Philosopher's Stone* and *Downton Abbey*.

*Offer available by visiting the admissions office on the day of your visit, cannot be pre-booked.

alnwickcastle.com / 01665 511100

15% DISCOUNT*

The Bowes Museum

BARNARD CASTLE, COUNTY DURHAM – DL12 8NP

Outstanding collections of art, fashion and design housed in an impressive French-style public museum, with a café and shop, set in 22 acres of beautiful parkland.

*Tickets must be pre-booked via The Bowes Museum website using discount code EHeritage10.

thebowesmuseum.org.uk / 01833 690606

10% DISCOUNT*

Caernarfon Castle

Cadw

English Heritage Members can gain half-price admission to Cadw attractions during the first year of membership and free entry in subsequent years.

From Chepstow Castle near the River Severn to Beaumaris Castle on Anglesey, Cadw protects historic monuments and sites across Wales so they can continue to inspire generations to come. Whether visiting Valle Crucis Abbey in Llangollen, the last Cistercian abbey built in Wales, or revelling in the medieval grandeur of bishops' palaces in St Davids, you can experience Wales' rich and diverse history at a discounted price or for free, depending on how long you've been an English Heritage Member. Cadw is part of the Welsh Government and is working for an accessible and well-protected historic environment.

Please check the Cadw website for opening days and hours.

Conwy Castle

Cadw, Ty'r Afon

Welsh Government, Bedwas Road
Caerphilly CF83 8WT
T. 03000 252239   E. cadw@gov.wales
W. gov.wales/cadw

Stirling Castle

Historic Scotland

English Heritage Members can gain half-price admission to Historic Scotland attractions during the first year of membership and free entry in subsequent years.

Situated in some of Scotland's most beautiful locations, Historic Scotland sites trace over 5,000 years of history. Whether walking in the footsteps of Roman troops on the Antonine Wall or exploring iconic Stirling Castle, childhood home of Mary, Queen of Scots, by visiting a Historic Scotland attraction you'll get a unique insight into Scottish history.

Pre-booking is recommended. Please check the Historic Scotland website for the latest opening times and information. A valid English Heritage membership card must be shown at the sites to gain entry.

Urquhart Castle

Historic Scotland

Historic Environment Scotland
Longmore House, Salisbury Place,
Edinburgh EH9 1SH
T. 0131 668 8999   **E.** members@hes.scot
W. historicenvironment.scot

Castle Rushen © Manx National Heritage

Manx National Heritage

Manx National Heritage welcomes English Heritage Members with free* admission to all its heritage attractions on presentation of a valid membership card.

Manx National Heritage is responsible for protecting and promoting the Isle of Man's natural and cultural heritage. It is a registered charity and looks after some of the island's most special places, spaces, archives and museum collections, making these available to people across the world. Whether discovering the story of legendary sea god Manannan or exploring Castle Rushen in the heart of the island's ancient capital, Manx National Heritage's sites will give you a unique insight into 10,000 years of history.

Admission charges may apply for some special events. Travel connections between the Isle of Man heritage sites are available on Victorian Steam Railway, Manx Electric Railway and Bus Vannin.

*Free admission applies to the Member only and children aged 17 years and under.

Laxey Wheel

Manx National Heritage

Kingswood Grove, Douglas
Isle of Man IMI 3LY
T. 01624 648000 W. manxnationalheritage.im

Rock of Cashel

OPW Heritage Ireland

As an English Heritage Member, you can get free entry to over 40 historic sites in Ireland, all under the care of OPW Heritage Ireland.

Explore prehistoric passage tombs at the World Heritage Site of Brú na Bóinne to discover the ancient history of this beautiful country. Rock of Cashel, meanwhile, is one of Ireland's most spectacular and iconic historical sites. Wherever you go, you can experience thousands of years of people and stories from the Emerald Isle.

Kilmainham Gaol

Swiss Cottage

OPW Heritage Ireland

For more information about OPW Heritage Ireland and their sites, please visit **heritageireland.ie** or find them on Facebook.

Heritage New Zealand Pouhere Taonga

Kororipo Heritage Park

English Heritage Members get free entry to all our properties.

Aotearoa New Zealand's peopled heritage reaches back centuries. Indigenous Māori named and claimed the landscape and left ancestral and sacred places including ancient rock art, fortified settlements, and large ornate wharenui (meeting houses) which are part of the contemporary landscape. The country's more recent heritage sites are tangible reminders of this South Pacific nation's connection to Great Britain as well its self-defining moments, from the Kerikeri Mission Station in Northland, to Kate Sheppard House in Ōtautahi Christchurch, to Hayes Engineering Works in the gold mining region of Central Otago. Heritage New Zealand Pouhere Taonga cares for 45 properties and sites where you can learn about the people and places that make New Zealand what it is today.

OUR SITES RANGE FROM IMPRESSIVE HOMESTEADS, TO CENTRES OF INDUSTRY AND INNOVATION, TO BATTLE SITES, AND MORE, INCLUDING:

Old St Paul's (Wellington) – where stunning stained glass windows help illuminate the glorious native timber interior of this 19th-century Gothic Revival church, a home away from home for US servicemen during the Second World War.

The Kerikeri Mission Station and Stone Store (Northland) – the Mission Station is New Zealand's oldest standing building, built in 1821-22, while the nearby Stone Store is one of the country's most photographed buildings.

Fyffe House (Kāikoura) – where a whale of a time is guaranteed, the property built as part of the early whaling industry and partly on whale vertebrae foundations.

Alberton and Highwic (Auckland) – impressive dwellings that were home to two prominent colonial businessmen.

Totara Estate (Ōamaru) – British dinner tables have featured our finest cuts of meat over many years, and Totara Estate is where New Zealand's billion dollar frozen meat industry began.

Heritage New Zealand Pouhere Taonga

More information on heritage sites to visit can be found on Heritage New Zealand's website **visitheritage.org.nz**. Our staff look forward to welcoming you. Please check opening hours on the website prior to your visit to avoid disappointment.

HERITAGE NEW ZEALAND POUHERE TAONGA

St George's Church, Portland, Dorset
© Churches Conservation Trust

St Mary's, Mundon, Essex before FoFC's rescue

Coanwood Friends Meeting House, Northumberland

Churches Conservation Trust

Open a church door to discover 1,000 years of England's history – from Anglo-Saxon carvings and medieval stained glass to grand Victorian architecture. With the Churches Conservation Trust help and your support these churches are kept open and in use – living once again in the heart of their communities. Entry is free, so push open the door and 1,000 years of history awaits you.

Discover more and see what's on near you at visitchurches.org.uk

Churches
Conservation Trust

Society Building
8 All Saints Street
London N1 9RL
T. 0845 303 2760
E. enquiries@thecct.org.uk
W. visitchurches.org.uk
Registered charity no: 258612

Churches Conservation Trust

Friends of Friendless Churches

Friends of Friendless Churches save disused but beautiful old places of worship of architectural and historical interest from demolition, decay and unsympathetic conversion. Working across England and Wales, they care for over 60 redundant places of worship and have helped hundreds more. They preserve these buildings for the local community and visitors to enjoy. Their churches are places for quiet study and contemplation, preserved for posterity as beautiful historic buildings.

Friends of
Friendless Churches

T. 020 4520 4458
E. office@friendsoffriendless churches.org.uk
W. friendsoffriendless churches.org.uk
Follow us on 📷 🇫 🐦
Registered charity no: 1113097

FRIENDS OF FRIENDLESS CHURCHES

Historic Chapels Trust

Historic Chapels Trust rescues non-Anglican places of worship in England that are no longer in use by their congregations. They aim to hand them on to future generations in good condition, as the physical record of religious life and a vital strand of our history. To visit their chapels and churches, please arrange a time with their local keyholder at the site first. Details of how to find the buildings and keyholders are on their website. Many of their chapels can be hired for concerts or other events – see details on their website.

Historic
Chapels Trust

Society Building
8 All Saints Street
London N1 9RL
T. 020 7481 0533 &
07741 016832
E. chapels@hct.org.uk
W. nationalchurchestrust.org/get-support/support-organisations/historic-chapels-trust
Registered charity no: 1017321

HISTORIC CHAPELS TRUST

HURTIGRUTEN EXPEDITIONS

BLOOM & WILD

Parkdean Resorts

VINTAGE

'A frank, funny and long overdue ode to teachers and teaching'
ADAM KAY

Let That Be a Lesson

A Teacher's Life in the Classroom

RYAN WILSON

SEASALT CORNWALL

WIGHTLINK
ISLE OF WIGHT FERRIES

As a thank you to you for your support, we've teamed up with brilliant brands to provide discounts on a fantastic range of items, along with exclusive competitions, experiences and content. Whether you're looking for theatre tickets, home appliances, wine, magazine subscriptions, clothing or holidays, you'll find an offer to help save money.

Redeeming your rewards couldn't be easier:
• Visit the Members' Rewards section on our website.
• Browse through the offers, which are grouped into food and drink, home and garden, family, travel, entertainment, lifestyle and outdoors.
• Follow the instructions to claim your reward and start making great savings!

Support us as you save

There are so many benefits to shopping through Members' Rewards. In addition to giving you access to great money-saving deals that can be used to cover the cost of your membership, the revenue generated by these partnerships also helps to support our vital work to care for England's historic sites. This means you will be playing your part in helping us to make sure England's story survives to be enjoyed by future generations.

Find out more

To see the full range of Members' Rewards on offer, visit **english-heritage.org.uk/rewards**

COTSWOLD outdoor

BEER52

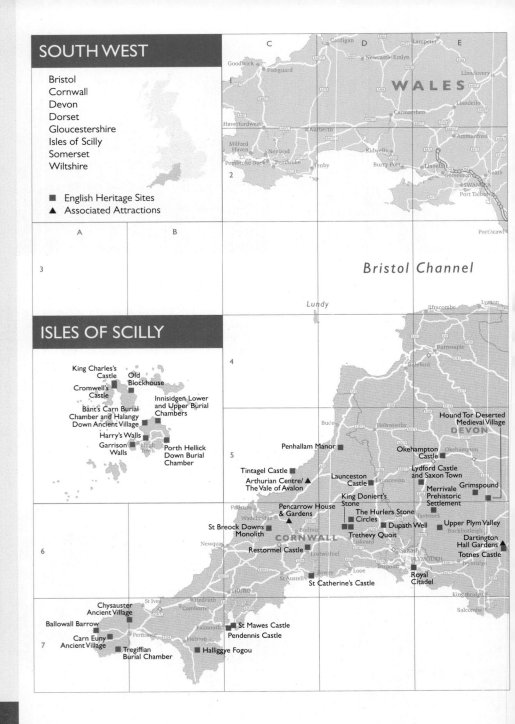

SOUTH WEST

Bristol
Cornwall
Devon
Dorset
Gloucestershire
Isles of Scilly
Somerset
Wiltshire

■ English Heritage Sites
▲ Associated Attractions

ISLES OF SCILLY

WALES

Cardigan
Lampeter
Goodwick
Fishguard
Newcastle Emlyn
Llandovery
Haverfordwest
Carmarthen
Llandeilo
Narberth
Ammanford
Milford Haven
Neyland
Kidwelly
Pembroke Dock
Pembroke
Tenby
Burry Port
Llanelli
Gorseinon
Neath
SWANSEA
Port Talbot

Porthcawl

Bristol Channel

Lundy

Ilfracombe
Lynton
Barnstaple
Bideford

King Charles's Castle
Old Blockhouse
Cromwell's Castle
Innisidgen Lower and Upper Burial Chambers
Bant's Carn Burial Chamber and Halangy Down Ancient Village
Harry's Walls
Garrison Walls
Hugh Town
Porth Hellick Down Burial Chamber

Penhallam Manor
Bude
Holsworthy

Hound Tor Deserted Medieval Village
DEVON
Okehampton Castle

Tintagel Castle
Arthurian Centre/ The Vale of Avalon
Launceston Castle
Lydford Castle and Saxon Town
King Doniert's Stone
Merrivale Prehistoric Settlement
Grimspound
Padstow
Pencarrow House & Gardens
Wadebridge
The Hurlers Stone Circles
Tavistock
St Breock Downs Monolith
CORNWALL
Bodmin
Dupath Well
Upper Plym Valley
Buckfastleigh
Newquay
Trethevy Quoit
Liskeard
Dartington Hall Gardens
Restormel Castle
Lostwithiel
Saltash
PLYMOUTH
Totnes Castle
Ivybridge
Fowey
Looe
Torpoint
Royal Citadel
St Austell
St Catherine's Castle
Kingsbridge
TRURO
Redruth
Camborne
St Ives
Salcombe
Chysauster Ancient Village
Ballowall Barrow
Penzance
St Mawes Castle
Carn Euny Ancient Village
Pendennis Castle
Tregiffian Burial Chamber
Falmouth
Helston
Halliggye Fogou

A   B   C   D   E

1

2

3

4

5

6

7

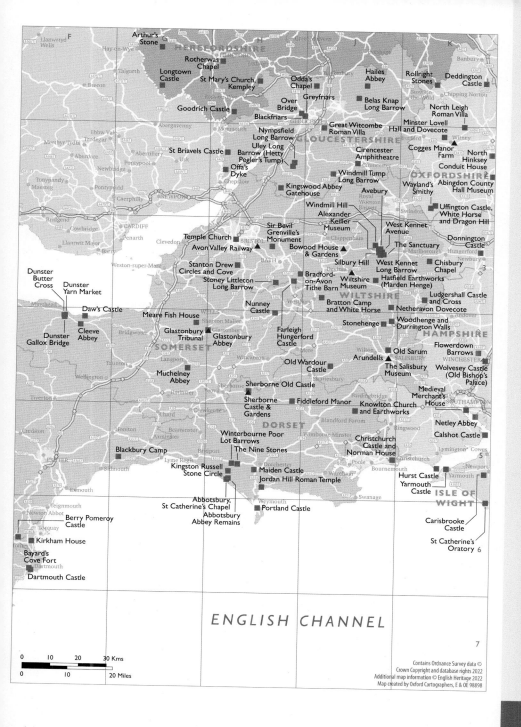

HEREFORDSHIRE

Arthur's Stone

Hay-on-Wye

Rotherwas Chapel

Longtown Castle

St Mary's Church, Kempley

Odda's Chapel

Hailes Abbey

Rollright Stones

Deddington Castle

Greyfriars

Over Bridge

Belas Knap Long Barrow

North Leigh Roman Villa

Goodrich Castle

Blackfriars

GLOUCESTER

Great Witcombe Roman Villa

Minster Lovell Hall and Dovecote

Nympsfield Long Barrow

GLOUCESTERSHIRE

Cogges Manor Farm

North Hinksey Conduit House

St Briavels Castle

Uley Long Barrow (Hetty Pegler's Tump)

Cirencester Amphitheatre

OXFORDSHIRE

Offa's Dyke

Windmill Tump Long Barrow

Wayland's Smithy

Abingdon County Hall Museum

Kingswood Abbey Gatehouse

Avebury

Uffington Castle, White Horse and Dragon Hill

Windmill Hill

Alexander Keiller Museum

West Kennet Avenue

Donnington Castle

Sir Bevil Grenville's Monument

The Sanctuary

Temple Church

Bowood House & Gardens

Silbury Hill

West Kennet Long Barrow

Chisbury Chapel

Avon Valley Railway

Stanton Drew Circles and Cove

Bradford-on-Avon Tithe Barn

Wiltshire Museum

Hatfield Earthworks (Marden Henge)

Stoney Littleton Long Barrow

WILTSHIRE

Ludgershall Castle and Cross

Dunster Butter Cross

Dunster Yarn Market

Nunney Castle

Bratton Camp and White Horse

Netheravon Dovecote

Daw's Castle

Meare Fish House

Farleigh Hungerford Castle

Stonehenge

Woodhenge and Durrington Walls

HAMPSHIRE

Cleeve Abbey

Glastonbury Tribunal

Glastonbury Abbey

Flowerdown Barrows

Dunster Gallox Bridge

SOMERSET

Old Sarum

WINCHESTER

Muchelney Abbey

Old Wardour Castle

Arundells

The Salisbury Museum

Wolvesey Castle (Old Bishop's Palace)

Sherborne Old Castle

Medieval Merchant's House

SOUTHAMPTON

Sherborne Castle & Gardens

Fiddleford Manor

Knowlton Church and Earthworks

DORSET

Netley Abbey

Blackbury Camp

Winterbourne Poor Lot Barrows

Christchurch Castle and Norman House

Calshot Castle

The Nine Stones

Berry Pomeroy Castle

Kingston Russell Stone Circle

Maiden Castle

Hurst Castle

Kirkham House

Jordan Hill Roman Temple

Yarmouth Castle

ISLE OF WIGHT

Bayard's Cove Fort

Abbotsbury, St Catherine's Chapel

Portland Castle

Carisbrooke Castle

Dartmouth Castle

Abbotsbury Abbey Remains

St Catherine's Oratory 6

ENGLISH CHANNEL

0 10 20 30 Kms
0 10 20 Miles

Contains Ordnance Survey data © Crown Copyright and database rights 2022
Additional map information © English Heritage 2022
Map created by Oxford Cartographers, E & OE 98898

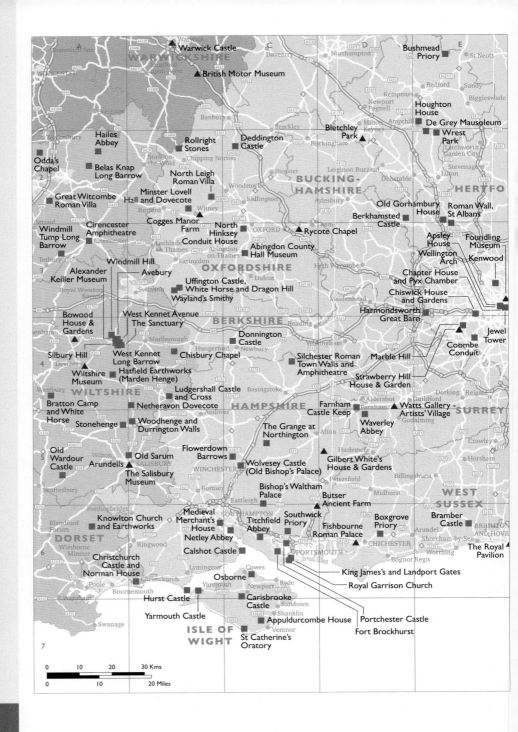

Warwick Castle

British Motor Museum

Bushmead Priory

St Neots

WARWICKSHIRE

Houghton House

De Grey Mausoleum

Wrest Park

HERTFO

Bletchley Park

Hailes Abbey

Rollright Stones

Deddington Castle

BUCKING-HAMSHIRE

Odda's Chapel

Belas Knap Long Barrow

North Leigh Roman Villa

Great Witcombe Roman Villa

Minster Lovell Hall and Dovecote

Old Gorhambury House

Roman Wall, St Albans

Cogges Manor Farm

Berkhamsted Castle

Apsley House

Foundling Museum

Windmill Tump Long Barrow

Cirencester Amphitheatre

North Hinksey Conduit House

Rycote Chapel

Wellington Arch

Kenwood

Windmill Hill

Abingdon County Hall Museum

Chapter House and Pyx Chamber

Alexander Keiller Museum

Avebury

Chiswick House and Gardens

Uffington Castle, White Horse and Dragon Hill

Wayland's Smithy

OXFORDSHIRE

Harmondsworth Great Barn

Bowood House & Gardens

West Kennet Avenue
The Sanctuary

BERKSHIRE

Jewel Tower

Silbury Hill

West Kennet Long Barrow

Chisbury Chapel

Donnington Castle

Silchester Roman Town Walls and Amphitheatre

Marble Hill

Coombe Conduit

Wiltshire Museum

Hatfield Earthworks (Marden Henge)

Strawberry Hill House & Garden

Bratton Camp and White Horse

Ludgershall Castle and Cross

Netheravon Dovecote

HAMPSHIRE

Farnham Castle Keep

Watts Gallery - Artists' Village

SURREY

Stonehenge

Woodhenge and Durrington Walls

The Grange at Northington

Waverley Abbey

Old Wardour Castle

Flowerdown Barrows

Gilbert White's House & Gardens

Arundells

Old Sarum

WEST SUSSEX

The Salisbury Museum

Wolvesey Castle (Old Bishop's Palace)

Butser Ancient Farm

Bishop's Waltham Palace

DORSET

Knowlton Church and Earthworks

Medieval Merchant's House

Titchfield Abbey

Southwick Priory

Boxgrove Priory

Bramber Castle

Fishbourne Roman Palace

Netley Abbey

The Royal Pavilion

Christchurch Castle and Norman House

Calshot Castle

King James's and Landport Gates

Osborne

Royal Garrison Church

Hurst Castle

Carisbrooke Castle

Yarmouth Castle

Appuldurcombe House

Portchester Castle

ISLE OF WIGHT

St Catherine's Oratory

Fort Brockhurst

0   10   20   30 Kms

0   10   20 Miles

F · G · H · J · K

CAMBRIDGE
Newmarket
Moulton Packhorse Bridge
Bury St Edmunds
Bury St Edmunds Abbey
Stowmarket
Saxtead Green Post Mill
Framlingham Castle
Saxmundham
Leiston Abbey
Aldeburgh
Woodbridge
Orford Castle

Duxford Chapel
Haverhill
Lindsey St James's Chapel
Ipswich
Hadleigh
Sudbury

Audley End House and Gardens
Royston
Saffron Walden

Winchester Palace
London Wall
Prior's Hall Barn
Halstead
Lexden Earthworks
Bishop's Stortford
Bluebottle Grove
Braintree
Great Dunmow
Colchester
St John's Abbey Gate
St Botolph's Priory
Felixstowe
Mistley Towers
Harwich
Landguard Fort
Walton-on-the-Naze

RDSHIRE
Waltham Abbey Gatehouse and Bridge
ESSEX
CHELMSFORD
Witham
West Mersea
Maldon
Clacton-on-Sea

Milton Chantry
Hill Hall
Tilbury Fort
Cutty Sark
Ranger's House - The Wernher Collection
Stow Maries Great War Aerodrome

Hadleigh Castle
Southend-on-Sea
Lullingstone Roman Villa
Temple Manor
Faversham Stone Chapel (Our Lady of Elverton)
Reculver Towers and Roman Fort
St Augustine's Abbey Conduit House

Eltham Palace and Gardens
Eynsford Castle
Upnor Castle
Rochester Castle
Isle of Sheppey
Herne Bay
Powell-Cotton Museum
Margate
St Augustine's Cross
Ramsgate
Richborough Roman Fort and Amphitheatre

Home of Charles Darwin, Down House
St Leonard's Tower
Kit's Coty House and Little Kit's Coty House
Old Soar Manor
Sutton Valence Castle
Maison Dieu
Faversham
CANTERBURY
Sandwich
St Augustine's Abbey
Deal Castle
Walmer Castle and Gardens

Tonbridge
KENT
Ashford
Canterbury Cathedral
Deal
Dover
St John's Commandery
Dover Castle
Knights Templar Church

East Grinstead
Royal Tunbridge Wells
Bayham Old Abbey
Tenterden
Horne's Place Chapel
Folkestone
Hythe
Western Heights, Dover

Crowborough
EAST SUSSEX
Uckfield
Rye
Lydd
New Romney
Dymchurch Martello Tower

Burgess Hill
Battle
Camber Castle

Lewes Castle and Museum
Michelham Priory House & Gardens
Hailsham
Bexhill
1066 Battle of Hastings, Abbey and Battlefield
Hastings

Anne of Cleves House Museum
Lewes
Pevensey Castle
Newhaven
Eastbourne

ENGLISH   CHANNEL

Berkshire
Buckinghamshire
East Sussex
Hampshire
Isle of Wight
Kent
Oxfordshire
Surrey
West Sussex

■ English Heritage Sites
▲ Associated Attractions

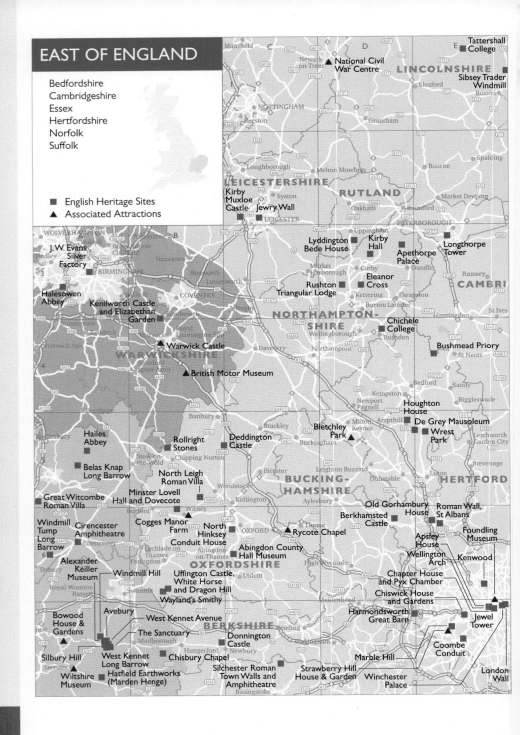

EAST OF ENGLAND

Bedfordshire
Cambridgeshire
Essex
Hertfordshire
Norfolk
Suffolk

■ English Heritage Sites
▲ Associated Attractions

Tattershall College
Sibsey Trader Windmill
National Civil War Centre
LINCOLNSHIRE
Sleaford
Boston
Mansfield
Newark-on-Trent
Grantham
Spalding
NOTTINGHAM
Becston
Bourne
Loughborough
Melton Mowbray
Market Deeping
LEICESTERSHIRE
RUTLAND
Kirby Muxloe Castle
Syston
Oakham
Stamford
PETERBOROUGH
Jewry Wall
LEICESTER
Uppingham
Lyddington Bede House
Kirby Hall
Apethorpe Palace
Longthorpe Tower
CAMBRI
Market Harborough
Corby
Oundle
Ramsey
Rushton Triangular Lodge
Eleanor Cross
Kettering
Thrapston
Burton Latimer
St Ives
NORTHAMPTON-SHIRE
Chichele College
Huntingdon
Wellingborough
Rushden
Bushmead Priory
Northampton
St Neots

J.W. Evans Silver Factory
BIRMINGHAM
Nuneaton
Bedworth
Lutterworth
Rugby
COVENTRY
Halesowen Abbey
Kenilworth Castle and Elizabethan Garden
Kenilworth
Royal Leamington Spa
Warwick
▲ Warwick Castle
Daventry
WARWICKSHIRE
Stratford-upon-Avon
▲ British Motor Museum
Bedford
Sandy
Biggleswade
Kempston
Newport Pagnell
Houghton House
Evesham
Banbury
Brackley
Bletchley Park
Milton Keynes
Ampthill
De Grey Mausoleum
■ Wrest Park
Letchworth Garden City
Hailes Abbey
Rollright Stones
Deddington Castle
Buckingham
Leighton Buzzard
Luton
Stevenage
Belas Knap Long Barrow
Stow-on-the-Wold
Chipping Norton
Bicester
Dunstable
HERTFORD
Great Witcombe Roman Villa
North Leigh Roman Villa
Woodstock
BUCKING-HAMSHIRE
Aylesbury
Tring
Windmill Tump Long Barrow
Minster Lovell Hall and Dovecote
Kidlington
Old Gorhambury House
Roman Wall, St Albans
Cirencester Amphitheatre
Cogges Manor Farm
Witney
OXFORD
Thame
▲ Rycote Chapel
Berkhamsted Castle
Apsley House
Foundling Museum
Alexander Keiller Museum
North Hinksey Conduit House
Lechlade on Thames
Abingdon County Hall Museum
Abingdon-on-Thames
High Wycombe
Wellington Arch
Kenwood
OXFORDSHIRE
Windmill Hill
Uffington Castle, White Horse and Dragon Hill
Swindon
Didcot
Chapter House and Pyx Chamber
Chiswick House and Gardens
Avebury
Wayland's Smithy
West Kennet Avenue
Maidenhead
Harmondsworth Great Barn
Jewel Tower
Bowood House & Gardens
The Sanctuary
Marlborough
BERKSHIRE
Reading
Donnington Castle
Newbury
Wokingham
Marble Hill
Coombe Conduit
Silbury Hill
Devizes
West Kennet Long Barrow
Chisbury Chapel
Hungerford
Silchester Roman Town Walls and Amphitheatre
Strawberry Hill House & Garden
Winchester Palace
London Wall
Wiltshire Museum
Hatfield Earthworks (Marden Henge)
Basingstoke

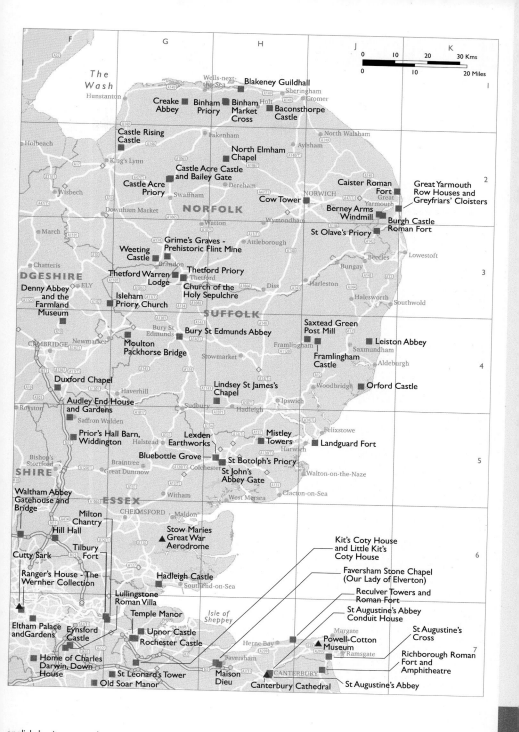

The Wash

Hunstanton

Holbeach

Blakeney Guildhall
Sheringham
Wells-next-the-Sea
Holt
Cromer

Creake Abbey
Binham Priory
Binham Market Cross
Baconsthorpe Castle

Castle Rising Castle
Fakenham
North Walsham
Aylsham

King's Lynn
North Elmham Chapel

Castle Acre Castle and Bailey Gate
Dereham

Wisbech
Castle Acre Priory
Swaffham

Downham Market

NORFOLK
Watton

Caister Roman Fort
Great Yarmouth Row Houses and Greyfriars' Cloisters

NORWICH
Cow Tower
Great Yarmouth

Wymondham
Berney Arms Windmill
Burgh Castle Roman Fort

March

Attleborough
St Olave's Priory

Chatteris

Grime's Graves - Prehistoric Flint Mine
Beccles
Lowestoft

CAMBRIDGESHIRE

Weeting Castle
Brandon

Bungay

ELY
Denny Abbey and the Farmland Museum

Thetford Warren Lodge
Thetford
Diss
Harleston

Isleham Priory Church
Thetford Priory
Church of the Holy Sepulchre

Halesworth
Southwold

SUFFOLK

CAMBRIDGE
Newmarket

Bury St Edmunds
Bury St Edmunds Abbey

Saxtead Green Post Mill
Leiston Abbey

Moulton Packhorse Bridge

Framlingham
Saxmundham

Stowmarket
Framlingham Castle
Aldeburgh

Duxford Chapel

Haverhill
Lindsey St James's Chapel

Woodbridge
Orford Castle

Royston
Audley End House and Gardens

Saffron Walden

Sudbury
Hadleigh
Ipswich

Prior's Hall Barn, Widdington
Halstead

Lexden Earthworks
Mistley Towers
Landguard Fort

Félixstowe
Harwich

Bishop's Stortford

Bluebottle Grove
Braintree
Great Dunmow
Colchester
St Botolph's Priory
St John's Abbey Gate

Walton-on-the-Naze

HERTFORDSHIRE

Witham
West Mersea

Waltham Abbey Gatehouse and Bridge

ESSEX
CHELMSFORD
Maldon
Clacton-on-Sea

Milton Chantry
Hill Hall

Stow Maries Great War Aerodrome

Kit's Coty House and Little Kit's Coty House

Tilbury Fort

Cutty Sark

Hadleigh Castle
Southend-on-Sea

Faversham Stone Chapel (Our Lady of Elverton)

Ranger's House - The Wernher Collection

Lullingstone Roman Villa
Isle of Sheppey

Reculver Towers and Roman Fort

Temple Manor

St Augustine's Abbey Conduit House

Eltham Palace and Gardens
Eynsford Castle

Upnor Castle
Rochester Castle

Margate
Powell-Cotton Museum

St Augustine's Cross

Home of Charles Darwin, Down House

Herne Bay
Faversham
Ramsgate

Richborough Roman Fort and Amphitheatre

St Leonard's Tower
Old Soar Manor

Maison Dieu
CANTERBURY
Canterbury Cathedral
St Augustine's Abbey

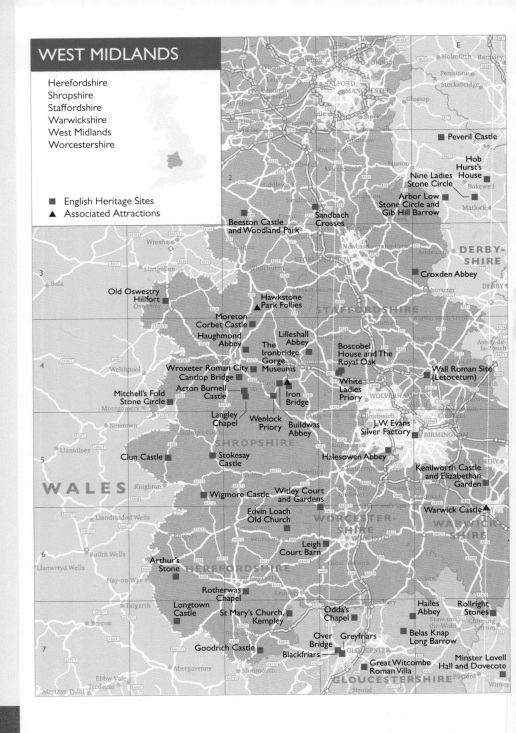

WEST MIDLANDS

Herefordshire
Shropshire
Staffordshire
Warwickshire
West Midlands
Worcestershire

■ English Heritage Sites
▲ Associated Attractions

Peveril Castle

Hob Hurst's House

Nine Ladies Stone Circle

Arbor Low Stone Circle and Gib Hill Barrow

Beeston Castle and Woodland Park

Sandbach Crosses

Croxden Abbey

DERBY-SHIRE

DERBY

Old Oswestry Hillfort

Hawkstone Park Follies

STAFFORDSHIRE

Moreton Corbet Castle

Haughmond Abbey

Lilleshall Abbey

Boscobel House and The Royal Oak

Wall Roman Site (Letocetum)

The Ironbridge Gorge Museums

Wroxeter Roman City

Cantlop Bridge

Acton Burnell Castle

White Ladies Priory

Mitchell's Fold Stone Circle

Iron Bridge

WOLVERHAMPTON

Langley Chapel

Wenlock Priory

Buildwas Abbey

J. W. Evans Silver Factory

BIRMINGHAM

Clun Castle

Stokesay Castle

Halesowen Abbey

Kenilworth Castle and Elizabethan Garden

WALES

Wigmore Castle

Witley Court and Gardens

Warwick Castle

WARWICK-SHIRE

Edvin Loach Old Church

WORCESTER-SHIRE

Leigh Court Barn

Arthur's Stone

HEREFORDSHIRE

Rotherwas Chapel

Longtown Castle

St Mary's Church, Kempley

Odda's Chapel

Hailes Abbey

Rollright Stones

Belas Knap Long Barrow

Over Bridge

Greyfriars

Goodrich Castle

Blackfriars

GLOUCESTER

Great Witcombe Roman Villa

Minster Lovell Hall and Dovecote

GLOUCESTERSHIRE

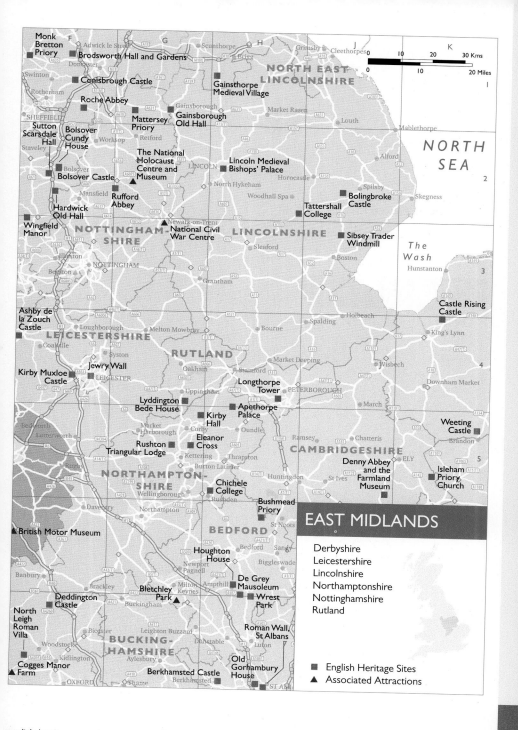

Monk Bretton Priory
Brodsworth Hall and Gardens
Adwick le Street
Doncaster
Scunthorpe
Brigg
Grimsby
Cleethorpes

NORTH EAST LINCOLNSHIRE

Swinton
Rotherham
Conisbrough Castle
Roche Abbey
Gainsthorpe Medieval Village
Market Rasen
Louth
Mablethorpe

SHEFFIELD
Sutton Scarsdale Hall
Bolsover Cundy House
Mattersey Priory
Gainsborough Old Hall
Gainsborough
Worksop
Retford

NORTH SEA

Staveley
Bolsover
Bolsover Castle
Mansfield
The National Holocaust Centre and Museum
LINCOLN
Lincoln Medieval Bishops' Palace
Horncastle
Alford
Spilsby
Skegness

Hardwick Old Hall
Rufford Abbey
North Hykeham
Woodhall Spa
Tattershall College
Bolingbroke Castle

Wingfield Manor
NOTTINGHAM-SHIRE
Newark-on-Trent
National Civil War Centre
LINCOLNSHIRE
Sleaford
Sibsey Trader Windmill

The Wash

Ilkeston
NOTTINGHAM
Boston
Hunstanton

Beeston
Grantham

Ashby de la Zouch Castle
Loughborough
Melton Mowbray
Bourne
Spalding
Holbeach
King's Lynn
Castle Rising Castle

LEICESTERSHIRE
Coalville
RUTLAND
Oakham
Market Deeping
Wisbech
Downham Market

Kirby Muxloe Castle
Jewry Wall
LEICESTER
Syston
Stamford
PETERBOROUGH
March

Longthorpe Tower
Uppingham
Lyddington Bede House
Apethorpe Palace
Kirby Hall
Corby
Oundle
Ramsey
Chatteris
Weeting Castle
Brandon

Bedford
Lutterworth
Rugby
Market Harborough
Rushton Triangular Lodge
Eleanor Cross
Kettering
Thrapston
Burton Latimer
Huntingdon
St Ives
CAMBRIDGESHIRE
Denny Abbey and the Farmland Museum
ELY
Isleham Priory Church

NORTHAMPTON-SHIRE
Chichele College
Wellingborough
Northampton
Rushden
Bushmead Priory
St Neots

British Motor Museum
Daventry
BEDFORD
Sandy

Banbury
Bedford
Biggleswade
Houghton House
Brackley
Newport Pagnell
De Grey Mausoleum
Wrest Park
Deddington Castle
Bletchley Park
Milton Keynes
Ampthill
Buckingham
Leighton Buzzard

North Leigh Roman Villa
Bicester
Woodstock
Kidlington
Dunstable
Luton
Roman Wall, St Albans
Old Gorhambury House

Cogges Manor Farm
BUCKING-HAMSHIRE
Aylesbury
OXFORD
Thame
Berkhamsted Castle
Berkhamsted
ST ALBANS

EAST MIDLANDS

Derbyshire
Leicestershire
Lincolnshire
Northamptonshire
Nottinghamshire
Rutland

■ English Heritage Sites
▲ Associated Attractions

Scale: 0 — 10 — 20 — 30 Kms
0 — 10 — 20 Miles

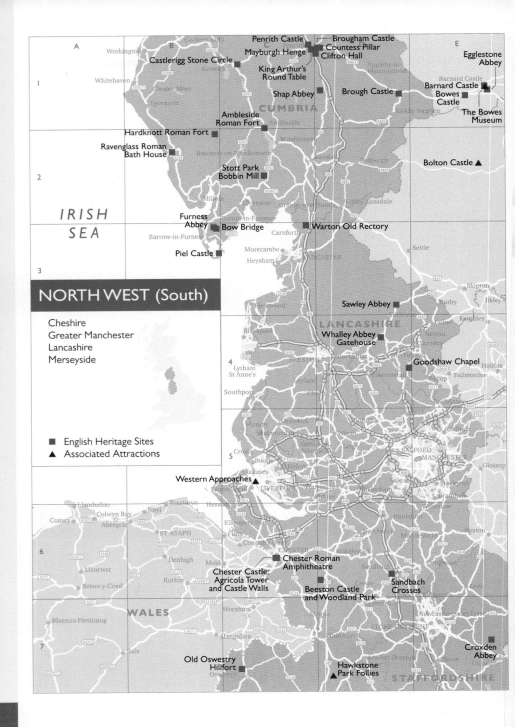

A

Workington

Whitehaven

Cockermouth

Castlerigg Stone Circle

Keswick

Penrith Castle
Mayburgh Henge

King Arthur's
Round Table

Countess Pillar
Clifton Hall

Brougham Castle

E

Egglestone
Abbey

Appleby-in-
Westmorland

Barnard Castle

Barnard Castle
Bowes
Castle

Cleator Moor

Shap Abbey

CUMBRIA

Egremont

Brough Castle

Kirkby Stephen

The Bowes
Museum

Ambleside
Roman Fort

Hardknott Roman Fort

Ravenglass Roman
Bath House

Ambleside

Windermere

Bowness-on-Windermere

Kendal

Sedbergh

Bolton Castle ▲

Stott Park
Bobbin Mill

Millom

Ulverston

Dalton-in-Furness

Grange-over-Sands

Kirkby Lonsdale

IRISH

SEA

Furness
Abbey

Bow Bridge

Carnforth

Warton Old Rectory

Settle

Barrow-in-Furness

Piel Castle

Morecambe

Heysham

LANCASTER

Skipton

Ilkley

3

NORTH WEST (South)

Cheshire
Greater Manchester
Lancashire
Merseyside

Fleetwood

Blackpool

LANCASHIRE

Sawley Abbey

Kirby

Keighley

Colne

Nelson

Burnley

Whalley Abbey
Gatehouse

Goodshaw Chapel

Halifax

Todmorden

4

Lytham
St Anne's

PRESTON

Leyland

Blackburn

Chorley

Rawtenstall

Bacup

Rochdale

Southport

■ English Heritage Sites
▲ Associated Attractions

Crosby

Bootle

5

Wallasey

St Helens

SALFORD

MANCHESTER

Oldham

Stockport

Glossop

Bramhall

Western Approaches ▲

Birkenhead

LIVERPOOL

Widnes

Runcorn

Warrington

Llandudno

Conwy

Colwyn Bay

Abergele

Rhyl

Prestatyn

Heswall

Ellesmere Port

Flint

ST ASAPH

Denbigh

Mold

Connah's Quay

CHESTER

Northwich

Knutsford

Middlewich

Wilmslow

Macclesfield

Buxton

6

Llanrwst

Betws-y-Coed

Ruthin

Chester Castle:
Agricola Tower
and Castle Walls

Chester Roman
Amphitheatre

Sandbach

Beeston Castle
and Woodland Park

Sandbach
Crosses

Congleton

Blaenau Ffestiniog

WALES

Wrexham

Llangollen

Nantwich

STOKE-ON-TRENT

Whitchurch

Newcastle-under-Lyme

Bala

7

Old Oswestry
Hillfort

Oswestry

Hawkstone
Park Follies

Market Drayton

Stone

Croxden
Abbey

STAFFORDSHIRE

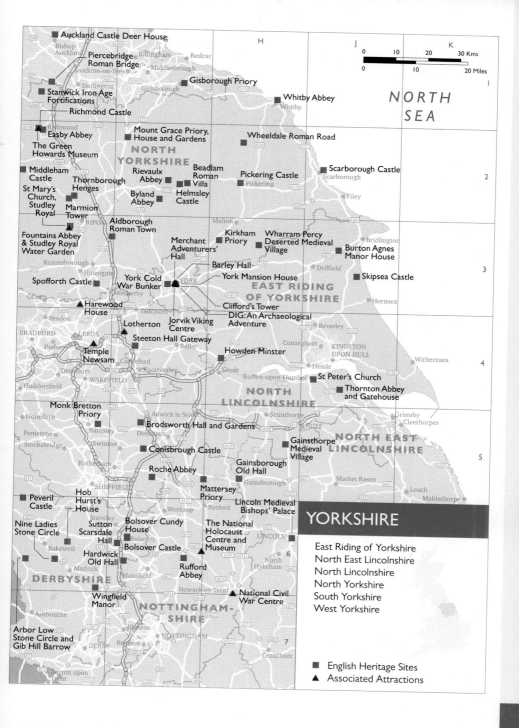

Auckland Castle Deer House

Bishop Auckland

Piercebridge Roman Bridge

Stockton-on-Tees

Stanwick Iron Age Fortifications

Richmond Castle

Easby Abbey

The Green Howards Museum

Mount Grace Priory, House and Gardens

NORTH YORKSHIRE

Middleham Castle

Rievaulx Abbey

Thornborough Henges

St Mary's Church, Studley Royal

Byland Abbey

Marmion Tower

Fountains Abbey & Studley Royal Water Garden

Aldborough Roman Town

Spofforth Castle

York Cold War Bunker

Harewood House

Lotherton

Jorvik Viking Centre

Temple Newsam

Steeton Hall Gateway

Monk Bretton Priory

Brodsworth Hall and Gardens

Conisbrough Castle

Roche Abbey

Peveril Castle

Hob Hurst's House

Nine Ladies Stone Circle

Sutton Scarsdale Hall

Bolsover Cundy House

Bolsover Castle

Hardwick Old Hall

Wingfield Manor

Arbor Low Stone Circle and Gib Hill Barrow

DERBYSHIRE

NOTTINGHAM-SHIRE

Billingham   Redcar

Middlesbrough

Guisborough

Gisborough Priory

Whitby Abbey

Whitby

NORTH SEA

Wheeldale Roman Road

Beadlam Roman Villa

Pickering Castle

Helmsley Castle

Scarborough Castle

Filey

Malton

Kirkham Priory

Wharram Percy Deserted Medieval Village

Merchant Adventurers' Hall

Barley Hall

York Mansion House

Clifford's Tower

DIG: An Archaeological Adventure

Burton Agnes Manor House

Skipsea Castle

EAST RIDING OF YORKSHIRE

Hornsea

Howden Minster

KINGSTON UPON HULL

Withernsea

St Peter's Church

Thornton Abbey and Gatehouse

NORTH LINCOLNSHIRE

Adwick le Street

Gainsthorpe Medieval Village

NORTH EAST LINCOLNSHIRE

Grimsby

Cleethorpes

Gainsborough Old Hall

Market Rasen

Louth

Mablethorpe

Mattersey Priory

Lincoln Medieval Bishops' Palace

The National Holocaust Centre and Museum

LINCOLN

Rufford Abbey

National Civil War Centre

NOTTINGHAM

YORKSHIRE

East Riding of Yorkshire
North East Lincolnshire
North Lincolnshire
North Yorkshire
South Yorkshire
West Yorkshire

■ English Heritage Sites
▲ Associated Attractions

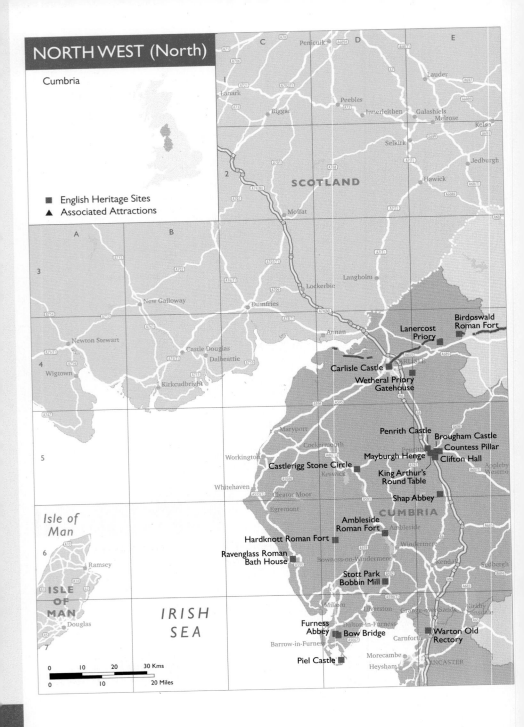

Cumbria

■ English Heritage Sites
▲ Associated Attractions

SCOTLAND

Penicuik
Lanark
Biggar
Peebles
Innerleithen
Galashiels
Melrose
Kelso
Lauder
Selkirk
Jedburgh
Hawick
Moffat

CUMBRIA

Langholm
Lockerbie
New Galloway
Dumfries
Annan
Newton Stewart
Castle Douglas
Dalbeattie
Wigtown
Kirkcudbright

Lanercost Priory
Birdoswald Roman Fort
CARLISLE
Carlisle Castle
Wetheral Priory Gatehouse

Maryport
Cockermouth
Workington
Whitehaven
Cleator Moor
Egremont

Penrith Castle
Brougham Castle
Countess Pillar
Mayburgh Henge
Clifton Hall
Castlerigg Stone Circle
Keswick
King Arthur's Round Table
Appleby
Westmo
Shap Abbey

Ambleside Roman Fort
Ambleside
Hardknott Roman Fort
Windermere
Ravenglass Roman Bath House
Bowness-on-Windermere
Kendal
Sedbergh

Stott Park Bobbin Mill

Milom
Ulverston
Grange-over-Sands
Kirkby Lonsdale

Isle of Man

Ramsey

ISLE OF MAN

Douglas

IRISH SEA

Furness Abbey
Dalton-in-Furness
Bow Bridge
Carnforth
Warton Old Rectory
Barrow-in-Furness
Piel Castle
Morecambe
Heysham
LANCASTER

| 0 | 10 | 20 | 30 Kms |

| 0 | 10 | 20 Miles |

english-heritage.org.uk

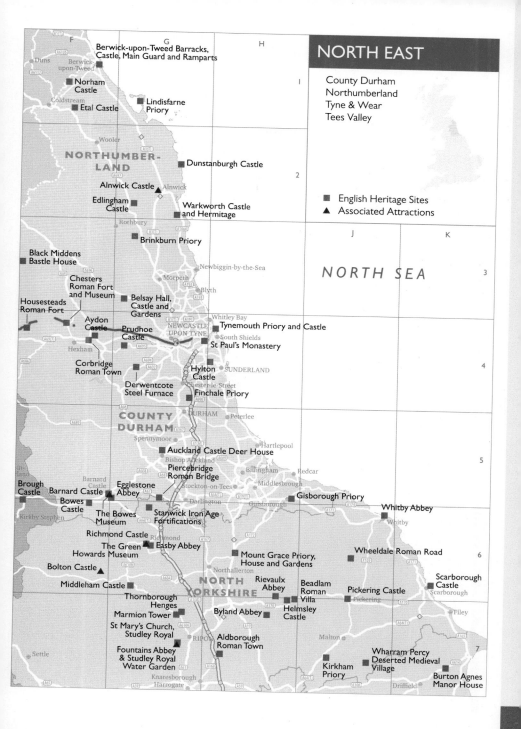

NORTH EAST

County Durham
Northumberland
Tyne & Wear
Tees Valley

■ English Heritage Sites
▲ Associated Attractions

NORTH SEA

Berwick-upon-Tweed Barracks, Castle, Main Guard and Ramparts

■ Norham Castle

■ Etal Castle

■ Lindisfarne Priory

NORTHUMBER-LAND

■ Dunstanburgh Castle

Alnwick Castle ▲ Alnwick

■ Edlingham Castle

■ Warkworth Castle and Hermitage

■ Brinkburn Priory

Black Middens
■ Bastle House

Chesters Roman Fort and Museum

Housesteads Roman Fort

■ Belsay Hall, Castle and Gardens

■ Aydon Castle

Prudhoe Castle

Tynemouth Priory and Castle

St Paul's Monastery

Corbridge Roman Town

Derwentcote Steel Furnace

Hylton Castle

Finchale Priory

COUNTY DURHAM

■ Auckland Castle Deer House

Piercebridge Roman Bridge

Brough Castle

Barnard Castle

Egglestone Abbey

■ Gisborough Priory

Bowes Castle

The Bowes Museum

Stanwick Iron Age Fortifications

Whitby Abbey

Richmond Castle

The Green Howards Museum

Easby Abbey

Bolton Castle ▲

Middleham Castle

Mount Grace Priory, House and Gardens

Wheeldale Roman Road

NORTH YORKSHIRE

Rievaulx Abbey

Beadlam Roman Villa

Pickering Castle

Scarborough Castle

Thornborough Henges

Byland Abbey

Helmsley Castle

Marmion Tower

St Mary's Church, Studley Royal

Aldborough Roman Town

Fountains Abbey & Studley Royal Water Garden

Kirkham Priory

Wharram Percy Deserted Medieval Village

Burton Agnes Manor House

Glossary

Whether at a prehistoric monument or an art deco palace, you can understand more about our sites with these helpful explanations of just a few of the features you may come across when visiting.

PREHISTORIC SITES

Barrow
Artificial mound of earth, turf and/or stone, normally constructed to contain or conceal burials. Long barrows date from the early Neolithic period, round barrows mostly from the early Bronze Age.

Fogou *(pronounced foogoo)*
A stone-built tunnel, generally within a settlement, exclusively in west Cornwall and Scilly. Their purpose is still debated; suggestions have included storage, refuge from attack, and ritual.

Henge
Circular or sub-circular enclosure defined by a bank and (usually internal) ditch, with one or two (rarely more) entrances. Of ceremonial/ritual function, they contain a variety of internal features, sometimes including timber or stone circles. They date mainly from the late Neolithic period, 3000-2400 BC.

Stonehenge, Wiltshire

Sarsen
A large sandstone boulder. In the chalklands, these boulders were often used as standing stones. They get their name from 'Saracen' in the medieval sense of 'pagan, heathen'.

Trilithon
A structure composed of two large upright stones supporting a third, lintel stone.

ROMAN SITES

Basilica
A high-roofed rectangular hall used for legal and administrative purposes. It usually forms part of an important public building, such as the principia.

Hypocaust
An underfloor heating system found in expensive houses and bath-houses.

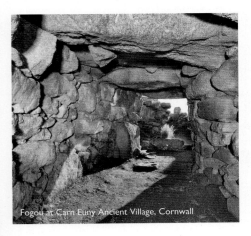

Fogou at Carn Euny Ancient Village, Cornwall

Housesteads Roman Fort, Northumberland

Inscription
Writing carved into stone. The Romans adorned buildings, memorial stones and religious objects with inscriptions.

Legionary
A citizen soldier of the Roman army. They were organised into legions of around 5,000 soldiers.

Principia
The command centre of a Roman fort, where the unit's standards and pay were kept.

Vicus
A settlement of military veterans, traders and civilians outside a Roman fort.

CASTLES

Barbican
An outward extension of a gateway, forming an enclosure outside the castle's main defences.

Scarborough Castle, North Yorkshire

Crenellation
The head of a castle wall, comprising higher sections (merlons) alternating with lower openings (crenels or embrasures).

Garderobe
A latrine, usually discharging into a cesspit or through an outlet into a moat or ditch.

Hoard or Hourd
Covered timber gallery overhanging the top of a wall, for the defence of the wall below.

Machicolation
An opening at the head of a wall or in a vaulted ceiling, allowing defenders to shoot weapons or drop stones onto attackers.

Dover Castle, Kent

MONASTERIES

Chapter House
The room in which the monks or nuns held daily meetings, including the reading of a chapter of the Rule of the monastic order.

Day Stair/Night Stair
Stairways leading from the dormitory for day and night-time use: the day stairs led to the cloister, the night stairs to the church.

Order
The international grouping to which each monastery or nunnery belonged, following a particular Rule (e.g. Benedictine, Cistercian, Carthusian).

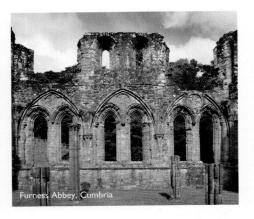
Furness Abbey, Cumbria

Reredorter
A building containing the latrines, sometimes flushed by a channel of running water.

Warming house
The only room in a monastery where a communal fire was kept burning during the winter months.

COUNTRY HOUSES

Coach house
A structure, often close to the stables, in which coaches or carriages were kept under cover.

Drawing room
Derived from 'withdrawing room', space in the house used by the members of the family for recreational purposes after dinner or for receiving guests.

Osborne, Isle of Wight

Orangery
Building, either attached to the house or separate, for keeping orange and other citrus fruit trees warm over winter.

Portico
The centrepiece of a house's facade, usually forming a covered way over the entrance.

Scullery
Room within the service wing of a country house, in which meat and vegetables were washed and prepared, and crockery, cutlery and other utensils were cleaned.

Audley End House and Gardens, Essex

HISTORIC PARKS AND GARDENS

Grotto – An artificial rocky cave or a small garden building, sometimes decorated with shells.

Ha-ha – A dry ditch which divides the formal garden from the parkland without interrupting the view.

Parterre – A level space in a garden occupied by ornamental flowerbeds, often symmetrical in design.

Topiary – Trees or shrubs pruned and trained into shapes, particularly geometric, bird or animal forms.

Patte d'oie – A layout where several straight paths or avenues radiate from a single point. Patte d'oie means 'goose foot' in French.

Details of OS LandRanger and Explorer map references are provided for easy location of each property, with specific map numbers (LandRanger; Explorer) followed by the grid reference.

NB. Contains Ordnance Survey data © Crown Copyright and database rights 2016. Additional map information © English Heritage 2023. Map created by Oxford Cartographers Ltd.

MIX
Paper | Supporting responsible forestry
FSC
www.fsc.org   FSC® C014496

English Heritage Handbook 2023/24

For English Heritage:
Louise Dando, Tom Dennis, Johanna Lovesey, Tersia Boorer, Richard Leatherdale, Tom Moriarty and Charles Kightly.

Design and Publishing:
Ledgard Jepson Ltd.
For Ledgard Jepson Ltd:
David Exley, Bev Turbitt, Andrea Rollinson, Rod Harrison.

Cover Concept and Art Direction:
Tony Dike (for English Heritage).

Cover Artwork: Ed Kluz.

Print: Produced by GGP Media GmbH, Pößneck, Germany.

Images: All images in this handbook are © English Heritage or © Historic England unless otherwise stated.

The following symbols indicate facilities available at the English Heritage properties listed in this handbook.

ACQ.1945	Date property came into the National Collection
🚹	Adult changing facilities
🎧	Audio tours
🚼	Baby changing facilities
🍴	Café
🎠	Children's play area
♿	Disabled access
🐕	Dogs allowed on leads
▣	Educational resources
🎭	Events
E	Exhibition
👪	Family learning resources
🎬	Film/TV location

❄	Gardens
📖	Guidebook available
🏠	Holiday cottage to let
🐄	Livestock grazing on/around site
🚉	Local railway station
🚹🚺	Male/female toilet
🚻	Non-gender specific toilet
Ⓜ	Museum
OVP	OVP – admission free for Overseas Visitor Pass holders
♣	Park
P	Parking
⛱	Picnic area
🐕	Registered assistance dogs allowed only
🛍	Shop
☕	Tearoom
♿	Toilets with disabled access
⚠	Site may contain hazardous features

Please note: All of our sites have uneven surfaces due to their historic and/or outdoor nature so please wear appropriate footwear. Please observe site signage, barriers and staff instructions. Please supervise children closely. Metal detecting, smoking, fires, BBQs and unauthorised commercial photography and drones are prohibited at all our properties. Damage to our sites is a crime.